T

THE STEAM
LOCOMOTIVE
A History

THE STEAM LOCOMOTIVE

A History

DAVID ROSS

TEMPUS

For Jane and George Nissen

First published as *The Willing Servant: A History of the Steam Locomotive* in 2004
This edition 2006

Tempus Publishing Limited
The Mill, Brimscombe Port,
Stroud, Gloucestershire, GL5 2QG
www.tempus-publishing.com

British Library Cataloguing in Publication Data.
A catalogue record for this book is available from the British Library.

ISBN 0 7524 3916 2

Typesetting and origination by Tempus Publishing Limited
Printed in Great Britain

Contents

The Significance of Wheels   8

Introduction   9

Acknowledgements   12

1   Ancestry and Beginnings   13

2   Coming of Age   27

3   Trials and Triumphs   39

4   The Basics Confirmed   49

5   Pushing out Frontiers   57

6   Adjustments to the Nervous System   69

7   Engineers and Aesthetics   75

8   Gauges and Growing Pains   83

9   Mid-Century Perceptions   87

10   Coke, Coal, Culm, Logs, Bagasse and Oil   99

11   The Need for Growth   105

12   But How do you Make it Stop?   113

13   Magniloquence and Minimalism   117

14   Compounding   127

15   The Racing Years   137

16   Superheating   145

17 A Hundred Years On   151

18 Imperial and Royal   161

19 'Great Things Were Expected'   165

20 Big Boilers   171

21 Across Tundra, Veldt and Pampas   177

22 'Foreign Devils' Fire Carts'   183

23 Engines of the Imagination   189

24 Bigger Engines   201

25 Express Elegance   209

26 The Search for Super-Power   215

27 Getting Away from Stephenson   225

28 The Standardisers   231

29 Record Breakers   241

30 The Iconic Locomotive   251

31 On the Footplate   257

32 The Biggest Engines   261

33 A Sort of Zenith   273

34 A Consideration of Chimneys   281

35 War Engines   287

36 Post-war Engines   299

    A Smoky Epilogue   333

    Bibliography   337

    Index   341

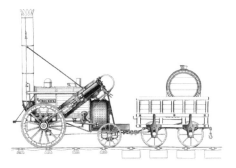

And the Iron Horse, the earth-shaker, the fire-breather, which tramples down the hills, which outruns the laggard roads, which leaps over rivers, which grinds the rocks to powder and breaks down the gates of the mountains, he too shall build an empire and an epic. Shall not solitudes and waste places cry for gladness at his coming?

Statistics and Speculations Concerning the Pacific Railroad, 1853

It is the embodiment of the age, an instrument of power, speed, noise, fire, iron, smoke – at once a testament to the will of man rising over natural obstacles, and yet, confined by its iron rails to a pre-determined path, it suggests a new sort of fate.

Leo Marx, *The Machine in the Garden*

The Significance of Wheels

Steam locomotive people, whether professional or amateur, owe a debt of gratitude to Frederick M. Whyte, Mechanical Engineer of the New York Central Railroad. Around 1900, numerous efforts were being made to come up with a straightforward classification system for steam locomotives. Whyte's was by far the best, and it has survived. Taking it as a basis that the steam locomotive (facing west, the 'course of Empire' in the USA) potentially has carrying wheels, driving wheels and then further carrying wheels, he set out the number of each, including zero if necessary. Thus a locomotive with no front carrying wheels, six driving wheels and no trailing wheels, would be an 0-6-0. If it had a four-wheel bogie in front of the driving wheels, it would be a 4-6-0; or with two trailing wheels as well, a 4-6-2. Whyte's system worked remarkably well, taking in articulated engines by an additional digit, as in 2-6-6-2, which indicated two sets of six driving wheels, with a two-wheel bogie fore and aft. Garratt-type locomotives, in effect two engines pivoting under a central boiler, were denoted by a plus sign between the two wheel notations, as in 4-6-2+2-6-4. It provided an admirable shorthand compared to the wordy or ambiguous descriptions necessary before. In France, it was adapted to show the number of axles rather than wheels, and there a 'Pacific' became a 2-3-1 rather than a 4-6-2. In German practice, the number of driving axles was indicated by a letter of the alphabet, from A (single driver) to F (six axles), and thus a 'Pacific' was 2C1. The addition of T after the wheel notation indicated a tank locomotive in all these codes. Just about the only thing that might have defeated Whyte is a freakish design of 1862 by the indefatigable Jules Pétiet of the *Nord* railway in France, a tank engine with a single driving axle at each end, and three separate carrying axles in between – in Whyte's notation a 2-2-2-2-2, which implies three pairs of unconnected drivers in the middle! The Germanic A111A is more specific in this case.

Introduction

This is a life-story, though the subject is a species rather than an individual. It first appeared on earth, after a few false starts, in 1804. For twenty years it led a precarious and largely hidden existence. Then from 1825 it began to roar up and down in full public view. Very soon after that it crossed the Atlantic from Great Britain and colonised North America; it was already pushing through Europe too. It became recognisable world-wide in many hundreds of varieties and established itself as humanity's strongest helper on land. A wonderful gift to the age-old human urge to be on the move, it was a willing servant in commerce, industry, and warfare. With it, many things previously impossible could be accomplished, and in a host of activities good and bad, its service was great beyond measure. Now it is all but extinct, other than in the railway equivalents of zoos and safari parks. It deserves to have its story told.

Books on railway subjects tend to be, like the two former classes of Chinese travel, hard or soft. 'Hard' ones are written for the committed enthusiast. Assuming a shared world of knowledge and interest between writer and reader, they are rich in technical detail, numbers and the kind of jargon teased by Myles naGopaleen on page 191. 'Soft' ones are written for the leisure reader with a more tenuous and sedate interest in trains and travel; they generally are to do with what goes on in the train rather than in the engine, and have much more of the human element. Not many bridge the gap, but this book sets out to be one of them. It is more of a biography than an engineering history. Many technical details are included when they are integral to the story, but, I hope, are made clear in a painless way. Equally, I have sought to trace the steam locomotive's impact on the human imagination, which very soon became a two-way process. From the beginning, the locomotive was used to embody or reflect a whole variety of attitudes and ideas arising in the society of the time. Other writers, including Leo Marx in the USA, and Ian Carter and Michael Freeman in Great Britain, have explored the imaginative and cultural impact of the railway as a whole. My focus is much narrower, but readers of these authors will recognise some of the same quotations taken from the slender presence of railways in Literature, though they may be used to different effect.

The aim is to follow the all-round development of the main-line railway locomotive across the world, and so I have not gone up the alluring side-tracks on which one might find specialised types like the Shay and Heisler geared logging engines: intriguing variants of the species, which were capable of climbing a 1:10 slope with a load behind. Nor have I entered the industrial enclaves where thousands of small but interesting and often venerable steam engines were once to be found. Some readers may feel I have done little justice to some experimental types; but then their part in the story is very small, and none gave rise to a family of locomotives in regular use. Other readers may identify other gaps in what is, after all, a wide-ranging subject.

Another aim is to provide accurate information. In reading books and articles on locomotives and railways, both by amateurs and by engineers, one finds frequent conflicts of fact. To give only one example, two distinguished writers on engineering history, from opposite sides of the Atlantic, state respectively and flatly, that for general benefit the Stephenson valve gear was never patented; and that it was 'of course' patented. As some encouragement to readers of this book, I can only say that the facts in it, which are very numerous, have been checked against the historical record as carefully as the author can manage.

The steam locomotive, during its spread across the world, produced a great number of sub-species: far too many to be individually recorded. In tracing its beginning, rise to greatness, maturity and decline, I have had to be selective, and to concentrate on the main schools of locomotive design, though I have often and deliberately used far-flung products of these nurseries as examples. The lifetime of the steam locomotive almost exactly parallels the human experience of an industrialised world; and we abandoned it at very much the time when people began to have serious doubts about the purpose and destination of, even the need for, our hectic pursuit of technological innovation. That may help to explain the benign aura that now surrounds its memory. For it was not an environmentally-friendly machine. It burned fossil fuels, mostly, and discharged large amounts of sulphur and other un-digested chemicals into the air. It had a tendency to set line-side woodlands on fire. Its larger depots lived under a pall of smoke. When its demise was announced, the vast majority of people were pleased. The few, some of them professional engineers, others enthusiastic amateurs, who argued for a new generation of steam power, were regarded as die-hards and eccentrics.

And yet, even at the time, there was some regret expressed, and even sometimes by those who commanded the cutting-torch. As he introduced the British Railways' modernisation plan in June 1955, the chairman was moved to say: 'Somehow both the diesel and the electric locomotive lack the glamour which surrounds the mighty steam engine pounding through the night with the light of the fire glowing in the faces of the crew. There is something here of real importance, and we are honestly seeking a means to avoid losing all the romance which has attached to this great iron horse.' Inevitably, they failed to do so. The sources of true glamour always lie deep, and cannot be cosmetically reproduced. Of all the mechanical creations of humanity, the steam locomotive, with its warmth, its apparent breathing, its hissings and shrieks and occasional involuntary gushings of water, was the one that most seemed to possess life. With its fiery heart and smoky breath, it touched deep and ancient human feelings and re-evoked myths that had grown around the use of fire and the creation of life itself. For many people, to contemplate a locomotive gave the same sense of satisfaction that others felt in viewing the lines of a thoroughbred horse. Another reason for its appeal was that to give of its best, it needed skilled coaxing and physically hard work from its human masters. Its behaviour often suggested struggle and harsh effort, toiling with loads many times its own weight. Sometimes it blew up or went off the rails. But its failures were rare, and its contribution colossal. It was our most willing servant.

Now it is possible to look back on it and think of it as 'the Good Machine' – an alternative title for this book. If nostalgia for a selectively remembered past helps to justify this name, there are also better reasons. Primality is one – it was the first powered machine to become part of everyday life. Its man-ifestation of Obedient Power is another. To a race that still retains a strong nomadic instinct, its gift of mobility was precious. Its benefits were shared and open to all: compared to the train, the motor car is a selfish, exclusive machine. Then there was a certain simplicity in the way that it worked and revealed its workings, which was more akin to the animal than to the later technological world. In the intentions of its first builders, and in almost all its uses, it was wholly benevolent (ironically, the other vehicle which loco-motive works could be readily adapted to build was the battle tank, whose whole purpose was to cause death and destruction). The pages which follow trace the story of involvement between people and machines, of excite-ments and disappointments, high moments and low ones, dreams dashed and dreams fulfilled, international collaboration and rivalries, through the eventful two centuries that we have shared with the steam locomotive.

Acknowledgements

Though the opinions in this book are the author's own, or so he would like to think, the information it contains has been extracted, compared and distilled from a great variety of sources. Grateful thanks are owed to the Librarian of the Stephenson Locomotive Society, Reg Carter, and to Brian Lewis and Frank Jux; also to Terry Silcock, Librarian of the Railway Correspondence and Travel Society, to Philip Atkins and Lynne Thurston at the National Railway Museum, York, the London Library, the Science Museum/Imperial College Library, and the Bibliothèque Municipale, Mulhouse. For help with illustrations I am also very grateful to Ted Nevill of TRH Pictures, Keith Moore of the Institution of Mechanical Engineers, the Stephenson Locomotive Society, Bob Bourquin of Timken, Gideon Grimmel, Graeme McClare, Assistant Secretary of the New Zealand Railway & Locomotive Society, and Campbell McCutcheon.

ONE

Ancestry and Beginnings

There was nothing new about railways in the year 1804. In European countries from Transylvania to Scotland, wooden-wheeled trucks had been running on wooden rails in mine galleries for 200 years or more; the earliest printed reference to railways is from 1556, when G. Agricola's *De Re Metallica*, a treatise on mining, was published in Basel. Cast-iron rails had been in use in a few up-to-date places since the mid-eighteenth century. But the motive power employed on these tracks had always been animal, human or gravity. There was nothing new about steam engines, either, although they were not very common. More than a hundred years before, the Frenchman Denis Papin and the Englishman Thomas Savery were both attempting to build steam engines: Papin using high pressure in his 'Digester', while Savery set the English pattern of low pressure. Thomas Newcomen made improvements, in 1707, to the atmospheric steam engine developed by Savery in 1698; and by 1711 he had built a pumping engine whose hissing, clanking life went on for sixty years. Though they made steam, these engines used atmospheric rather than steam power. Steam was raised, not to expand, but to condense. Passing from the boiler into the cylinder, it cooled and condensed, forming a partial vacuum within the more-or-less sealed cylinder. Atmospheric pressure then forced up the piston, which, as it rose, drew water up the pipe. The water was discharged through a one-way valve; and with the next admission of steam, the engine then repeated its motion. Through the eighteenth century such engines continued to be chiefly used for pumping water out of mine shafts. Large and slow-acting, they were fixed in very substantial frames and the movement they generated was exclusively upwards and downwards.

The notion of applying steam power to make a vehicle move was first tried out with some effect in France. In 1769, Nicolas Cugnot constructed a three-wheeled steam carriage which could travel short distances at speeds of up to 4mph. He had been an officer in the artillery and wanted to find an effective alternative to horse-teams for moving heavy guns. His idea was still a little ahead of its time, and like many pioneering devices, Cugnot's carriage, with a clumsy ratchet drive on the single front wheel, was not a practical success. It indicated what might be done when engineering had advanced somewhat further. His second steam carriage, of 1771, is preserved in Paris. But the fall from power of his political patron, the duc de Choiseul, left his work officially ignored in France. The advances came in Great Britain. In the year of Cugnot's first carriage, James Watt patented his development of the steam engine, with separate steam condenser. The Watt engine was able to work faster than the Newcomen type, and was more versatile: it could impart a rotary motion and so drive machines as well as pumps. In 1775 Watt and the businessman Matthew Boulton set up a factory in Birmingham to build steam engines. The crankshaft had already been invented but it was someone else's patent, and so Watt used the more cumbersome but freely available 'sun and planets' rotary motion. In this, the connecting rod was attached to an eccentric cog-wheel which meshed with a fixed cog on the driving shaft. His employee and fellow-Scot William Murdock, also a gifted inventor, began to experiment with a small steam engine which could drive a carriage. Such a machine would need a high-pressure boiler, but Watt, always an advocate of low-pressure steam, discouraged him. Murdock did build two or three small steam-powered self-propelling tricycle engines, and was responsible for a very important invention. This was the slide valve, a sliding plate moved by the reciprocal to-and-fro action of the piston, alternately covering and exposing an aperture and so making it possible to admit steam to the cylinder and exhaust it after it had done its work. As it happened, he was based in Redruth, Cornwall, at this time, and it is known that the young Richard Trevithick was given a demonstration of one of his models in action in 1790. By now the potential of a more compact and mobile steam engine was being actively explored in several countries. In France and America men were struggling with the technicalities of using steam power to drive boats.

The amount of brain-power now being applied, and of work now being done, meant that the arrival of the steam locomotive was only a matter of time, whether in the new American republic, in France, or in Great Britain. In America, the boatbuilder and engineer Oliver Evans had obtained the right to make and use 'steam waggons' as early as 1786. In Philadelphia, Pennsylvania, cradle-town of American steam power, he fitted a steam engine to an amphibious machine, *Oruktor Amphibolos*, in 1804, and invented a form of belt drive to move it under its own power by turning either a stern-mounted paddle wheel, or road wheels. Evans did not have the funds or backing to pursue his steam road drive. But even apart from the slender thread of coincidence or causality linking Murdock and Trevithick, it is no surprise that it should have been a Cornishman who built the first effective locomotive. As tin, copper and lead mining were the main industries of Cornwall, the farthest south-western county of England, it was quite normal that young Cornishmen should be familiar with the working of steam engines. These were numerous in the Cornish mines, whose ancient and often waterlogged workings, in narrow, winding seams, often extended out under the sea. Some were already venerable Newcomen engines, others were more recent Boulton & Watt products, but all operated at low steam pressure, only a few pounds greater than that of the atmosphere, and worked through large cylinders. As they were fixed in position, their cumbrous dimensions were not of themselves a handicap, except that they took up a great deal of space on what often were constricted and sloping sites. They were also great coal guzzlers. Cornwall had no coal and it was expensive to bring in. The men who owned and operated the Cornish mines had a tendency to think more about the running costs of their engines than about the very real savings the engines brought.

Richard Trevithick, born in 1771 at Illogan, near Camborne, was the son of a mine captain and land agent. His natural affinity for engines could not have had a better nursery. By the age of fifteen he was employed as a mechanic on pumping and winding engines and soon became involved in the long wrangle between the Cornish engineers and Boulton & Watt, over failures to pay royalties, and patent infringements. Several reasons thus existed for Cornish mine-owners to wish for engines that were smaller and more fuel-efficient, and that would owe nothing to Boulton & Watt. Motive and opportunity were both present for a clever young engineer. Trevithick had the ability, and, hardly less important, the will-power and perseverance, to pursue the concept. It would necessarily involve a boiler working at higher pressure. By the late 1790s he was successfully building stationary engines of this type, in Cornwall and beyond. Unlike the sighing, hissing giants which preceded them, these engines, rather alarmingly for bystanders, 'puffed', as the exhaust steam was discharged from the cylinders, and they were often known as the 'puffing engines'.

Trevithick did good business with stationary engines, for which there was a rapidly growing demand, but, having achieved a compact, relatively light engine, his abiding dream was to apply it to road traction, although there was no public demand for this at all. In 1801, after experimenting like Murdock with designs in miniature, he built a 'steam road carriage'. Any plans or drawings of it made at the time no longer exist. Unlike the machines of Cugnot and Murdock, it was four-wheeled, with the boiler set on a frame. It probably required two operators, one to steer and the other to work the engine. Its career was extremely brief; overturning on its second run, it was wrecked. Trevithick's next venture with motive power, in 1802, was in London, where he built a 'steam carriage' that really was the first automobile, with built-in passenger compartment and its own engine. The 'Trevithick Dragon' was demonstrated in Oxford Street, but nobody wanted to buy such a noisy, uncomfortable, jolting conveyance, and people were afraid that it would frighten the horses. Trevithick returned to the more profitable business of building stationary engines, but remained obsessed by the concept of the locomotive engine. In 1802 he built a boiler for William Reynolds, at the Coalbrookdale ironworks, by the Severn river, with a working pressure of 145psi (pounds to the square inch). Such unprecedented high pressure was anathema to the cautious Watt, who believed that these boilers were too dangerous (at least one of Trevithick's stationary boilers did explode, killing three men, at Greenwich, south-east London, on 8 September 1803: though the cause was careless operation). There is some tenuous documentary evidence to suggest that he built a locomotive at Coalbrookdale, but no record of any performance, other than a paragraph in a local publication, *History of Madeley*, almost eighty years later, stating that:

> An accident, we believe a fatal one, which happened to one of the men on starting the engine led Mr Reynolds to abandon the machine, but he by no means lost faith in the invention.

What happened at Coalbrookdale remains obscure, though it seems most likely that Trevithick built an engine which could have run on wheels, but was actually used for pumping. But the next year he was in South Wales, building stationary steam engines for the ironworks and new coal pits that were being established there. It was a boom time for industry. War with France was driving the economy upwards. New reserves of coal were being found under bare and unproductive hillsides. Fortunes were being made and a generation of entrepreneurs, home-grown or incoming, had taken charge of developments, and was making itself immensely rich in the process.

One of these new men was Samuel Homfray, who in 1784 had set up an ironworks at Penydarren, at the edge of the new mining town of Merthyr Tydfil, a raw sprawl of terraced housing growing faster than any community in the world. Homfray was a partner in the Penydarren Tramroad, laid in 1800-1802. Built with L-shaped cast-iron plate rails bolted to stone blocks, the right angles facing outwards, it ran for 9.75 miles, including a short tunnel, to the wharves of the Glamorganshire Canal at Abercynon. Trucks, known as trams, loaded with iron ingots, ran to the canal, pony-hauled but assisted by the downwards gradient; and once emptied were pony-hauled back up to the works. Trevithick was employed to build a stationary engine for the ironworks, but he quickly communicated his enthusiasm for steam-powered traction to Homfray. Which man decided that Trevithick's next motive experiment should run on rails rather than a roadway is not known, but Homfray made a celebrated wager with another notable ironmaster, Richard Crawshay of the nearby Cyfarthfa Works. He put 500 guineas on his assertion that a steam-powered engine could pull a load of 10 tons along the Penydarren Tramroad, and return with the empty trams. Crawshay took him on. A third local ironmaster, Richard Hill of the Plymouth Ironworks, held the stake. By mid-February 1804, the locomotive, built on site, was ready. A trial was conducted on the 13th, of which Trevithick recorded in a letter to his scientist friend Davies Gilbert, that: 'It work'd very well, and ran up hill and down with great ease'; and it was with some confidence that Homfray appeared at the demonstration run on 21 February. The engine was mounted on the rails, fired up, and set off with its load of 10 tons of bar iron in tram wagons. Trevithick, a giant in physique as well as in his enthusiasms, walked in front of his creation, operating the rudimentary controls. Around seventy excited men and boys added 4 tons of humanity to the load, perching and clinging somehow to the train. The journey, with many pauses, took four hours and five minutes. No *frisson* of excitement ran through the nation. Media interest was reflected only in a 'Letter from Merthyr Tydfil' published in *The Cambrian* on 24 February, which described the scene and was not wholly unaware of its epoch-making implications:

... it performed the journey without feeding the boiler or using any water, and will travel with ease at the rate of 5mph. It is not doubted that the number of horses in the Kingdom will be very considerably reduced ...

No complete details of this primal railway engine survive. It was not built purely as a locomotive; the axles were bolted to the boiler, but the four wheels were detachable so that it could be mounted, using the axle beams, on a frame. Indeed, part of the exercise seems to have been to prove the versatility of the Trevithick high-pressure engine. It was to be shown to a visiting 'engineer from Government' – Mr Goodrich of the Navy Board in London – performing such tasks as raising water, winding coal tubs, and operating a hammer, as well as pulling loaded wagons. It is likely that the firebox was in front, below the chimney, which was set to the side, with the fire-door alongside; and that it pushed a truck holding a supply of coal, of which two hundredweights were burned during the journey, and water. When the fire needed stoking, the train was stopped. The boiler was cast iron, with a return flue of wrought iron. The single cylinder, with a diameter of 8.25in (21cm) and the enormously long stroke of 54in (137.2cm), was set horizontally into the rear end of the boiler. The long piston rod was attached to the centre of a cross-bar, which drove the two left-hand wheels (via a set of geared cog-wheels) and a flywheel on the right-hand side. This latter was a necessary feature in a stationary engine to provide starting motion if the piston should stop on dead centre, from where it could exert no leverage on the crank. There does not seem to have been a water-feed arrangement, and the boiler was topped up from external supplies of cold water. A fusible plug was inserted in the boiler as a safeguard against excessive heat: and the locomotive historian Dendy Marshall credits Trevithick as the likely inventor of this valuable safety device. Another very important feature was identified by Trevithick in a letter to Davies Gilbert on 20 February: 'The fire burns much better when the steam goes up the chimney than when the engine is idle.' He returns to this point in a later letter, clearly aware of its importance. Trevithick was first to produce and record the function of exhaust steam in creating a draught that increased the combustion in the firebox. The weight of the engine was around 5 tons, and its best speed was reckoned at 5mph. The gauge of the tracks appears to have been between 4ft 8in and 4ft 9in – almost identical to that of the colliery tramways of north-east England. The rails had been laid by a professional contractor, Curl, and it is likely that this was already a 'standard' gauge for industrial tramroads, derived from the optimum dimensions of a pony-hauled tram-truck.

Although Homfray won his bet, matters were complicated by the fact that for the engine to pass through the tunnel, which was only 8ft high, the tracks had to be removed. The pernickety Richard Hill apparently considered this a breach of the terms. The height of this tunnel, passing under the Plymouth Ironworks, has caused problems in establishing the engine's dimensions. In the letter of 20 February, Trevithick wrote, in his somewhat phonetic English, 'the Chimny is but 8 feet above where the steam is delivred into it'. This suggests that the chimney top would be over 10ft above the ground, too high to fit in the tunnel. The upper part of it may have been detachable, but very hot metal tubes were not easy to detach, and some mystery still attaches to this aspect of the machine.

The locomotive made few runs after the first demonstrations. It cracked or broke the brittle, flanged tram plates and its jerky movement tended to pull the draw-hooks out of the trams. On one run it was derailed, and had to be brought back by ponies, and ponies resumed their role as tram pullers. Trevithick recorded that in July 1804 it was working a steam hammer. For some years it was used as a stationary engine, probably with its role as a locomotive forgotten. Nor did it create a wave of demand for steam locomotives: the interest was both short-lived and mostly local. The 'engineer from government' never came. Trevithick received only one order for a second railway engine, from a north-eastern mine-owner, Christopher Blackett. This was duly built on site, to plans sent by Trevithick, but it, like the first one, was too heavy for the tracks, which in this case were made of wood. Richard Trevithick continued to build stationary engines whilst struggling to interest the world in the locomotive. He returned to London in 1808 with an engine which he called *Catch-me-who-can*, built for him by the iron-founders Hazeldene and Rastrick of Bridgnorth, which ran on a circular track inside a high wooden wall set up on an open space near Euston Square. People paid two shillings – a substantial sum – to see it, and could ride behind it if they were daring enough. A later form of motive power, the electric locomotive, would have a similar introduction at the Berlin Trades Exhibition in 1879: however reluctantly, the developers of new technology had to use showmanship to captivate an indifferent or suspicious public. But once again, London showed little interest. After some weeks a rail broke, the engine ran into the ground and was damaged; Trevithick could not afford to repair it, and the circular showground was closed down and dismantled. The engine was later installed in a Thames barge.

In 1808, Trevithick received an invitation from Christopher Blackett to build another engine, this time to run on iron rails. But he declined. Never short of ideas and enthusiasms, he wanted to try something new. The father of the steam locomotive was a brilliant engineer and ambitious for wealth and fame, but, unlike his younger and longer-lived contemporary George Stephenson, he had no head for business. Despite his years of obsessive effort on the locomotive, both fame and fortune remained as far off as ever. He had no means of knowing that north-east England would be the real nursery for his child. Restless but always resourceful, he continued his career as an engine builder and mining engineer as far afield as Colombia and Peru. His adventures led him to the mining camp of Cerro de Pasco, high in the Peruvian Andes, a place then accessible only by mule-path, but which would in the future be home to some remarkable steam locomotives. Nineteen years later, in 1827, in one of the striking coincidences that often arise in life, Trevithick, returning virtually penniless to England, met George Stephenson's twenty-four-year-old son Robert, also homeward-bound from his own 'gap years' in the silver mines. The encounter, in the port of Cartagena in Colombia, was perhaps embarrassing to both, but Stephenson lent the older man £50 to assist him on his way. Trevithick continued to experiment and to take out patents, including one in 1832 on a means of re-heating steam, a fore-runner of the superheater. Before his death, in London, in 1833, he saw the first steam-powered railways well-established, but with no profit or — at least at the time — credit to himself.

Trevithick's vision of a railway carrying passengers and making the stage-coach obsolete was prescient but still in the realm of prophecy. Between 1808 and 1812, experimentation seems to have subsided, and even after that, the place of the locomotive was to remain firmly among the spoil heaps, engine houses and smoke-stacks of heavy industry, pushing and pulling wagon-loads of coal and pig-iron. False starts were still being made. In 1812, the brothers William and Edward Chapman patented a locomotive which hauled itself along a track on a fixed chain; it was used at Heaton Colliery in Northumberland, but soon was abandoned. In the same year, the Middleton Railway in Yorkshire, founded as a colliery horse-drawn line in 1758, experimented with rack-and-pinion drive, in which traction was obtained by cog-wheels mounted on the locomotive, which meshed with toothed racks laid alongside the rails. Its first two engines were built by Fenton, Murray & Wood, of Leeds, an established builder of stationary engines, for John Blenkinsop, superintendent of the Middleton Colliery. Matthew Murray was responsible for their design, though Blenkinsop specified the rack system. Topically named *Salamanca* and *Prince Regent*, these were the first steam locomotives in regular use. They were true locomotives, with two cylinders, each driving one side, and Trevithick's flywheel was not needed. Nevertheless, £30 was paid to the owners of Trevithick's patent. Murray developed his own form of slide valve to admit steam to the pistons, and this became the model for other early locomotive builders. Murray and Blenkinsop were interested in sales of their 'steam carriages', and supplied one to the Kenton and Coxlodge Collieries in Northumberland, in 1813. But the cog-wheel traction was slow and uncertain. A Middleton engine was the first to be reliably recorded as having killed its driver, as the result of a burst boiler. The incident was reported with a gruesome relish in the *Leeds Mercury* of 15 February 1814: '… the unfortunate engine-driver was literally blown to atoms, and his mutilated body scattered in all directions.'

Another innovation of 1813 was an engine mounted on four wheels but pushed along by a pair of jointed iron legs and feet, operated from a single cylinder. This machine was patented by William Brunton in May 1813, and one was put to work on the Newbottle colliery wagon-way in County Durham. The walking engine or 'steam elephant' worked there until 31 July 1815, when its new boiler exploded, killing at least three people. A sister engine may have survived until as late as 1827, but chiefly as a curiosity. In 1814, a steam locomotive was built by William Stewart of Newport, Monmouthshire, for the Parkend Colliery in the Forest of Dean. Stewart had undertaken to convey its coal for half the rate paid for horse transport, which was £3,000 a year. The colliery company used the threat of the locomotive to get this rate reduced to £2,000. Offered an uneconomic £1,000 a year to provide his locomotive and its services, Stewart indignantly withdrew, though he was 'obliged to abandon the engine to that Company in lieu of a small sum they had advanced to him for his assistence in its completion'. The tale is not untypical of relations between unwary engineers and their customers. But the focus shifts to the north-east of England, where further concentrations of coal-based heavy industry had been established.

The leading advocate of steam traction was Christopher Blackett, of the Wylam Colliery in the hinterland of the town of Newcastle upon Tyne.

With his manager William Hedley, Blackett organised a set of practical experiments with hand-propelled vehicles on gradients, in the first scientific attempts to measure the adhesion of wheel on rail, and how much tractive effort was required to pull a given weight. The tests were made from around 1811, and the results gave them faith in 'smooth wheels'. In 1813, a few years after Trevithick's refusal to build a second locomotive for him, Blackett commissioned two new engines. Built at Wylam Colliery by Hedley, they were popularly known as *Puffing Billy* and *Wylam Dilly*, and in altered form can still be seen at the Science Museum, London, and the Royal Scottish Museum, Edinburgh, respectively. They are the oldest railway engines to be preserved. Originally they had flangeless wheels for running on flanged track, as at Penydarren. In an effort to stop them breaking up the track, they were both for a time remounted on two four-wheel trucks to spread their weight, with a drive-train of cog-wheels turning every axle. Not far away was Heaton Colliery, where the Chapman chain-drive engine had been set up. William Chapman had also patented the pivoted truck or bogie system on which his failed locomotive was mounted. It is not clear whether the Wylam trucks were pivoted or whether they allowed only for independent lateral movement of the axles: from the details available, the latter is more likely. The nature of the cog-drive could have allowed for only minimal articulation of the trucks, if any at all, without jamming on one side and disengaging on the other. A twenty-six-year-old blacksmith at Wylam, Timothy Hackworth, joined in the care and maintenance of these erratic steeds and would himself become a notable locomotive builder. *Wylam Dilly,* incidentally, had a nautical interlude when it was taken off its wheels and used to power a paddle-tug during a strike of the Tyne keelmen, or coal-boat crews, in 1822: the first instance of a steam engine being used by one group, the coal-owners, to spoil the plans of another group. Already its innocence as humanity's universal friend was being compromised.

Before the advent of the steam locomotive, the largest self-powered land machine had been a toy built by a Jesuit priest, Father Verbiest, at Peking, to divert the Chinese Emperor, around 1681. This little cart had a fire-tray, with an 'aeolipile', something first described by the Greek philosopher Hero of Alexandria in the first century of the Common Era. It was a spouted vessel from which a jet of vapour was directed on to a vaned wheel. Now builders and would-be builders were engaged with machines that weighed 5 tons and more. They were working in the dark, with very little theory or science to rely on. Mechanical engineering was not yet a textbook subject, though the starting of *Mechanic's Magazine*, in 1823, showed the general interest in this new applied science. Despite the Penydarren example, and Blackett's research, there was considerable doubt about whether a metal wheel, on a metal rail, would be able to exercise any traction at all when pulling a heavy load. This doubt was not entirely misplaced, and wheel-slipping would remain a problem with steam locomotives to the very end (it is by no means unknown with diesel and electric traction also). Rails were still a problem, even when it was accepted that the flanges should be on the wheels rather than on the rails. Although wrought iron rails were in use, and were more resistant to wear than cast-iron, progress in this department was badly needed. In 1820 a patent was granted to the English industrialist John Birkinshaw for the making of rolled malleable iron rails, and with these the locomotive gained a track on which it could run without fear of cracks and breakages.

The popular by-name of the Newcastle region, 'Geordie-land', is a tribute to its most famous son, George Stephenson, born in 1781 and in his prime in the 1820s. He and his son Robert would bring the sporadically-produced and breakdown-prone invention of Trevithick's into an everyday reality. His father was a stoker at Killingworth colliery, close to Wylam, and George grew up in a place that already took the steam engine for granted. Unschooled, he became the enginewright at Killingworth. In 1814, aged thirty-three, he built his first locomotive, named *Blücher* after the military commander of Britain's Prussian ally in the war against France, and it made its first run on 25 July. Stephenson's confidence, ability and ambition took him far beyond Killingworth and within a few years he was known not only as the prime steam engine expert in England, but also as an accomplished all-round engineer. In 1814 Robert was a promising boy of eleven, receiving a better education than his self-taught father, though his six months at Edinburgh University was an unusually brief sojourn. The Stephenson family was determined to 'get on' in life. It was this drive and managerial quality, linked with great technical ability and understanding, rather than inventive brilliance, that made George and Robert the fathers of modern railways.

Only a handful of locomotives had, so far, been built. There had been more widespread experimentation with powered ships, which offered a wider platform to support a steam engine. The serious business of bulk inland haulage was carried on by canals, some of them very new and others still being constructed. Canals were very expensive to build and in both political and commercial terms the 'canal interest' was a strong one.

The sight of a few puffing, hissing, clanking 'iron horses' trundling wagons between the pit-head and the canal wharves, frequently breaking down, regularly running off the tracks, or breaking them, was not something to instil fear into those who were still investing large sums in canal building. The locomotive's potential seemed to be as an auxiliary to the canal barge, rather than a threat to the canals' very existence. Few people supposed that the 'steam carriage' could ever pull a heavy load uphill, and on a number of colliery and quarry sites, stationary steam engines were set up at the top of slopes, hauling wagons up by means of a rope.

The greatest problem for the first locomotive builders was to provide an effective drive system between the cylinders and the wheels. Matthew Murray had set a pattern of vertically-mounted cylinders, standing up above the boiler and partly mounted inside it, as was normal with stationary steam engines. Trevithick's horizontally-mounted cylinder was forgotten. In the cylinders of his first locomotives, George Stephenson followed Murray's example, but, though he used a cog-wheel drive, he did not employ the rack and pinion system. Blenkinsop's system was very slow and the wheels were liable to miss their fit and spring out of the rack. The method would be rediscovered for mountain railways later in the century, but Stephenson was well aware of the Blackett-Hedley experiments and never seems to have doubted that rails alone would suffice. Another factor perhaps played a part – from the beginning, progress in locomotive design was hedged about by patent protection. To build a locomotive on the Murray-Blenkinsop model would require payment of royalties, or invite prosecution. Both the very real prospect of making mechanical improvements, and the urge to avoid unnecessary costs, drove mechanics to contrive alternative solutions as well as completely new ones.

For Stephenson, Hackworth and their generation, there was no lack of opportunity for invention and improvement. In his first few designs, George Stephenson explored a number of different drives, including a sprocket-and-chain system that gave four-wheel drive. It was in 1825, through practical experiment, that he settled on the system of side rods driving crank axles, though at this time the cylinders and connecting rods were still mounted vertically. The early builders also had to work out a means of suspension. The track-beds were rough and uneven, and an axle-load of 3 tons was quite enough to break a cast-iron shaft if it received a jolt – broken crank-shafts would go on being a nightmare for successive generations. With the builder himself at hand, and the locomotive never travelling very far from the workshop, first aid could be readily applied, and preventive devices could be tried out.

Technical progress was soon to be recorded for publication. Among the little community of technically-minded men in Newcastle was Nicholas Wood, colliery viewer (supervisor) at Killingworth and author of the first manual of steam railway operation, *A Treatise on Rail-Roads*. When it was first published in 1825, George Stephenson was worried that it might give away too many secrets, and wanted to censor it. But it soon required amendment and was in a fat third edition by 1838, by which time there were numerous other books on the new phenomenon, in German, French and Russian as well as English.

TWO

Coming of Age

In 1821, to propose to build a railway, though enterprising and very modern, was not in itself startling. Public railways, using horses, had been known since 1803, when the Surrey Iron Railway was opened between Wandsworth and Croydon in South London. Another early line, the Kilmarnock and Troon Railway in Scotland, had tried using a six-wheeled, chain-drive steam locomotive, built by George Stephenson, in 1817, but the rails could not stand up to it, and the line reverted to horse-traction. The great novelty of the Stockton & Darlington Railway, incorporated in 1821, was that it was laid with Birkinshaw's new rails, 'fish-bellied' in form, 2in deep at the end of each 12 or 15ft section and 3.25in deep in the middle, and resting on stone sleepers. Its main business was to transport coal from the mines around Darlington to the loading staithes at Stockton, on the Tees estuary, and passengers were very much a secondary consideration. Ominously for the canal interest, a canal option had also been considered, and rejected in favour of a 'railway or tramroad.' In 1822, George Stephenson was appointed Engineer to the line. As a public railway it required an Act of Parliament, and in May 1823 the original Act enabling construction of the line was amended and a new word officially entered the vocabulary:

… it shall be lawful for the proprietors to make and erect such and so many loco-motive or moveable Engines as the said Company shall from time to time think proper and expedient, and to use and employ the same in or upon the said Railways or Tramroads or any of them, for the purpose of facilitating the transport conveyance and carriage of Goods, Merchandise and other articles and things upon and along the same Roads, and for the conveyance of Passengers upon and along the same Roads.

In the dry language of bureaucracy the locomotive thus duly if belat-edly received its birth certificate, though the name had not yet caught on and it would often be referred to as a 'travelling-engine'. In the same year Stephenson, with Edward Pease of the Stockton & Darlington, Michael Longridge of the Bedlington Ironworks, and his own son Robert (now aged twenty) founded Robert Stephenson & Co. for the purpose of building locomotives, with a factory at Forth Street in Newcastle. This was the world's first purpose-built locomotive works, though it no doubt looked very much like the existing iron foundries. Locomotive business was not very brisk at first, and the factory also made rails, wheels, wagon parts and so on. Its third locomotive to be ordered was its first to be delivered, as the Stockton & Darlington company's No.1, in September 1825, a few days before the line's opening. This was the celebrated and still preserved *Locomotion*. In design it conformed to the pattern of Stephenson's colliery engines, with vertical cylinders, their connecting rods linked by cross-bars, driving eccentric cranks on the wheels, and it was the first locomotive to have outside coupling rods. A four-wheel 'convoy cart' was provided, wooden-sided, with a sheet-iron water tank. It hauled the line's inaugural train on 27 September 1825, with George Stephenson as the driver. Appropriately enough, the train was formed of thirty-one coal wagons, with the company's single passenger carriage in the mid-dle. *Locomotion's* first boiler exploded in January 1828, killing the driver, after which the engine was substantially rebuilt by Timothy Hackworth. Later a third boiler was fitted. The speed of technical developments very soon made *Locomotion* obsolescent, but it worked regular services until 1841, and in deference to its primacy, it was used to head ceremonial proces-sions at the opening of new lines by the company. In the later 1840s it was used as a pumping engine, and in 1857 it was placed on a pedestal at North Road Station, Darlington. It is now in the Darlington Railway Museum.

Twenty-one years after the Penydarren exploit, the steam locomotive might be said to have come of age. It had emerged from the obscure con-fines of coal-yards and ironworks to operate a public service. The first train, said to have around 500 people in it, or on it, plus a band, attained a maxi-mum speed of 15mph, and, said a contemporary account, 'nothing could exceed the beauty and grandeur of the scene.' Timothy Hackworth was appointed Locomotive Foreman to the line, in charge of all engines, car-riages and trucks – the first of a long line of Master Mechanics and Chief

Mechanical Engineers who would rule, with varying degrees of autocracy, eccentricity, genius and skill, the locomotive departments of many hundreds of railway companies all over the world. It was not until 1833, however, that regular passenger services were worked by steam on the S&D; prior to that horses were used, and the world's first passenger steam railway was the Liverpool & Manchester, opened in 1830.

The locomotive's fame had spread. In 1812, the Grand Duke Nicholas, the future Tsar of Russia, who would inaugurate the St Petersburg-Moscow Railway, inspected the locomotives of the Middleton Railway. In 1815, a French engineer, M. Andrieux, visited it, and other visitors, mostly connected with the mining industry, came to view the Wylam and Killingworth engines. The chief engineer of the French *Corps Royal des Mines*, M. de Gallois, noted in his 1818 book *Des Chemins de fer en Angleterre*, that at Killingworth: '*les ouvriers appellent ces machines Iron Horses, chevaux de fer*', though the earliest known use of this term was applied to a solitary engine built by a mining engineer, Taylor Swainson, which ran briefly at Whitehaven, Cumberland, in 1812. The French visits do not appear to have resulted in any construction, but also in 1815, two German visitors came to see the Middleton Railway, one of them being Friedrich Krigar, Superintendent of the Royal Iron Foundry in Berlin. On his return, two engines of the Murray-Blenkinsop type were built at the Royal Foundry, one of which went to the mines of Upper Silesia; the other to the western Saar coalfield. Both were failures: the Silesian one, intended to haul coal between Königsgrube and Königshutte, was defeated by 'passive resistance, fear and aversion,' according to Dr C. Matschoss, quoted by Dendy Marshall in his authoritative and indispensable history of the earliest locomotives. The other simply failed to work properly, was laid aside, and sold for scrap in 1835.

The Forth Street works were naturally a place of great interest to anyone who wanted to observe the cutting edge of technical progress, and foreign visitors appear to have been shown round with a proper pride and remarkably little anxiety about trade secrets. William Strickland, sponsored by the Pennsylvania Society for Internal Improvement, came from the USA in 1825, and wrote a *Report on Canals and Rail Roads*. Two further Prussian engineers, Karl von Oeynhausen and Heinrich von Decken, came in 1827 and published their book, *Über Schienenwege in England* (On Railways in England), two years later. No travelogue, it was a closely detailed account of current locomotive design. Another visitor was a French engineer, Marc

Seguin, in the winter of 1825-1826. He was thirty-nine, well-off, well-educated, well-connected, a savant, a nephew of the ballooning Montgolfier brothers. On earlier visits to England he had made the acquaintance of leading scientists like Sir Humphry Davy and Michael Faraday. Although his main field had been the design of suspension bridges, for which he devised the stranded wire cable, he was interested in steam power in all its aspects. In 1824 he had designed a steamship for taking passengers on the Rhône, but its boiler, imported from the London makers Martineau & Taylor, had been inadequate to develop enough steam. Seguin realised that far more steam could be produced if the boiler could incorporate a greater heating surface than the firebox and the single or return flue provided. He designed a boiler fitted with tubes, through which heated air was drawn from the firebox, and obtained a patent for it on 22 February 1828, in a form related to stationary engines. From 1826 he was involved in the first French railway, from St Etienne to Andrézieux, and was a partner in and Chief Engineer of the line from St Etienne to Lyon. In the early spring of 1828 he purchased two locomotives from Robert Stephenson & Co. Allowed into France free of import duty by special ministerial dispensation, these were four-wheeled engines with low-slung vertical cylinders between the two wheels on each side; one was sent to the workshops of Alfred Hallette in Arras for testing; the other was sent straight to St Etienne. It was found that the Stephenson boilers could only produce 300kg of steam per hour, insufficient for the haulage requirement, and that the maximum speed was only 3.7mph (6km/h). Both locomotives were soon taken out of service, though at least one survived until August 1858, when it was offered for sale at the scrap value of Fr2,400, about £100 sterling.

By mid-May 1829 the building of a locomotive of Seguin's own design was well under way. It had a boiler holding forty-three copper tubes, though otherwise it incorporated most of the Stephenson mechanism, including vertical cylinders. Tests on it were first referred to in a report of the Council of the St Etienne-Lyon Railway on 20 October 1829, and on 7 November 1829, on test at Lyon-Perrache, it successfully hauled seven (four in some accounts) wagons laden with 15 tons of iron up a slope of 1.4 per cent and round a curve of 500m radius. It was stopped and successfully restarted in the middle of the gradient. Its increased heating surface produced 1,800kg of steam per hour, and the increased power produced a speed of 25mph (40km/h). A dozen locomotives were built to this design. None have been preserved, although a faithful modern replica has been built. A large double bellows was incorporated into the original design, mounted on a cart which also held the water tank, and pushed by the locomotive. Driven by a fan-belt from the cart's leading axle, this ventilator produced a current of air as long as the locomotive kept moving, which was passed back through a flexible connection into the ashpan and thus supplied a draught to the fire, which was at the front end of the boiler. The hot gases from the firebox were driven through the boiler tubes and back to the chimney, which was above the firebox but not directly linked to it. Once Seguin had worked out the effect of the blast-pipe – this was not something he learned on his English visits – the bellows was abandoned. Above the firebox was a water tank, fed from the tender cart, intended to preheat the water before it was pumped into the boiler space.

Seguin's method of locomotive design, scientific, theoretical, analytical but with a hard practical intention, was to typify the French approach just as the Stephensons' pragmatic, try-it-and-see style, with an intuitive feel for what was possible, would characterise English practice. From these early days, the two schools set off on divergent tracks, and the differing attitudes are realised and amusingly touched on by Seguin in his book (pp.458-9). The two pioneers were themselves very different types, Seguin a peppery *haut-bourgeois* Frenchman, father of nineteen children, opinionated and prone to fall out with his colleagues; George Stephenson a widower since 1805, with the one son upon whom he doted; a shrewd provincial Englishman with a fund of common sense and self-confidence that enabled him to hold his own in any intellectual or aristocratic gathering of his class-obsessed country. But for a time they worked together with a common purpose, both being very much aware that technical progress was necessary for the locomotive to become really useful – and for demand for its use to increase. The Stephensons and Seguin retained a mutual friendly respect, and fittingly, in the 1860s, the French engineer Jean Albert Perdonnet – another visitor to Newcastle in 1828, and later Director of the *Ecole Centrale* in Paris – arranged the casting of a prize medal bearing the heads of both George Stephenson and Marc Seguin.

An intriguing question arises here, the first but not the last to arouse ripples of nationalistic feeling about who invented certain features of the locomotive. The tubular boiler was the first vital improvement to the primitive steam locomotive. All the early engines had a single flue from firebox to chimney, or sometimes a single return flue. In the latter case the firebox was positioned at the front end and the flue was U-shaped, returning to exhaust up the chimney. Robert Stephenson was still building engines with single-flue or, at the most, double-flue boilers, when in 1828 he built the *Lancashire Witch* for the Bolton & Leigh Railway, in Lancashire, with two side-by-side furnace flues. But by May 1829, when he began to build the *Rocket*, he used a boiler fitted with twenty-five copper tubes. Where did he get that idea from? In English railway lore, the tubular boiler was proposed to the Stephensons by Henry Booth, who became their partner in the project. Booth, though a businessman rather than an engineer, was keenly interested in the mechanical aspects of the railway, and invented a form of screw coupling. But the tubular concept was certainly not original to Booth: the Frenchman Jean-Constantin Périer had described a tubular boiler in 1773, and Joel Barlow, US Consul in Paris, took out a French patent on a form of tubular boiler in 1793 (probably on behalf of his compatriot, the pioneer steamboat builder Robert Fulton); and in 1826 an English engineer, James Neville, obtained a patent in England for a vertical tubular boiler. Extension of the heating surface was clearly one of the current ideas of the time, though some at least of those earlier tubular boilers contained water tubes, not gas flues. Dendy Marshall notes that Booth denied any knowledge of Seguin's boiler, and also states that *Rocket's* tubular boiler and Seguin's were 'utterly unlike' each other. Apart from the copper tubes, this was certainly the case; Seguin's boiler had a separate firebox, at the chimney end, and the heated gases went from this into a single flue, helping to warm the water tank as they did so, and then passed backwards through the tubes. Stephenson's engine also had a firebox separate from the boiler, but at the opposite end from the chimney, and the gases went straight from it, forwards, into the tubes, as would happen with virtually all subsequent locomotives. Seguin began to build his locomotive before Robert Stephenson started on the *Rocket*, and both were completed at much the same time. How much detailed discussion, if any, there was between Stephenson and Seguin on the subject of locomotive design is unknown. It may be noted, though, that Robert Stephenson did not patent the tubular boiler as fitted to *Rocket* and, in modified form, to all his subsequent engines, while on 16 October 1829, Seguin applied for a further French patent specifically related to the tubular boiler in locomotives. In a long and somewhat defensive statement submitted to Samuel Smiles in 1857, when that worthy person was revising his *Lives of the Engineers*, Robert Stephenson rather played down the part of Booth:

... various claimants have arisen for the merit of having suggested the multi-tubular boiler as a means of obtaining the necessary heating surface. Whatever may be the value of their respective claims, the public, useful and extensive application of it must certainly bear date from the experiments made at Rainhill. M. Seguin ... states that he patented a similar multi-tubular boiler in France some years before ... but certain it is, that the perfect establishment of the success of the multi-tubular boiler is more immediately owing to the suggestion of Mr Henry Booth ... and to my father's practical knowledge in carrying it out.

The French engineer Anatole Mallet echoed this in reaching a sensible verdict through the haze of ancient steam that hangs around this question. Seguin, he said, was first, but he only built a boiler. Stephenson was second, but he built *'une véritable chaudière de locomotive'* – a real locomotive boiler. Dendy Marshall also accepts that Seguin 'was the first to propose the application of boilers with horizontal tubes to railway engines' (p.236). Though Forth Street made the idea its own, credit for the invention of the tubular locomotive boiler must certainly stay with Seguin. From autumn 1829, the steam locomotive was an Anglo-French machine.

Seguin did not make further developments of his locomotive design. He fell out with his co-directors in 1834 and left the St Etienne-Lyons Railway, though he maintained his interest in the new traction and in 1839 contributed to the rapidly increasing number of books on railways, with *De l'influence des chemins de fer et de l'art de les construire et de les tracer.* The engineers who followed him would return to using English-built locomotives, though of a sort more powerful than the pair supplied in 1828.

One wonders how many inventors, visionaries and mechanical dabblers abandoned work with a curse or a sigh as the news spread that a successful steam locomotive had been developed. For others, however, the news was exciting and promising. One who would have been pleased but not surprised was John Stevens, the American inventor who was first to operate a steamboat with a screw propellor, and was a pioneer supporter of railways as superior to canals. In 1825 he built and ran a small steam locomotive on rails in his garden. Another American enthusiast was the young Horatio Allen, assistant engineer of the Delaware and Hudson Canal Company. This concern was set up to transport coal, in the most industrialised region of the United States. It did not lay the first American railroad, having been preceded by a few short quarry lines in Massachusetts and Pennsylvania, but its chief engineer, John B. Jervis, unlike many canal managers, saw the railway not as something to be opposed, but as an opportunity to be embraced. By his own account, in 1827 Allen 'decided to go to the only place where a locomotive was in daily operation and could be studied in all its practical details.' During his stay in England, Allen ordered four locomotives on behalf of the Delaware & Hudson, three from Foster, Rastrick, of Stourbridge in the Midlands, and a single one from Robert Stephenson, at a price £100 higher. All were intended for use on a feeder line between Carbondale and the canal at Honesdale. The first to be delivered was the Stephenson locomotive, landed on 15 January 1829. Although sometimes said to have been named *America*, it was actually *Pride of Newcastle*, a four-wheeler of similar design to the *Lancashire Witch*. It was exhibited in steam at Dunscomb's yard in Water Street, New York, with the wheels raised off the ground to show the motion going. Its later fate is unknown but it never appears to have run on rails. Almost certainly it ended up as a stationary engine. A cylinder from it is preserved at the Smithsonian Institution. Better recorded is the first of the Foster, Rastrick engines, known as the *Stourbridge Lion*. Landed at West Point Foundry, New York, in May 1829, it too aroused great interest and was steamed for public display, though again there were no rails there for it to run on. Transferred by canal to Honesdale, it became the first full-size steam locomotive to work in the United States, on 8 August 1829.

The track of the new line, beams of hemlock wood topped by iron strips, was supported by a curving wooden trestle, 30ft high, over Lackawaxen Creek, and when Allen's colleagues saw the engine, they had grave doubts about its axle-loading. Jervis's requirement had been that this should not exceed 1.5 tons, but it was at least half a ton more than this. Allen took the controls alone for the demonstration run. In his own, much later words:

> … believing that the road would prove safe, and preferring, if we did go down, to go down handsomely and without any evidence of timidity, I started with considerable velocity, passed the curve over the creek safely and returned without accident to the point of departure.

According to the later (1870) recollection of a local figure, the Hon. John Torry, some people described the engine as 'looking like an enormous grasshopper, having three or four times the usual number of legs. Its driving wheels were of oakwood, banded with a heavy wrought-iron tire, and the front was ornamented with a large, fierce-looking face of a lion, in bold relief.' A local paper, the *Dundaff Republican*, described it as 'a plain, stout work of immense height.' Despite local excitement, the event was not a happy or auspicious one. A cannon, introduced to signal the departure, was fired prematurely and shattered the arm of one Alva Adams, which had to be amputated. For all Allen's bravado, the engine was not used again. It was taken off the track and later fenced round with boards. For fourteen or so years it remained in its makeshift shed, then finally the boiler was removed to Carbondale for a stationary engine, and what remained was sold for scrap. The other engines did not come into service at all, and the line was regraded as a gravity-worked one. Jervis confirmed to the locomotive historian William H. Brown on 17 July 1870 that 'only the *Lion* was set up'. Allen departed from the Delaware & Hudson soon after. But he and Jervis remained close friends and, both surviving to over ninety years, they were to play further parts in the development of the American steam locomotive in the course of eminent careers.

Incidentally, accounts of Jervis, even today, often refer to him as the designer of the *Stourbridge Lion*. This mistake may be put down to the fact that he did design later locomotives; though a certain reluctance to accept that America's first full-size locomotive was a wholly English product can also be discerned. Had Jervis been responsible for the design, the manufacturers, Foster, Rastrick, would certainly have been taken to task over the two-ton axle loading which made the locomotives unusable. John Urpeth Rastrick, who designed the *Stourbridge Lion*, was an experienced foundryman and second only to Trevithick as a locomotive-builder; and was soon to be one of the three referees at the Rainhill trials. Typically of engineers of the time, he was able to design and build bridges and lay out railway lines as well as build machines. The separation of mechanical and civil engineering into separate disciplines had yet to happen. His main contribution to locomotive design was the glass gauge showing the boiler water-level, which made its first appearance on his engines, and quickly came into universal use. The Stourbridge engines, as the 'grasshopper' reference suggests, were essentially of the primal type, with a vertical cylinder sunk into each side of the boiler, a forward-placed firebox, and crosshead frame supporting the motion. Rastrick's colliery engine *Agenoria*, which is preserved, is of identical type. *Pride of Newcastle* was a more advanced design, for during 1828 and

1829, important developments had taken place, and others were at hand, in the north of England.

In late 1827, Timothy Hackworth produced a new locomotive for the Stockton & Darlington, the first to have six coupled wheels. Though George Stephenson's locomotive for the Kilmarnock & Troon Railway, in 1817, had been an 0-6-0, it had chain drive. In fact Hackworth's was a drastic rebuild of an unsuccessful four-wheeler built by Robert Wilson of Gateshead in the previous year, and contemptuously called 'Chittaprat' by the engine-men. Reincarnated, it had a larger boiler than any previous engine, and was proudly named *Royal George*. A meticulous practical engineer, Hackworth was concerned with providing enough steam, and getting effective traction on the rail. The first concern led him to more than double the heating surface of the 'Locomotion' type; the second to provide six coupled wheels, joined by connecting rods. Other novelties which would become standard were spring-loaded safety-valves and self-lubricating bearings, with built-in oil reservoirs. The two front axles were supported on a single leaf spring on each side. But perhaps the most important new aspect was Hackworth's use of the exhaust steam, once it had left the cylinders. Some of it was diverted to provide a jet below the grate, to stimulate the fire. Some was used to heat the boiler feed water: either this or a contemporary engine of George Stephenson's, *Experiment*, was the first to heat its own feed water. But most was sent up the chimney, through a narrow aperture which passed it in a succession of blasts, rather than mere puffs, with each return of the piston rod. This reduction of the opening to the blast-pipe was a crucial feature in improving the draught: forcing the fire to a greater heat, and so generating more steam, as the engine moved along. In other respects, the engine retained many primitive features, including vertically-mounted cylinders, which drove directly on to the rear coupled wheels, though in a neater arrangement than the old Killingworth types. The boiler, 13ft (395.9cm) long and 4ft 4in (132cm) in diameter, contained a single U-shaped return flue, as Trevithick had used in his engines. *Royal George* was by far the most reliable locomotive yet built. In its first year it conveyed 22,442 tons of coal at a cost reckoned to be £466, against an equivalent cost for horse haulage of £998. It was eventually sold in 1840, for £550 – a handsome profit after thirteen years' work.

By 1828, Robert Stephenson, who had returned to his eponymous company in 1827 from his three-year stint as a mining engineer in Colombia, had also embarked on new designs. The first was the already-mentioned

Lancashire Witch, whose cylinders were not set vertically but placed to the rear of the boiler, at an angle, and drove the front set of wheels. Leaf springs were fitted to the wheels. The elbowing grasshopper limbs were gone. Similar cylinders were fitted to five six-wheeled engines built in 1829, including one ordered by Samuel Homfray for the Sirhowy Railway in Wales, and another ordered by Major George Washington Whistler for the Baltimore & Ohio Railroad. Shipwrecked off the Scottish coast, this engine was the first of many to be lost at sea; though unlike most it seems to have been salvaged, and used as a stationary engine. It never reached the USA. These engines show a significant stage of development on the way towards the design of the *Rocket*, in the same year.

THREE

Trials and Triumphs

The steam locomotive, like the race that invented it, was destined to be a competitive beast, constantly matched and measured against rivals of its own species. The appearance of the very first locomotive was prompted, or encouraged, by a wager. In a similar way, the appearance of the first 'main-line' locomotive was prompted by a prize competition. It would have happened anyway, but the sense of rivals at work undoubtedly drove Robert Stephenson and his associates to produce something that represented the best of proven experience in their still limited field. Most important in their eyes was the reward of the locomotive contract for the newly-built Liverpool & Manchester Railway. The celebrated trials at Rainhill Level, on the new line, which took place from 6 to 14 October 1829, not only secured them the contract but the accompanying publicity spread their fame across the world. To open-minded people, the steam locomotive was now established beyond doubt as a machine that was going to revolutionise land transport.

On the eve of the trials, matters did not look quite so obvious. A strong body of opinion within the Liverpool & Manchester believed that a series of stationary hauling engines was the most reliable way of handling the traffic. To them, the trials were not to find the best locomotive, but rather to show that locomotives were simply not up to the job. The entry conditions of what the judges called 'the Ordeal' were demanding. The locomotives had to weigh a maximum of 4.5 tons on four wheels, or 6 tons on six wheels. Their boilers had to be tested to a pressure of 150psi (10.5kg/cm^2), though the stipulated working pressure was only 50psi (3.5kg/cm^2). They had to complete a 70-mile course and pull a 20-ton train at 10mph. They had to consume their own smoke. Some of these stipulations reveal the public's genuine anxiety about locomotives. Many fears were expressed, that cows would lose their milk or abort their calves; that high speeds (i.e. 30mph) would cause asphyxiation; that boilers would explode with fatal results. The loud puffing and mechanical clanking noises made by locomotives alarmed people. Smoke, its destructive chemical properties not yet fully understood, was seen simply as an offensive nuisance. Consequently, though the earliest engines had burned coal, all the steam engines entered in the trials burned coke, which is virtually smokeless, if not fumeless.

It was very soon apparent that there were only three serious contenders: the *Rocket*, entered by the Stephensons with Henry Booth (who was also Treasurer of the L&M), the *Sans Pareil*, entered by Timothy Hackworth, and the *Novelty*, entered by the Swede John Ericsson and the Englishman John Braithwaite. All were four-wheelers. The two other entrants were a small steam engine, *Perseverance*, built by Timothy Burstall, of Leith, a pioneer of powered road coaches; and a horse-propelled 'Cyclopede'. A brief appearance was made by a 'manumotive' entered by an enterprising American visitor, Ross Winans, who had been sent over to England by the Baltimore & Ohio Railroad. Operated by two men, it was certainly incapable of fulfilling the conditions, and the *Liverpool Courier* of 7 October noted that it had damaged a wheel in collision with the solid *Sans Pareil*. But we shall meet Winans again. The hearts of the watchers were won by *Novelty*, which unlike the others ran almost silently, its fire kept going by a bellows; and, without a train, reached over 30mph – the fastest land speed yet attained. But, as George Stephenson observed, the lightweight *Novelty*, when it came to pulling a train, had 'no guts'.

Hackworth by now had plenty of experience with coal-hauling, and *Sans Pareil* was more robust, certainly the most powerful of the competitors. In fact it was heavier than the conditions allowed. Near the end of the tests, its feed pump failed to work, the water level in the boiler fell, and the fusible plug between the boiler and firebox melted, filling the firebox with steam and water, and effectively ending its chances. Hackworth was deeply disgruntled; as John Dixon, one of George Stephenson's 'young men' wrote immediately afterwards:

> Timothy has been very sadly out of temper ever since he came ... he openly accused all G.S.'s people of conspiring to hinder him of which I do believe them innocent, however he got many trials but never got half of his seventy miles done without stopping. He burns nearly double the quantity of coke

that the Rocket does and mumbles and roars and rolls about like an Empty Beer Butt on a rough Pavement and moreover weighs above 4.5 tons consequently should have six wheels and as for being on Springs I must confess I cannot find them out either going or standing neither can I perceive any effect they have. She is very ugly...

The cylinders of *Sans Pareil* had been cast at Stephenson's works, hence the designer's suspicions, or excuse for failure. Tempers often ran high – a great deal was at stake, hard work and hard cash, against possible reward, fame and fortune. The early locomotive engineers were far from being a band of brothers, combining in tenderly nursing along their infant phenomenon. Burstall's son James had been found one day inside the Forth Street works, and was promptly ejected. Technical and commercial rivals, all guarded their own secrets jealously whilst looking long and hard at the products of the opposition: the days of openness were gone.

Rocket was the only contestant to satisfy the conditions. It incorporated great advances made in the five years since *Locomotion*. The chimney was fitted with a blast-pipe, a feature which has caused controversy. It has been suggested that on the very eve of *Rocket's* first test, the Stephensons, noting the powerful blast of *Sans Pareil*, altered the exhaust of their locomotive to provide a similar forced draught. This is quite possible, though Robert denied it, writing to Smiles in the statement already quoted from: ' ... to the best of my recollection, the prize was won without any alteration having been made in that part of the engine.' All the engines had to be constantly tinkered with and adjusted, merely to keep them running. But later accusations included burglary of the shed in which *Sans Pareil* was kept overnight. Through the nineteenth century and into the next, a fierce argument would be maintained by those who believed that the Stephensons had received too much credit for early developments, and Hackworth too little. They had some right on their side. But the Stephensons had long been aware of the value of the blast-pipe in forcing air into the fire. Trevithick had discovered this effect when he directed exhaust steam up the chimney of his first locomotive. Since then, builders had tried to keep a balance between the positive aspect of this, and the negative ones, which included excessive fuel consumption and the shooting of sparks and embers out of the chimney. The Stephenson engines, mostly travelling short distances, had only a modest blast; steam could be raised again at the end of the journey. Hackworth, with a longer line to operate, needed to generate steam as the locomotive went along, and had adapted or built his to provide a more powerful draught. George and Robert Stephenson were no doubt powerfully curious to know just what *Sans Pareil's* blast-pipe width was, but allegations of industrial espionage remain unproven. In any case, the twenty-five 3in tubes in *Rocket's* boiler generated enough steam and power to more than fulfil the haulage and speed requirements. The cylinders were set beneath and behind the boiler, at an angle of 35°, and drove the rear wheels via connecting rods. The firebox was made of copper and the wheels were fitted with springs. The four-wheel, wooden-framed tender was the first vehicle to have outside bearings. *Rocket* did not break down. *Mechanic's Magazine*, which favoured *Novelty*, could only complain of *Rocket* that: 'the faults most perceptible in this engine, were a great inequality in its velocity, and a very partial fulfilment of the conditions that it should 'effectually consume its own smoke'.' It also, of course, later perpetrated the first running-down of a member of the public by a locomotive, when on the railway's opening day it fatally injured the eminent Parliamentarian William Huskisson. At that time and for some years to come, unwary people were at serious risk from the sudden approach and terrible momentum of the steam locomotive. America fitted bells as a warning following a Massachusetts state edict of 1835; early Stockton & Darlington engines had bells, though Britain came to prefer the whistle (invented for the stationary engine by Adrian Stephens, a friend of Trevithick's, and first recorded in railway use in 1835, after a locomotive on the Leicester & Swannington Railway ran into a herd of cows) – American locomotives eventually had both bells and whistles.

As a public event, the trials were a great success and received worldwide publicity. Reporting events on 12 October, *The Times* noted that the astonishment of spectators at the *Rocket* 'was complete, every one exclaiming involuntarily, "The power of steam is unlimited!"' The railway company benefited in other ways too. *The Times* recorded on 24 October that: 'Such has been the good effect of this competition on the public mind, that the selling price of the Company's shares has advanced no less than ten per cent … Ten per cent in a total capital of 650,000l makes the net sum gained by this judicious scheme of competition no less than 65,000l.'

Rocket in its turn was almost immediately superseded; but its great contribution was to show that the steam locomotive could give consistent performance at a much higher level of work than before. The anti-locomotive agitators went quiet. The L&M sold the engine for a satisfactory £300 in 1836, and in much-altered form it can still be seen in the Science Museum, London. In the year of the Rainhill trials, Thomas Carlyle, a leading way-marker of nineteenth-century thought, characterised the era in *Signs of the Times* as 'The Mechanical Age' – the age of machinery, he emphasised, 'in every outward and inward sense of that word'. Carlyle did not consider this to be a good thing, but he nevertheless acknowledged a reality that many others preferred to ignore.

Meanwhile the Forth Street works benefited from an order for a further eight locomotives of the 'Rocket' type. These were far from being replicas: on each successive engine some improvement was made. *Rocket* itself was adapted before going into regular service. The angle of the cylinders was greatly reduced, with consequent improvement to its stability. The original high-set moving 'elbows' imparted a disturbing wiggle and pitch to the motion. Given the almost complete lack of protection for the men on the footplate in these early engines, especially the four-wheelers, it can only have been the slow operating speeds that prevented drivers from being pitched off and seeing their engines trundle on down the line without them. Luckily, if this happened, a fast-reacting man could heave himself on to one of the trucks as it rolled by, and clamber forwards to regain control. The most significant alterations were first incorporated in *Northumbrian*, delivered to the L&M on 31 July 1830. It was the first locomotive to have an integral boiler and firebox, and a smoke-box as a separate chamber. With the importance of the blast-pipe fully recognised, the rudimentary fittings of *Rocket* in this respect were adapted to the basic form of a chamber in front of the boiler, with the blast-pipe from the cylinders fitted in its lower part, and the chimney above. This would be found in all steam locomotives except those later fitted with condensing apparatus or Franco-Crosti boilers. It formed part of a self-serving system, known to later engineers as the 'Stephenson cycle'. Steam had to be produced in sufficient quantity to supply the cylinders. The production of steam required combustion: the more steam needed, the more heat was demanded. Combustion requires air, and the rate of combustion depends on the rate of air supply. The exhaust steam blast carried with it smoke and combustion products from the firebox, and air was drawn into the furnace to replace these. A hotter fire produced more steam, which created more draught, which in turn made the fire hotter. Forced draught devices, like Seguin's bellows, were no longer needed once this combination of events was understood. Strangely enough, though, it would be almost the end of the steam locomotive's life before the functions of blast-pipe and draughting system were subjected to close technical analysis. For 120 years, this vital aspect of steaming would be left to guesswork and 'tweaking' of the smoke-box fittings not only in prototypes but also in production locomotives.

By luck or shrewd calculation, the supporters of steam on the Liverpool & Manchester Railway found a helpful ally in the attractive form of Fanny Kemble, aged twenty-one, who had just made a sensational acting debut in London, playing the heroine in *Romeo and Juliet*. She was the first but far from the last young female beauty to be involved in promoting mechanical marvels; but she was more articulate than most. In the summer of 1830, after being shown the locomotive *Northumbrian* by an avuncular George Stephenson, and riding both on and behind it, she recorded her impressions:

> A common sheet of paper is enough for love, but a foolscap extra can alone contain a railroad and my ecstasies … We were introduced to the little engine which was to drag us along the rails. She (for they make these curious fire-horses all mares) consisted of a boiler, a stove, a small platform – a bench, and behind the bench a barrel containing enough water to prevent her from being thirsty for fifteen miles, the whole machine not bigger than a common fire engine. She goes upon two wheels, which are her feet, and are moved by bright steel legs called pistons … The reins, the bit and bridle of this wonderful beast is a small steel handle, which applies or withdraws the steam from its legs or pistons, so that a child might manage it… This snorting little animal which I felt rather inclined to pat, was then harnessed to our carriage, and, Mr Stephenson having taken me on the bench of the engine with him, we started at about ten miles an hour… On the return journey … The engine was set off at its utmost speed, 35mph, swifter than a bird flies (for they tried the experiment with a snipe). You cannot conceive what the sensation of cutting the air was; the motion as smooth as possible. I stood up, and with my bonnet off, 'drank the air before me'. I had a perfect sense of security, and not the slightest fear. When I closed my eyes the sensation of flying was delightful and strange beyond description.

The Liverpool & Manchester, the first railway to employ exclusively steam traction, was opened formally on 15 September 1830. At that time the rails had already been laid for a new public railway in South Carolina, to link

Charleston and Hamburg. Its chief engineer was the ever-buoyant Horatio Allen, who had not lost his enthusiasm for steam power. Always ready with a quotable phrase, he reported to his Board that:' … in the future there was no reason to expect any material improvement in the breed of horses, while, in my judgement, the man was not living who knew what the breed of locomotives was to place at command.' This time, however, the engines were to be home-produced. An order was placed with the West Point Foundry, New York, and the first US-built engine for regular service was shipped in parts to Charleston, assembled there, and steamed for the first time on 2 November. This was the famous *Best Friend of Charleston* – a four-wheeler, with a vertical boiler mounted at the rear end of the frame, its weight balanced by the cylinders and water tank at the other end. The design, by E.L. Miller – who had also been at Rainhill – owed nothing to British practice though it had some resemblance to Ericsson's *Novelty*, and, like *Novelty*, was a precursor of all tank engines, with a well tank fitted inside the frame. *Best Friend* was recorded as hauling a five-car passenger train at 20mph (32km/h). Public service on the line began in January 1831, the first American railroad to work a regular steam-powered schedule. The locomotive's career was short. Early safety valves were simple devices and, with boiler pressures rarely exceeding 50psi (3.5kg/cm²), it was not uncommon for drivers or firemen to get a little more steam by tying down the valve. This dangerous trick was tried by the *Best Friend's* fireman on 17 June 1831. Apparently because the noise made by the valve was annoying him, he fastened down the valve and sat on it, while the engine was on the turntable and the driver was examining the waiting train of lumber wagons. Shortly afterwards the boiler exploded. According to the *Charleston Courier* of 18 June, 1831, the fireman suffered a broken thigh. The driver, Nicholas Darrell, however later said that the man had died of his injuries. The engine was rebuilt, with a centrally-placed vertical boiler, and appropriately renamed *Phoenix*.

Such hazards of steam locomotion were no discouragement to would-be drivers. To be at the controls of the fastest thing on earth, so new, so powerful, so noisy, was an excitement and a source of prestige. And the drivers were paid well. From the early days, each was assigned his own locomotive. On the Stockton & Darlington Railway, which set the pattern, drivers were paid a basic retainer, whether their engine was used or not, plus a working rate based on the tonnage of goods or the number of passengers. In April 1828, the best-paid driver was making over £37 a week (he was William Gowland, and had charge of the reliable and husky *Royal George*). From this he had to pay his fireman, and also a driver-fireman, so that two men were always available to operate the locomotive. Nevertheless, it made him probably the highest-paid working man in the country. Not that the job was easy. The driver customarily worked a ten-hour day, or longer, on his exposed footplate. To start the engine, it was necessary to prise the wheels into movement with a long crowbar before jumping on board. Getting it into reverse gear was tricky: another S&D driver, William Chicken, was specially famous because he could reverse in the dark.

Best Friend had an immediate home-built predecessor in the tiny locomotive Tom Thumb, designed in 1829-1830 by the philanthropic millionaire Peter Cooper with the assistance of Ross Winans, who had begun as a supplier of horses to railroads, but had returned from England convinced of the future of steam power. It was built at Cooper's Scranton Ironworks. With a horse-power scarcely greater than that of a single horse, it was regarded purely as an experimental model. On 28 August 1830, it was demonstrated with a passenger carriage containing twenty-four 'disinterested gentlemen, of the first respectability', and some wagons, a total load of about 4.5 tons, on the horse-hauled line that formed the original section of the Baltimore & Ohio Railroad. Its single cylinder drove a crank, and a fan-belt attached to one of the wheels actuated a bellows to stimulate the fire. To meet the return trip, the stage-coach operators Stockton & Stokes had put their best horse with a carriage on the parallel track from Relay House. In a somewhat bathetic episode, the horse got off a to a faster start until the locomotive developed its full tractive power and drew ahead. Then the fan belt slipped, the fire went down, steam was lost, and the horse was first to the end of the line. The incident was much publicised and illustrated. Loftily ignoring it, Winans noted that the true purpose and success of Tom Thumb's thirteen-mile run was to establish that: 'curvatures of 400ft radius offer no material impediment to the use of steam power on railroads, when the wheels are constructed with a cone ... The engineers in England have been so decidedly of opinion that locomotive steam engines could not be used on curved rails, that it was much doubted whether the many curvatures of the Baltimore and Ohio Railroad would not exclude the use of steam power.' The cone referred to meant that the wheel surface and its flange did not meet at right angles, but the flange was conic in section, so that on a curve, when the inner wheel inevitably pressed harder on the rail, the pressure was somewhat relieved. Again it was a question of adapting the locomotive to different circumstances.

Despite such rather uncertain beginnings, America proved to be, for a variety of reasons, a favourable home for the steam locomotive. Having crossed the Atlantic, it quickly spread and established itself. The USA was a new country, with few cities and many scattered towns. It was rich in woodlands (and almost immediately wooden billets began to be used as fuel rather than expensive coke). There was a sense of national expansion, of wide frontiers, of great distances that needed to be covered as quickly as possible. Trade and industry were developing fast, based on crops and primary products like coal, ore and lumber, which needed heavy haulage power. Not least, there was an open-minded attitude to inventions and ideas that speeded up business and made life more convenient. Although it was an invention from the Old World, the New World adopted – and adapted – the locomotive with enthusiasm. The countries of continental Europe were a little slower to follow.

FOUR

The Basics Confirmed

But in 1830, the momentum of development was still with England. Robert Stephenson's team in Newcastle were not resting on their post-Rainhill laurels. There was much to do before their products would be free of criticism for unreliability and difficulty of operation. Other builders were also coming forward. In 1830 a Liverpool foundry, Edward Bury & Co., supplied a locomotive to the Liverpool & Manchester Railway which was in many respects a trend-setter. Bury's foreman, and probably his chief designer, James Kennedy, had worked for a time at Forth Street. Named *Liverpool*, this engine's cylinders were set horizontally, at the front, and completely out of sight, inside the frames. The frames were slender iron bars, between which the internal driving rods could be seen, attached to a crank axle between the rear wheels. The four wheels were of an unprecedented diameter, 6ft. The firebox was shaped like a D, with a flat front and its sides and back forming rather more than a semi-circle. Its top was domed and set above was a smaller steam dome, the first of its kind. In its original form, there was also a bellows fitted beneath the tender to provide draught to the fire. Although it formed the basis of Bury's later engines, it was not itself a success; George Stephenson thought *Liverpool's* wheels were too big and was reluctant to test it. During the testing period, it also made some runs on the Bolton & Kenyon Railway, where in July 1831 it killed its driver – and in this case the fireman too – when a wheel broke and it went off the rails, crushing them against a bank. The L&M rejected it, but, rebuilt, it remained in use on the colliery line for many years.

Also in 1830 the Stephensons brought out a new locomotive which followed the Bury model in the placement of its cylinders. However, the true pioneer of inside-cylinder design was Goldsworthy Gurney, the Cornish surgeon who built the first successful steam road vehicles, and whose work was well-known to the railway builders. The first Stephenson inside-cylinder design, *Planet*, was also the first locomotive which could be said to form a class. Up to then, engines had been one-offs, each incorporating improvements or experiments, as the designers and builders struggled with the business of making mobile steam power effective. By late 1830, things were settling down somewhat, and a whole series of locomotives was built in very much the same manner, all four-wheelers, some of them 0-4-0s, but the majority being 2-2-0, with a single driving axle. In particular, *Planet* confirmed some basics of what was to become the prevailing British style, with horizontal cylinders, set within the frames, and placed at the front. The aim was practical, to get better stability of running through better distribution of weight, and to situate the cylinders closer to the boiler's heat, but the 'invisible drive' stylistic effect also seems to have pleased British engineers. Not all followed this policy: in 1834 George Forrester of Liverpool built the first engines with horizontal outside cylinders, 2-2-0 types for Ireland's first railway, the Dublin & Kingstown. But in general, inside cylinders would remain a hallmark of British locomotive design, despite their inconvenience of access and the need to provide expensive crank axles. The outside 'sandwich' frame, of ash or oak planking, reinforced by iron plates on both sides, and with outside bearings, became another typical feature, and for the first time, the boiler was attached to the frame, rather than itself forming the main structural member. As with *Northumbrian*, boiler and firebox were a single unit. One of the main reasons for the outside frame was to provide support in the event – all too frequent – of the crank axle breaking. This axle was also protected by inside bearings. A small railed footplate was by now being provided, but British designers saw no need to provide a cab to shelter the enginemen.

It was not obvious at the time that the 'Planets' confirmed the basics, and in any case there was still enormous scope for experimentation and improvement. In 1831, Stephenson built two 0-4-0 'Planets' as heavy goods engines for the Liverpool & Manchester Railway, with coupled wheels of equal diameter. At 10 tons they were heavier than the passenger engines, and their names, *Samson* and *Goliath*, indicate how they were viewed at the time. Many others followed. Two of these were fitted with piston valves in 1832, the first examples of what would later become universal, but slide valves, less complicated in practice if less efficient in theory, remained standard for another six decades. Railway workshops were still little more than slightly glorified blacksmith's shops, and men like Hackworth had to devise machine tools and work systems to cope with the steadily increasing workload of maintenance and repair on a growing fleet of locomotives. The fuel burned by these, as with all early British locomotives, continued to be coke, because of adverse public opinion of coal smoke.

The 'Planet' design was elaborated into Stephenson's 'Patentee' class of 1833, on a 2-2-2 wheelbase, with trailing wheels set behind the firebox, which allowed for a somewhat longer boiler, reduced the axle-load on the driving axle, and gave the engine a more stable ride. This aspect was important, as the engines had rigid frames, with fixed wheels, and the four-wheelers especially were prone to pitch up and down and generally make life on the footplate highly uncomfortable. There was little understanding as yet of the problem of balancing in steam engines. Heavy cranks going round at high speed caused unsteadiness in lightweight locomotives. By 1837, John Braithwaite, on the Eastern Counties Railway in England, had begun to fit balance weights to the driving wheels to counteract the movement of the cranks. This method was continued and improved by William Fernihough on the same railway and the practice gradually became universal. Once again, English empiricism was backed up by French science. The French engineer Louis le Chatelier made a detailed study of locomotive balancing and in 1845 published *Etudes sur la stabilité des machines locomotives en mouvement*, a work which saved other designers a great deal of trouble, trial, and error. The 'Patentees' and 'Planets', despite their possession of a full-length frame, used it only to support the boiler and the axle bearings. The cylinders were fixed to the boiler, and the tender drawbar was attached to the base of the firebox. In later designs, these would normally be attached to the frame.

For several years from 1831, a railway map of Britain, Western Europe and North America would have shown only a modest and random scattering of short and unconnected lines. Many of these were still operated wholly or partly by horses. But the improvements brought about in Britain encouraged the building of new lines, and from now on any railway entrepreneur would automatically include the price of locomotives and their ancillary requirements in costing a new railway. At this time, however, a distinct characteristic of the steam locomotive emerged. Just because it ran well across the vales and gentle slopes of England did not mean that it would do the same in the more rugged terrain of the Allegheny foothills or the deep valley of the Delaware. The builders of American railroads, in a hurry to get their investment back, did not shrink from steeper slopes and tighter curves than would have been thought desirable in England. The rails still were wooden blocks laid lengthwise, with thin iron straps hammered down on top: these 'strap-rails' often broke and left curled-up ends, a menace to the next engine. American conditions required an American solution, and in 1831, borrowing the Liverpool & Manchester's idea, the Baltimore & Ohio Railroad set up a competition to find a suitable American-built locomotive. The prize was $4,000 for the winner and even $3,500 for the runner-up. Among the stipulations were that the entries should not weigh over 3.5 tons (very light-weight, but the railways with their strap-rails were preoccupied with axle-weight), and that they must on a level rail be capable of drawing by day 15 tons, including the weight of the wagons, at 15mph. Up to five entrants may have duly appeared on 27 June 1831, but only the *York*, built by the clockmaker Phineas Davis, of   York, Pa., fulfilled the conditions. It was a small vertical-cylindered engine, on four wheels with outside bearings, dubbed 'the Grasshopper' because of its upward-jutting rods; but the B&O ordered it and a few more of the same, and some were still at work fifty years later. Davis was killed in an accident with one of the 'Grasshoppers' in 1836: the first of several designers who would be victims of their own creations.

Among the reasons for amending British designs may also be that American engineers, contemplating a newly-assembled locomotive shipped out by Bury or some other British maker, felt that they could add something to this rather meagre beast. Perhaps they even felt a patriotic necessity to turn the product of the old imperial state into something more distinctively typical of the Land of the Free. There was also the matter of fuel. The narrow British chimney, built to pipe out smoke and fumes from coal or coke, was unsuited to wood smoke and when wood was burned in the firebox the sharp blast puffed out hot ash, sparks and burning fragments, with consequent fire hazard. Whatever the reasons, the British designs were often remodelled by American owners. *John Bull*, a four-wheel, inside-cylinder engine, of the 'Planet' goods class, built to the 4ft 10in (147.2cm) gauge, was a typical case. Shipped in parts from Robert Stephenson & Co. to the Camden & Amboy Railroad, it was assembled at Bordentown, New Jersey. Its cost was almost $4,000. On 12 November 1831 it pulled a demonstration train for members of the New Jersey legislature, in a highly satisfactory manner; and went into regular service on partial completion of the line in September 1833, along with three other Stephenson types which had been built at Hoboken. *John Bull* had not long been running before modifications were made. By early 1832 a leading truck and pilot had been fitted. This latter item, complete with cow-catcher, set to become typical of the American locomotive, was added by the C&A's engineer, Isaac Dripps, who had come from Belfast, Northern Ireland, as a child with his parents, learned the mechanic's trade, and would in due course become superintendent of motive power on the great Pennsylvania Railroad. Later *John Bull* was equipped with headlight, cab, bell and whistle. It was untypical only in its survival. By the late 1840s it was being used only on lightweight passenger trains, and in 1849 it was jacked up for use as a boiler testing-plant for new engines. In the 1850s it was already regarded as an antique, and though most old engines went for scrap or drastic rebuild, *John Bull* somehow survived, and in 1876 was shown as 'America's first locomotive' (which of course it was not) at the Centennial Exhibition in Philadelphia. It was partially restored at this time. In 1885 the Pennsylvania Railroad, which had absorbed the Camden & Amboy in 1871, presented the engine to the Smithsonian Institution. It made a run from New York to Chicago in April 1893. Since 1940 it has been a static exhibit. The original tender was a four-wheeler adapted from a C&A car. The present one dates from the mid-nineteenth century. Built as an eight-wheeler, it was changed to its present four-wheel form in order to better represent the original. But, as with many another ancient locomotive, there is little of *John Bull's* original fabric remaining.

The demands of US railroad operation soon left the four-wheeled locomotive behind, and new designers came forward with new ideas. The most notable of these was John B. Jervis. His first known design, the *De Witt Clinton*, with four coupled wheels, for the Mohawk & Hudson Railroad, was not a great success, but incorporated three features unseen before. One was a protective roof for the crew, an early form of the cab; another was an integral tank built into the tender; the third was all-iron wheels – previous locomotives had had wooden wheel-centres. An early image of *De Witt Clinton* shows it hauling a set of cars closely modelled on the stage-coaches of the time. A contemporary account describes how on the first trip, in August 1831, the carriages, linked by 3ft iron chains, were jerked so abruptly into motion that some of those sitting on top fell off. Sparks from the engine's pitch-pine fuel set the outside passengers' clothes smouldering and ignited their parasols. For the return journey, wooden posts were wedged between the coaches, and this early form of buffing gear prevented further unseemly tumbles.

In 1832, Jervis came up with another new design, again for the Mohawk & Hudson. This was a single-driver engine, built by the West Point Foundry. Named *Experiment*, it announced the first great American contribution to the development of the steam locomotive. It was the first in the world to incorporate a leading truck, or bogie. The four-wheel truck had an outside frame and bearings, with suspended springs. The 4-2-0 wheel arrangement became the first distinctively American type, and flourished between 1835 and 1842. The swivelling action of the truck kept engines on the road where a rigid wheel arrangement might have derailed on undulating or irregularly-laid track. *Experiment* had other unusual features, including driving wheels set to the rear of the firebox. Among the specified fittings was 'a good and convenient hand force pump, with copper pipes to connect with the water tank on the tender waggon' – effective injection of feed water into the boiler was one of the as-yet unsolved problems of locomotive design. The engine had two inside cylinders and link motion modelled on that of the Stephenson 'Planets'. The outside frame was of seasoned white oak, strengthened with iron braces, and supporting outside bearings for the driving wheels. Originally it was built as an anthracite burner, but poor steaming led to rebuilding of the firebox for wood burning in 1833. Despite this, it was claimed that *Experiment* achieved a speed of 62mph (99.7km/h) in 1832. Later renamed *Brother Jonathan*, the locomotive was rebuilt in 1846 as a 4-4-0.

The truck was adopted by all American railways, for use on 'road engines' – those which went out on the line with freight or passenger trains. Only those which stayed in the yard to do switching duties would not be provided with a truck. But at this time the concept of the switcher was still in the future, and the same engines both went out on the road and did such shunting and train marshalling as was required. Britain was slow to adopt the leading bogie truck as used by Jervis, but its origins have provoked some debate. William Chapman had patented a pivoting bogie in England in 1812, and by 1832, also the year of Chapman's death, illustrations of his 'frames', as used in the re-wheeled *Puffing Billy*, had appeared in more than one book on locomotive design. Chapman, however, proposed his bogie either as a trailing one, or as one of a pair of four-wheelers, operated by a drive-train of gear wheels. The American historian of early locomotives, Zerah Colburn, wrote in 1869 that:

In 1828 the engineers of the B&O Railroad visited England and the late Robert Stephenson once informed the author that he suggested to them, what is now the chief distinguishing feature of all American rolling stock, viz., the 'Bogie' to be applied to the engines intended to work round curves of six-chain radius, at that time proposed to be adopted. The bogie, which had grown out of William Chapman's invention of 1812, was then, Mr Stephenson stated, in regular use on the quays of Newcastle.

Although this sounds authoritative, and Colburn had no pro-British axe to grind, the British historian E.A. Forward pointed out that no bogie engines were built by Stephenson before 1833, and the identity of any bogie engines working on the quays of Newcastle is unknown (*Newcomen Transactions*, No.28). Unlike Chapman's, Jervis's was a leading bogie for attachment to a rod-driven locomotive. His truck was quite different in purpose and design, and his claim, as declared to William H. Brown in a letter of 17 July 1870: 'I was the inventor of, and put in successful operation, the locomotive truck', is entirely reasonable. Jervis did not patent his contribution to locomotive design, and the locomotive historian John H. White Jr. has ascribed this to Jervis' wish to make it generally available. But perhaps some awareness of Chapman's pioneering work also played an equally honourable part. In Britain, a rigid wheelbase remained the rule for a long time, the only exception being a rear bogie in an 0-2-4 locomotive built in 1833 in Dundee, for the Dundee & Newtyle Railway in Scotland. This was partly because British track was made of iron and more solidly laid; and partly because British locomotives were typically small and short.

By 1837, the concept of railways in England had grown from links between provincial towns to that of a national network, and on no line was this smallness of locomotives more noticeable than the great new London & Birmingham Railway of 1838, where Edward Bury had obtained the post of Chief Mechanical Engineer and provided a range of lightweight 2-2-0 types from his own works. Bury was, as we have seen, an original designer, and his iron bar-frames became a standard in the USA, to which he exported a number of locomotives in the 1830s. The bar frames reduced weight and gave the engines a typical see-through look beneath the boiler barrel. His standard engine for the L&B had the circular outer firebox surmounted by a characteristic small 'haycock' copper dome, as first used on the Liverpool, and it was under-powered from the start, with a boiler pressure of 50psi (3.5kg/cm2). There were fifty-eight of them, cheap and reliable, but four or more could be seen on the heavier trains. Bury held on to the contract until 1847, by which time the traffic demands were quite beyond his engines. His business continued for some time, however, and maintained its small-engine emphasis, which suited many lines well enough. The engines themselves were well made and some Bury types built for other lines have survived. One of his 0-4-0 goods engines, built by Fairbairn & Sons for the Furness Railway in 1861 and affectionately known as 'Coppernob', has been preserved, and another is still displayed at Kent Station in Cork, Ireland. Bury, though a capable engineer, was primarily a businessman and felt he was on to a good thing in making large numbers of small engines, rather than smaller numbers of larger ones. It was also the case that Robert Stephenson's attempt to provide a bigger goods engine, the 'long-boiler', with all the wheels set between the cylinders and the firebox, was a bad design with a dangerous propensity to pitch and roll. But Bury's approach was short-sighted. The locomotive's impetus towards greater size and power could not be arrested by one man's opportunism. Quite apart from such self-interested efforts to hem in development, however, a certain conservatism was setting in among British locomotive engineers. Britain was the true home of the locomotive, they felt, and there was a definite resistance to 'foreign' ideas.

FIVE

Pushing out Frontiers

So far, the only purpose-built locomotive works was that of Robert Stephenson & Co. in Newcastle. But as the number of railway companies increased, the demand for new locomotives grew. The natural people to enter the business of locomotive construction were iron founders, who already had the equipment necessary to cast boilers and cylinders, and build frames and wheels; and as we have seen, businesses like Foster, Rastrick in England, and the West Point Foundry in New York State, were early in action. Among others were Murdoch & Hill, of Glasgow, who began that city's visceral connection with the steam locomotive by building two engines, following the already outdated 'Killingworth' design, for the Monkland & Kirkintilloch Railway in 1831. Edward Bury's firm was already exporting its locomotives to the United States and France.

One or two railway companies were by now large or ambitious enough to build their own locomotive works, like the Liverpool & Manchester. But most were too small and new. At their inception, they might only want a few locomotives; perhaps only a single one. Germany's first railway, the Nuremberg-Fürth line of 1835, was intended to open with a home-built locomotive. But at a late stage, the project collapsed, and a 2-2-2 engine of the 'Patentee' type was hurriedly ordered from Robert Stephenson & Co., and arrived in time for the ceremonial opening on 7 December 1835. Named *Adler*, it was the first fully operational locomotive in Germany. *Adler* ran until 1857, when the wheels and motion were salvaged and the boiler sold for scrap. The first successful German-built engine was *Saxonia*, built by a very gifted young engineer, Johann Andreas Schubert, in 1837-1839 for the Dresden-Leipzig Railway.

In the early 1830s it was plain that there was a growing international market for steam locomotives. The British had been exporters from the first, but it was not long before they met competition. Not only did they find American manufacturers knocking at the doors of their European customers, but Britain itself became an importing market. In 1831, William Norris, an entrepreneur rather than an engineer, set up shop as a locomotive manufacturer in Philadelphia. Pennsylvania and the adjacent state of New Jersey were the heartland of the US railway system and this region would eventually have a concentration of the major works. Norris had been involved with railways for some years. With Colonel S.H. Long of the US Topographical Corps of Engineers, he had built a locomotive of the 4-2-0 arrangement in 1829. It had outside-mounted cylinders, a belt-driven fan to assist combustion, and a boiler which combined tubes at each side with a 'combustion chamber' in the middle. In December 1830 Long and Norris patented a method for fixing tyres to driving wheels. Between 1832 and 1836, they built a few locomotives, but Long withdrew from the business in 1834. Growth came from 1836 with the success of another 4-2-0 with outside cylinders, *The Washington Country Farmer*, for the Philadelphia & Columbia Railway. Eight broadly similar engines were supplied to the Baltimore & Ohio in 1837-39. They represented a combination of British and American ideas, with Bury bar-frames and circular fireboxes, a front bogie with inside bearings, and outside cylinders. The Norris engines performed well on the B&O gradients. Their longer, larger boiler saved them from the lack of power experienced by Bury's 2-2-0s in England. Norris was by now heading a rapidly-growing business. In 1838 he arranged with the Birmingham & Gloucester Railway in England to supply a test engine to work on its then-building 1 in 37 Lickey incline, between Bromsgrove and Blackwell, south of Birmingham. This was the nearest thing to a mountain line that Great Britain yet had, and it remains to this day the steepest main-line gradient in the country. The test, in May 1839, was not a success, but Norris had a first-rate salesman in his European agent, and the B&G was prevailed on to buy the engine, *England*, and nine others. With a mixture of English and proudly American names like *Niagara*, *Philadelphia* and *New York*, they were delivered between November 1839 and May 1842, at a cost of between £1,500 and £1,600 each, including 20 per cent import duty, and excluding tenders. The railway was prepared to pay a substantial premium for power and reliability (though in the latter respect the engines varied widely). The Norris engines were Britain's first imported locomotives, and also the first front-bogie locomotives to work in Britain. Eventually the B&G had twenty-six Norris locomotives, nine of them built under licence in English works.

A year after Norris, another new firm was set up in Philadelphia, by Matthias W. Baldwin (1795-1866). The son of a carriage builder, he had trained as a jeweller, and became a highly skilled mechanic in miniature. In 1825 he became a partner in a business making bookbinder's tools and cylinders for calico printing. As a tool for this trade he built a very small steam engine, which was so effective that its fame spread and he got orders for more. Then in 1830, when steam locomotives were very much a hot topic, he was asked by the proprietor of the Philadelphia Museum, Franklin Peale, to build a miniature locomotive. This he did, and it was inaugurated on 25 April 1831, running inside the Museum grounds, and able to pull four passengers on two miniature cars. In 1832 he was asked by the Philadelphia, Germanstown & Norristown Railway, previously horse-reliant, to build them a full-size locomotive. The result was *Old Ironsides*, a four-wheeler very much on the English 'Planet' pattern. Baldwin by this time was seeking business as an engine-builder, and the next order came from E. L. Miller of the Charleston & Hamburg, looking for something to supplement his *Phoenix* (ex-*Best Friend*). It was a 4-2-0, the design based on Jervis's *Experiment*, and named after the purchaser. In 1832, five locomotives were built in Baldwin's works. A typical one of these was the 4-2-0 *Lancaster*, for the Philadelphia & Columbia Railroad, bought by the Commonwealth of Pennsylvania for $5,500 including the tender. The 4-2-0 design had acquired a reputation for effective and reliable operation, and until 1842 it was the only model Baldwin would offer, though it did come in three different sizes, weighing from 26,000 to 23,000 and 20,000lbs. A reputation for sticking to tried-and-true design did Baldwin no harm at all, and survived his occasional departures from it. His company was destined to become America's largest manufacturer of steam locomotives. Other businesses followed, including that of Thomas Rogers of Paterson, in 1835. Though a number of small builders opened up around New York and in New England, Pennsylvania and New Jersey had by far the greatest concentration.

Patents were always of great concern to these early builders (and would be just as much to later ones). It was no longer possible to patent a steam engine as such, as Boulton & Watt had done in the previous century, but any new or different auxiliary device offered the chance of taking out a patent. This had two advantages: first of all, if it was a real improvement, it drew customers. Secondly, other builders would pay for the right to incorporate it in their machines, and could be pursued through the law if they simply copied it. Consequently, patent-hunting, and patent-protecting, became two great sports in all the industrialised countries, and patent lawyers became a particularly rich sub-species in a generally well-heeled profession. The fact that a patented invention worked did not necessarily mean great success. The French designer Claude Arnoux patented an alternative to the bogie in 1839, consisting of two guide wheels fixed to the front corners of the locomotive frame almost at rail level, and set at an angle of about 15° to the horizontal. Their rims ran along the inner sides of the rails, whose joints had to be suitably adapted to provide a smooth surface. John Stevens' garden railway in 1825 had used a similar guide-wheel method. The system was used on locomotives of the Paris–Sceaux suburban line from 1846 to 1891, but no other took it up (although the Paris *Métro* would use something similar on its pneumatic-tyred lines much later). Even when the prospect of significant improvement was much less obvious than in the early days, the inventive spirit and the urge to improve produced a range of mechanical freaks, oddities and one-off designs all through the century and into the next.

There were frequent problems, when inventions were simultaneous and very similar, or made in different countries. Also, there was very often room for argument over what constituted a new invention. An interesting dispute came up in the mid-1830s. The American 4-2-0, with its single driving axle, soon came to be considered as lacking tractive power, especially on freight trains. A natural remedy was to add another set of driving wheels, thus increasing the adhesive weight of the locomotive. This was first done by Henry R. Campbell, engineer of the Philadelphia, Germanstown & Norristown Railroad. He patented his design for a 4-4-0 locomotive in 1836 and the first was built by James Brook of Philadelphia. Campbell's engine was the biggest of its time and it was estimated that it could pull a 450-ton (457t) train at 15mph (24km/h) on level track – a gain in tractive effort of over 60 per cent on the standard Baldwin 4-2-0.

Campbell and Brook were almost pipped to the post by two other Philadelphian engineers, Andrew Eastwick, of Garrett & Eastwick, and his foreman Joseph Harrison (who as Norris's foreman had been responsible for the effective 4-2-0 design). They brought out a 4-4-0 for the Beaver Meadow Railroad in the same year of 1836. Campbell threatened to sue them for infringement of his patent, and there was considerable legal and legalistic argument until it was accepted that Eastwick and Harrison had the right to proceed with their design. In fact their engine, *Hercules*, was a more advanced machine than Campbell's. Among the as-yet unresolved problems of the locomotive was the matter of suspension. Although individual wheels were now fitted with springs, little attention had been given to the overall problem of keeping a locomotive steady on the road when travelling at speed. Pitching, wobbling, and yawing were things drivers had come to expect, and on a slow-speed four-wheeler or a 4-2-0 they did not matter too much. But when it came to planning a larger, faster engine, with driving wheels coupled together, suspension became an issue that had to be tackled. Campbell did not try, and his 4-4-0 was liable to pitch itself off the track when the road was in any way uneven. *Hercules* had its coupled wheels fitted to a truck frame in a partly successful attempt at equalising the axles and thus enabling the wheels to ride dips and humps in the track. The problem was solved a few years later when Harrison developed his patent equalising lever in 1838. This was a major step towards the design of larger locomotives. The driving axles were connected by leaf springs and connecting levers, attached to the main frame on each side, which spread the effects of road shocks among the axles and thus helped to ensure that all wheels kept in contact with the rails. In effect, the engine had three-point suspension, based on the bogie pivot and the two driving axles. As often happened in the early days, Timothy Hackworth had devised a very similar leaf-spring equaliser on the *Royal George* in 1827, which worked well but was not copied by others. Despite its superior traction, the railways were slow to take up the 4-4-0, and it was only after 1840 that production went up rapidly. From 1845, even the conservative Baldwin had to accept that it had superseded the 4-2-0. Later it became known as the American Type and was the most popular wheel arrangement in the USA and Britain in the nineteenth century. If Campbell had been able to demand a royalty on each one built, he would have become hugely rich.

Nobody could re-invent the steam locomotive, but opportunities for inventors and patent-hunters remained: there were many aspects that could be improved, or were crying out for improvement. Brakes, safety valves, reversing gear, water supply to the boiler, control of steaming, reduction of smoke and sparks – all these aspects were still manifestly imperfect. The urge to improve them was bolstered by the increasing demand from the traffic managers for more power and greater speed. Already the time was past when 30mph seemed a terrifying pace. Speeds of 60, even 80mph were now being claimed, with little supporting evidence.

The expanding railway system was creating great demand for new engines, not only in Britain and America but in Europe, and as well as being used on British lines, locomotives of 'Planet' or 'Patentee' type were exported in large numbers and became the basis of early locomotive practice in the Low Countries, the German States, Russia, and the Italian States, among other countries. They were also influential in British North America. The Champlain & St Lawrence, opened on 21 July 1836, was Canada's first railway. The 0-4-0 *Dorchester*, which pulled the first train, was a lightweight version of the Stephenson 'Samson' type, first built for the Liverpool & Manchester Railway in 1831. Linking Amsterdam and Haarlem, the Holland Iron Railway Company was the first Dutch railway, opened in 1839, with 5ft 10in gauge until 1866 when it was relaid to standard gauge. Its first two engines, *Snelheid*, 'Speed', and *De Arend*, 'The Eagle', were built by Longridge & Co. of Bedlington, England (the Stephensons' erstwhile partner had set up on his own). They were essentially of the Stephenson 'Patentee' type. Although *De Arend* was scrapped in 1857, a full-size working replica was built in 1938 for the centenary of the line. But American competition, as exemplified by the energetic William Norris, was very close behind. The Champlain & St Lawrence's second engine was a Norris 4-2-0. Austria's first engine, delivered in April 1838, was another Norris design was widely copied by early builders in Austria and in Germany.

Stephenson's factory could not keep up with demand and others were licensed to produce locomotives to Stephenson design. Since every new railway had to set up its own workshops for maintenance and repair, local variations very soon began to appear. In France, there had been little progress since the work of Seguin, and Stephenson's supplied an 0-4-0 locomotive to the St Etienne line in 1832. The new Paris-Orleans Railway used numerous English locomotives of 2-2-2 arrangement. Another 2-2-2, a modest machine of 1839, was the first locomotive built by André Koechlin at what would later become the great works of the *Société Alsacienne de Constructions Mécaniques*, with its headquarters at Mulhouse in Alsace. Twenty-three were built and sold to a variety of railway companies between 1839 and 1842, including three which went to the *Chemin de Fer du Nord*. Stephenson influence was strong, as seen by the inside cylinders and outside frames, but the boiler pressure was upped to 85psi (6kg/cm^2), improving their tractive effort. Although several French companies used single-wheelers up to the 1850s and beyond, these never became a 'standard' type in France as they did in England.

Russia's first steam-powered railway was built in 1836, between the Vyskii factory and the Mednyi copper mine. Its locomotive was of the 'Planet' type, built by E.A. Cherepanov, a serf-mechanic who had been sent to England to look at engines. A replica is on display at the Railway Cultural Centre in Ekaterinburg. The first Russian public railway, between St Petersburg and Tsarskoe-Selo, opened on 30 October 1837. A religious service was held to solemnise the event, and members of the imperial family threw holy water on the locomotive wheels. Such proceedings were not unusual in Catholic and Orthodox countries, but uncommon in others, where a brass band and a cannon or two were more likely to be the accompaniment. One of the engines was supplied by Timothy Hackworth. By no means a conventional design, it was a double-acting ram or trunk engine, with connecting rods pivoting directly on the piston, and no piston rods as in the conventional locomotive. This experimental design was not a success; and a few years later the Tsar would turn to American engineers to set up a locomotive-building works within his vast empire. The approach was made to Eastwick & Harrison of Philadelphia following the appearance of their 4-4-0 *Gowan & Marx* for the Philadelphia & Reading Railroad. Its name came from a London banking firm that did business with the P&RR. It featured the equalising lever linking the coupled axles, developed by Eastwick & Harrison in 1838. The boiler was based on the Bury 'haycock' type, but with an oblong rather than a round firebox, giving it a somewhat larger grate than other engines, which helped it to develop more power. The boiler pressure is quoted as varying between 80 and 130psi (5.6-9.1kg/cm^2). Its valve gear, patented by Eastwick in 1835, was rather cumbersome, as it required movement of the valve ports, rather than of a sliding valve, in order to engage reverse gear. A 6-ton tender was fitted. On 5 December 1839, *Gowan & Marx* pulled the first train between Reading and Philadelphia, and on 20 February 1840 it hauled a 423-ton (429t) train of 101 cars on this line. Even at little more than walking pace, this was a great achievement. Reports of its performance aroused great interest in Europe, and inspired the official invitation to its builders to set up a factory in St Petersburg, where the locomotives for the St Petersburg-Moscow railway would be built. In 1843 Eastwick & Harrison opened their new works, and between then and 1862 they built several hundred engines. One of the first was an outside-cylindered 0-6-0, for goods haulage. A two-wheel front truck was soon added, making it a 2-6-0 type, later known as 'Moguls', and the first of several thousands all over the world.

Italy saw its first locomotives in 1839, in the form of three 2-2-2 engines supplied by Michael Longridge's works at Bedlington, Newcastle, for the Naples-Portici Railway. Two were named, *Bayard* and (rather aptly) *Vesuvio*; the third, a goods engine, was anonymous.

Among all these early railways, there had been little variation of gauge. The English colliery tramway gauge of 56.5in (143.5cm) was most common, but anything in excess of 60in (152.4cm) was rare until 1838, with the construction of the Great Western Railway, between London and Bristol, when the gauge, as specified by its engineer, Isambard Kingdom Brunel, leapt to 84.25in (214cm). Although he was a great and visionary engineer, Brunel's contribution to the development of the steam locomotive was minimal. Never afraid of thinking big, he said about his gauge, compared with the 'standard' one: 'Looking at the speeds which I contemplated, and the masses to be moved, it seemed to me that the whole machine was too small for the work to be done, and that it required that the parts should be on a scale more commensurate with the mass and the velocity to be attained.' His broad gauge was not followed up anywhere else (the first Russian railway, of 72in (182.9cm) gauge, pre-dated it). According to his own testimony, the design of the line's first locomotives was left to the builders, though subject to his approval. Attempting to produce something worthy of the wide gauge, of its imperious young engineer's reputation for originality and his demand for speed (30mph was to be a minimum average), the builders came up with some remarkable-looking engines, distinguished by huge wheels up to 10ft (304.8cm) in diameter, and including two, *Thunderer* and *Hurricane*, in which the 'engine' part with cylinders, motion and driving wheels, was mounted on a separate frame in front of the boiler part, to which it was linked by flexible steam pipes. A tender brought up the rear. A most improbable claim was made that *Thunderer* had covered 28 miles at 100mph in September 1839. Nearly all were poor or hopeless performers in regular service. The best were two enlarged 'Patentees' built by Stephenson's and originally intended for export to the USA. One of these, *North Star*, though rebuilt in 1854, survived the end of the broad gauge and was not broken up until 1906. Fortunately, Brunel's assistant, Daniel Gooch, was a true locomotive man, and he designed a family of Great Western engines that, with little alteration, served the line well until the broad gauge was finally done away with in 1892.

The Gauge Act of 1846 declared for the narrower 'standard' gauge, but the English 'battle of the gauges' stimulated both locomotive design and running, as the exponents of each strove to prove their superiority. GWR engines had a massive look even though they did not utilise the full potential of the wide gauge. The stability of the engines and the solidity of the permanent way, combined with excellence of locomotive design, made it one of the fastest railways in the world in its main-line expresses. Gooch had tested the way in 1846 with a 2-2-2 *Great Western*, of similar working dimensions to the subsequent 'Iron Dukes', which was reputed to have run from London Paddington to Swindon, 77.25 miles (124.3km), in seventy-eight minutes, in June 1846. The only significant later alteration was to fit a second set of front carrying wheels to spread the weight. Twenty-two locomotives of the 4-2-2 'Iron Duke' class were built at the company's new Swindon works in 1847-51. It was a tribute to their quality, as well as to the GWR's later complacency, that when the older engines were scrapped in the 1870s, they were replaced by almost identical designs, differing only by having cabs and 140psi (9.8kg/cm²) pressure. They were very solidly built with outside sandwich frames and also three plate frames inside, running from the back of the two inside cylinders to the front of the firebox; all five held bearings for the driving axle, though the carrying wheels were supported by the outer frames only. The front carrying wheels were on independent axles fixed to the frame: the bogie had not yet come into use in England. The boiler was domeless, and steam was taken from a perforated pipe which ran to a regulator box inside the smokebox. The big driving wheels, of 96in (243.8cm) diameter, were originally flangeless.

The Great Western's broad-gauge engines were ultimately sterile, with no direct successors, though the company would produce a new dominant strain on the standard gauge in the early twentieth century. But in the mid-nineteenth century, they were the uncontestable giants and champions of British railroading. From then until 1880 they ran the country's fastest trains. In 1848, the 9.50 Paddington-Bristol mail train was allowed fifty-six minutes to travel the 53 miles (85km) from Paddington to Didcot, non-stop; and twenty-nine minutes for the next 24.25 miles (39km) to Swindon. As in other countries, it was the demands of the mail service which forced the railway companies to increase the speeds of the fastest trains. Most locomotives ran slowly; the speed of freight trains was usually less than 10mph.

In most countries, development proceeded on the 56.5in (143.5cm) gauge. By the later 1840s, the few short lines on the world railway map had increased in number, grown longer, and in many areas formed a network. There were still huge blank spaces, in Asia, Africa and Australia. South America had only one line, the Georgetown-Plaisance, in British Guyana, opened in 1848. But everywhere plans for new railways were being made. The steam locomotive was poised to spread across all the inhabited continents, and its growing band of acolytes were making preparations on a large scale. If not extraordinary, it is certainly striking that the format established at such an early point by the Stephenson-Seguin combination should prove to be an effective basis for nearly all further developments of the steam locomotive. Although engineers would hunt for, and experiment with, radical change, the basic boiler-cylinders-valve gear package of the 1830s would remain essentially unaltered 120 years later. Not everyone followed the Stephenson line in all respects, however. On the Stockton & Darlington, Timothy Hackworth continued to use the return-flue boiler, with the firebox at the front end, alongside the sideways-placed chimney; the whole design requiring a three-part set of coal cart, engine and water tender. In 1848 W. and A. Kitching built the last locomotives of this type. The cylinders, set at the rear, and at a steep angle, drove the front coupled wheels, which were of Hackworth's distinctive perforated pattern. One of these engines, *Derwent*, has been preserved.

In 1842 another patent locomotive design appeared, the brain-child of an English engineer, Thomas Russell Crampton, at that time an assistant to Daniel Gooch on the GWR, and, therefore, at home with the concept that locomotives could and should go fast. His aim was to bring similar speed to the standard gauge. Like other engineers of the time, he was convinced that for stability while moving, the locomotive's centre of gravity must be kept as low as possible. The patent Crampton had a low-set boiler and large-diameter driving wheels placed behind the firebox (something John Jervis had already done in the USA; it is not known whether Crampton was aware of this), and also had the relatively large heating surface and high boiler pressure he was familiar with from the Gooch engines. His first engines, two 4-2-0s, were built in 1846 for the English-owned Liège & Namur Railway in Belgium. They were the only two Crampton engines ever to work in Belgium, and only a handful were ever ordered by railways in Britain. In America, a couple of unwieldy Crampton types, with a six-wheel front bogie, were designed by Isaac Dripps and built by Norris for the Camden & Amboy Railroad. But Cramptons proved to be highly successful in France, beginning with a set of twelve double-framed 4-2-0 engines, with cylinders between the frames, for the Nord railway in 1848. The PLM also used Cramptons, and on the *Est* railway they hauled the main Paris-Strasbourg expresses from 1852 into the 1890s. An ex-PLM Crampton, sold to the *Est* and fitted with a double-barrel boiler, reached a speed on test of 89.5mph (144km/h), with 157 tons. This was probably a world speed record for the time (20 June 1890). By this time, of course, the virtue of a low centre of gravity had long been shown to be a myth, and though the European Cramptons worked well, they did not present a path for development. No more than 350 or so were built, but their speed and free steaming, due to generous steam passages, preserved their interest for engineers and designers. One of the *Est* engines, *Le Continent*, is preserved.

One of Crampton's many ideas was to put two of his engines back-to-back, with coal bunkers above their boilers, and a double-ended water-tender between them, in effect a 4-2-0+0-2-4, to provide heavy haulage. Certainly his single-driver engines were at their best with light-weight trains. But to satisfy the requirements of new customers and new demands to cover longer distances with heavier trains, further improvements to the basic locomotive were urgently needed.

SIX

Adjustments to the Nervous System

Attempts to describe the steam locomotive's working often brought forth analogies with the anatomy of living creatures. The boiler was the heart; the cylinders the lungs. In this scheme of things, the valve gear was usually described as the nervous system of the steam locomotive, as it controlled the motion of the 'limbs'. Its function is to open and close the ports or openings that control admission of steam to the cylinder, and exhaust from it, at the appropriate points of the piston's movement. Steam must enter where it will push the piston back and, having done its work, be free to exhaust before the piston returns, or the problem of back-pressure occurs, slowing down the piston's movement. In the earliest days this was all the valve gear was expected to do, apart from providing a means of re-positioning the valve in order to initiate reverse movement. However, it had been appreciated even before the invention of the locomotive that the ability to cut off the admission of steam before the piston had completed its stroke, would be a great advantage. Steam admission through the whole length of the stroke was only needed when starting off, or pulling a heavy load at very low speed; at other times it was more economical to cut off admission at an earlier point, employing the expansive potential of the steam already in the cylinder to move the piston. This conserved both steam and fuel. But it was to take some time before 'cut-off' could be applied in a controllable and adjustable way.

The valve gear fitted to early locomotives had never been very satisfactory, and many builders had tried to improve it, often, as George Stephenson remarked, showing 'the danger of too much ingenuity' in the process. The vital piece was the slide valve, as devised by Matthew Murray in 1812, whose movement opened and closed the ports; as the piston moved from left to right, so the valve moved from right to left, and vice versa. Later, the slide valve was lengthened (given more 'lap' in engineering-speak) so that during part of its movement it closed off both the entry and exit openings of the cylinder. This gave the steam more opportunity to work expansively. George Stephenson's friend Nicholas Wood had the idea of operating the slide valves from slip-eccentrics fitted to the driving wheel centres. These could be set in such a way as to move the valve before the piston had completed its stroke, and so to cut off the steam supply before the exhaust port was opened. The amount of cut-off thus given could not be changed by the driver, however. The other function of the valve gear, to engage reverse, remained cumbersome. To get the eccentrics to slip into reverse mode, the engine had to be pushed backwards with the help of a horse or crowbar. By the early 1830s the inconvenience of this arrangement was causing delays and annoyance among the operating staff, and deep cogitation among designers.

'Lead' and 'lap' were the keys to effective operation between valve chest and cylinder. Lead defines the extent of valve opening to let steam into the cylinder before the piston comes to the end of its stroke. As the piston returns, it meets this steam supply. The main effect of lead is to enable the cylinder to take steam more readily, and to give a cushioning effect on the moving parts. It can also help in starting if the engine stops on 'dead centre' with the connecting rod and crank in the same plane as the axle. Lead had to be carefully judged: too much, and it let in steam behind the piston before it had completed its return stroke. Lap, essential to the expansive working of steam, defines the extent by which a slide valve in its central position overlaps the edges of the steam ports. A longer lap also meant a longer valve travel to keep the cut-off unchanged. Both lead and lap were measured in short units: a variation of half an inch made a substantial difference.

These valve events were fairly well understood; the problem was at the other end: how was the driver to adjust the valve setting while the locomotive was moving? Builders began using a 'gab' or hook gear, each with his own variations. Essentially, it required fixed eccentrics on the axles, rather than the old slip eccentrics. These were joined by a rod to a gab — a catch which might be V-, X-, or Y-shaped, and which moved forwards and backwards as the wheel turned. The gab could be operated from the footplate, to connect with either of two pins set at opposite ends of a rocking arm which itself was fixed to the valve spindle. Each pin delivered opposite motion to the other. The Liverpool engineer George Forrester devised a double-eccentric gear in 1834, with one eccentric on the driving axle for each direction of motion. Between the gab-hooks was a space in which lay a pin fixed in the valve spindle. Running forwards, the top gab was lowered onto the pin and imparted its horizontal motion. To reverse, it was raised out of the way, and the lower gab brought up to connect with the pin, which could then be moved in the opposite direction by the other eccentric. This basic method became standard in Britain and North America until 1842 in Britain and the 1850s in America. It was the best yet, and allowed for a degree of lead in both forward and reverse gear, though it still did not allow the driver to control the extent of steam cut-off, and several designers were struggling with how to accomplish a variable cut-off.

Then in 1842 two young men at the Stephenson works, William Williams, a gentleman apprentice, and William Howe, a pattern-maker, worked out how to eliminate the clumsy hit-or-miss detachable gabs by a linked gear. Williams came up with the notion of the slotted link-piece, along which one end of the valve rod could slide. The 'link' was fixed in a curved slot which joined the ends of two connecting rods fixed to eccentrics on the driving axle. One eccentric delivered forwards motion; the other backwards. Simply raising or lowering the link by means of a lever in the cab would move the valve into the desired position, setting the gear for forwards or reverse motion. Very importantly, it also soon became clear that it could provide intermediate cut-off positions, to allow for variable steam expansion in the cylinders. Although the general form of the Stephenson link motion seems to have been anticipated by the American William James in 1832, James' design had been forgotten (the engine it was fitted to exploded), and it was this 1842 version that came into use in locomotives all over the world. It was the first really effective locomotive valve gear, and remained the most popular form throughout the world for over a century. The new system was first called Williams' motion, then, universally, Stephenson's link motion. Later there would be bad blood between Williams and Howe as to who deserved more credit for the design. Surprisingly, the system was not patented: Robert Stephenson & Co. were usually quick to protect their inventions. Other British engineers, notably Daniel Gooch of the Great Western and Alexander Allan of the Grand Junction Railway, swiftly took up the concept of expansive link motion and patented their own modifications. John Gray of the Hull & Selby Railway had patented a form of valve gear in 1838, and it was in the course of an action brought by him against the mighty London & North Western, in 1851, for infringement of his patent, that William Howe, called as a witness, claimed to be the inventor of the link motion. Asked why it had not been patented, he replied: 'I do not think one was ever applied for. There seemed to be a doubt whether it would act effectively or not.' He added that he himself: 'had not been in a condition to take out a patent.' It seems likely that Robert Stephenson & Co. were not immediately aware of the full significance of the discovery; and the wrangle between the designers made the question of ownership a difficult one. What was soon beyond all doubt was that the Stephenson link motion, allowing the point of cut-off to be adjusted from the footplate while the locomotive was in motion, was a great step forward. From now on, the locomotive driver had far more effective control over the steaming of his engine, as well as finding it much easier to engage reverse gear.

Though by far the best available solution, it was not a perfect one (a perfect one was never found), and work on the nervous system continued. In Belgium, railway development had been under state control from the outset. The main workshops were at Malines, north of Brussels, and in the year that the Stephenson link motion was developed, a young man of twenty-two started work there. He was Egide Walschaerts, possessor of one of the most frequently mis-spelled names in railway history. His strong mechanical aptitude led to his promotion in 1844 to foreman at the Brussels-Midi locomotive shops. In that year his radial valve gear arrangement was patented. Lighter than the Stephenson gear, which required two eccentrics for each cylinder – and so meant four eccentrics on one driving axle – it required only a single crank to operate each valve, with the reverse motion obtained by allowing it to rock on bearings at its mid-point. A fixed amount of lead for either direction, at all points of cut-off, was obtained by means of a combination lever taking part of the motion of the valve from the crosshead. It was neat and efficient, especially when fitted outside the wheels, to valves set above the cylinders, but beyond Belgium it would be largely ignored for several decades. Walschaerts was not a qualified engineer, and his post as a foreman was too lowly for him to be able to apply for patents in his own name – a situation like that of William Howe at Stephenson's in England. He found a nominee, F. Fischer, who consented to file the patent in his own name, which led to the system sometimes being known as the Fischer valve gear. By 1848 the inventor had devised an improved version, in essence the modern Walschaerts valve gear. This was fitted to a Belgian State Railways inside-cylinder 2-2-2. Apparently the trial was successful, although it was the private Belgian companies, not the State Railway, that adopted it for their outside-cylinder locomotives. Here, as in other countries, the Stephenson gear remained the preferred form for inside-cylinder machines. In 1848 a German designer, Edmund Heusinger, chief engineer of the Taunus Railway, unaware of the Belgian patent, devised a valve gear almost identical to Walschaerts' 1848 version, and took out a patent on it in 1849. Some dispute ensued as to whether Walschaerts or Heusinger was the true inventor of the radial valve gear. Heusinger eventually acknowledged that the Belgian had priority, but in central Europe the arrangement continued to be known as the Heusinger gear.

During the steam era well over 100 different designs of valve gear were devised, but only a handful were adopted on a large scale. Apart from fulfilling the vital aim of providing good steam distribution, an effective valve gear had to be reliable, economical in space and weight, and easy to maintain. The Stephenson type answered these needs. American designers were surprisingly slow to adopt it, and it did not come into general use among them until around 1855. This was, partly at least, because many of them had developed their own partial solution to the problem. But with its ruggedness, simplicity and effectiveness, particularly when fitted inside the frames, the Stephenson gear became supreme until the end of the nineteenth century. Early in the twentieth century, the Walschaerts gear largely replaced it, for reasons that will be seen. Meanwhile, for forty-one years, Walschaerts remained as foreman at Brussels-Midi, with no further professional advancement. He died in 1901, a few years before his valve gear came into almost universal use.

Another extremely welcome addition was invented in France by the Parisian scientist Eugène Bourdon. To pursue the anatomical analogy, it did not tighten up the nervous system, but was more comparable to a blood-pressure meter. Although rather uncertain mercury gauges had been around since before the Rainhill trials, he devised the first really effective steam pressure gauge in 1849. It was a simple device, consisting of a curved metal tube, sealed at one end, with its other end open to the boiler. It reacted to increases of pressure inside the boiler by a straightening movement which was recorded on a calibrated dial. Of all the supplementary inventions, this was the one which was taken up most rapidly by locomotive builders everywhere. Engine crews had often felt like men riding on the back of a tiger, which might at any moment turn and rend them: fear of the exploding boiler had lain heavy on them, and often inhibited their performance. Bourdon's gauge was exhibited at the Great Exhibition in London in 1851, and American rights were bought on the spot by the equipment manufacturer E.H. Ashcroft. As it came into general use, boiler explosions became less frequent; engines were worked more closely to their optimum steam generation capacity; and there were substantial fuel savings.

SEVEN

Engineers and Aesthetics

Up to now in the locomotive's story, the European nations have appeared largely in the role of customers to builders in Britain and America. From 1837, the American locomotive builder William Norris had been making determined efforts to interest European railways in his engines. One of his contacts was a dynamic German industrialist, August Borsig of Berlin, who, perhaps more inspired than Norris would have wished, set up his own works and brought out his first engine, based on the Norris 4-2-2, in 1841. By 1843 his works produced their twenty-fourth engine, *Beuth*. It had bar frames and a tall Norris-style firebox, but also showed strong English influence, notably in its 2-2-2 wheel arrangement and its use of the very new Stephenson's link motion, though *Beuth* did not take advantage of the facility for intermediate cut-off positions. By 1845 Baldwin as well as Norris was supplying his products to Germany. William Norris, ousted from the Philadelphia works by his brother Richard, actually set up a factory in Vienna in 1844, but by 1848 it had gone out of business and he returned to the USA. That year of revolutions was a bad one for business. But Norris designs formed the first products of such great locomotive works as Esslingen, from 1847, and Henschel, from 1848, as well as the already-mentioned Borsig. Europe, especially industrialised northern Europe, was a potentially lucrative market, though economic slumps and political upheavals could ruin a locomotive builder whose business had expanded too fast, just as with any other capitalist enterprise. The railway companies and systems, as they grew and began to amalgamate, also showed a tendency, distressing to the independent builder, towards designing and building their own locomotives. This had begun in Great Britain, where the Grand Junction (later London & North Western) and the Great Western had both laid out huge new plants on greenfield sites at Crewe and Swindon respectively. Soon the Great Northern would follow suit at Doncaster. The Austrian State Railway Works were established at Vienna. But the demand for new motive power was such that there was plenty of room for everyone.

At the end of the 1840s, a decade of sometimes confused progress, the locomotive was much improved. It had shown its ability to climb gradients, but it had yet to encounter real mountain country. Now there was a plan to link Vienna, capital of the Austro-Hungarian empire, with Trieste, the empire's main seaport, on the Adriatic. To reach the southward-leading valleys from the Danube basin, the Semmering Pass had to be crossed. At an altitude of 2,880ft (878m), it was the lowest of the Alpine passes, but it offered an unprecedented challenge to the locomotive. As at Rainhill, almost twenty years earlier, there was a strong body of opinion, perhaps not very technically informed, but extremely vocal and sometimes highly-placed, which held that cable working from fixed engines was the only possibility; or perhaps an atmospheric railway (that doomed attempt to provide non-locomotive traction had not yet collapsed): steam and adhesion could not possibly cope with the length and steepness of the inclines. A competition was duly arranged, with a prize of 20,000 florins for the winning builder. Though no British or American builder formally entered the competition, émigré Britons were closely involved with three of the challengers. The country which had cradled steam power was experiencing a diaspora of skilled engineers, men whose ambition took them abroad to greener pastures. There was usually no shortage of job opportunities at British locomotive works, but the great expansion was for fitters, pattern-makers, riveters — positions in the lower strata of the ever-widening industrial pyramid. The top posts remained vastly more limited in number.

Some interesting locomotives took part in the Semmering trials, but none that was a convincing world-beater. The prize was won by *Bavaria*, a long-wheelbase eight-wheeler with outside cylinders and outside frames, built by Josef Anton Maffei, who had set up as a locomotive builder in the Bavarian capital, Munich, in 1837. Maffei was of Italian descent; his designer was Joseph Hall, an Englishman. Driven partly by chain and partly by connecting rods, *Bavaria's* small wheels helped it to pull a 132-ton train up the 1 in 40 grade at 11.4mph (18km/h). But in service the chain drive failed constantly, and the boiler was taken off and used in a stationary engine at the line's Maribor workshops. The contribution of the Austrian State

Railway Works was the creation of its Scottish director, John Haswell. The first eight-coupled engine to be built in Europe, like Bavaria, it had a wooden-lagged boiler, which was beginning to be rather old-fashioned, but in other respects was highly up to date. Though its test performance was inferior to the other's, it was a more durable engine. Another Englishman, John Cockerill, who had established a locomotive works at Seraing in Belgium, entered *Seraing*. This engine had some resemblance to an original design of Horatio Allen's for the South Carolina Railroad. *South Carolina*, as that was called, was designed in 1831 and delivered in January 1832, the first of four. They were double-enders, with a central firebox, and four boilers, set in parallel between the firebox and smoke-box. A steam dome was set to one side of the smoke-box top. Inside cylinders drove the crank axles, one forwards, one in reverse, or vice-versa. The wheels, one pair on the carrying axle, one on the driving axle, were set in trucks. Allen's enterprising design, much discussed with John Jervis who at the time was planning the *Experiment*, was a complete failure in operation. *Seraing* was an altogether more serious locomotive. Its form anticipated the Fairlie double-locomotive that would be widely used on many mountain and narrow-gauge lines later in the century, and also harked back to old Puffing Billy and its four-wheel trucks. The Semmering trials proved that steam locomotives could do the job, and gave confidence to railway developers looking at the higher Alpine passes; later experience taught the Austrians that a good conventional locomotive with eight coupled wheels was a better answer than anything specially contrived. Other main-line railway operators in mountain country, including British India, had to learn that lesson for themselves.

The very earliest designs paid scant heed to aesthetics. It was enough to put all the pieces together in a way which balanced, worked, and fitted the gauge. But even a year before the Rainhill trials, Robert Stephenson was expressing concern about the appearance of his locomotives, particularly the moving parts above the boiler. He wrote to his partner Michael Longridge: 'I have been talking a great deal to my father about endeavouring to reduce the size and ugliness of our travelling-engines, by applying the engine [i.e. cylinders and motion] either on the side of the boiler or beneath it entirely...' These discussions resulted in the laterally-placed cylinders of *Lancashire Witch* and the even lower placing of *Rocket's* cylinders. Appearance, as well as well as mechanical considerations, was influencing design. For the same reasons, the paint scheme of *Rocket* and its successors was chosen to make the locomotives look as colourful, shiny and attractive as possible. A touch of flamboyance in the presentation of a portentous new machine was natural, especially at that time. The locomotive emerged in the late stage of the Romantic era of European culture, and its full flush in America: Sir Walter Scott lived until 1832, the same year in which Goethe died; Victor Hugo was then only thirty, Hector Berlioz a year younger. Edgar Allan Poe was twenty-three; Herman Melville was a boy of thirteen.

In the later nineteenth century, although even white and yellow locomotives could be seen (in Egypt and China respectively) green became the most common colour. This has been ascribed to a belief in the early years that dark green was a restful colour to the eyes of enginemen, unlikely to distract their attention from the fixed signals and landmarks they had to look out for. However, the durability of green pigment — much better than blue, for example — may have counted too. Whatever views were held of locomotives by aestheticians trained in the various *beaux-arts* academies and traditions, the engine builders treated the appearance of their creations very seriously. Steam locomotive design lent itself to working in curves and circles; the builders made extensive use of copper, which could take a high polish, and within a few years the early functionalism was overtaken by a more decorated style which applied classical fluting to steam-pots and finely-turned copper caps to stove-pipe chimneys.

Names played a similar part. Virtually all early railways named their engines. The practice was borrowed from the shipping tradition, and quite soon locomotive names showed as much variety and inventiveness as those of ships. Grand and imposing associations were popular. Occasionally they suggested a brusque impatience with the whole business, as with *Ant, Snake*, and *Bat*; but most sought some kind of aptness and sometimes even wit. Classical references were common. Royal names were popular in countries that still had kings: Sweden's first passenger locomotive was *Prins August*. Mythology was regularly raided: the first engine in Denmark was *Odin*. A public-relations shrewdness was often also detectable, as with the 2-2-2 *Jenny Lind* designed by David Joy for the London & Brighton Railway. Named after a much-admired Swedish singer, it also happened to be an excellent performer, partly because of its unusually high boiler pressure, 120psi (8.3kg/cm^2). Other lines wanted 'Jenny Linds', and its builder, E.B. Wilson of Leeds, went on to build more for home and export. Names were often changed, or swapped between engines. The first locomotive to run in California, *Elephant* of the Sacramento Valley Railroad in 1849, was later renamed *Garrison* after the line's president; and ended its days as *Pioneer*. Sometimes the public, or the railway staff, took a hand, and gave a locomotive type an unofficial name which endured. Ross Winans' 0-8-0 freight engines of the Baltimore & Ohio, in the mid-1840s, were meaningfully called 'Mud-Diggers' by the men who had to work them. J.C. McConnell's 2-2-2 engines of 1851, for the London & North Western Railway, were christened 'Bloomers' through some suggestive resemblance to Mrs Amelia Bloomer's pioneering designs for ladies' clothing. Variations on the 'coffee-pot' theme were bestowed on the smallest tank engines in most countries.

In the early decades of railways, enginemen's cabs were usually notable by their absence. Drivers and their stoker assistants were considered the equivalent of coach drivers, who had no shelter, though more chance of wearing several layers of waterproof clothing. Early builders were preoccupied by the need to maintain light axle-loads, and any unnecessary weight was both undesirable and added to the expense in a competitive market. The lack of a cab for the crew is one of the features that separate the locomotives of the first three decades from their mid-century successors. The provision of shelter on the footplate, slow and uneven, began as a result of 'severe weather and the democratic inclination of the United States', according to the locomotive historian John H. White Jr. The use of cabs became more common as locomotives travelled greater distances, and also as railway-building moved closer to the Arctic Circle and to higher altitudes. The attitude of enginemen was mixed at first. A hardy and conservative breed, some of them felt it was effete to have a cab, or that a cab would obscure the driver's view of the track ahead, and make it more difficult to jump free if a collision were imminent. Early cabs were often added by the railway company after the engine had been delivered, and they were normally made of wood. By 1855, all new locomotives in North America were provided with cabs from the outset, and they became part of the overall design, usually with a side window. In Europe, with less democracy, or better weather, it was 1870 before the same thing could be said, and even then the shelter was often minimal, hardly more than a spectacle-board with vestigial side-panels which would only later – and not in all cases even then – assume the form of windowed sides.

In the increasingly important and self-aware field of modern technology, a significant event happened in 1847. The Institution of Mechanical

Engineers was founded in London, with George Stephenson as its first President. It was established in anger, by Stephenson's fellow engineers, when the Institution of Civil Engineers asked the great man, the evidence of whose handiwork lay across many countries, to submit a description of his work to support his application for membership, like some tyro in the profession. Stephenson balked at this. He was sixty-eight, and it was to be the last year of his life. Like some minor cult object originating in an obscure region, but which later assumes great significance and attracts worshippers across the world, so the locomotive was no longer a local phenomenon tended by isolated groups of devotees. It had gained universal acceptance, and now had its national priesthoods and hierarchies. Similar bodies were formed in other countries. The new Institution's name confirmed the separation of engineering into specialised fields, though the Institution of Civil Engineers, founded in 1818, retained an interest in mechanical matters. The title of engineer marks one of the interesting divergences between the English of England and that of America; in England, the engineer was the man who designed and built the machine; it was maintained by mechanics and driven by a driver. In the USA, an engineer could be a designer of machines, but also, logically enough, he was the man who drove the engine. Mechanics maintained it, but their status rose higher than in Britain: the Master Mechanic, on the west side of the Atlantic, was the opposite number of the Chief Mechanical Engineer on the east. Germany followed the English model with its *Lokomotivführer*. In France, the engine driver's title of *mécanicien* reflected a greater degree of technical competence than was asked of his Anglo-American counterparts. In Italy he was a *macchinista*, as he also was in the Netherlands, a machinist. The title of his footplate assistant, everywhere, reflected the importance of the fire: he was the fireman or stoker. His French label, *chauffeur*, would be borrowed in due course for the motor car.

Mechanical engineering covered a far wider range than in earlier years: the steam engine was being put to a great variety of uses. By far the most dramatic of these new uses happened in France, where the balloon and the airship had long been a special study. In 1852 a twenty-seven-year-old scientist, Henri Giffard, built a steam engine so light and compact that it could be used to drive a dirigible airship. With Giffard at the controls, the first successful powered flight took place that year. His fame is, therefore, greatest in the history of aviation, but he learned his steam technology in the workshops of the *Chemin de Fer de l'Ouest* at Paris, after graduating from the *Ecole Centrale* in the French capital. In the course of his efforts to make a lightweight steam engine, he conceived one of the basic features of the modern steam locomotive. This was the injector. It looked like an unspectacular piece of plumbing, but it made a huge difference to the effectiveness of the locomotive. Before this time, the only way to get water into the boiler was by means of a pump, and these pumps, as we have noted, required the engine to be in motion for them to work. But engines were often at rest for long periods. A scientist in the Seguin and Bourdon tradition, Giffard based his work on Venturi's Law and other fundamental rules of pressure, velocity and acceleration, and his device was based on the conversion of velocity (the speed of steam in this case) into pressure. A stream of live steam drawn from the boiler sucked the air out of the pipe and drew the feed water after it through a set of cones and nozzles. The mixture of condensed steam and cold water came through at sufficient pressure to easily force its way into the boiler through a one-way 'clack' valve. The injector could be used in motion or at rest, it had no moving parts, and the steam helped to warm up the cold water as it passed through. Giffard patented his invention in May 1858, but the world of locomotive engineering (largely Anglophone still) did not immediately sit up and take notice. Samples were sent to some major locomotive builders, including Sharp, Stewart of Manchester, England, who took it up with enthusiasm. A visitor to their works in early 1860 was William Sellers, a Philadelphia manufacturer of ancillary railroad equipment, from whistles to turntables. He secured the right to patent and sell the injector in the USA. In England it had already been seized on by a very able chief engineer, John Ramsbottom of the London & North Western Railway, and put to work on his new 2-2-2 'Problem' class, of which the first to appear was named *Lady of the Lake*. By mid-century, the LNWR works at Crewe in England were among the world's biggest. This Crewe-built class of sixty engines, short and lightweight, but with a relatively high boiler pressure of 120psi (8.4kg/cm^2), was straightforward and reliable in operation and all survived (though rebuilt in the 1890s) into the twentieth century. The first ten fed their boilers through pumps driven from the crosshead; the rest, from November 1860, were fitted with the Giffard injector.

In its early form the injector was not utterly problem-free, and in the USA especially its acceptance was only partial until the mid-1870s. Its parts could loosen; it needed a strong, unvaried steam flow; it was sensitive to bad water. Often it was used in conjunction with a feed pump, or two injectors were fitted. It also needed cold water to make it work. The feed pumps installed on many later locomotive types were needed because they had feed-water heaters, and the original injectors did not work with hot feed water. Before the end of the century, though, the use of the injector was universal in France and Britain, and very common in all other countries.

The 'Problem' class had other claims to fame in the locomotive story. They were the first to be fitted with a screw-operated reverser, a more sensitive device than the reversing lever. This had a handle in the cab, fixed to the end of the screw rod, and provided a wider range of cut-offs to the driver. They were also among the first to have water pick-up apparatus, enabling them to refill their tender tanks, without stopping, from water troughs placed between the rails. With these, non-stop running was now governed only by the coal capacity of the tender. Both these devices were invented by Ramsbottom. He also patented an improved form of spring-loaded safety valve, said to be foolproof – tampering with safety valves was still a problem, often because they went off prematurely, losing vital steam pressure. Ramsbottom's valves were widely used, and functioned with an austere efficiency that characterised all his work, though he was said to be a genial and friendly individual. He died a wealthy man, from the income generated by his patents rather than his salary. So did Giffard, who left his fortune to the State for investment in charitable purposes.

EIGHT

Gauges and Growing Pains

In 1830, a railway of 30 miles' length had seemed a major undertaking. By the 1850s, many lines stretched for hundreds of miles. London and Edinburgh, Paris and Amsterdam, New York and Chicago, Berlin and Vienna were all linked by railway. The lines on the maps were joining up to form large-scale networks. The history of the development of railways of course goes far beyond the scope of the locomotive's life story, though in classic pulling oneself up by one's own boot-straps style, longer lines needed bigger engines, and bigger engines in turn made possible yet more ambitious railway undertakings. In 1853, the first steam locomotives to run in India arrived at Bombay (Mumbai) from the Vulcan Foundry in England: the Class Q34 2-4-0 for the Bombay-Thana 5ft 6in (167.5cm) gauge line of the Great Indian Peninsula Railway, India's first public railway, which opened on 16 April 1853. They were standard English 2-4-0s, with inside frames and bearings, but on arrival in India were fitted with long-canopy cabs to ward off sun and monsoon rain. For the next twenty years, engines of this type, usually with larger cylinders, would run most of the passenger trains on India's developing railway system. One of them, *Sindh*, is preserved. Another survival of that period is the East Indian Railway's restored tiny 2-2-2 *Fairy Queen* of 1855, built by Kitson & Co., of Leeds. In 1854, the first locomotives to run in Brazil and Australia were delivered. In 1856, the Cairo-Alexandria line inaugurated railways in Africa. Also in 1856, through trains began to run from Montreal to Toronto. Further south, plans for the first trans-continental line were already in hand. Even further south, Argentina's first locomotive, built in England and suitably named *La Portenta*, began to work between Parque and Floresta in 1857. The national gauge was set at 5ft 6in, because the locomotive had been built to that gauge for an Indian railway whose order was cancelled.

On the longer lines, individual locomotives did not traverse the full distances with their trains. About 70 miles was usual, before a change of engines was made. This might be because the line changed ownership, but it was in any case made necessary by other factors. One was the fuel capacity of the tender. Small four-wheeled tenders were still common and had to be re-stocked every hundred miles or so. Also, locomotives were still assigned to specific drivers. There were as yet no regular lodging facilities for engine crews, and drivers expected to return to their home depots at night.

Whilst new inventions were improving the locomotive's efficiency and safety, they were also changing in other ways. From the time of the Liverpool & Manchester Railway, a distinction had been made between passenger and freight engines; the former expected to go faster but with a more light-weight train, while the latter toiled along slowly with a much heavier load. This distinction remained, though passenger trains were becoming heavier, and the speed of freight trains was by now expected to get some way into double figures. Consequently, both types grew larger.

The homeland of these evolutions was the United States. From the 1850s onwards, almost every increase in locomotive size, length and wheel arrangement would originate there. Europe still had some vital contributions to make, but would rarely inaugurate a new phase of growth. And Great Britain, though it would produce some locomotive classes of great distinction, and remain the world's prime exporter of steam locomotives, had made the last of its great contributions with Ramsbottom's safety valves and his water-troughs. Towards the end of the nineteenth century, an increasing divergence in locomotive size became apparent between those coming from the building works of the British railway companies, constructing locomotives largely for their own use, and those of the independent builders, like Beyer Peacock of Manchester, Dübs of Glasgow or Robert Stephenson of Newcastle. Although the independents could and did build for the home market also, their survival and growth were based on supplying the export market. And, whereas at the beginning new railways in other countries had been grateful for the standard British types and the standard British size, it did not take long for them to start to stipulate their own special requirements when placing orders. The most accommodating buyers were the railways in British colonies — India, South Africa, Australia — where the lines of trade were firmly fixed with the 'mother country' and the railway officials, including the mechanical engineers, were men who had learned their business in Britain and who based their operating practice on British methods. Thus the growing railway system of India was provided with hundreds of 0-6-0 freight locomotives, with inside cylinders, purely because such locomotives had become the backbone of freight operations in Britain. India's lines were mostly built either to the metre gauge (39.4in) or to a 66in (167.6cm) gauge, and the basic small 0-6-0 was simply widened or narrowed as necessary. Among other countries which more or less tamely accepted British practice was Argentina, where most railways were British-owned (those that were French-owned of course looked to Lille or Paris for their locomotive stock). One colony quickly became an exception. This was Canada, where for a number of reasons, not least geographical proximity and cross-border rail links, locomotive design followed that of the United States, with only a few exceptions. Eastern North America suffered from break-of-gauge problems until a phase of expensive standardisation was gone through in the 1880s: the Canadian Grand Trunk and some New England lines were laid to 5ft 6in (167.6cm) and other lines, including many in the southern states, were laid to 4ft 10in (147.6cm).

British design, for home usage anyway, was increasingly inhibited by the constraints of the loading gauge. No locomotive could exceed 13ft 6in (411.5cm) in height and 8ft 6in (260cm) in width, and some lines required less than this. Thousands of bridges and hundreds of tunnels had been built to these dimensions. The high platforms of British stations, so convenient to the passengers, were a further problem to locomotive designers and contributed to the retention of inside cylinders, whose inaccessibility made maintenance more expensive. One outside-cylinder 2-2-2 built at the LNWR's Wolverton works by J.C. McConnell in 1850, was known as 'Mac's Mangle' because of its effect on lineside fittings. Only New Zealand would have even tighter constraints than Britain – admittedly its lines were of only 42in (106.7cm) gauge, but then, so were South Africa's, which had a generous loading gauge. Most countries could take higher and wider locomotives than Great Britain – most notably Russia, where a height of 16ft 6in (502.9cm) and sometimes more was permissible, and North America, another terrain of wide open spaces. Not that British inventiveness ceased: in many other aspects of railway life, from interlocking points and signals to the automatic token exchanger for single-line working, its continuing vitality was displayed. But in locomotive design a crushing conservatism, a preoccupation with external appearance, and a freezing indifference to what was happening outside their own little worlds characterised the attitude of all too many chief mechanical engineers. Partly responsible for this was the social and commercial system in which these men rose to their positions. Britain had not set up a system of technical universities and colleges comparable with those of continental Europe; and British locomotive engineers lacked the theoretical knowledge and academic training of their counterparts elsewhere. They were – had to be – professionals: but they learned normally as 'gentleman apprentices' on the shop floor or at the draughting-table. Often they had been with the same company since their teens. Equally professional were the men who ran the traffic department. They knew about timetabling, carriage rates, refreshment halts, cost management, and double-entry book-keeping. It was from their ranks, and much more rarely from the locomotive department, that general managers emerged. The directors were a mixture of businessmen, local notables like mayors or aldermen, and aristocrats. The general manager was sometimes invited to join the board; his senior officers rarely were. But the officers ran their own domains. The chief mechanical engineer, in particular, was effectively answerable to no-one. Very few managers or directors had the technical competence to question him. And normally he was also in charge of the locomotive running sheds as well as of design and construction. Thus the British chief mechanical engineer enjoyed great power. He designed the engines, controlled the building works, and employed the drivers. If the engines were defective, it would be a brave driver who complained. In most cases the engines worked acceptably; sometimes brilliantly. But by no means always.

In other countries, railways also had their chief engineers, sometimes as powerful and autocratic as their British counterparts. But usually locomotive running was a separate responsibility, which meant that there was some sort of dialogue between the designers and the people who had to take their products out on the road.

NINE

Mid-Century Perceptions

The Great Western Railway of England was a lordly concern which went its own way from the start, with a fine sense of its own worth. One distinction however fell to it by accident: a GWR engine was the first to be a subject of fine art. In 1844 the English painter J.M.W. Turner exhibited his celebrated study *Rain, Steam and Speed – the Great Western Railway*, at the Royal Academy. He was seventy years old, but still unique for his time in his depiction of light and atmosphere. The picture shows a train crossing the Thames at Maidenhead, in a violent squall of wind and rain. The locomotive is portrayed heroically – it and the bridge are solid new constructs which defy the wild elements, and cut across the older, gentler landscape of river and roadway. In front of the engine a racing hare can be seen: the old and now outmoded symbol of speed. But Turner's attitude to the locomotive is ambiguous, and some critics have seen it as an image of divisiveness, even death, rather than vital energy. Such appreciation of an industrial product as a subject for fine art, not uncommon in early nineteenth-century Britain, was already beginning to change. Between Turner and the Impressionists, few artists would consider the railway, or other aspects of modern industry, as a fit or desirable subject. A contemporary of Turner's, John Martin, who did depict industry on a grand scale, rendered it as sharply detailed visions of Hell and of humanity over-reaching itself with metallic splendours; for him 'the steam locomotive was no less a source of satanic imagery than the fiery furnaces of the Black Country' (Michael Freeman). In a famous painting of a modern Armageddon, he has a train tumbling into the Pit. The railway companies cannot have been pleased. But from their early days in Britain and the United States they utilised, and benefited from, a more representational style of art.

Even before it opened, the Liverpool & Manchester Railway commissioned a series of engravings for public sale. Pride in its own achievement had something to do with this, but more important was the desire to impress and familiarise the public with the new form of transport. Rudolf Ackerman, who was using steam power in his printing works, published vast numbers of railway prints, from original drawings by T.T. Bury, I. Shaw, and others. These have great period charm. A higher standard of depiction was attained by John Cook Bourne in his famous lithographs of work on the London and Birmingham and Great Western Railways. But all were art enlisted in the service of commerce; despite their clear detail, they are not objective portrayals of the railway scene. One Ackerman print was suppressed because it showed a locomotive in the Edge Hill Tunnel at Liverpool at a time when the company's enabling act authorised only cable traction inside it. It is notable that the engines are usually shown as incidental items in these pictures: they are subdued and small, and the focus is on grand landscape works and architecture. Although locomotives were the most strikingly novel aspects of the railway, they were also the most alarming to the public at large (early names like *Fury* and *Acheron* are rather surprising in this context; one might have expected *Tranquillity* instead). Close-up depictions would not have been reassuring to apprehensive travellers, and were rare at first.

Thirty years later, the lithographic reproductions of Nathaniel Currier and James Ives, produced in vast numbers in the USA, show a more robust readiness to put locomotives in the foreground, but their great enterprise was independent of the railroad companies. With them too, however, it is the railway in the landscape, and its involvement with people, that are of most interest. Currier and Ives were showing the new America to itself, in bright, metallic colours, and railways were a crucial part of their subject matter, with locomotives as the animating element. 'Almost overnight the steam locomotive became an instrument of continental implications,' wrote Lucius Beebe in *Hear the Train Blow*. 'Only fifteen years after the coming of the trains the country was swept to a crescendo of emotional intensity by the phrase "manifest destiny." The United States was going places and, by tunket, it was going there in style aboard the railroad'.

On a different note, railway disasters provided a rich source for etchers and engravers, and the companies could do nothing to prevent newspapers and magazines regaling the public with scenes of locomotives plunging off embankments, colliding at high speed, and exploding their boilers.

The rivalries and idiosyncrasies of railway companies were mocked by cartoonists, and a famous *Punch* cartoon shows English broad-gauge and standard-gauge engines scowling at each other: faces on smoke-box fronts go back a long way before Thomas the Tank Engine. Louring 'Railway Dragons' and 'Railway Juggernauts' frequently appeared in cartoons during the railway mania years in the mid-1840s. 'I come to dine, I come to sup; I come, I come, to eat you up!' announces a backwards-advancing loco-motive through its fire-door mouth to a terrified middle-class family at their Christmas dinner, depicted in a George Cruickshank cartoon. A more cheerful extension of railway awareness came in light music, beginning around 1830 with *Railways Now Are All The Go, With Steam, Steam, Steam*, a music-hall song. Of the same general date is Bryan's *Characteristic Rondo*, a musical piece composed to reflect a journey by train from Manchester to Liverpool. The score is annotated to show the various stages of the jour-ney, the crescendo being reached as it plunges into the tunnel at Liverpool. A similar exercise was done in France by Charles-Valentin Alkan, with *Le Chemin de Fer* (1844), though the first railway song in French comes from 1835, with music by Charles Plantade: *Titi au Chemin de Fer de St Germain en Laye, ou Impressions de voyage d'un gamin à Paris*. The boy in the title is making a railway trip to Paris. Special musical tributes were sometimes written for grand openings, like Christian Lumbye's *Copenhagen Steam Railway Galop*, celebrating the first Danish railway in 1847. There were not many such pieces among the vast range of parlour music, but works like D'Albert's *Express Galop* from around 1855, with its atmospheric cover pic-ture of an engine crossing a viaduct by night, show how the rhythms of steam were becoming part of the general background to life. The American engineer Thatcher Perkins, Superintendent of Machinery on the Louisville & Nashville Railroad, received an unusual tribute in 1871 in the publication of a song-sheet, *Number Twenty-Nine*, composed by Will S. Hays, 'respect-fully dedicated by the Employees of the Road', and with his 4-4-0 No.29 lithographed on the cover. One or two greater composers showed hints of interest. Mikhail Glinka inserted deliberate railway rhythms into *Farewell to St Petersburg* in 1840. Hector Berlioz composed a cantata to someone else's words, *Le Chant des Chemins de Fer*, in 1846, a bread-and-butter job for the grandiose opening of the Nord railway at Lille. Rossini is said to have dis-liked trains, and his *A Train Journey* for solo piano builds up to a crash. Several members of the Strauss family composed railway pieces; Johann Strauss the Elder with *Eisenbahn Lust Wälzer*, 'Railway Pleasure Waltzes', in 1836; the younger Johann, though sharing Rossini's view, contributing altogether a jollier piece in *Excursion Train Polka* of 1899. In this century and the next, a number of scions of musical families entered the service of the locomotive; the first seems to have been Max von Weber, designer of engines for the railways of Saxony, and the son of the court composer Carl Maria von Weber.

The locomotive, compared to the horse and the ship, has proved stoutly resistant to incorporation in high literary culture. Among the few poets to make even passing reference to it was the Frenchman Alfred de Vigny, who was not favourably impressed. In *La Maison du Berger* of 1844, he complained that the hurrying pace of the train destroyed the contemplative, gradual quality of travel, and in a famous line likened the experience of travel behind a locomotive to: '… un brouillard étouffant que traverse un éclair', a stroke of lightning passing through a suffocating fog. By then, the first large-scale railway disaster had already occurred, in 1842, at Bellevue in France, with seventy-three dead — the cause was a broken axle on one of the train's two Bury-type locomotives. One of the earliest books to note the locomotive's existence is A. W. Kinglake's eastern travel tale, *Eothen*, published in 1844. In ironic mode, the writer records an imaginary dialogue conducted — through the interpretation of a dragoman — between a British traveller and an Ottoman pasha. The visitor is endeavouring to recount the mechanical wonders of his country. The pasha responds with eagerness:

> I know it — I know it all — the particulars have been faithfully related to me, and my mind comprehends locomotives. The armies of the English ride upon the vapours of boiling cauldrons, and their horses are flaming coals! whirr! whirr! all by wheels! — whiz! whiz! — all by steam!

One of the few English poets of distinction to try to capture the imaginative impact of a locomotive was Elizabeth Barrett Browning. A few lines in *Aurora Leigh* note:

> *First, the shrill whistle, then the distant roar,*
> *The ascending cloud of steam, the gleaming brass,*
> *The mighty moving arm; and on amain*
> *The mass comes thundering like an avalanche o'er*
> *The quaking earth…*

This was not Mrs Browning at her best; and the steam locomotive seemed doomed to inspire bad verse among English writers: few of them much worse than T. Baker, who lived from around 1817 to some time after 1857, the year in which he published his *The Steam Engine: or, the Power of Flame: An Original Poem in Ten Cantos*. A verse history of railways, its flavour is well given by his lines on the death of Huskisson at the wheels of *Rocket*:

> *Thus fell the great financier in his prime!*
> *This fatal chance not only caused delay,*
> *But damped the joy that erst had crown'd the day.*

At a humble literary level, the locomotive was generally welcomed as a token of progress and future prosperity, as put in artless style by one minor versifier, Ned Farmer:

> *'Tis destined, you'll find, to befriend all mankind,*
> *To strew blessings all over the world;*
> *Man's science, they say, gave it birth one fine day,*
> *And the flag of King Steam was unfurl'd.*

More ambitiously, various minor poets attempted the anthropomorphic approach, as if the locomotive could express its own thoughts. Typical of these was Cosmo Gordon Monkhouse's *Night Express* of 1865:

> *Little I know or care*
> *What be the load I bear.*
> *Why thus compelled I seek not to divine.*
> *At man's command I stir,*
> *I, his stern messenger!*

The same line of thought can be found among American political economists, though expressed from a different angle. But the opposition also had its bards; the chorus to an English pro-coaching song of the 1830s went:

> *Let the steam pot*
> *Hiss till it's hot —*
> *Give me the speed*
> *Of the Tantivy Trot.*

French poets after Vigny did not consider the locomotive as a subject, though in 1873 Paul Verlaine, shut up in Mons jail for wounding his implacable co-adventurer Arthur Rimbaud, wrote with wistful eloquence of the sounds of the engines at night beyond the prison walls. The generally negative or unresponsive English and European attitude was not shared in the United States, whose writers lived in a larger, wilder landscape and could perceive the role played by the railway in humanising and uniting a vast tract of the planet. Ralph Waldo Emerson noted in his journal:

> I hear the whistle of the locomotive in the woods. Whenever that music comes it has its sequel. It is the voice of the civility of the nineteenth century saying, 'Here I am!'

This was an essentially American reaction. Americans were able to integrate their sense of the great outdoors with an enthusiasm for new inventions that stimulated their imagination. In July 1844 Nathaniel Hawthorne was peacefully contemplating the minutiae of nature on a woodland path near Concord, Mass., when:

> 'But, hark! there is the whistle of the locomotive – the long shriek, harsh, above all other harshnesses, for the space of a mile cannot mollify it into harmony. It tells ... of all unquietness; and no wonder that it gives such a startling shriek, since it brings the noisy world into our slumberous hollow.'

The great American advocate of the simple life, Henry David Thoreau, wrote about his beloved and deeply-observed pond in *Walden*:

> The Fitchburg Railroad touches the pond about 100 rods south of where I dwell ... when I meet the engine with its train of cars moving off with planetary motion, when I hear the iron horse making the hills echo with his snort like thunder, shaking the earth with his feet, and breathing fire and smoke from his nostrils (what kind of winged horse or fiery dragon they will put into the new mythology I don't know), it seems as if the earth has got a race now worthy to inhabit it.

When he wrote this in 1854, the iron horse was still a relatively small beast. The locomotive often aroused a curious sense of past mythology come to life, as if old dreams of dragons had been in anticipation of its arrival. Not for nothing were numerous early engines named *Prometheus* – there was more than a hint of primeval force in something that moved, with rods flailing like arms, and seemed most powerfully to breathe, and had fire secreted in its iron belly. And yet it was most modern and up to date. Two great American poets recorded their visions of it. In *To a Locomotive in Winter*, Walt Whitman saluted it as it moved in:

> *… the snow, the winter day declining,*
> *Thee in thy panoply, thy measur'd dual throbbing and thy beat convulsive,*
> *Thy black cylindric body, golden brass and silvery steel,*
> *Thy ponderous side-bars, parallel and connecting rods, gyrating, shuttling at thy sides …*
> *Thy matrical, now swelling pant and roar, now tapering in the distance,*
> *Thy great protruding headlight fixed in front…*

A better shot was had by the reclusive Emily Dickinson, who, in *I Like To See It Lap The Miles*, ignores the detail to capture the movement through space, the way in which the verges of the track come close and retreat, and the contrasts and combination of power and control inherent in the locomotive:

> *I like to see it lap the Miles –*
> *And lick the Valleys up –*
> *And stop to feed itself at Tanks –*
> *And then – prodigious step*
>
> *Around a Pile of Mountains –*
> *And supercilious peer*
> *In Shanties – by the sides of Roads –*
> *And then a Quarry pare*
>
> *To fit its Ribs and crawl between*
> *Complaining all the while*
> *In horrid – hooting stanza –*
> *Then chase itself down hill –*
>
> *And neigh like Boanerges –*
> *Then – punctual as a Star*
> *Stop – docile and omnipotent –*
> *At its own stable door –*

As Leo Marx points out in *The Machine in the Garden*, however, it did not need poets to bring the symbolic value of the locomotive into play:

> A locomotive is a perfect symbol because its meaning need not be attached to it by a poet; it is inherent in its physical attributes. To see a powerful, efficient machine in the landscape is to know the superiority of the present to the past.

He quotes from John Stuart Mill in the *Edinburgh Review* of October 1840 to underline this:

> ... the steam engines, the railroads, carry the feeling of admiration for the modern, and disrespect for ancient times, down even to the wholly uneducated classes.

It was in serious and thoughtful books and essays on modern life and political economy, especially in the United States, that the role of the locomotive was most considered. In the June 1846 issue of *Hunt's Merchant's Magazine*, Charles Fraser wrote of 'The Moral Influence of Steam', exploring the idea that steam power upset that 'great law of the universe, which makes labor the portion of man, and condemns him to earn his bread by the sweat of his brow'. This theme echoes through the 1840s and 1850s. Writers saw steam power as a historical culmination, not (as we do) as the first accelerative phase of a technological era. Classically-educated, they tended to write in terms of the past. Theodore Parker, a prominent apologist for the new, wrote in the April 1850 issue of *Scientific American*:

> At the voice of Genius ... Fire and Water embrace at his bidding, and a new servant is born, which will fetch and carry at his command ... and run errands up and down the continent with men and women on his back ... The Fable of Orpheus is a true story in our times.

These were the palmy days of the steam locomotive, when it blazed as brightly in symbolic significance as its own paint and polish shone in sunlight, or as its red fire lit up the darkness. In the century's great wave of scientific and technical innovation, humanity had assumed a creativity that was almost godlike. A mechanical slave, the mighty locomotive would meekly do the bidding of its driver and never ask why. It was a perception that encouraged a materialist view of life, and may partly explain why, at a higher aesthetic level, the railway was dismissed or ignored in England. John Ruskin, the most prominent Victorian critic of art and morals, could not abide it and when he travelled, he deliberately hired post chaises to 'cut the railway'. To him it was part of what another critic referred to as 'the hideous prose of modern life'. This frostily detached view, which extended to technology in general, had a deeply discouraging effect on imaginative writing. The first novel in which the railway plays a significant part, though not a vital one, is Charles Dickens's *Dombey and Son*, of 1847-1848. Dickens was concerned with the social impact of the railway as a whole; and he saw it as one of the main agents of change taking humanity into a new world which threatens as much as it promises. Inevitably perhaps, he made use of the dramatic potential of the locomotive for destruction. The annihilation of the unpleasant Mr Carker by an advancing engine is, with the suicide of Tolstoy's Anna Karenina, one of the two great railway deaths in literature. Dickens' example did not spark a reaction from other novelists in Britain, which never produced a serious novel with the railway at its centre. Nor, more surprisingly, did the United States, where Herman Melville and Mark Twain were not at all inhibited about weaving technological elements into great themes.

The public at large had its own perceptions, influenced by the creative fire of artists and writers, but much more by daily experience and common sense. Anyone born in the year of the Stockton & Darlington Railway was still only twenty-five at mid-century, but by then the existence and activity of the steam locomotive had long ceased to be a matter of amazement and wonder. People had become accustomed to living in an age of constant technological improvement, in which railways were only a part. Some shared Ruskin's doubts about the nature of this as 'progress'. William Wordsworth, Poet Laureate of Great Britain, who had in his youth welcomed the forward march of science, was now writing lines like: 'Is there no nook of English ground secure From rash assault!' (*On the Projected Kendal and Windermere Railway*). Despite his attack on 'a false utilitarian lure' there is more than a hint of 'Not in my back-yard' in the Lakeland-dwelling poet's attitude. Many less articulate citizens similarly felt that the railway was a good thing, so long as it did not come too near.

But it entered their lives in various and sometimes subtle ways, affecting even their daily language. A few locomotive metaphors soon became current: a wild person 'went off the rails'; lively children had to 'let off steam';

someone ready for a big task had 'a full head of steam' and went for the job 'at full throttle'; but a project brought up short 'hit the buffers'. Time gained a new precision, 'railway time observed in clocks as if the sun itself had given in', observed Dickens in *Dombey and Son*. The first postage stamp to show a locomotive was a 3-cent US issue of 1869, which featured a typical wide-stacked 4-4-0. Peru also showed engines on stamps in 1870, but none of the European postal services did so before the twentieth century. Perhaps the earliest banknotes to show locomotives were those of the St Lawrence & Champlain Railway in Canada, which issued its own currency in 1837 with a picture of *Dorchester* or a similar four-wheeler, and its train.

Already the locomotive had begun to recruit its army of lay admirers, who were captivated by its mechanism, movements, colour, smell, warmth and noise, and its intense presence, which left a particularly deep emptiness when it had gone. For them its appeal went beyond the glamour of fast travel, 'here now, sixty miles away in an hour's time'. They felt some deep inner response to the smooth, oiled, regular movement of revolving and reciprocating parts, to the mystery of shining brass-framed gauges glimpsed on the boiler back-head; to levers and handles that held huge power in check; they appreciated above all, perhaps, that transient, majestic moment when steam hissed forth, stillness gave way to motion, great wheels began to turn, and the object of contemplation, slowly at first, then with increasing rapidity, moved itself away, leaving a pleasant void in the imagination which was almost a small nirvana.

This capacity for beguilement by machines was chiefly noticeable among men and boys of the Anglo-American and northern European countries. Perhaps it was partly because these were first to know the locomotive, and could have some proprietorial feelings towards it. It owed a lot to the existence of a growing middle class, with an involvement in business and commerce and a keen interest in what made the new industrial economy tick. They were people who used the railway, for business and pleasure; it was familiar and friendly, its locomotives were willing servants. In England especially, many of these locomotive enthusiasts were clergymen, a curious minor detail of social life that would continue for 100 years. From around 1850, with the development of photography, some railway observers would also take photographs, at first only of locomotives standing at station plat-forms; later, as the science developed, of moving ones. This blend of hobbies was itself a sign of relative wealth and leisure; and the almost obligatory small boy who appears by the engine in many such Victorian pictures, to give it scale, is invariably an Eton-collared child of the bourgeoisie. From as early as 1835, he would be likely to have a toy engine or train at home. Made mostly in France and Germany, they were made of sheet tin or brass, and marketed internationally, with different models and colours to correspond to national styles (while almost every railway in Europe had a 'Patentee' or two, this was not a difficulty).

Even those homes without a resident locomotive enthusiast were likely to have some railway-related items. Prompted or approved by the railway companies, iconic locomotives were blazoned on cups, plates and vases by chinaware makers. As early as 1811, the Leeds Pottery Co. produced pottery representing the Middleton Railway engines before they were even built. By 1830, Staffordshire ware mugs, jugs and plates showed locomotives and railway scenes. The Ackerman prints in England, and those by Currier and Ives in America, were immensely popular. In 1840, a French company produced a cafetière in the form of a four-wheel locomotive of red porcelain and metal. To have such items on display did not necessarily show a special interest in railways; it was simply to be modern.

For peasants and proletarians, it was another matter. The trains that roared by the great estates and latifundia of Russia and Italy were no more part of the life of the workers in the fields than were shooting stars. As for the industrial workers, the railway used them, as did the rest of industry. For most of them their acquaintance with steam power was too close, too intimately linked with drudging toil, too demanding of life and energy, for any possibility of romance or admiration to arise. The locomotive did not belong to them, but to the boss, like Crawshay Bailey, the Welsh ironmaster:

> *Cosher Bailey had an engine:*
> *It was always wanting mendin';*
> *And according to her power,*
> *She could do four mile an hour.*
> *Did you ever see, did you ever see,*
> *Did you ever see*
> *Such a funny thing before?*

So went one folk song, more concerned to poke fun at the big man and his enthusiasms than at his engine. Only the driver, himself an aristocrat of the working class, might rise above this, lavishing extra polish and decoration on his locomotive. In some heroic cases, his devotion went far beyond surface shine:

> *Then up the road he hurtled, against the rock he crashed;*
> *The engine it turned over, poor George's chest was mashed.*
> *His head was at the firebox door; the flames were rolling high:*
> *'I'm glad I was born for an engineer, on the C & O road to die…'*

> *The doctor said, 'Dear George, my darling boy, be still;*
> *Your life may yet be saved, if it is God's precious will.'*
> *' Oh, no,' cried George, 'That cannot be; I want to die so free,*
> *I want to die on the engine I love, One Hundred and Forty-three.'*

– and even better known than George Alley of the Chesapeake & Ohio was Casey Jones, of the Illinois Central, commemorated in Wallace Saunders' rendering of a folk-poem:

> *Casey pulled up Reno Hill,*
> *Tooted for the crossing with an awful shrill,*
> *Snakes all knew by the engine's moans*
> *That the hogger at the throttle was Casey Jones.*
> *He pulled up short two miles from the place,*
> *Number Four stared him right in the face,*
> *Turned to his fireboy, said, 'You'd better jump,*
> *'Cause there's two locomotives a-going to bump.'*

Heroic drivers entered railway folklore, and occasionally an engine did too. The North British 4-4-0, No.224, that went down with the Tay Bridge disaster in 1879 was later retrieved from the sea-bed, repaired and put back in service. The Scottish railwaymen knew it as 'The Diver' and among the public a completely false belief grew up that it was never allowed to run over the rebuilt bridge.

TEN

Coke, Coal, Culm, Logs, Bagasse and Oil

Coal, with its high calorific value in relation to weight, was the prime locomotive fuel in most countries. But for over thirty years, in much of North America, and other places where wood was plentiful and coal expensive, most locomotives burned wood. American engineers established the right kind of firebox and grate for this fuel, and a magnificent array of spark-arresting smokestacks, as varied as the helmets at some grand cavalry convention – each one containing a patent device – was paraded by successive locomotive types. These often dwarfed the still modest-sized boilers. The locomotive's needs created a lumber supply industry right across the country, and cordwood was stored in vast amounts. One of the earliest specialised locomotives was a saw-engine on the Utica and Schenectady Railroad, which could go out to where the loggers were at work, by the side of the tracks. As the railroads spread, the supply of cordwood became a substantial industry and the engines, by one estimate, devoured over a million acres of forest trees between 1830 and 1865. After that year, consumption of wood fell rapidly, in favour of coal. The great forests of the north-east had been largely eradicated and the price of wood was going up. But also, coal production was increasing, the price of coal was falling, and coal was more than twice as effective, pound for pound, in heating value, as the best pine or hardwood. By the end of the nineteenth century, from around half a million tons of wood a year in 1860, the American railroads were burning only a few thousand tons. The use of wood as a main fuel source went on much longer in some countries, including Finland, Thailand, and Angola, all of which had ample forest resources (or planted them specially in the case of Angola) and little or no coal reserves, and which burned wood as well as coal or oil until steam power was phased out.

On the earliest British railways, engines consumed coke, which burned well, reached a high temperature, and created little smoke. Coke is the residue of high-quality coal that has been heated in an airless atmosphere to over 1000°C ; and though a supply was available as a by-product of coal-gas manufacture, all railway companies found it necessary to establish their own coking plants to provide sufficient fuel, and principal locomotive depots could be picked out from afar by their tall smoke-stacks. But coke was expensive, and by the 1840s engineers were looking for ways in which coal might be used instead. Coal was much cheaper as it needed no processing, and most of the busiest railway lines were close to, or built over, coalfields. With the spread of other uses of steam power, the old stipulation against smoke was increasingly ignored, and every industrial town was being coated with a gradually thickening layer of soot. Nevertheless, the legal obligation in many places to avoid smoke helped to drive on the process of developing an effective coal-burning firebox. A complicating factor was that coal is by no means a uniform substance; its chemical content and its density vary widely, as does the way it burns. Railway companies wanted to use the coal that was cheapest, which usually also meant nearest, and not necessarily of best quality. In east central Europe, there were large deposits of 'brown coal' or lignite, with a lower calorific value, requiring a wider firebox in order to create sufficient steam for heavy load-pulling: with a consequent influence on locomotive design. At the same time, designers were striving to find an alternative metal to copper, which was very suitable for fireboxes but also very expensive. Wrought-iron designs came and went with great rapidity, and most designers went back to copper. British designers stayed with copper-lined fireboxes to the last, though the Germans and Americans in due course found that reliable steel fireboxes could be made.

In the late 1850s, work was going ahead both in Britain and the USA on how to make coal burn better in locomotives and produce less smoke. Both countries had large reserves of coal, both bituminous and anthracite. Not for the first time, the same solution was reached by different inventors in each country, at much the same time. It was far more simple than any of the many previous efforts, which had involved double fireboxes and special devices of various kinds. An arch of flame-resistant firebricks was built across the upper area of the firebox, and a deflector plate was attached to the fire-door. These deflected and lengthened the flames from the fire, increased the heat of combustion, improved steam generation, and reduced the production of smoke. In the USA, George S. Griggs, Master Mechanic of the Boston & Providence Railroad, patented a brick arch in December 1857, though the idea seems to have been first put into practice by Matthew Baird, a partner in the Baldwin Works, on some engines in 1854. Griggs's design did not include a deflector plate. The pioneer design work in Britain was done on the Midland Railway, with James Kirtley as chief mechanical engineer. The man responsible was his assistant Charles Markham, who perfected the method by the end of 1859, after a long and strenuous period of experimentation. He used the combination of arch and deflector plate. From 1860 onwards, the firebrick arch was incorporated into all fireboxes, and coal became the standard fuel on most lines.

The first British class to have the improved coal-burning firebox from the start was the Midland's inside-cylinder, outside-framed 0-6-0 design of 1863, with a boiler pressure of 140psi (9.8kg/cm²) – 315 of this class were built up to 1874, and they formed the mainstay of the MR goods traffic. Numerous members were still in service in the late 1940s and the last was not withdrawn until 1951.

In the United States, other inventors were giving attention to fireboxes. Although US main-line railways were mostly built to the same 'standard' gauge as in the UK, the permissible width of a locomotive was greater. This was exploited by Ross Winans, who had become something of a maverick among American locomotive suppliers. Around 1840 he established a factory at Baltimore, next door to the Baltimore & Ohio's Mount Clare workshops. He shared the general preoccupation with developing a coal-burning firebox; in his case, also one that could cope with relatively low-grade coal. Such fuel required a wide grate in order to develop a fire that was sufficiently large and hot. In 1848 Winans built an oddly shaped locomotive which he called the 'Camel', with a very wide, backwards-sloping firebox at the rear, taking up the full width available. The fireman stood on the tender and plied his shovel. The driving cab had to be displaced to a position over and around the boiler. This was the only type of locomotive that Winans' factory would build, to a final total of around 300. It was also the first coal-burning locomotive to be produced in quantity, and the original one, *Camel*, was supplied to the Boston & Maine. After road tests, the B&M turned it down and it was sold to the Reading Railroad. Its performance, incidentally, appears to have been good, but apart from its appearance, it incorporated a number of idiosyncrasies and novelties unlikely to appeal to a Master Mechanic. The front tube of the apparent double funnel was an ash hopper, with a door at the base. Firing the huge box was a fireman's nightmare; Winans had incorporated feed-hoppers into his design, to get the coal to the front of the fire, but the firemen objected to the double task of shovelling coal from the floor up to the firing platform of the tender, and then into the hopper. There were significant shortcomings in the design, with a major main structural problem in the link between the firebox and the boiler. Unsupported by wheels or frame, the firebox had a tendency to sag. The boiler itself was weakened by the huge steam dome, which probably accounts for the relatively low pressure employed. A feed-water pump injected cold water at the side of the firebox, unnecessarily reducing the heat of the hottest part of the boiler. The placing of the firebox made the tender-locomotive drawbar link a difficult one. The drawbar, passing through the ashpan, would frequently become red-hot in operation.

Winans persevered with steadily larger fireboxes. He found regular customers in the Baltimore & Ohio (in which he was a large shareholder) and Philadelphia & Reading lines, both of which ran slow-speed, heavy coal trains. The 'Camel' was ill-suited to speeds over 15mph (24km/h), and few others expressed interest in it. In service, the design had its merits. John H. White Jr. quotes a run recorded around 1859, when the P&R 0-8-0 *Susquehanna* took a train of 110 four-wheel coal cars from Pottsville to Philadelphia, 95 miles (152.8km), at 8mph (13km/h). It used 4.5 tons of coal, costing $2.50 per ton. The fuel cost, of 11.74 cents a mile, compared very well against those of a wood-burner, which could run to 25 cents a mile. But by 1862, demand had ceased, and Winans closed his factory. His 'Camels' laboured on for a long time; the last of the breed, on the B&O, went for scrap at the Mount Clare shops in 1898.

Ugly and not greatly loved, they could claim to be the ancestors of the most successful wide firebox design of all, John H. Wootten's patent of 1877. He was General Manager (and former Master Mechanic) of the Philadelphia & Reading Railroad. It operated among anthracite mines, and he observed that there were vast heaps of anthracite waste, known as culm. He designed his wide firebox to burn culm, which it did most effectively, and established the wide, shallow firebox as the best for low-grade fuel. His first wide-box engines had rear cabs, but the cabs were moved forward to where there was marginally more space. The engines thus built were known as 'Camelbacks' or 'Mother Hubbards'. Unlike the old 'Camels', they could go very fast. Several thousand were produced up to 1918, mostly as ten-wheelers, though in 1906 the Erie Railroad acquired three 0-8-8-0 'Camelback' Mallets. The design, like that of the 'Camels', was confined almost entirely to America, and was not copied anywhere else. In 1878 a 4-4-0 'Camelback' was shown at the Paris Exposition and subsequently tested by French and Italian companies, without being taken up. On British lines, of course, the loading gauge would have put it out of the question – but one wonders what a forthright but conservative British designer, Patrick Stirling for example, would have said of a locomotive that appeared to have carried away a signal box on top of its boiler.

In the late 1940s, in Ireland, one old engine was adapted, and a completely new one built, to use peat as fuel, but the "turf-burners" did not enter commercial use. More successfully, Belgian and northern French railways frequently used coal in briquette form, shaped blocks formed from coal dust and tiny pieces, bonded together, which could be stacked in a bunker, taking up less space than the heap of mixed lumps carried in tenders elsewhere. While coal was always king, in many places engineers were finding that locomotives, especially smaller ones, could burn all sorts of material that the founding fathers had never contemplated. In tropical areas, a prime one was *bagasse*, the residual stalks and leaves of the sugar plant, still used in some of the last surviving steam locomotives, working on sugar plantations in Cuba and Java. Other kinds of waste were used, including the otherwise unusable greasy waste material from Yorkshire woollen mills, which kept a few small, smelly tank engines going inside factory precincts. These were very localised, but a very significant step forward was taken in Russia in the late 1870s, where Thomas Urquhart, one of the many expatriate Scottish engineers who found their way to the corners of the world, was superintendent of the Grazi-Tsaritsin Railway. In southern Russia, neither coal nor wood was readily obtainable, but the region had large, recently discovered, oil deposits. Urquhart began experimenting with ways of using heavy oil as a fuel. From 1882, he was using it in regular service, and three years later 143 locomotives of the line were adapted to burn oil. Like some other initiatives, this one was slow in having an effect beyond the railway on which it began. But around thirty years later, many railways turned to oil as a fuel for steam locomotives, especially large ones. This was Russia's only important contribution to locomotive development outside its own wide borders.

ELEVEN

The Need for Growth

By the 1860s, the steam locomotive was equipped with most of the features which it would retain. Two important areas were still the subject of debate, experiment and collective head-scratching among engineers. These were the vexed questions of brakes; and of how, if possible, to make the steam in the boiler even hotter and drier. They still remained blank areas on the design maps, with only tentative and incomplete lines of exploration. Meanwhile, the already-made improvements continued to be incessantly tweaked and altered. In the wider industrial background, work was also going on from which the steam locomotive would greatly benefit. Most important was the improvement in manufacturing process that enabled steel to be produced in large quantities. From 1856, when Sir Henry Bessemer's converter was introduced, the special properties of steel: strength, lightness, stress and heat resistance, became available to locomotive builders. Before that, steel's use had been limited, due to its high expense. Among the first to apply the technology of steel were the great Krupp Ironworks at Essen, Germany. A steel tyre for locomotive wheels was developed there in 1851 and assiduously marketed to railway companies on an international basis. After testing, the potential customers were rapidly convinced. A steel tyre could do five times the mileage of the former wrought- or cast-iron tyres fitted to locomotive driving wheels. As John White Jr. noted, 'The acceptance of steel tires is unparalleled for its speed and completeness in an industry noted for its aversion to innovation.' The Krupp tyre joined the French injector as part of a locomotive's basic equipment. As a result of such improvements, the way was open to build locomotives that were substantially larger and more powerful than any that had yet appeared.

Long-distance routes were opening up. High politics and internal strategy brought about the construction of the first trans-continental railways in the USA, Russia and Canada; and later, in Australia. Commerce came puffing at the rear. The American Civil War hastened the plan for the first coast-to-coast link, which was completed on 10 May 1869, at Promontory Summit, Utah, when the 4-4-0s *Jupiter* of the Central Pacific Railroad and No.119 of the Union Pacific, came gently to a halt, pilot to pilot on the single track, with the golden spike between them. Bottles were passed around, and toasts were drunk. The moment was commemorated in typical manner in Bret Harte's *Locomotive Dialogue*, beginning:

> *What was it the engines said,*
> *Pilots touching, head to head,*
> *Facing on the single track,*
> *Half a world behind each back?*

– and ending:

> *Said the Union: 'Don't reflect or*
> *I'll run over some director!'*
> *Said the Central: 'I'm pacific,*
> *But when riled I'm quite terrific.*
> *Yet this day we shall not quarrel;*
> *Just to show these folks this moral:*
> *How two engines, in their vision,*
> *Once have met without collision.*

As the telegraphers passed on the news, there were celebrations across the country, including Sacramento, where 'thirty Iron Horses gaily bedecked and drawn up into line screeched out a concert of joy.' The two engines were modest forerunners of the giants which would wheel huge trains across the prairies in years to come. Trains in the West were still light-weight, as were the tracks. It was in the industrial East that the demand for more power was loudest. But the progress towards a satisfactory big engine was slow. As early as 1838 Isaac Dripps had built something called 'The Monster' for the Camden & Amboy Railroad. It had eight wheels – but was not strictly an 0-8-0 as its second and third driving axles were linked by spur gears, not connecting rods. It had a lever drive of extreme complexity, but worked well enough for four larger versions to be built in 1852-54. There were no imitators, and Dripps reverted to a more conventional drive system. Ross Winans' 'Camels', though powerful in their day, had a number of disadvantages, not least their very slow speed. A few other one-off big engines were built, including a 0-8-0 for the B&O in 1848, but no proper class yet appeared.

The 'ten-wheeler', as the 4-6-0 was originally known, did not play a part in the growth process. Although later it would become very numerous, it was little used until late in the century, by which time larger types had already emerged. The first 4-6-0 has been credited to Septimus Norris, whose family works built a ten-wheeler, *Chesapeake*, for the Philadelphia & Reading Railroad in March 1847, and who tried unsuccessfully to patent the wheel arrangement. But few railroads wanted the type, which was felt to offer little advantage over the 4-4-0. Indeed, in the USA it always seemed either too big or too small, though in Canada the Northern Railway used several 4-6-0 classes in large numbers; and in Europe, whose first 4-6-0 tender engines were designed by Cesare Frescot for the Upper Italian Railways in 1884, it was to become a standard mixed-traffic type in most countries (except Italy, as it happens, where the 2-6-2 was ultimately preferred). It found most favour in Britain, during the twentieth century, where it was used for fast expresses as well as freight and stopping trains.

In 1862, the Erie Railway catered for its freight engine needs with the new Class 250 2-6-0. At this time the Erie wanted to increase the power on its coal trains, previously pulled by 4-4-0s, and selected the 2-6-0 type as a standard freight locomotive to work on its 6ft (182.7cm) gauge line. The change to an additional coupled axle was prompted by the invention by Levi Bissell of his 'safety truck' in 1857. In this, the single front carrying axle was set in a frame which pivoted behind the axle, giving it much more freedom to 'find the road' and lead the locomotive into tight curves, while the extra coupled axle increased the locomotive's tractive power. Ten were ordered from Danforth, Cooke & Co. of Paterson, New Jersey, in 1862, and proved very successful, and further orders followed. With two outside cylinders in typical American fashion, it was an anthracite burner. It had a novel grate, formed of iron tubes linking the water spaces at front and rear of the firebox, an invention of James Millholland of the Philadelphia & Reading Railway. The 2-6-0 type with swivelling 'pony truck' acquired the by-name of 'Mogul'. It was the success of the 'Mogul' that brought about the first really successful 'big' engine.

In 1866, the Lehigh & Mahanoy was a new coal-carrying line with severe gradients, on which even its largest engines, 4-4-0s and 2-6-0s, could only cope with lightweight trains. Its Master Mechanic Alexander Mitchell designed for it what he called a 'super' freight locomotive in 1865, with eight coupled wheels, of 4ft (121.9cm) diameter, and a front pony truck. Some trouble was found in getting a builder; Matthew Baird of Baldwin pooh-poohed the design and suggested a Baldwin model instead. But Mitchell was convinced of the potential of his design, and eventually Baldwin took on the job, in April 1866. By August, the engine was in service. During construction the line merged with the Lehigh Valley Railroad, and the name of the new locomotive, *Consolidation*, was chosen to celebrate the event. The newest developments were incorporated, including steel tyres from Krupps, and a steam injector. The engine cost $19,000 to build, plus $950 war tax, but the railway was eminently satisfied with its investment. James I. Blakslee, the Superintendent, wrote to Baldwin: 'She is a perfect success … I am satisfied she can out pull any machine ever built of her weight. She has plenty of speed and will make any curve that your ten-wheelers dare make … you may calculate on orders for more.'

The real success of *Consolidation* was not in tractive power, which could be matched by an 0-8-0; but in its ability to operate with a heavy load on a sharply curving track at higher speeds than any railway had dared to attempt before, and with a maximum axle load of no more than 8.4 tons (8.5t). Nevertheless, in all respects this was a locomotive at the leading edge of design. Its truck was not a Bissell type but a modified form patented by William Hudson, superintendent of the Rogers Locomotive Works, with a heavy equalising lever linking the truck frame to the leading coupled wheel spring hangers. This made a great improvement to the suspension, which had been a problem in the earliest 'Moguls'. The long boiler, 15ft (456.8cm) from firebox to smoke-box, could make plenty of steam, at a maximum pressure of 120psi (8.4 kg/cm^2), and its big cylinders delivered the power to the wheels. A single injector was supplemented by feed-water pumps on both sides, worked off return cranks on the rearmost coupled wheels.

Further engines of the class were duly ordered. Other companies were keenly interested, though they were at first cautious about purchasing, partly because of its great length and greater cost. But steadily the 2-8-0 won its reputation as a heavy freight hauler. It was found to be as advantageous on narrow gauge as it was on standard gauge. In 1876 it was adopted as the Pennsylvania Railroad's standard freight locomotive, and from then the type grew very rapidly in popularity. Its greater capital cost was soon offset by the work it did. The Erie Railway supplemented its 'Moguls' with 2-8-0s, and its managers calculated in 1878 that fifty-five 2-8-0s did the work of a hundred 4-4-0s. The 2-8-0 became the most widely-built freight engine in the United States and came to dominate long-distance freight services in almost every country. However, large as it seemed in 1866, *Consolidation* soon began to look quite small. Its success launched the American trend towards ever-larger and more powerful steam locomotives.

The USA was not the only country where bigger engines were being asked for. In India too there was a real need for pulling and pushing power beyond what was so far available. The 5ft 6in (167.5cm) gauge main line into the Deccan from Bombay climbed steeply up the long 1 in 37 Ghat inclines of the Great Indian Peninsula Railway, a gradient far beyond the powers of the small engines so far supplied from Britain. The GIPR's locomotive superintendent, J. Kershaw, designed the Class Y43 4-6-0 tank engines specially for this task. Five were built in 1862 by Sharp, Stewart of Manchester, the first locomotives of the 4-6-0 wheel arrangement built in Britain, and also the most powerful yet built there. They were banking engines, intended to push trains up the gradient, and were of unusual design, with a thin chimney poking through saddle tanks set over the smoke-box and the front end of the boiler, and with sandwich-type outside frames. The very short front bogie, wider than it was long, with tiny wheels, was not pivoted but could slide laterally. The inside cylinders, at 20 by 24in (50.8 by 60.9cm) were the largest yet fitted to a British-built locomotive. The boiler pressure was 120psi (8.4kg/cm²), and they weighed just over 50 tons (49.7t). Sledge brakes, operating on the rails, were fitted. As first supplied, they had no cabs, despite the Indian climate. In service they turned out to be indifferent performers, but they confirmed the important principle that colonial and foreign customers could specify their own designs. While the British works could provide an off-the-peg design if necessary, this meant that they essentially had to offer a bespoke service, like a high-class tailor's. In the USA, things were different – the now very large works of Baldwin produced an annual catalogue of models from which prospective buyers could choose. Divergence from the list was not encouraged. As a result the Americans could usually offer very speedy delivery. To some degree they also achieved cost savings, but response to customer demand meant regular changes in design, mostly towards larger sizes and wheel configurations.

In France, when the *Nord* railway, serving the industrialised north-east, had a need for heavier freight power, its chief mechanical engineer, Jules Pétiet, took the chance to try something new, and in 1863 he designed an 0-6-6-0 tank engine for freight work. It had two sets of cylinders and two sets of driving wheels, set under a very large boiler, whose heating surface at 212.4sq ft (197.3m²) was more than double that of the stand-ard French '*Bourbonnais*' 0-6-0 freight locomotive. This 'duplex' drive was fixed in the frame, and some lateral motion of the coupled wheels at each end was allowed in order to give a bit of flexibility to the long wheel-base. Articulation had not yet arrived. Apart from its drive system, the most remarkable aspect was the absence of a front chimney. The exhaust emerged in the usual place but was piped backwards over the boiler and firebox, used on the way both as a feed-water heater and a steam drier, and finally discharged through a chimney mounted above the cab. Although unsat-isfactory in performance, with poor steaming, the engine was in several ways ahead of its time. Twenty were built, but were soon abandoned though not wasted: in a remarkable instance of locomotive resurrection, from their remains a series of forty conventional 0-6-0 shunting tanks was brought forth.

In the 1860s 'big engine' in most countries meant an 0-8-0, and these were rare. The 0-6-0 was the standard, and if more power were needed, two could always be employed. It was quite late in the century before larger engines of 2-8-0 configuration appeared in some numbers in Australia and Austria. In 1892 the 4-8-0 was introduced in South Africa. Another type that would later dominate freight traffic on railways throughout the world had its origin in 1886 on the Dom Pedro Segundo narrow gauge railway in Brazil. This was the 2-10-0, first built by Baldwin. The long wheelbase of five coupled axles meant that its early progress on standard gauge was slow, until developments in central Europe increased its ability to pour itself round curves. Quicker progress was made by a more self-evidently flexible type of big engine, with a shorter fixed wheelbase, the 2-8-2, of which the first was also a Baldwin product, in 1897. First known as 'modified Consolidations', they were built for Japan's 3ft 6in (106.5cm) gauge and acquired the name of 'Mikado' after one of the titles of the Japanese emperor. The key to the design, as with the first 4-6-2, was the need for a large, wide firebox to burn low-grade coal. This was placed wholly behind the driving wheels, and a two-wheel truck was inserted to support it and balance the locomo-tive. Like the standard 'Consolidation' it had two outside simple-expansion cylinders driving on to the third coupled wheels. It was very successful, and by 1902 Baldwin were building 2-8-2s for US lines, at first for those like the Bismarck Washburn & Great Falls, which also used low-grade coal. But soon the advantage of the big firebox in a heavy freight engine was recognised by lines which used good steam coal, and 'Mikados' of considerably greater tractive power were produced. It became India's standard heavy freight locomotive. Always particularly well-adjusted to narrow-gauge tracks, it was also frequently used on the American standard gauge for both passenger and freight work, the freight engines often assisted by a booster engine fitted to the trailing bogie. 'Mikados' were built in the USA right up to 1946, the last being the Great Northern Railroad's Class 0-8.

By 1900, whatever any railway's relative criteria of size might be, 'big' engine types were available if wanted.

TWELVE

But How Do You Make It Stop?

Like a universal law, it seemed to be decreed from on high that progress in locomotive design would be answered by increased demand from the operating side. With bigger engines, civil engineers felt more confident about constructing mountain lines. Traffic managers, especially on lines which competed for the same traffic, wanted heavier trainloads so that they could offer cheaper ton/mile prices; on lines which enjoyed a monopoly they wanted the same thing, not to reduce prices but to swell the profits and the shareholders' dividend. These demands for speed and power inevitably raised another issue, which had long been scandalously neglected by the railway companies. Trains carrying 400 tons of freight, or as many passengers, were by now not unusual. But that large tonnage with its great momentum and those vulnerable passengers whirled along at 60mph or more were protected by only the most rudimentary and inadequate braking systems. It was surprising that there were not more disasters than actually did occur.

The patent of Stephenson's 'Patentee' locomotive had included a steam-powered brake, operated by a lever from the footplate. In practice, few if any of the 'Patentees' actually incorporated this feature. British locomotives normally had brakes fitted to the tender wheels. These were not intended to slow down the train in motion, but merely to hold the engine in position while it was stationary. Shutting off steam, and (if possible) yanking the valve gear into reverse mode, were the only ways of slowing the locomotive. A whistle signal to the guard warned him to apply the brake in his van at the end of the train. Between the tender and the guard's van, the trucks or carriages, however numerous, had no brakes at all (except on some freight lines, on which individual wagons with pin-down brakes were used). The inability to come to a fully controlled stop was not only a serious disincentive to speed, but a cause of innumerable minor front- and rear-end collisions. But the worst accidents were usually caused by trains breaking in two on gradients when couplings failed, with the breakaway part being unable to stop.

The responsibility was not with the locomotive builders, but the railway companies, which for many years shied away from the cost of installing proper continuous braking systems, and the governments which let them get away with it. The locomotive, as power generator, was the key to effective braking. But locomotive driving wheels had no brakes at all. Received wisdom among engine designers was that to have brake-shoes pressing on the driving wheels would impose such strains as to force the axles out of their blocks, and bend the connecting rods. Much in the way of received wisdom had been challenged and found wanting, as in the notion that a locomotive must have a low centre of gravity, but the brake shibboleth endured.

It was on the Pennsylvania Railroad in 1869 that George Westinghouse first successfully demonstrated his continuous brake, operated by compressed air. Any diminution in the air pressure automatically applied brakes throughout the train. The compressor was a simple steam-powered pump, attached to the side of the locomotive. The railway companies did not rush to use it. It took another twenty years and several appalling accidents for the British government to make the use of an automatic continuous brake compulsory on passenger trains. Many British companies opted for a vacuum system rather than compressed air; though an air pump was still required in order to maintain the vacuum in the brake-pipes.

In the interest of avoiding wheel-brakes, some builders fitted locomotives with sledge-brakes, which pressed down on the rails: these were especially popular on steeply-graded lines. But they were not satisfactory, sometimes scraping the rails, sometimes being applied so hard that they lifted the wheels off the rails altogether and threatened to derail the engine. Counter-pressure braking, which had been advocated in the 1840s by the French engineer Louis le Chatelier, author of the study on locomotive stability, was used on some railways with long downhill gradients until late in the century. To use the pistons to pump steam back into the boiler was possible, but it created intense heat. Le Chatelier's system allowed for the admission of hot water to the cylinder, which vaporised with a cooling effect. But gradually, it became noticed that some engines actually had brakes fitted on the driving wheels, and suffered no ill effects as a result of using them. The over-riding need for effective control of speed and stopping ensured that driving wheel brakes became a regular practice on new locomotives in Britain from the mid-1860s, and in America from around 1875. In 1889, though, about half of the American locomotive stock was still fitted only with the old tender hand-brake. In 1897 the *Railway Magazine* reported that Westinghouse, now with works in London, Paris and Hannover as well as Pittsburgh, had had orders to fit the air brake system to 49,548 engines. The slightly asthmatic, rhythmic puff-pant of the Westinghouse pump became a familiar addition to the range of sounds produced by locomotives. Fast freights were also eventually fitted with automatic continuous brakes, though most freight trains had only pin-down brakes. The consequent need for brakemen was responsible for the little rear look-out cab fitted on many locomotive tenders, especially in the USA and Germany, as a refuge for the train's head brakeman.

THIRTEEN

Magniloquence and Minimalism

A growing literature of technical magazines and books helped engine designers and repairmen, especially those who worked in relative isolation on new lines in Africa and Asia, to keep in touch with what was going on at the centres of their profession. The engineering societies held regular meetings and published both the papers presented and the discussions that followed. An element of self-promotion and company propaganda came into all this. Chief engineers were keen to show handsome, posed pictures of their latest designs, and to produce a carefully-drafted and vetted descriptive text. They were less keen to go into details that might give away a trade secret or – even worse – expose some unsuspected deficiency to the sharp and critical eye of a rival. Often they were even less ready to give verified figures relating to such fundamental matters as steam generation and fuel consumption. In many cases the damning truth about a design – though long known to the suffering locomotive men – did not emerge until after its creator's retirement or death. Some senior engineers also travelled abroad to see things for themselves, their trans-oceanic journeys greatly speeded up by improvements in steam-ship technology. The great exhibitions which began in the mid-nineteenth century, shop windows on a vast scale for the national range of products and a stage for the national ethos on which to parade itself, always had an important railway component. New engine types were put on show, painted and polished, and all kinds of ancillary equipment were also displayed and demonstrated. Business as well as the desire for corporate prestige was a prime motive. Apart from the general public, who came to be educated and awed, customers and potential customers came to buy, from all over the world. Often, especially if they were Americans, they would make a dramatic on-the-spot purchase. But not only Americans got carried away. In 1862 a 2-2-2 express passenger locomotive was shown by the Caledonian Railway at the London International Exhibition. Built at the company's own St Rollox Works in Glasgow, it went back to a Caledonian design of 1859, by Benjamin Conner, based in turn on the old 'Crewe type' with its typical curvaceous front-end view. A cab was provided – something more common on Scottish than English locomotives at the time. Among the grandees touring the Exhibition was the Ottoman Viceroy of Egypt, Said Pasha. He was so enamoured of the locomotive that he arranged to buy it. To impress the populace, he wanted a locomotive that would convey his state train at 70mph, and the 98in (248.7cm) driving wheels of the engine promised speed. Later he arranged for the purchase of two more, which were built for him by Neilson & Co., of Glasgow.

The exhibitions had their baby-show aspect, and it was customary for a panel of eminent judges to award medals for the best entries. These were awarded purely on the basis of appearance and whatever information was published in the technical literature. Many were of international scope: it was even possible for an English locomotive to receive a gold medal at a Paris exhibition.

Despite this, national styles were steadily pulling away from one another. In the 1870s, in America, size was already making a difference. But in the course of twenty years, the whole American 'look' changed considerably. By the 1850s, and probably well before, designers were very conscious of the aesthetic aspect of their engines: William Mason, a leading Massachusetts builder, wrote in 1853: 'We want them, of course, strong workers, but we want them also good lookers… we shall hope to see something soon on the rails that does not look exactly like a 'cooking stove on wheels'.' At the depots, drivers added their own finishing touches, with elk-horns fixed to the great lanterns, profiles of Indian braves on the smoke-box doors, or brassy eagles on the sandbox.

Basic features of the mid-century American 4-4-0 – the most typical engine – had been level-set cylinders, a long-wheelbase truck, exposed wheels, a deep, narrow wood-burning firebox, bar frames, big wooden cab, and an eight-wheel tender. Valve gear was much improved, with Stephenson link motion normally replacing the old gab gear. The relative smallness of boilers and the prevalence of wood burning had combined to make the American locomotive distinctive by a great flared or diamond-shaped smokestack and its large cab. In between these features, the boiler, increasing in diameter from front to back, 'wagon-top' style, would support a substantial brassbound dome and a sandbox. The boiler and its lagging would be protected by an outer shell of Russia iron, which could be, and was, painted or polished to a state of extreme effulgence. By 1870 the boiler was reaching a diameter which meant that, even with the American clearance, the structures on top had to be somewhat reduced in size. Wood burning was on the way out and a squat stove-pipe chimney replaced the massive old stacks. The driving wheels were still fully exposed, and any running plate along the boiler side was set high and offered little more than a toe-hold. These, with the height, the length, the open space between bar-frames and boiler, the bell, the boiler-mounted sandbox, and the cow-catcher, all contributed to the generalised profile which now announced 'American locomotive'. A reaction to the gaudy colours of previous decades set in after the 1860s, fuelled by shareholders who did not want to see their dividends reduced by the use of gold leaf in locomotive decoration. Most American locomotives were painted black, with the New York Central taking the lead. Names became rare, and US locomotives were mostly known by number, as in the folk song 'Wreck of Ol' Number Nine':

> *On a dark and stormy night,*
> *Not a star was in sight,*
> *And the north wind came howling down the line;*
> *There stood a brave engineer,*
> *With his true love so dear,*
> *And his orders, to take out Number Nine.*

These changes reflected the new policy increasingly adopted by most rail-roads of pooling locomotives and crews, ending the dedicated-driver era and with some consequent diminution of the driver's status. They also showed that a difference in perception had come about. The locomotive had ceased to be seen as the romantic harbinger of a new era for human-ity, or even as a special and unusual machine; it was simply a workaday piece of equipment, of quantifiable cost, to be fully exploited. Decoration was expensive, and money was often tight. In 1877 the Philadelphia & Reading Railroad saved over $100,000 by sacking its locomotive polish-ers. Bright colours remained on British locomotives, and on those in the British sphere of influence, though the biggest line, the LNWR, opted for shiny black. Economy was the alleged reason. Its chief mechanical engineer, Francis Webb, has sometimes been credited with saying, long before Henry Ford, that the engines could be any colour the directors liked, so long as it was black. What he actually said, at a meeting of the Institution of Civil Engineers in 1885, was that he: 'had once been attacked by a member of the shareholders' Audit Committee for painting the engines black. His reply was that when they paid ten per cent he would line them in gold.' Most other countries eventually opted for black, in varying degrees of shine, with green reserved for express engines in Germany and Russia, among others.

European railways remained content, for the time being, with small engines, or somewhat larger versions of the small engines of the 1850s and 1860s. In France, the favoured express type was the 2-4-2, rather than the 4-4-0 of British and American usage. With the generous French height allowance of 14ft (426.7cm), this produced a generation of locomotives that seemed very short in relation to their height; seen at speed from in front, they seemed like piled-up structures toppling forwards. Boilers were set low, chimneys and domes were lofty, and there was plenty of external equipment and pipework. Water supplies in France were often impure or hard, and feed-water heaters and purifiers were considered necessary by most lines. To the French, a locomotive was a work-horse, and external working parts only enhanced its dramatic sense of activity and energy. In addition, it was scientifically preferable to place working parts where they functioned best; and economically desirable to make them easily accessible. The French designers saw beauty in a combination of factors, which might be best expressed in overall terms as the locomotive's visible fitness for its task.

On the other side of the Straits of Dover, a very different set of views on locomotive appearance prevailed. Yet, oddly, one of the most effective and admired French locomotive types, the 4-4-0 Class 2 '*Outrance*' of the *Nord*, introduced in 1870, was based on a British model. Outrance means 'utmost' and these engines regularly gave their utmost on heavy boat trains up the long gradients of the rolling country north of Paris. The *Nord*'s chief engineer, Jules Pétiet, had taken as his model Archibald Sturrock's 2-4-0 class of 1866 built for the English Great Northern Railway, but added a four-wheel leading bogie. Sturrock was a believer in high steam pressure, as was Pétiet, but these Sturrock engines were not otherwise highly regarded, and were rebuilt by his successor, Patrick Stirling, as 2-2-2s. The '*Outrances*' with their four carrying wheels and slightly larger dimensions, were very successful and continued to be built up to 1885. They had outside frames, maximum boiler pressure of 145psi (10kg/cm^2), two inside simple-expansion cylinders and long Belpaire fireboxes. An un-British feature was the forward-angled outside steam pipes running from a header behind the chimney down to the steam-chests. The cab was of the minimalist type, little more than a frame for the spectacle-glasses. The design became thoroughly cosmopolitan; used by the Madrid Caceres & Portugal Railway in Spain, and built for it by Hartmann in Chemnitz, Germany; and by the French-owned Rosario & Puerto Belgrano Railway in Argentina. The '*Outrances*' of the latter, class 21, were built in 1910 by Schwarzkopff in Berlin: a French design, based on an English model, on a South American railway, from a German builder.

German railways and locomotive builders, despite early flirtations with America, showed a strong British influence until a thoroughly German school of locomotive practice emerged towards the end of the nineteenth century. Their engines often had an English look, exemplified in a tidy external appearance, a low running plate, and splashers covering much of the wheels. Indeed, the most 'English' of designers, Charles Beyer of Beyer Peacock, was an immigrant to Britain from Saxony; one of many Germans who contributed to the great sweep forward of British industrial development. Within that overall appearance, German design was often more experimental and open-minded. One of its landmark engines is the 0-4-0 *Landwührden* built in 1867 by Georg Krauss of Munich for the Oldenburg State Railways. One of Krauss's associates was Richard von Helmholtz, designer of the Krauss-Helmholtz leading bogie which would be used in many European locomotives. The company eventually merged with Maffei to become Krauss-Maffei. *Landwührden* was shown at the Paris Exhibition of 1867 where it won a gold medal for design and workmanship. Among its features was a well tank incorporated in the riveted box-frame, for heating feed water. Taken out of service in 1900, it is preserved, without its tender, in the Nürnberg transport museum.

Lying between France and Germany, with a racing ground on the level terrain of Flanders, and with heavy industry spreading in the hilly country of the Borinage and around Liège, Belgium developed a locomotive style very much its own. The leading figure was Alfred Belpaire, from 1864 the chief mechanical engineer of the Belgian State Railways (and so the ultimate boss of the humble Walschaerts), and later the Administrative President. He was responsible for the second great Belgian contribution to the steam locomotive, the type of firebox that bears his name. Belpaire was challenged by the fact that the coal most readily and cheaply available was of relatively low calorific value, crumbly, and with a high ash content. Such fuel did not burn well in the small narrow round-topped fireboxes typical of European locomotives. He designed a new firebox, longer than the traditional type, with a flat top, as wide as possible, higher at the front and tapering back towards the cab, and blending in with the curve of the lower half of the boiler. This firebox provided much more combustion space and in particular brought heat to the upper part of the boiler, where steam was actually made. It had a larger grate area than before, with a floor of thin steel plates riveted together and providing a better access for air to the fire.

The Type 1 2-4-2 express passenger locomotive of 1864 was Belpaire's first major design. Naturally, it had the firebox he had developed, and which would be used by many others for almost a century to come. It contributed to a distinctive appearance – a tall, high-shouldered box at the end of the boiler barrel, requiring the latter to taper outwards to meet it. Cockerill of Seraing built the first examples, and most other Belgian and some French constructors supplied later engines. In all 153 were built, up to 1884. It had outside frames, with two inside cylinders, and the running plate was raised over the wheels to clear the coupling rod cranks. A stove-pipe chimney was originally fitted, with the dome placed right behind it. Other modern equipment included Giffard injectors. Westinghouse brakes and pumps were fitted from 1878, and roofed cabs were provided from 1882. Between 1889 and 1896 the Type 1s were re-boilered and at that time a massive square chimney was added. It was this, with the high-shouldered firebox, that gave the unmistakable Belgian look, in which the Belgians took some pride. It might appear bizarre, but it was theirs. Until 1890 the Type 1s ran express trains on all lines except that to Luxembourg; from then to the 1920s they were on secondary services, and the last of the class survived until 1926.

In a curious postscript to Belpaire's regime, however, the Belgian State Railways, under the locomotive management of his successor J.B. Flamme, did something most unusual by purchasing large numbers of locomotives originally designed for a foreign railway, and which could hardly have been more different to the Belpaire engines. With deep, narrow, round-topped fireboxes and thin chimneys, they were 4-4-0s and 0-6-0s designed by J.F. McIntosh for the Caledonian Railway in Scotland. One of his 'Dunalastair II' 4-4-0s had won a gold medal at the Brussels Exhibition of 1897. Flamme and others travelled to Glasgow, and liked the simplicity and robustness of the designs. A deal was done; the Caledonian's own works were not allowed to build for outside customers, but the plans were made available, and five 'Dunalastairs' were built by Neilson's and delivered to Antwerp in December 1898. Hundreds were to follow over the next few years, all built in Belgium, their trim, distinctly Scottish appearance making an intriguing contrast with Belpaire's massive-funneled engines.

In east Central Europe, the Austro-Hungarian empire sprawled across an array of what were later to be independent states, from Austria itself through Bohemia and Hungary and down into northern Italy and the Balkans. Railway development was piecemeal and the design of locomotives reflected this. Most were small, with many tank engine types, and 0-6-0s predominating among tender engines. Even more than in France, the imperial engineers were happy to clap on external fittings. Impure water was a frequent problem, and purifiers and feed-water heaters were considered essential. Most locomotives were built at one or other of the by-now established works in Vienna, and there was often a basic resemblance, modified by such aspects as chimney styles, the placing of domes and sandboxes. But detail parts, like nuts, bolts, pins and rods, were completely unstandardised.

Typical of the early 1870s was the 0-6-0 Class 335 of the Hungarian Railways (MÁV), introduced in 1869. The MÁV state-owned system began in 1867 and as it progressively enfolded lesser railways, a wide variety of locomotive types was inherited, all very similar in general respects but whose lack of standardisation made the provision of spare parts extremely difficult. A start on standardised locomotive classes was made, and this goods engine, with the series 238 2-4-0 passenger engine of the same year, was the first fruit of that policy. They handled most of the country's freight, working on independent lines as well as those of MÁV. With outside frames, simple expansion working through two outside cylinders, and Stephenson link motion actuating inside valves, it was in most respects typical of the older Austrian tradition, and constructed by Austrian builders. Though with inevitably slightly different dimensions, it was very similar to the Class 33 0-6-0 of the Austrian *Staats Eisenbahn Gesellschaft*, built at the StEG's own works from 1866. The boiler diameter was quite small, and a considerable array of domes and water-treatment cylinders was placed on top, together with a tall stove-pipe chimney, usually with some form of spark arrester fitted at the base or the top. One is preserved.

The Imperial Austrian Railways were formed from the *Kaiserin Elisabeth Bahn* and other lines in 1884, and encountered the same problems as MÀV had. Most of the engines were outside-framed 0-6-0 and 2-4-2 types. In due course, a firm and confident hand would design a splendid range of imperial standard locomotives. But even then, smaller types would show a tendency to develop on their own, enhanced by the urge of the empire's non-Austrian countries to do things in their own way. The 0-6-0 side-tank type of Class 97, which originated on the *Kaiserin Elisabeth Bahn*, was typical of many others in this respect. Eventually the Imperial Railways had 225, and many others were built up to 1913 for privately-owned railways in the various parts of the empire. Although the main dimensions remained the same, a great many individual variations and alterations in detail of domes, chimneys, etc., appeared. One of this class was the first locomotive to be built in Czechoslovakia, by the PCM works, in 1900.

In Britain, though such writers as John Ruskin would have considered the use of the two words together to be an oxymoron, and the designers might have been embarrassed by it also, locomotive aesthetics continued to be a prime concern. Designers, it seemed, began by drawing a straight line at buffer-beam level, all the way from the front of the engine to the rear of the tender. The design itself, whether large- or small-wheeled, was then made above this line. Large wheels were half-concealed by splashers. A determination to conceal the works, as much as possible, was usually evident, and engines with outside cylinders were far outnumbered by those which moved in a mysterious way with their connecting rods and valve gear hidden inside the frame. It was also generally accepted that the fewer external additions, the better. A much-praised engine, exhibited at the 1862 Exhibition in London, was Beyer's *Dom Luiz*, a beautifully proportioned 2-2-2 type built for the South Eastern Railway of Portugal. Other than a tall, slim, shapely chimney at one end, and a nicely-curved safety-valve casing at the other, nothing was built on to the boiler. No cab added its undesirable verticals to the rhythm of horizontal lines and carefully-placed circles. It set an austere standard to which many others aspired, though to some continental eyes, British engines seemed as naked as plucked and prepared chickens.

An apogee of British nineteenth-century design was reached by Patrick Stirling's 4-2-2 No.1, built in 1870 by the Great Northern Railway at its own works in Doncaster. British railways retained use of the 'single driver' locomotive long after most other countries had adopted multiple-coupled types. The reasons for this attachment to what foreigners considered an archaic wheel arrangement include the insularity and conservatism of the railway company engineers and managements, most of whom controlled their own building shops. But some factors favoured the single driver. Distances in Britain were relatively short: the GNR's main line was just over 200 miles (322km) long; and carriages were still relatively lightweight in the 1870s. All the stabling equipment, particularly turntables, was built for short engines. The quality of the track was generally high, so that the relatively heavy main axle-load of a single-wheeler, in this case 15 tons (15.2t) was not a great problem. A single-wheeler was also cheaper to build than an engine with more axles. Designers believed that it was more free-running than a coupled engine.

Nevertheless the British urge towards minimalism went far beyond concerns with efficiency, and in some respects it actually got in the way. Stirling's engines were obsessively plain and simple. He disliked any sort of appendage and few of his engines had domes; he also disliked bogies, and greatly preferred the cylinders to be inside and out of sight. A bluntly-spoken Scotsman, he likened the movement of an outside-cylinder engine to 'a laddie running with his breeks down'. The 4-2-2 with 8ft (243.6cm) drivers, of which No.1 still survives in preservation, went against his cherished prejudices by having a front bogie – necessary to bear the weight – and outside cylinders, which were required by the height of the driving axle. Yet despite such 'blemishes' this was Stirling's favourite among his numerous designs. The underlying psychology offers intriguing speculation to the amateur psychologist. One may speculate on why many designers, like William Dean of the Great Western, should put voluptuously rounded domes on their boilers, while the company's first designer, Daniel Gooch, along with Stirling and some others, avoided domes altogether. Gooch used a higher pressure than other engineers of his time, and may have felt that a dome would weaken the boiler. By Stirling's day, this was not a worry. For whatever reasons, it was in Britain, perhaps more than anywhere else, that the notion of the steam locomotive as somehow anthropomorphic, took a strong hold. There was also the conscious parallel, expressed by Fanny Kemble, and clearly felt by the early engineers, with the horse: a sense of the fine, spare lines of a thoroughbred animal comes through in some of the British designs. But it remains the case that all were more constrained by the loading gauge than by their creators' subconscious minds. British locomotives had little space to spare for pumps and heaters; also, still fitted with quite small boilers, they needed all their steam for the work they had to do.

This work was by no means a matter of dainty little trains. The Great Northern's Kings Cross-Leeds expresses weighed up to 250 tons in the early 1880s, and these were allowed twelve and a half minutes for the 8-mile (12.9km) climb at 1 in 200 from the start to Potter's Bar. In October 1875, the single-driver No.22 ran from Kings Cross to Peterborough, 76.25 miles (122.7km), in ninety-two minutes with an eighteen-carriage train, an average speed of 49.75mph (80km/h). In the 1890s, with steel-tyred wheels and heavier rails, the eight-footers turned in some remarkable performances, with speeds up to 83mph (133km/h) recorded. To do this, the engines had to be 'thrashed' along by their drivers, and the simplicity and robustness of the design allowed this to happen time after time. One writer likened the passage of a Stirling single at full speed to a volcanic eruption. Such fire-throwing, though wasteful and dangerous, was the only way to extract enough performance from a boiler with a heating surface of 1165sq ft (108m²), and a maximum pressure of 140psi (9.9kg/cm²); and Stirling's express engines were typical of those of other lines in this respect. The thrashing of engines was certainly *le vice anglais*.

FOURTEEN

Compounding

The parallel progress of marine steam technology had produced very large engines by the 1860s, and by 1870 compound working was a regular feature. Steam engineers had been aware of the possibilities of compound expansion since the Englishman Jonathan Hornblower took out a patent in July 1781 on an engine which passed steam from one cylinder into another. Locomotive engineers took note of how the marine engine used its steam in compound expansion, passing it, at lower pressure, into additional, larger cylinders in order to extract the maximum possible effort from it. The locomotive, with its use of high-pressure steam in a single pair of cylinders, was wasteful by comparison. However, the requirements of ships and locomotives were very different. Ships' engines were built to operate at a steady pace for days on end. Locomotives had to cope with far more frequent acceleration and deceleration, starts and stops. The amount of space available was very different too. Locomotives could, and did, become longer, but unlike ships they could not get higher or wider. To accommodate the principle of compounding to the railway engine was nevertheless an intriguing problem which engineers in several countries tried to tackle. As early as 1850, John Nicholson, a driver on the Eastern Counties Railway in England, invented a 'continuous expansion' system (which his superior, James Samuel, patented for him), and a Mr Edwards of Birmingham patented a tandem (two-cylinder) high- and low-pressure system in 1853. But these did not lead to any sort of fruition. In 1868 or 1869, an Erie Railway locomotive was rebuilt as a compound by the Shepard Ironworks at Buffalo, NY: but it was not duplicated and must be presumed a failure.

The first successful compound engines were designed in France, where compounding was to become a high art, by the Swiss-born engineer Anatole Mallet; and built at Le Creusot in 1876. Two small 0-4-2 side-tank engines, they worked trains of two-decker carriages on the short Bayonne-Biarritz Railway, which linked these neighbouring cities in the extreme south-west of France. In compounding, the low-pressure cylinder must be larger than the high-pressure one, as it operates with only partially expanded steam to do equivalent work. In the pioneer engines, the two 'cross-compound' cylinders were mounted outside, and gave rise to the nickname of *La Boiteuse*, 'lame one'. On one, whether for aesthetic or commercial reasons, the small high-pressure cylinder was apparently given a false casing to match the large high-pressure one. At the Paris Exposition of 1878, where this engine was shown, Mallet, whose enthusiasm for compounding was already well-known to his fellow-engineers, was complimented on having produced a 'normal' engine.

An independent figure, attached to no railway, Mallet did not have a ready opportunity to build on his success, though further compounds on his principles were built in France and Russia. Then in 1884 he patented a four-cylinder compound design, intended for light railway use, which would in due course lead to very great things in the USA and elsewhere. A few years before, in 1879, he addressed the Institution of Mechanical Engineers, in London, where one of his listeners was Francis W. Webb, Chief Mechanical Engineer of the London & North Western Railway, at that time the busiest and richest railway company in the world. Webb was open to ideas, if they suited his requirements, one of which was economy in operating costs, including fuel. He began experimenting with compound engines almost immediately, converting an elderly 2-2-2 engine to the Mallet pattern. He settled on a three-cylinder system, with the large low-pressure cylinder between the frames. Between 1882 and 1890 he brought out several different compound classes, both passenger and freight, using a new valve gear, designed by David Joy, of 'Jenny Lind' fame. Until 1897, the passenger engines had two driving axles, one driven by the inner cylinder, the other by the outside cylinders, and the driving wheels themselves were not joined by a coupling rod. When G.A. Sekon wrote his *Evolution of the Steam Locomotive*, in 1899, Webb was still in command at Crewe, a power in the land, and the writer had to pick his words carefully. Nonetheless, he indicated: 'Whether the four driving wheels work well together, or whether, on the other hand, there exists a considerable amount of either slip or skidding is another matter.' In fact the driving wheels, on starting, sometimes commenced to revolve in contrary directions. Men with crowbars, as in the earliest days, had to get them going.

Webb's compound engines numbered less than a tenth of the LNWR's 2900 locomotives. They have perhaps been mocked over-much. Complex and expensive, they marked the opposite to the Crewe works' previous policy of building cheap, sturdy and simple designs. Having invested his professional credibility in compounding, Webb appears to have shut his eyes to the inadequacies of his own compound designs. The class of 1889, known as 'Teutonics', were the best performers, and the most reliable in service – sufficiently so to be entrusted with Queen Victoria's royal train. No. 1304 *Jeanie Deans* ran the 'Scotch Express' between Euston and Crewe between 1891 and 1899, loading up to 300 tons (305t), at an average speed of just under 50mph (80km/h) in the down direction, and 52.3mph (84km/h) on the more favourably graded up service; and kept good time. No. 1306, Ionic, achieved 708,546 miles (1,140,240km) up to 1904. But it does not compare with the two million miles (3,218,500km) of Webb's earlier simple-expansion 2-4-0 'Precedent' *Charles Dickens*. In 1893, the LNWR sent the second engine of the 'Greater Britain' class, the 2-2-2-2 No.2054 *Queen Empress*, to the Columbian Exhibition in Chicago in 1893; in a complete antithesis of normal policy, it is said to have been painted white. It made some demonstration runs, but if sales were hoped for, there were no takers. Webb also produced 111 examples of a three-cylinder 0-8-0 goods type, with coupled wheels. His final compounds were four-cylindered, also with coupled wheels, but still indifferent performers. All his compounds were heavy coal users, and needed more repair and maintenance than simple-expansion engines. Whenever possible the operating staff ran them double-headed with simple-expansion types. It took years for the LNWR to come to grips with the fact that their splendid works at Crewe were turning out new locomotive types of dubious performance and heavy operating cost. Four years after Webb's unwilling retirement in 1903, most of his compounds had been scrapped or converted to simple expansion, and a process of rapid replacement by simple 4-4-0 'Precursors' and 4-6-0 'Experiments' was well under way. Webb was not the only British designer to adopt compounding; the Midland Railway went on to develop a highly effective compound three-cylinder 4-4-0, and continued to build them, but his example made most other British designers regard compounding with something between suspicion and holy dread, though independent builders constructed many compound locomotives for overseas customers.

British reservations were not shared in other countries. Webb's work, which was widely publicised (though poor performance figures were hushed up) did much to spread the international feeling that compounding was the big new thing. The principle was taken up independently and vigorously in Germany by August von Borries, a great technician who was chief mechanical engineer on the Hannover Division of the Royal Prussian Railways. Von Borries travelled widely, including to the USA, and was responsible for much of the technical improvement that made Germany a major player in modern steam locomotive development. In 1880 he introduced a two-cylinder compound 2-4-0 for passenger trains. The cylinders were mounted outside, with the high-pressure one supplied via an external steam pipe from a large dome. He followed this in 1889 with a four-cylinder compound. Both were successful in operation. But at Hannover, von Borries was in an outer division of the large Prussian system, and other development work was by then going ahead which would eclipse the interest in compounds there, and on many other railways also. The von Borries two-cylinder system attracted interest on certain lines in the British Isles, unrelated to the LNWR and its activities. With it, the cylinders could be fitted inside the frames, in accord with the designers' desire to keep the moving parts of locomotives as far as possible unseen, and this led to the compound 4-4-0s and 4-2-2s designed by T.W. Worsdell on the Great Eastern and North Eastern Railways, between 1884 and 1893; as well as Britain's first compound freight locomotive, an 0-6-0 of 1885. These locomotives gave satisfactory performance. The von Borries system was also used in Ireland by Bowman Malcolm on the Belfast & Northern Counties Railway between 1890-1908.

Development in compounding took a leap forward with the system developed on the Nord line in France by the English-born Alfred de Glehn and the Frenchman Gaston du Bousquet. Their first product was a 2-2-2-0, of 1885, rebuilt as a 4-2-2-0 in 1892 (the driving wheels were originally not coupled, and as with Webb's compounds, in effect each axle was driven by a separate 'engine', hence the unusual notation). It used four cylinders, with high-pressure outside, driving the second of the two axles; low-pressure inside, driving the leading axle. Each cylinder had an independent set of valve gear, and cut-off could be adjusted independently for high and low pressure, through two regulators. The driver could also close off the low-pressure cylinders and send all exhaust steam up the blast-pipe. Expertly applied, it meant that the engine could exert almost 50 per cent additional tractive effort on starting. It was a system of great flexibility, to cope with different loads and conditions, but it was undeniably complex to maintain and operate. The French practice of having highly trained drivers, who had served time as workshop fitters, was ideally suited to the management of compounding. Although other compounding systems were also used in France – the only country that really made compounding work for express services – it was the de Glehn/du Bousquet system, as improved by André Chapelon from 1928, that became the nearest thing to a national standard.

In 1900 two prototype four-cylinder compound 4-4-2s were produced, rapidly followed by line production, the class ultimately numbering thirty-five. The first were built by the *Société Alsacienne de Constructions Mécaniques* at Mulhouse, where de Glehn was director of engineering; others were built by the J.F. Cail shops at Lille. The production engines had coupled driving wheels, but retained other features of their predecessors, including the Belpaire firebox and the outside bearings on the front bogie. Boiler pressure was high for the time, at 228psi (16kg/cm^2), and the firebox had a large grate area, 33.4sq ft (2.76m^2). From the beginning they were star performers, though after 1912, with Schmidt superheating and enlarged high-pressure cylinders with piston valves, they made their best achievements. One English authority wrote: 'their hill-climbing capabilities have probably never been excelled by any locomotive of comparable size and power.' Such abilities were essential on the heavy Calais boat trains, often loading up to 393.6 tons. On level track the 'Atlantics' ran these trains at a steady 75mph (120km/h).

The English Great Western Railway, in process of developing a new range of locomotives, paid the French a compliment by buying three of the compounds, and derived much benefit though it did not in the end adopt compounding. The great and equally lordly Pennsylvania Railroad in the USA bought one for similar reasons. Even more gratifyingly, seventy-nine were bought by the Royal Prussian Railways. At home, the Nord 'Atlantics' ran into the 1930s, some of them by then fitted with wide-diameter chimneys and Lemaître blast-pipes, and with eight-wheel bogie tenders holding 6.8 tons (7t) of coal and 5,070gals (6,000US) of water. No.2.670, as modified in 1912, is preserved at the French Railway Museum, Mulhouse.

From around the turn of the century, many other countries seized on compounding. By 1907, railways in Abyssinia, Argentina, Denmark, Italy, Norway, Russia (almost 300 were in use on the Trans-Siberian line in 1915), Sweden, Switzerland and the United States were among those using compound locomotives, which became common enough for locomotive observers and admirers from now on to note of any locomotive type whether it used simple or compound working. The chief benefit looked for was fuel economy, and this was of particular interest to American railways, where the increase in size of the locomotives had naturally also led to an increase in appetite. During the 1890s, the compounding concept was enthusiastically taken up by Samuel M. Vauclain. The son of one of Baldwin's first workmen, he became works superintendent, then a partner in the business, and ultimately its President and one of the USA's great railroad men. In 1889 he patented his system in which high- and low-pressure cylinders are mounted outside in pairs, low pressure below high pressure, each pair driving a common cross-head. Like the earlier tandem compound system which it largely replaced, which had the high-pressure cylinder set in front of the low-pressure one, it obviated the need for internal drive (American engineers had detested crank axles from the very first). A by-pass valve allowed live steam to enter the low-pressure cylinders on starting. The Vauclain system was not without problems, partly caused by the heavy reciprocating masses required to counteract the piston thrust, and partly by difficulty in balancing the work of the high- and low-pressure cylinders. In 1902 Baldwin built their 20,000th locomotive, and also their heaviest yet, the first of a 2-10-0 freight class for the Atchison Topeka & Santa Fe Railroad. It was also the first four-cylinder Vauclain compound. The drive was to the middle coupled wheels, which were flangeless. The four cylinders were formed in a single casting with the steam-chests and half of the smoke-box saddle. A single piston valve actuated both cylinders on each side.

Vauclain's compounding system was popular for several years, being used on locomotives in Russia and other countries as well as on other US locomotives: as many as 2,000 up to 1907. But it was not a lasting solution, since any inequalities of steam distribution to the four cylinders set up stresses which affected the riding of the locomotive as well as reducing its efficiency. The powerful double thrust on the connecting rods, though it provided a strong tractive effort, created severe problems of stress. Vauclain would continue to develop his ideas on compounding. He was an inventive engineer, with many other patents to his name, including those for a flexible locomotive boiler, which was fitted, though not for long, to six locomotives of the Santa Fe in 1910-11. More portentous for the future of American steam was the appearance in 1904 of the first big Mallet locomotive, an 0-6-6-0 built by Alco for the Baltimore & Ohio Railroad. Affectionately known as 'Old Maud', it took its turn for a while as the world's largest locomotive, and heralded even mightier things to come.

Anatole Mallet had patented the basic design in France in 1884: in essence it consisted of a single large boiler which served to power two engine units. The front of these was mounted in an independent frame which pivoted beneath the locomotive's main frame. The rear one was fixed in conventional style to the main frame. Its cylinders received steam at full pressure from the boiler (235psi; 16.45kg/cm^2 in 'Maud's' case), and passed the exhaust steam by flexible wide-diameter pipes to the front unit.

The very first articulated compound Mallet was an 0-4-4-0T 23.5in (60cm) gauge locomotive built in Belgium, by the *Ateliers Métallurgiques* of Tubize, in 1887, for the French specialist in narrow-gauge locomotives, Decauville, and the type won favour on a number of narrow-gauge mountain lines. In 1889 the Gotthard Railway commissioned a single 0-6-6-0T, and twenty-six followed on the Swiss Central Railway. All had the standard Mallet form of semi-articulation, the front (low-pressure) power unit mounted on a pivot set behind the wheels; the rear, high-pressure power unit being fixed to the frame. They were intended for heavy haulage, and fitted for steam heating to pull passenger trains as well as goods trains. Maximum service speed was 34mph (55km/h). The four cylinders, outside-set, were operated by slide valves. As Mallet drivers all over the world would learn, care had to be exercised on starting, since, despite the presence of a valve to admit live steam to the low-pressure cylinders on starting, the fact that the two sets of wheels were independently coupled made the 'high-pressure' wheels more likely to slip. Much to Mallet's chagrin in later life (he died in 1919), the Americans would revert to simple expansion on the giant locomotives that bore his name: he was a firm believer in compounding to the last. But then, it was his child. Over 5,000 Mallets would be built, of wildly varying size, up to 1961. Almost the only countries with a developed railway system not to use Mallets were Britain and Australia.

James E. Muhlfeld, Superintendent of Motive Power of the B&O, had an interest in European developments that was by no means common among his peers in the USA, who were quite as complacently insular as their British counterparts. He was responsible for the introduction of Walschaerts valve gear into the USA; and he saw the Mallet's potential for heavy haulage on the winding Allegheny grades. The new 0-6-6-0 was put to work on freight trains in the Western Pennsylvania mountains. It satisfied the requirement to provide high power – with a tractive effort reckoned at 71,500lb (32,426kg) – and maximum adhesive grip in banking heavy trains on the long, curving mountain grades, without the problems of a long rigid wheelbase, which included serious stresses on curves and heavy wear on wheels and rails. About eighty of this type were built, of which some were converted to 2-6-6-0. On later Mallets, American railroads generally preferred the 2-6-6-2 configuration, which made better provision for the use of a wide, deep firebox, supported by the trailing wheels. American locomotive designers inherited a dread of putting engines with no front bogie out on the road that went right back to the days of John Jervis, and survived until the end of steam. Only slow-moving, limited-range yard switchers – quite often converted road engines with bogie removed – might be 0-6-0s, 0-8-0s or 0-10-0s. Meanwhile such types trundled freely, if at modest speed, with freight trains on main lines throughout Europe.

Alco, builder of the Mallet, was the American Locomotive Company, a new name, but in fact the result of a merger in 1901 of eight long-established businesses, including some of the oldest, like Brooks, Rhode Island, and Danforth & Cook, who had combined to create a strong rival to the mighty Baldwin. Rogers joined in 1905. Alco remained second in size to Baldwin, who left central Philadelphia in 1906 for a huge new works on a greenfield site at Eddystone, 12 miles out.

After 1907, and the arrival of superheating, compounding became rarer on American railroads, though it was maintained for a few years more on articulated locomotives. Apart from a brief hesitancy in the early 1920s, it was clear that as far as most designers and operators were concerned, a big boiler and efficient simple-expansion cylinders could develop the necessary tractive power, with far fewer operational and maintenance problems.

Italy was one of the countries which most avidly pursued compounding in the first decade of the twentieth century, as the new national company, the *Ferrovie Statale*, developed its locomotive stock from 1905. But prior to that, an interesting compound class appeared in 1900, in the form of the Class 500 4-6-0 of the Adriatic Network (RA), known to railwaymen as Mucca, 'Milch Cow'. Designed by Giuseppe Zara, with the prototype built at the RA works in Florence, this was a cab-forward design, with the driver and fireman at the front. Coal was carried in bunkers fitted alongside the firebox, and a six-wheel water-tank tender was attached at the cylinder end, with a flexible hose link to the injectors. It had the Italian four-cylinder compound arrangement devised by Plancher, having both high-pressure cylinders to one side, and both low-pressure ones to the other. All drove the second coupled axle. Walschaerts valve gear was fitted; one outside piston valve distributed steam to both cylinders on each side. Inequalities between high- and low-pressure steam supplies caused the engine to 'hunt' uncomfortably from side to side; the system was really only suited to low speeds. The cylinders were mounted on an extension of the frame beyond the smoke-box; in normal service, this back-to-front engine ran permanently 'backwards'. Designed for mixed-traffic, the Class 500 was recorded as hauling goods trains up to 817 tons (830t), and as maintaining 56mph (90km/h) on passenger service. Designated Class 670 of the State system from 1905, the forty-three-strong class remained in service into the 1940s. Although it solved the problem of a clear front look-out, and also obviated any drifting steam or smoke, the cab-forward design was emulated in Europe only by one or two experimental locomotives, including a 4-4-6 built by Schneider of Le Creusot to the design of M. Thuile, engineer to the port of Alexandria (he was killed when it derailed during a test run). Two semi-streamlined cab-first design 4-4-4 engines of 1904, forming Class S9 of the Royal Prussian Railways, were built by Henschel & Sohn, of Kassel, always at the cutting edge of German steam technology, The boiler and tender were encased in a carriage-like body, with the chimney protruding from the roof. The driver's controls were mounted in a V-shaped front cab; the fireman sweated in an enclosed compartment in the middle of the loco-bunker unit. These incidentally were the first locomotives to have a corridor link to the leading carriage. They were three-cylinder un-super-heated compounds, intended for express passenger work, and one was said to have reached 89.4mph (144km/h) with a 160-ton train, but the concept was not pursued in Germany. Crewmen referred to them as the *Möbelwagen*, 'furniture vans'.

The cab-front layout was repeated in a mighty but similarly one-company progeny in the USA, where a range of huge cab-forward articulated locomotives was built by the Southern Pacific Railroad, up to 1944. These however were oil-fired, which made more sense, and were simple-expansion.

Compounding continued to have its supporters in Europe and elsewhere, and these included two of the greatest of steam locomotive designers, Karl

Gölsdorf and André Chapelon. There was no doubt that compounding worked; there was also no doubt that it was difficult to design an effective compound system, and even then, usually difficult to make it work to proper effect. The uncertainty of designers in this matter is shown by the frequent tendency, when producing prototype locomotives, to build both compound and simple versions. Though the use of compounding became steadily less common, it was never abandoned, particularly not in France, where compound express locomotives dominated long-distance services. As late as the 1940s, the Great Northern Railway of Ireland brought out a new class of compound 4-4-0 locomotives.

FIFTEEN

The Racing Years

Most passenger train services were slow; some were very slow. Almost all freight services were even slower, though from quite early in the nineteenth century, railways had, of necessity, identified certain bulk perishable items as 'fast freight' and given them express treatment. These included fish, fruit, fresh flowers, and other produce which had to be delivered quickly to be saleable. From the 1840s, a few railways had run prestige services at average speeds of 60mph (96km/h) or even more. Usually, these had been mail trains. Post office contracts were lucrative, but in return the postal authorities demanded a better than average standard of performance. By the 1880s, when braking and signalling systems had been greatly improved, there was a real possibility of a general improvement in train speeds. On many lines, the increase in traffic also required a speeding-up, in order to create time paths for additional trains. Railway writers and journalists were taking a greater interest in timings; making comparisons, and urging on the sluggards. Professor Foxwell's and Lord Farrer's book *Express Trains, English and Foreign*, published in 1889, was widely read. It did not shrink from acerbic criticism, as in its remarks on the flaccid speeds of the North Eastern Railway in England: 'The North Eastern metals traverse a district ever memorable in railway history, and its main track is comparatively level; neither easy gradients, nor proud memories can prevail against an unexcitable executive and consciousness of a safe monopoly.' Other railway managements would see nothing but common sense in the North Eastern's attitude. Where there was no monopoly, competition provided a spur: many cities were now linked by more than one railway line. From 1875, travellers from London to Edinburgh had a choice of three routes. Two lines were in competition between Toronto and Montreal, and between New York and Philadelphia. In 1880 there were many people who, like the now seventy-one-year-old Fanny Kemble, could still remember when 30mph was either exhilarating or terrifying, but all had long since become accustomed to speed and comfort of a very different order. The track on main lines was being steadily renewed with heavier rails, which could stand up to the pounding of bigger locomotives and heavier trains. In all the technical ways, the scene was set for the pursuit of high speeds.

In many countries, train speeds were limited by government edict setting a maximum which must not be exceeded. This was the case in France, Spain, and Germany. In Great Britain and the USA, there were no such constraints. Speed limits were set by the civil engineer, for curves, viaducts and other places where prudence was required or stress should be at a minimum. Otherwise, it was up to the driver to maintain his timetable. Both countries had certain stretches of track favourable to high-speed running. In Britain these included the Caledonian Railway's line between Perth and Forfar, the North Eastern's between York and Darlington, the Great Northern's south of Grantham; and the Great Western's between London and Bristol. In the USA, the line from Camden to Atlantic City, the lines leading to Fort Wayne, Indiana, and the line to Jacksonville, Florida were among the high-speed sectors.

The amount of railway racing that went on was very limited. Most railway companies had a monopoly in their territory. Most took a dim view of very high speeds, as damaging to the track, putting undesirable strains on the locomotives, and greatly increasing their coal consumption. During the economic recession and consequent reduced traffic of 1857-1859, the Chicago & Rock Island Railroad found that by enforcing speed reductions it could reduce locomotive running costs from thirty to twenty-one cents a mile. Such steps were much more appealing to a profit-conscious management than a speed increase.

In Britain, the notion of railway 'racing' first took root in 1871, when the thrusting Superintendent of the Great Northern, F.P. Cockshott, openly told his Midland Railway opposite number that whatever time the Midland took on its route between Leeds and its London terminus at St Pancras, the Great Northern would leave later and arrive sooner in its adjacent terminus at Kings Cross. Cockshott kept up this aggressive stance for twenty years, supported by the performance of the high-pressure single-driver engines of Archibald Sturrock and Patrick Stirling; primarily the latter's 'eight-footers', though his slightly smaller-wheeled 2-2-2s (7ft 6in, 228.6cm) also played a part. The next serious outbreak of rivalry arose in 1888, between the London & North Western Railway, with its head-quarters at Euston Station, London, and the Great Northern. A burst of competitive schedule-paring took place on the London-Edinburgh routes that summer, with the best journey time reduced from nine hours to seven hours and thirty-two minutes. This was ended by a pact, agreeing on an eight-hour time from Euston and seven and three quarters from Kings Cross. These occasions were a relatively gentle prelude to what came later, and the maximum train speed recorded was 76.6mph (127km/h) by a Stirling 4-2-2 on the Great Northern's 'Flying Scotchman' express, on 31 August 1888. With the construction of the Forth Bridge, and the rebuilding of the fallen Tay Bridge, the racing ground extended all the way from London to Aberdeen, 539.7 miles from Euston by the West Coast route and 523.7 miles from Kings Cross by the East Coast. A real fear of traffic loss, especially of high-premium first-class passengers, haunted Euston, and the LNWR General Manager, George Findlay, wrote to *The Times* on 9 October 1889 to proclaim that the West Coast lines would always do the journey to Aberdeen as fast as the East Coast. The locomotives of three companies from Kings Cross, and of two from Euston, were involved. The two routes eventually converged at the lonely signal-box of Kinnaber Junction, 38 miles south of Aberdeen. By coin-cidence this old Gaelic-Pictish place-name means 'head of the convergence', though of streams rather than iron roads. The first train to be offered to the Kinnaber signalman got the road, and won the race.

Matters came to a head in the summer of 1895. Between 15 July and 22 August, the average speed of the fastest trains between London and Aberdeen rose from 45.5 to 63.25mph (73.2 to 102km/h). With its dis-advantage of a longer route and steeper gradients, the LNWR found a means of avoiding the constraints of the timetable by dividing the 'Tourist Express' into two sections. The second section followed the timetable and the station stops. The first section was unabashedly a racing train, under instructions to make the fastest time possible, and with engines standing by at Crewe, Carlisle and Perth to take the train onwards with the mini-mum delay. The East Coast companies, though they cut their timetable to the bone, punctiliously observed the published arrival and departure times. Every morning from 15 July to 19 August, the West Coast was first. On the 19th, the on-coming train bells from the previous stations rang simultane-ously in the signal box at Kinnaber Junction. The box was operated by the Caledonian, the other West Coast company, and its signalman gallantly gave the road to the opposition.

The sporting instincts of the nation were roused. Bets were made on which line would be first on each day, and what the best journey time would be. Newspapers reported the races in detail, and were keenly perused. For the first time since the early days — apart from accidents and scandals — railways became national news, and people who cared nothing for locomotives studied the form of North British or North Eastern 4-4-0 engines as avidly as if they were race-horses. A few people rode the trains specially, for no other reason than to be part of the race. Others were alarmed rather than excited; one traveller recalled that 'Some ladies in the next carriage kept up a continual screeching for the greater part of the journey.'

On the night of 20-21 August, the North British Railway, which ran the East Coast section from Edinburgh to Aberdeen, finally threw the gloves off, ignoring the timetable, and let the train go as soon as its new engine was coupled on at Waverley Station, with a clear road. But 80 miles further on, even as it went pounding uphill in the northern dawn, from Montrose towards Kinnaber Junction, the steam of the other train could be seen on the line above. The West Coast won with less than a minute to spare. Both trains had left London at 8pm. On the following night, the East Coast made a supreme effort and was first into Aberdeen, at 4.40am — something which not every passenger might have relished. Having thus made their point, the East Coast companies reverted to the timetable. But on the night of 22-23 August, the West Coast made a final gesture, doing the entire journey in eight hours and thirty minutes, at an average speed of 63.3mph (102km/h). The train was a lightweight one of three coaches; nevertheless for the LNWR 'Precedent' class 2-4-0 *Hardwicke*, a design of 1874, to take it over the 960ft (319m) Shap Summit at 60mph (96km/h) was a remarkable achievement; on the way down towards Carlisle, the maximum was 85mph (138km/h).

Usually known by the nickname of 'Jumbo', this inside-cylinder class was designed at Crewe, in the earlier, pre-compound days of F.W. Webb, to provide motive power on the London-Crewe-Manchester section of the LNWR. It proved to be a valuable and long-lived addition to the stock, and soon also showed its worth on the steep gradients of the Crewe-Carlisle section. Like many other British express types, the 'Jumbos' had to make up by hard thrashing what they lacked in maximum boiler capacity, and they stood up to the treatment very well, though at a high cost in fuel usage. One member of the class, *Charles Dickens*, employed exclusively on the Euston-Manchester run, recorded two million miles (3,218,500km) between 1882 and 1902; and continued on secondary duties until 1912. But as the locomotive historian E.H. Ahrons mused, 'it would be interesting to learn how much of the original engine remained in it'. The frames were less than an inch thick (2.2cm), and he was sceptical about their ability to withstand such intensive pounding for twenty years. The other racers of 1895 were 'Teutonic' compounds on the LNWR, 4-2-0 single-wheelers on the Great Northern, and 4-4-0s on the North Eastern (Worsdell's compounds), North British and Caledonian. These last were small engines with a boiler heating surface of 1,184sq ft (2,202cm²), but it was still a quite a professional feat for Driver Soutar, on one occasion to run the 150 hilly miles (241km) between Carlisle and Perth, non-stop, and with no chance to take on more water, at an average speed of a mile a minute. The tender tank capacity was 3,572 gallons, and at Perth it was completely dry.

A more regular long-term racing ground was the two lines between Philadelphia and Atlantic City, one operated by the Philadelphia & Reading (55.5 miles, 89.3km), the other by the Pennsylvania (58 miles, 93.4km). The tracks were parallel for much of the way, and at one point, outside Camden, they crossed each other on the level. The first train in sight got priority here. At both ends of the line, the trains ran through city streets, very slowly, with engine bells ringing, but out in the countryside, speeds quickly rose to the fastest yet timetabled in the USA. But often both lines beat the timetable.

The Philadelphia & Reading put its Baldwin-built 4-4-2 'Camelbacks' into service on this route. Its wide Wootten firebox was ideal for this 'Atlantic' type. First ordered by the Atlantic City Railroad of New Jersey in 1896, just before it was taken over by the Philadelphia & Reading Railroad, these engines used the Vauclain compound system. In a very modern touch, the driver and fireman communicated with each other by telephone. In the summer of 1897, this class was put on the 'Atlantic City Flyer', then the fastest scheduled service in the world, from Camden to Atlantic City in fifty minutes. The train despatcher's records, proudly reproduced in the Baldwin official history, show that the engines consistently beat this timing, with the best average speed being 71.2mph (114.5km/h) with six cars behind the tender. The load varied between five and six cars, with around 420 passengers. On the whole, the Reading seems to have had the best of it: the *Railway Magazine* of April 1904 names the Reading's Atlantic City-Camden service as the fastest train in the world, with a journey speed of 67.96mph

(109.4km/h); second comes the Pennsylvania, on the rival route, with 66.92mph (107.6km/h). In 1907, a new Class P5 'Atlantic' of the Reading, No.343, ran the 55.5 miles with a 260-ton load in forty-one minutes — an average of 81.3mph (131km/h), including a maximum of 96mph (155km/h).

A much longer competitive route was that between New York and Chicago, where the Pennsylvania Railroad had its mountain line through the Alleghenies, and the New York Central & Hudson River Railroad had the 'Water Level Route' following the old Mohawk & Hudson line. The NYC had every intention that its 'Empire State Express' between New York and Chicago should be a national showpiece of elegance, comfort and speed. Designed to be a racer, the one-off 4-4-0 locomotive No.999 ran the first or final eastern stage between New York and Albany; its driver, Charlie Hogan, was an acclaimed master of his trade. Built in 1893 at the line's own West Albany works, it was a typical American 4-4-0 with bar frames and two simple-expansion outside cylinders, but had unusually large coupled wheels. These 7ft 2in (218.4cm) diameter wheels carried it to a claimed world speed record of 112.5mph (180km/h) on 10 May 1893, running with a four-car train down a 1 in 350 gradient. On the previous day it had also been timed at a sustained maximum of 102.8mph (166km/h). Both speed achievements were timed by the train's conductor. Two acquaintances of the British speed-recorder, Charles Rous-Marten, also timed the train on 10 May and established a maximum of 81.8mph (131.7km/h), and this figure also later appeared in official reports. Speed records, unless confirmed by an experienced recorder, or by dynamometer car equipment, tend to be rather contentious matters. It was all wonderful publicity for the train and the line, however, and there is no doubt that No.999 was a very fast locomotive. Its performance in 1893 laid the basis for the celebrated 'Twentieth Century Limited' express. No.999, with some modifications, including standard 78in (198.1cm) coupled wheels, is preserved at Chicago.

Another famous American speed claim happened in 1901, and again competition for traffic was responsible — this time it was the mails. Post to and from the USA to the West Indies went by train between Washington DC and Jacksonville, Florida. and thence by ship. In that year, the Plant System (Savannah, Florida & Western Railway) and the Seaboard Line were competing for this US Mail contract. The 4-6-0 Class K9 of the Plant System was built for fast passenger work by Alco's Rhode Island Locomotive Works, though at 6ft (184.6cm) diameter its driving wheels were not particularly large. It achieved fame in March 1901 when a speed of 120mph (193.1km/h) was claimed for No.111. The postal authorities intended to award the contract to the line which could demonstrate a faster service. To test this, an eight-car mail train was split between the two companies at Savannah, and the first to reach its own terminus at Jacksonville, Florida, was to get the contract. The Plant System's first engine, No.107, was delayed by a hot axle box. No.111 took over the four-car train and ran from Jesup to Jacksonville, 115.9 miles (186.5km), at an average of 77.3mph (124.4km/h), including the reputed but unsubstantiated maximum of 120mph (193.1km/h) attained between Screven and Satilla. The Plant System duly obtained the contract. No.111 ran until 1942, when it was broken up for scrap.

All these racing and high-speed achievements were made by locomotives built in the last quarter of the nineteenth century. By luck or judgement, their designers had produced types that were exceptionally free-running. Although the technology of engine-construction had made great progress, there was still relatively little scientific understanding of the behaviour of steam and its passage from boiler to steam chest and thence to cylinder. Designers knew that the hotter the steam, the more efficient and economically the locomotive would work, if the driver applied the appropriate cut-off to allow for maximum expansion in the cylinders. To increase the heating surface, water-tube fireboxes were tried out by many designers, and to help maintain heat, exhaust steam was often passed through 'jackets' mounted around the cylinders. There was a certain hit-or-miss quality about these applications. But in Germany, on the Royal Prussian Railway Union (KPEV), scientific work was being pursued, patiently and methodically, which would completely transform the performance of the steam locomotive.

SIXTEEN

Superheating

Without the seven years' labour of Dr Wilhelm Schmidt of Kassel, it is likely that the steam locomotive would have gone out of use earlier than it did. The limitations of the traditional boiler design would have caused frustration and prompted more intensive work on the application of other forms of power. By the early 1900s both the internal combustion (i.e. combustion actually within the cylinder) engine and the electric motor had been applied to railway work. The advent of superheated steam helped to keep both these new developments on the periphery for another three decades.

'Of all the improvements made since George Stephenson outlined the basic form, the superheater remains the principal,' wrote E.S. Cox, an eminent English locomotive designer and author. Schmidt's was also the last great contribution to the development of the steam locomotive. There were new inventions still to come, but they were only of partial or local application and none attained anything like the universal application, and dramatic effect, of superheating. Schmidt was born in 1858 into a poor family in Saxony, and he became a locksmith before a combination of talent and good fortune won him a place in the Dresden Technical High School. His early work was done with stationary engines, and in 1894 he published in the engineering journal *Zeitschrift des Vereins Deutscher Ingenieure* details of a compound engine using high-temperature steam. Steam in the 1890s was still by far the prime technology, and it was typical of the methodical approach of the KPEV that it should provide access to an academically-trained scientist to work on boiler improvements. The chief mechanical engineer of the Berlin Division, Robert Garbe, was himself the holder of a doctorate, and it was he, not Schmidt, who would write the textbook on the application of superheated steam to locomotives. The underlying concept was by no means a new one.

Richard Trevithick, in 1828, had applied the principle of reheated steam in a stationary engine, and designers had long appreciated that hotter, drier steam would operate more efficiently in the cylinders. Various attempts at steam drying in locomotives had been made in France and England. In 1839 the locomotive builders R. & W. Hawthorn of Newcastle, England, had patented a steam chamber, fitted in the smoke-box, through which passed tubes containing hot furnace gases. A form of superheater using tubes set back into the boiler flues was drawn up in 1850 by M. Moncheuil, Locomotive Superintendent of the Monterau & Troyes railway, as a modification of a patent taken out by another engineer, Quillacq, but it does not seem to have ever been tested. J.C. McConnell had produced a ring-shaped smoke-tube superheater in 1852, improved in 1859, for which he claimed a 50 per cent increase in the power of the steam at the piston. These devices did not stand the test of real work. Despite these and other initiatives, including Pétiet's boiler-top steam drier, it was 'saturated' steam that drove the nineteenth-century locomotive. Possibly the superheater might have been developed even without Schmidt's work. But no other railway company or locomotive builder was pursuing the problem with the same blend of theoretical knowledge and painstaking practicality. Sir John Aspinall, on the English Lancashire & Yorkshire Railway, was supervising a similar attempt, but his 'steam-boxes', placed in an elongated smoke-box recessed into the boiler, did not provide conclusive results. These and other efforts were aimed at producing a moderate degree of superheat, while Schmidt was determined to achieve high superheat, in which the temperature of the saturated steam is lifted from around 368°F to a superheat of 572°F or more. An increase in temperature of this order would expand the volume of the steam by about a third.

Much of Schmidt's experimentation was carried out on the Prussian Class S3 4-4-0, designed by von Borries. This was a two-cylinder compound, generally regarded as efficient, with a boiler pressure of 171psi (12kg/cm²); a passenger engine with 6ft 6in (182.9cm) driving wheels. Several years of testing and measurement went on between 1895 and 1902, during which the centre of attention moved from the smoke-box to the boiler. Conditions in the smoke-box were of course very hot, but there was much greater heat within the boiler flues, conveying gases from the firebox to the smoke-box. In previous locomotives, steam was gathered in the dome, or in the upper part of a domeless boiler, and supplied direct to the steam-chest, which acted as a reservoir for the valve and cylinder chambers. In 1898 both Henschel and Vulkan built locomotives with Schmidt's first superheaters fitted in the smoke-boxes. But in Schmidt's final system, of 1902, the main steam-pipe led to a header, from which a set of narrow tubes were turned back inside widened flues in the upper part of the boiler, where the steam was subjected to the fierce heat of gases streaming from the firebox. The superheater tubes, known as elements, terminated in a second header from which the superheated steam was passed to the steam-chests. The whole assembly added only a ton or so to the locomotive's weight, but the increase in efficiency was dramatic. Once installed, it needed little in the way of management or controls; it became an integral part of the machine.

The chief benefit was that the very hot dry steam continued to expand in the cylinders and so not only gave more work for every ounce of steam produced, but also used less, giving greater economy in the use of coal and of water. Saturated steam, by comparison, was liable to condense in the cylinders and form water. Progress also brought its problems. Among the attendant disadvantages of superheating was that the hotter the steam was, the drier it was, and so more and better lubricant was needed where metal surfaces moved together in super-hot conditions. A special grade of superheat oil was produced, and various new kinds of automatic lubrication, controlled from the driving cab, were devised. Whether force-fed by a pump, or self-supplied on the sight-feed displacement system, the oil supply was married into a jet of live steam and so in atomised form carried into the main steam-pipe, or directly to the valve chests. The most crucial location was the valves, and the old-style slide valves were found to move much less freely with superheat than they had done with saturated steam. The abandonment of flat slide valves in favour of ring-shaped piston valves in actuating the work of the cylinders proceeded rapidly. Schmidt himself developed a broad-ring piston valve, which many railways used until, in Germany again, the narrow-ring piston valve was introduced during the 1920s and soon became universally used. According to J. N. Westwood, Schmidt was known to his German colleagues as *Heissdampf Willi*, 'Hot-Steam Willy', and certainly hot steam and high pressure were the dominant themes of his career. After the sale of his patent to the Superheater Company in 1910, he concentrated on the design of a high-pressure boiler for locomotives. He died in 1924, but the work of his later years would remain an item of interest to railways in several different countries.

Prussian design had already excited admiration, but German influence on international development took centre stage with the introduction in 1902 of Dr Garbe's Class G8 0-8-0 of the KPEV. In the Prussian Railways' classification, 'G' stood for *Güterzuglokomotive*, 'goods train locomotive'. The first really modern version of the steam locomotive, it became a staple work-horse on many railways. It was a modernised version of the G7 0-8-0 of 1893, with a round-topped firebox and a narrow grate, but unlike the G7, which had both simple and compound expansion versions, this was a simple-expansion type only, with two outside cylinders, piston valves, outside Walschaerts valve gear, and the final form of Schmidt superheater. In all these respects, it showed the way forward. In the next ten years over 1,000 G8s were built, and it became the standard freight engine of the KPEV. With a maximum axle-load of 14 tons (14.2t) and a compact wheelbase, it was a go-anywhere engine. No concessions to elegance or unnecessary aspects of finish were allowed for, but the G8, as unabashed in showing its rivets as Oliver Cromwell with his warts, put Prussian application and efficiency into reality. In 1913 a heavier G81 version was introduced, built first by the Hanomag works at Hannover but also by virtually every other German builder, twelve in all. Wartime service between 1914 and 1918 proved the value of this engine. The G8s hauled unprecedented loads and ran to far more demanding schedules than had been required of freight engines in peacetime. By 1921, a total of 5,087 had been constructed. In the period 1933-1941, 688 were rebuilt as 2-8-0s and classified G82.

The G8 was widely exported. German war reparations in 1918 spread them even further across European and Middle Eastern systems, as far east as Syria. It was not the cheapest 0-8-0 to build but its performance, economy and reliability were outstanding. Equally so was its durability. G8s were still working on heavy coal trains for the Turkish State Railways into the 1970s. Several are preserved, in Germany and other countries.

The very first locomotives to use Schmidt's fire-tube superheater were on the Belgian State Railways in 1901, but from the appearance of the G8, it became apparent to locomotive engineers everywhere, with varying degrees of consternation, or relish for what was now possible, that any of their productions, however new, large and splendid, however powerful and economical, was already obsolete if it did not use superheating. Although many others were later to develop their own patent versions – some of which, like the French Houlet superheater, gave even higher temperatures;

while others merely sought to evade Schmidt's patent – Schmidt's work was decisive. From around 1910, no modern boiler design, other than the very smallest kind, could be without a superheater, and thousands of 'saturated' locomotives were adapted to incorporate the new miracle equipment.

One of the side-effects of the superheater was to greatly reduce interest in compounding. Schmidt himself believed that superheating would replace compounding, and the trend-setting G8 had simple-expansion cylinders only. To most designers, with such an easy source of increased economy and efficiency now available, the improvements offered by compounding, more tricky to deliver and sometimes dubious or slight in effect, no longer seemed worth striving for. Only a few would persevere in combining superheat and compounding to extract the absolute maximum of performance and efficiency. Another side-effect was to popularise the use of Walschaerts valve gear, mounted externally and driven from an eccentric on a driving wheel crank pin, which worked more effectively with superheated steam than the internal Stephenson link gear. Ironically, this surge in use was just about to begin when Walschaerts died, in 1901. In outside cylinder locomotives, the Walschaerts-Heusinger gear, or some later derivative, was to become almost universal in the twentieth century.

The G8, and even more its passenger locomotive counterpart, the Class P8 4-6-0 which followed in 1906, and of which almost 4,000 were built, had another message for the locomotive world, which was not quite so obvious at the time. It was that a well-designed, medium-sized locomotive, with superheat and good steam distribution through piston valves, could undertake a very wide range of tasks. They established the concept of the 'general user' or 'pool' engine. At the time, most designers believed in specific locomotives for specific jobs and routes – and many would continue to do so for a long time to come. Associated with this belief was the general practice of allocating a particular driver to a particular engine: a system which had disadvantages as well as benefits. Inherent in the Prussian concept was that a locomotive could be passed on from one crew to another in order to be used to its maximum effect. There were no special idiosyncrasies, nothing extra to learn.

SEVENTEEN

A Hundred Years On

An unusual use of the steam locomotive was shown in 1902. On 24 September, at the Kentucky State Fair on Churchill Downs, two locomotives were set up on each end of a 2,000ft track, and put in motion towards each other before the crews jumped free. The staged collision took place before a crowd estimated at between 35,000 and 40,000 people. Weighing about 60 tons apiece, one doing about 35mph (56km/h), the other something between 15 and 18mph, the 4-4-0s piled into each other, with an effect described by one onlooker as: 'something like forcing two eggs together'. Spectators gleefully rushed to gather up fragments as mementoes. Similar events had been staged from the mid-nineties. Into this reduction of the locomotive to gladiatorial spectacle one might read a number of things, apart from the fact that there were plenty of old specimens available cheap. Underlying it was everyone's fear of a real-life train crash, as well as everyone's pleasure in seeing someone else's (supposedly) expensive property spectacularly destroyed. The symbolic value of the locomotive in expressing a vision of humanity's work-free future was long gone; if the Kentucky show can be dignified in any way at all, it is as a vision of humanity asserting its superiority to the machine, to the point of making it destroy itself. What was a locomotive, but just a big piece of commercial hardware, after all?

Two years later, 1904 brought the hundredth anniversary of the Trevithick locomotive's first outing. The *Railway Magazine* for March 1904 notes the event in passing, and says that the general press had for some reason been celebrating 10 February as the centennial day. Company centenaries would be celebrated vigorously from 1925 onwards, but the great day at Penydarren was given low-key treatment. A hundred years on from it, with the advent of the superheater, all the basic features that would characterise a modern steam locomotive were finally present. There were still a good fifty years of locomotive-building ahead; two generations of designers to come. In 1904 André Chapelon was a boy of eight. Nigel Gresley was a young engineer of twenty-eight on the Great Northern Railway; Richard Wagner was a twenty-two year old student of engineering in Berlin. Herbert William Garratt was forty, an obscure colonial engineer. William Woodard was thirty-one, as yet unknown among American designers. L. Dante Porta would not be born for another eighteen years. These would be among the great names of the future, indissolubly linked with the steam locomotive's story. But their role would be to deal with the elements that already existed and to employ new techniques and new insights that would standardise production and push efficiency, speed and power to their historic maxima. Of course, there was no general and simultaneous passing-on of the baton to new engineering chiefs at regular intervals. The international corps of engineers was formed both of newcomers and old-timers. In 1904, some notable engineers had recently died or retired, among them Alfred Belpaire (d.1893), John Haswell the Viennese Scot (d.1897), John Ramsbottom (also d.1897); August von Borries took up a teaching post at Charlottenburg in 1902. But many were in their prime, their work spanning the imaginary divide that separated the nineteenth and twentieth centuries. Samuel Vauclain was one of these, as were Gaston du Bousquet and Karl Gölsdorf. V.I. Lopushinskii was forty-eight, head of the technical section of the Vladikavkaz Railway's traction department, with the Russian O class 0-8-0 of 1890 behind him and the many thousands of the E class still to come. George Jackson Churchward had taken over as Chief Mechanical Engineer of the Great Western Railway the year before.

The world locomotive building industry was at its height. Whilst construction of new railways in western Europe had slowed down, new lines were still being built; and in lands where the railway was a late-comer, large-scale building was going on. There had been a general move to steel-framed and often steel-bodied cars, making passenger trains much heavier. Enormous freight traffic was generated by heavy industry, which had reached its full extent in forests of smokestacks spreading mighty plumes of atmospheric pollution whose effect was hardly questioned and whose extent was unmeasured. The population of the industrialised countries had soared in the century since the birth of the locomotive, creating a mass market for commercial and agricultural products which was dependent on distribution by railway. The demand for new locomotives was huge, damped only by occasional swings of economic recession. Railway companies were among the biggest businesses in the world (though some were also very small). In Britain there were over a hundred of them; in the USA far more than that. In France, however, there were only six major companies (after the *Etat-Nord* merger of 1909); in Germany each of the old states, the largest being Bavaria, Saxony, and Prussia, had its own system, with private feeder lines; in the Austrian Empire the imperial state system was dominant but the Austrian Südbahn and the Hungarian MÁV were also large railways. Russia had in effect a single system. All these and many other national arrangements and variations of railway management ensured an equally wide range of approaches to locomotive design and building.

In the early 1900s, and not without some regret, Britain finally ceased to build 'single-driver' locomotives. The introduction of steam-powered sanding gear had extended their lives by combating the huge wheels' tendency to slip on the rails. The mystique of their 'free steaming' and greater smoothness and steadiness in running compared to coupled engines was disproved by the performance of up-to-date designs like the French four-cylinder compounds. By 1904 it had to be acknowledged that single-wheelers were too small, and possessed insufficient traction, to be effective on the trains of the time. Even their legendary speed was revealed as unexceptional. In his *Railway Magazine* column of February 1904, Charles Rous-Marten noted that the highest recorded speed of a single-driver was 90mph (150km/h), by a Midland Railway 4-2-2 of the class built between 1896-1899, with 93in (236.2cm) wheels, while he had recorded higher speeds on various coupled engines. The single-drivers' doom had really been spelled out in 1895 with the Caledonian Railway's introduction of the 'big boiler' whose weight needed to be borne on coupled driving wheels. Now 4-4-2 and, increasingly, 4-6-0 types took over the main-line passenger services. With a perhaps myopic colonial loyalty, the British-owned Shanghai-Nanking Railway introduced a new class of 4-2-2s in 1905 (Class D) and built them until 1915.

Despite the huge proliferation of railway companies, a strong centralising influence was exercised on US locomotive design by the concentration of building in two great companies, Baldwin and Alco; from around 1916 the growth of the Lima Locomotive Company made it three. Most American railroads bought their engines from them; among the few to build much of their own locomotive stock were the Pennsylvania, the Norfolk &

Western, the Baltimore & Ohio, and the St Louis–San Francisco. The position was similar in Canada, where, though the Canadian Pacific did some building, the Canadian Locomotive Company and (from 1904) the Alco-owned Montreal Locomotive Works built most of the engines. In Britain, all the larger railways built most of their own locomotives; and the smaller lines normally designed their own and had them built by the private constructors. Among the latter the North British Locomotive Company of Glasgow was supreme, formed in 1901 by the amalgamation of Dübs, Neilson's, and Sharp, Stewart. But NBL and its rivals, like Beyer Peacock of Manchester and Vulcan Foundry of Warrington, were extremely reliant on export orders to maintain their business. Fortunately for them, imperial loyalties still generally prevailed in locomotive purchasing. In France, though building was shared between the big companies' own works and the independent builders like Cail of Lille and the Société Alsacienne, there was far more exchange of knowledge and design among the companies, encouraged by the government; and this was also true of Germany and Austria. The French locomotive industry was heavily supported, like the British, by orders from colonial railways. The only large Dutch builders, Werkspoor, sent locomotives to Java; the numerous Belgian works had a captive market in the Congo, and vied for business elsewhere. The Germans, late entrants to the colonial power-game, had few tied markets but companies like Henschel of Kassel, Krauss-Maffei of Munich, Schwartzkopff and Borsig, both of Berlin, built many engines for Spain, Portugal, Russia, Turkey, Denmark, Finland and Latin America, as well as for the home market. German design was very influential in Poland and the further east of Europe. In the summer of 1914, one of the very occasional instances of a British import happened when fifteen 4-4-0 engines were supplied by Borsig (always the most 'British' in look of the German builders) to the London Chatham & Dover Railway on the very eve of the First World War. Almost their first task was hauling troop trains to Dover, carrying the British Expeditionary Force to fight the Germans; and it does not seem that they were ever paid for. Few locomotives were exported from Austria, Czechoslovakia and Hungary, but the needs of the imperial system, pre-1918, and the separate national systems afterwards, kept the long-established locomotive works like Floridsdorf and StEG, outside Vienna, and the more recent Skoda of Plzen, and Budapest Locomotive Works, in steady production. The Scandinavian locomotive works also built mostly for home use, though Nydqvist & Holm (later Nohab) of Trollhättan, Sweden, were active exporters; and Frichs of Aarhus in Denmark also supplied wider markets.

Locomotive engineers were now a far-flung brotherhood (it was, in the manner of the times, an all-male profession) linked by those who changed jobs and countries, and by an ever-growing technical press devoted to mechanical engineering in general and locomotive engineering in particular. It was not always the well-remembered big names who were responsible for technical advances, and three of them, whose work spanned the late nineteenth and early twentieth centuries, may serve as examples for the rest of their kind. One provided Great Britain with its first 4-6-0 locomotive for home use, the second designed the world's first 4-6-2 or 'Pacific' class; and the third was responsible for the first home-built locomotive to run on the Japanese railways.

David Jones, who was born and learned his trade in Manchester, removed to Scotland and after a long stint as second-in-command, became the Locomotive Superintendent of the Highland Railway. This was one of the smaller main-line concerns, with its headquarters in the northern town of Inverness, but always of interest because of its long hauls through mountainous and scenic terrain. In the tourist season, its principal trains were very heavy and Jones had already been responsible for the design of some (by British standards) large and powerful engines when he introduced his 'Big Goods' in 1894. The first 4-6-0 on a British railway, it was built by Sharp, Stewart of Glasgow, and fifteen were ordered straight off the drawing board at the keen price of £2,795 each. At a time when single prototypes were often tried out first, this seems risky (next time the Highland tried it, under a later engineer in 1916, it was a disaster) but Jones had some reasons for confidence, arising from an unusual interaction between colonial and home locomotive practice. The resemblance of the Jones Goods to the very successful Indus Valley L-class 4-6-0, built by Dübs in 1880 for India, was soon noted, and it was supposed that David Jones, had acted at that time as a consultant to the purchasers. However, in a detailed Profile of the 'Big Goods', the locomotive historian Brian Reed noted that the HR's chief draughtsman, David Hendrie, had worked at Dübs' on the Class A 4-6-0 of the Nizam's State Railway in India – an enlarged version of the Indus Valley L class. The family resemblance among all three is distinct, and it seems that this untypical deference to a 'colonial' design paid off handsomely. (Hendrie went on to become the first Chief Mechanical Engineer of the South African Government Railways). In any case the 'Big Goods' were an immediate success. Their task was hauling goods trains on the main line between Perth and Inverness, with its long steep gradients, but they were often deployed on passenger trains in the peak summer season. The class remained in service for over forty years, and the first to be delivered, No. 103, is preserved. Although the Highland Railway had specific needs, the arrival of this engine was a sign of things to come, as British companies moved towards the big-engine philosophy that already prevailed in other countries.

Britain's first 4-6-0, eventually to become the country's most widely-used mixed traffic and passenger type, was built for its remotest railway. The 4-6-2 or 'Pacific' locomotive had its origin on an even more isolated system, in New Zealand. The first 'Pacific' class anywhere was the Class Q of New Zealand Railways, in 1901.

The NZR's Chief Mechanical Engineer, A.L. Beattie, was an immigrant to New Zealand from Yorkshire, England. Locomotive design was taken seriously on the NZR, which ran a long-distance 3ft 6in (106.5cm) gauge network over difficult terrain. Since 1878 it had partly shaken off colonial links and bought many engines from Baldwin, including some of the earliest 2-8-0s. It also built some of its own locomotives, at Addington, including the Class B 4-8-0 of 1896, about which a patriotic driver was moved to write:

> No more Yanks or Glasgow Tanks,
> Just give me an Addington 'B',
> She runs so sweet, it's quite a treat,
> To work on Three Hundred and Three.

Beattie wanted an engine with a wide firebox to burn lignite coal of low calorific value, mined on South Island, where they were intended to operate the main line passenger services. This need for combustive capacity, rather than anything else, prompted the placing of a trailing pony wheel to support the firebox. Having already been successfully done with the 4-4-2 locomotive, this was not in itself a novelty. The NZR tracks were light-weight and sometimes laid on an inadequate road-bed, so it was also important to spread the 75-ton weight of the new locomotive. Wide firebox technology was far better understood in Philadelphia than it was in Glasgow — or in Lille or Berlin for that matter. Britain, France and Prussia all used deep, narrow fireboxes designed to use high-grade steam coal. A Belgian or Bavarian builder could have coped, had they been asked. Thirteen of the Class Q were built by Baldwin. Beattie's specification was up to the minute in other ways. These were among the first engines outside continental Europe to have Walschaerts valve gear, and the outside-admission piston valves which it actuated were another modern feature (already in use on the Class B). The boiler pressure was 200psi ($14kg/cm^2$); they had bar frames, a dome-shaped sandbox, and Westinghouse air brakes. The 'Pacific' name, which became firmly attached to all 4-6-2s, is said to have arisen because it was shipped across that ocean to New Zealand, though its correspondence to the recently-named 'Atlantic' 4-4-2 type must surely also have played a part in bringing it into general use.

Baldwin built 'Pacifics' for US home use from 1902, beginning with one for the St Louis, Iron Mountain & Southern Railway, later absorbed into the Missouri Pacific. The usefulness of the wide supported grate, combined with six-coupled traction, was plain, and it very quickly became an international type. The big-wheeled express 'Pacifics' attracted most attention, but engines akin to the Q class, with fairly small-diameter driving wheels, usually between 50 and 54in (127-137.2cm), were widely used, on systems from Argentina to Thailand. The Malayan Railways acquired sixty of the H-class 4-6-2s between 1907 and 1914, for the long main line linking Singapore, Kuala Lumpur, and Penang. The original Q class was very successful in itself, running relatively leisurely schedules. Some were transferred to North Island lines, and the last one was retired from duty in 1957, having outlived many larger, fleeter and later locomotives of the same configuration. Incidentally, on the 'nothing-is-ever-as-new-as-you-thought' theme, a writer in Bulletin 87 (1952) of the US Railway and Locomotive Historical Society observed that the very first 4-6-2 was built by G.S. Strong at the Wilkes-Barre works of the Lehigh Valley Railroad in 1886 'and used for a time on that road'. This did not form a class, however, any more than putting two-wheel rear trucks on two ten-wheelers of the Chicago Minneapolis & St Paul Railroad did in 1893 (the trucks were later taken off).

The third engineer was the bearer of a famous name – perhaps too famous to support a career in his own country. Francis H. Trevithick was the third generation of his family to be a locomotive engineer. His father had been Chief Mechanical Engineer of the London & North Western Railway but had been too easy-going to retain the post under a management that demanded cold efficiency. Both Francis and his brother Richard emigrated to Japan and married Japanese wives. Japan had received its first locomotive in 1871, the 2-4-0 tank engine No.1 Ichigo, for its first railway, which opened from Shimbashi Station, Tokyo, to Yokohama on 14 October 1872. No.1, built by the Vulcan Foundry in England, can still be seen in the Tokyo Transport Museum. From 1878, Francis was Superintendent of the Tokyo Shimbashi works and in this capacity oversaw the construction of the first locomotive actually built in Japan, though 'assembled' might be more accurate, as most of its parts were prefabricated in Britain. The project was carried out at the railway's Kobe workshops. It was a two-cylinder compound 2-4-2, and the cylinders were cast in Japan. Numbered 860, it was a one-off, and, symbolically of the struggle which would ensue for the Japanese market, the next 'home product' was a Mogul put together from parts supplied from Baldwin in the USA. The pace of development was swift. The first independent locomotive works in Japan, Kisha Seizo Keisha, were established at Osaka in 1899. By 1912, the Japanese government announced that from then on locomotives for Japanese railways would be built in Japan. Before that time, Francis Trevithick had retired, though he was the last foreign railway official to remain in office, until 1904. Incidentally, his cousin Frederick Trevithick, who confusingly shared the same initials, was Chief Mechanical Engineer of the Egyptian Government railways from 1883 to 1912.

From 1902, the steam locomotive was potentially capable of virtually any task the traffic managers were likely to set it. The length and weight and even the speed of trains were now governed by other concerns: chiefly the weight of the rails and the quality of the track ballasting; the load-bearing strength of bridges; the length of platforms, crossing loops and sidings; and the effectiveness of the signalling system. A great deal of work went into what later became known as 'infrastructure' in order to provide for the improved performance and greater size of the locomotives. The consequence of this was soon felt in locomotive design. The deficiencies apparent in earlier generations had one by one been tackled and resolved. After the long haul uphill, a level plateau had been reached. The status of the locomotive designer was confirmed by the formation of an Institution of Locomotive Engineers in Britain (from 1911) and other countries. Mechanical Engineering had become an immensely wide field and a degree of specialisation was felt to be necessary. Around this time, for many engineers, the nature of their job seemed to change. They considered that the steam locomotive was as good as it was needed to be, and the task in drawing up a new design was how to make the most effective use of current knowledge, depending on local factors like the terrain, the type and quality of fuel, and the kind of services to be operated. A wide range of proven design options was available, backed up by any number of patent auxiliary devices from feed-water pumps to pyrometers which measured the degree of superheat; and new development concentrated on improving auxiliary equipment. In 1905 the first successful mechanical stoker was introduced by the Pennsylvania Railroad in the USA, and by 1911 the final version, feeding the fire from above with the aid of steam jets, was in use. These made it possible to use fireboxes of unprecedented size, and the old maximum grate area of around 50sq ft (4.6m^2) was left far behind. By 1913, the power reverser was also available. A further constraint on designers was provided by the commercial managements of the railways. Despite their continued monopoly of long-distance land transport, the economic state of many railways was precarious, partly because of competition from rival lines, partly because of their susceptibility to the down-turns in national and international economic life. Bankruptcies and mergers were common; some companies bought engines and defaulted on payment – throughout the industry, the demand for cost-cutting and economies of scale became ever more vociferous. Technical and economic factors, along with most engineers' sensible acceptance of their own average abilities, combined to make the majority of them content to be conservators, maintaining the existing basis of steam power. A locomotive chief in the first two decades of the nineteenth century could exercise choice in whether his new passenger engine would be a 4-4-2 'Atlantic' – believed by some to be the ideal lightweight express engine – or a 4-6-0; but outside (or multiple) cylinders, long-lap piston valves, Walschaerts valve gear and superheating were increasingly becoming standard items. Without these, his design would simply fail to achieve the kind of performance now regarded as routine. But there were also designers with abilities and ambitions beyond the average, and from these more might be expected.

1 A rare contemporary engraving of a Wylam Colliery locomotive at night, with the fire-door open. (Institution of Mechanical Engineers)

2 Among the cashmeres and Leghorn hats – an advertisement placed by the Liverpool & Manchester Railway in the *Liverpool Mercury* on 1 May, 1829, announcing their prize competition. (TRH Pictures)

3 A scale drawing of *Rocket*. (TRH Pictures)

4 A wonder to old and young – Phineas Davis's vertical-boilered *York*, winner of the B&O trials of 1831. The Irwin Myers drawing does not show any sort of coupling gear. (TRH Pictures)

5 Timothy Hackworth's *Derwent* of 1848 in steam at the 100th anniversary of the Stockton & Darlington Railway, 1925. (TRH Pictures)

The MASON TYPE
1857

6 Opening up the West – a Mason wood-burning 4-4-0 of 1857 is met by an ox-cart at a wayside depot. (TRH Pictures)

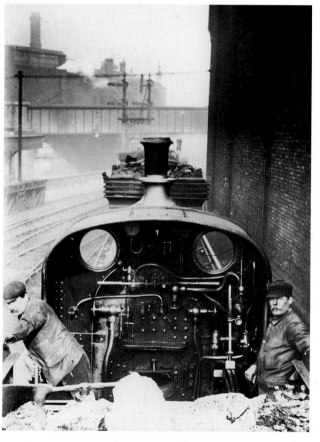

7 *Above:* The Mother Hubbard–
Wootten boiler combination: the
Central of New Jersey's Class P7s
Atlantic No.804, at Communipaw,
New Jersey, on 12 March 1931. A
lubricator pump is worked off the
front carrying axle. (SLS)

8 *Left:* A view into the Spartan cab
of the Great Northern Railway's
4-2-2 express engine No.1, as it
waits to back on to its train at Kings
Cross Station, London. (TRH
Pictures)

9 *Opposite:* One hundred and six
years old, built in 1860 for the
Graz–Köflacher Bahn in Austria,
and seen here in the engine shed at
Graz in 1966, this venerable 0-6-0
was only recently retired. (SLS)

10 At work in the Granada yards in 1963, this 0-6-0 locomotive, originally of the Madrid Zaragoza and Alicante Railway, was built in 1867.

11 The first big Mallet locomotive in the USA – the Baltimore & Ohio's 'Old Maud' of 1904. (SLS)

12 Karl Gölsdorf's 0-10-0 design of 1900 for the Imperial and Royal State Railways, here seen as 524.248 of the Czechoslovak State Railways in May 1967. (SLS)

Schweizerische Lokomotiv- und Maschinenfabrik Winterthur

Société Suisse pour la Construction de Locomotives et de Machines Winterthur

1-E-0 Normalspur-Güterzug-Lokomotive für die Schweiz. Bundesbahnen (Gotthard).
Locomotive type ‹Décapode› à voie normale pour trains de marchandises pour les Chemins de fer Fédéraux (Ligne du Gothard).

Spurweite *Écartement*	1435 mm	Heizfläche *Surface de chauffe*	265,8 m²	Leergewicht, Maschine *Poids à vide, machine*	76,1 T.
Triebraddurchmesser *Diam. des roues motrices*	1330 mm	Ueberhitzer *Surchauffeur*	Syst. Schmidt	Leergewicht, Tender *Poids à vide, tender*	16,2 T.

13 The ten-coupled locomotive for freight-hauling through the Alps on the Swiss Federal Railways' Gotthard line, as featured on a promotional card published by the builders, SLM of Winterthur. (TRH Pictures)

16 Staple locomotive-type of the old British Raj, and after – Pakistan Railways 5ft 6in gauge 0-6-0 No.245 has lubrication applied to a tender axle-box at Multan in 1981, before going on service. (SLS)

14 *Opposite above:* Crosti-boilered No.741.104 of the Italian FS, on a special excursion service at Catania, Sicily, in the 1980s. The heating drum door can be seen below the smokebox door. (SLS)

15 *Opposite below:* The British look in South America – this 4-6-2, No.171, of the Argentinian Central Railway, was built by North British Locomotive Co., Glasgow, in 1912. (SLS)

17 Photographed at Madium depot in 1972, this Indonesian veteran 2-4-0, No.01 of Class B50, was built by Sharp, Stewart in Glasgow in 1850. (SLS)

18 Ten new locomotives for the South Indian Railway are loaded on to a specialised 'Bel' ship, SS *Belray*, at Middlesbrough Docks, England, in 1927. (TRH Pictures)

19 Free roller: encouraged by the locomotive crew, three young ladies pull the roller-bearing fitted 'Four Aces' along the rails at Chicago, in 1930. (Timken)

20 Middle-Eastern 'Mikado' – a German-built 2-8-2 with a mixed train at the Damascus terminal in 1957. (TRH Pictures)

21 The New Zealand-American look – a Class A 'Pacific' designed by A.L. Beattie, with Vanderbilt tender. It was built in 1912 by NBL in Glasgow. (TRH Pictures)

22 *Opposite above:* Pennsylvania Railroad K4 'Pacific' No.3745 at speed near Englewood, Illinois, with the 'Liberty Limited' on 29 March 1941. (SLS)

23 *Opposite below: Chapelon Pacific No.231E.19* at Calais, on 15 May 1966. The breaks in the outer pipework suggest the locomotive is in line for repair or withdrawal. (TRH Pictures)

T4a · Class – Multi·Pressure Locomotive – Built at Angus Shops.

CYLINDERS	H.P. (1) ___ 15½ × 28″	BOILER PRESSURES		WEIGHT ON DRIVERS ___ 32055
"	L.P. (2) ___ 24″ × 30″	CLOSED CIRCUIT ___ 1350. lbs.		" OF ENGINE ___ 49530
DIAMETER OF DRIVERS ___ 63		HIGH PRESSURE ___ 850. "		" " AND TENDER _ 79530

26 German passenger and freight steam types at the depot in Rostock, in the former DDR: Class O1 'Pacifics' 0523 and 2048; 2-10-0s Class 44 0351 and Class 50 294, all still at work in 1974. (SLS)

24 *Opposite above:* The Finnish look – VR 4-6-0 No. 586 in typical southern scenery. The spark arrestor chimney cap can be clearly seen. (TRH Pictures)

25 *Opposite below:* Canadian Pacific No. 8000, the experimental 2-10-4 locomotive fitted with the Schmidt-Henschel high-pressure boiler. It was built at the line's own Angus shops. (TRH Pictures)

Schweizerische
Lokomotiv- und Maschinenfabrik
Winterthur

Société Suisse pour la Construction
de Locomotives et de Machines
Winterthur

1-C-2 Tenderlokomotive, 2 Zyl., Heißdampf, für die Portugiesischen Bahnen.
Locomotive-Tender à surchauffe à 2 cyl., pour les Chemins de fer Portugais.

Spurweite *Écartement*	1665 mm	Heizfläche *Surface de chauffe*	170 m²	Leergewicht *Poids à vide*	62,2 t
Triebraddurchmesser *Diam. des roues motrices*	1520 mm	Ueberhitzer *Surchauffeur*	Syst. Schmidt	Dienstgewicht *Poids en service*	82,5 t

27 Portugal imported its steam locomotives, mostly from Germany and Switzerland, as with this super-heated 2-6-4 tank engine type, for passenger service, a product of the SLM works at Winterthur. (TRH Pictures)

28 *Opposite:* The shapely front end of the LNER class A4 'Pacific'. No.2510 *Quicksilver* on the inspection pit at Cambridge locomotive depot in June 1937. (R.F. Roberts/SLS)

29 The Romney, Hythe & Dymchurch Railway in the 1930s. (J. & C. McCutcheon)

30 Two NSWGR 'Pacifics' of class 38, Nos. 30 and 13, head the first all-standard gauge 'Spirit of Progress' express from Sydney to Melbourne, in April 1962. (TRH Pictures)

31 The Giesl chimney is the most prominent feature on this narrow-gauge tank engine of the Volklemarkt-Eisenkappel line in Austria. It is pulling standard-gauge wagons on transporter trucks. (TRH Pictures)

AMERICAN LOCOMOTIVE COMPANY
NEW YORK

Class, 4 12 2 S 515, "Three-Cylinder."   Road Number, 9085

BUILT FOR THE UNION PACIFIC.

GAUGE OF TRACK	CYLINDERS		DRIVING WHEEL DIAMETER	BOILER		FIRE BOX			TUBES		
	Diam.	Stroke		Inside Dia.	Pressure	GAINES ARCH			Number	Diameter	Length
						Length	Width				
4'-8½"	Inside 27" Outside 27"	31" 32"	67"	90"	220 lbs.	184½"	108¼"		40 222	3½"	22'-0"

WHEEL BASE			WEIGHT IN WORKING ORDER—POUNDS				
Driving	Engine	Engine & Tender	Leading	Driving	Trailing	Engine	Tender
30'-8"	52' 4"	91'-6½"	81000	372000	62000	515000	308800

FUEL	EVAPORATING SURFACES, SQUARE FT.					SUPERHEATING SURFACE SQUARE FT.	GRATE		MAXIMUM TRACTIVE POWER	FACTOR OF ADHESION
Kind	Tubes	Flues	Fire Box	Arch Tubes	Total		LENGTH 144"	WIDTH 108¼"		
Simi-Bit. Coal	803	4459	529	62	5853	2560	Area 108.25Sq.Ft		96650 lbs.	3.84

Tender Type. 12-Wheeled.	Capacity, Water, 18000 Gals.	Fuel, 22 Tons

ORDER No. S-1701
August, 1930

32 The Union Pacific's mighty Class S 515, introduced in 1926 and built by Alco; the largest and most numerous class of rigid-framed locomotives with six driving axles. (TRH Pictures)

33 The locomotive in war: an improvised Union Army hospital train collects the wounded after a battle in the American Civil War. (TRH/US National Archives)

34 *Opposite above:* An American in France – ex-USATC 0-6-0T, now No. TU20 of the SNCF, was photographed at Calais on 15 May 1966. The notice on the tank side warns against accidents. (TRH Pictures)

35 *Opposite below:* Working back-to-back, NSWGR Garratts of Class AD60, Nos. 6042 and 6037, climb Fassifern Bank with a coal train from Newstan, on 7 December 1972. (TRH Pictures)

36 Mallet-type 2-8-8-0 Class DD52.07 of PNKA (Indonesian Railways). This was the last Mallet class to be built. (TRH Pictures)

37 'Pacific' No.840 of the Royal Siamese Railways was built in Japan in 1950 to the same specification as its wartime predecessors, except for being oil-fired. Photograph taken at Haat Yai, 3 September 1972. (TRH Pictures)

38 Cutting up a steam locomotive was no light task, as shown by this massive remnant of a Southern Railway H15 4-6-0 on the scrap line at Eastleigh, Hampshire. The severed superheater tubes have an uncomfortably organic air. (TRH Pictures)

39 Industrial lines saw the last workings of American steam, as with this 0-8-0 switcher of the Midland Electric Coal Corporation, still at work on 6 April 1963. (SLS)

40 The facsimile of Seguin's locomotive, complete with bellows-cart, in steam at Tenterden, England, on 18 July 1999. (Alan Barnes/TRH)

41 Engine in war – a heavily-loaded troop transport leaves camp, headed by a Nashville & Chattanooga 4-4-0, in this US Civil War scene. (Anne S.K. Brown/TRH)

42 The preserved Austrian 2-6-4, No.310.23, at the Railway Festival in Nürnberg, on 12 June 1994. (Gideon Grimmel)

43 The preserved P8, No.38 3199, Prussia's do-anything locomotive, at the Nürnberg Railway Festival, Germany, on 16 June, 2002. (Gideon Grimmel)

44 War engine – preserved Type 52 No.52.8195 at Nürnberg Hauptbahnhof, Germany, on 14 July 2002. (Gideon Grimmel)

45 *Opposite above, left:* Green light for the future – a locomotive brings in the New Year in this German greetings card of 1910. (SLS)

46 *Opposite above, right:* Steaming through the mountains – an Austrian postcard from the early twentieth century. The conical smokebox was a popular feature in central Europe. (SLS)

47 *Opposite below:* The locomotive reduced to blobs of light – an impressionistic yard scene on a German card of the early 1900s. (SLS)

48 The 'Crusader' express between Philadelphia and New York was the Philadelphia & Reading Railroad's version of the 'Hiawatha': the image, typically of North American postcard views, is quite free of smoke or even steam. (SLS)

49 Richmond, Virginia, was the only location in the world where three main-line railways crossed, one above the other. In this coloured view Chesapeake & Ohio 2-8-0 No.433 roars above a Seaboard Air Line 4-8-2, with a Southern Railway 'Pacific' on ground level. (SLS)

50 Locomotive as empire builder: the Canadian Pacific Railway's 'Colonists' Express', with 'Pacific' 1112, halts somewhere out in the prairies. The freight cars hold the immigrants' baggage. (SLS)

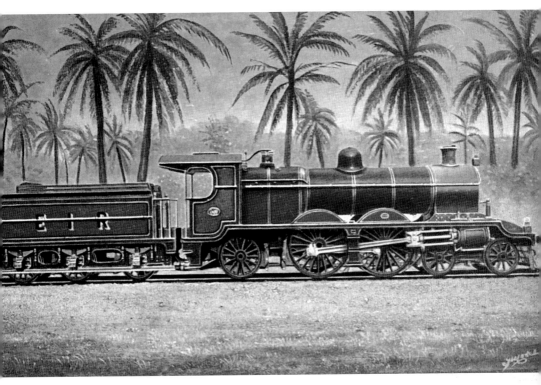

53 An East Indian Railways 'Atlantic', to a BESA design of the early 1900s. As the engine has no Indian features, like a tender canopy and headlamp, the view is almost certainly a British manufacturer's publicity shot, with suitably 'Indian' background added. (J. & C. McCutcheon)

51 *Opposite above:* Four ex-South African Garratt locomotives, now running on Mozambique Railways, await new crews at the start of a shift. (D. Burrows/TRH)

52 *Opposite below:* New Zealand Railways' preserved 4-8-4 Ka 942, with an excursion train at Kaikoura, on 13 September 1992. The tender message is 'Buy NZ-Made Goods.' (Graeme McClare)

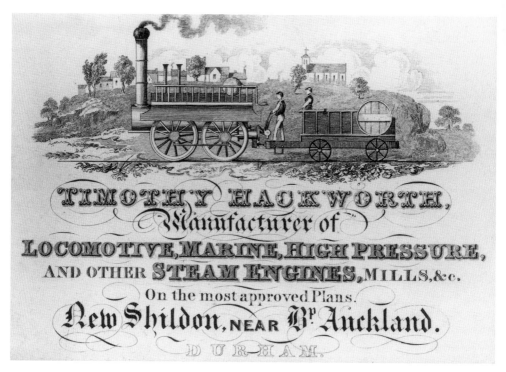

54 Timothy Hackworth's business card, from around 1830, shows a rather stylised 0-4-0 locomotive in a rural setting. It has inside cylinders driving from the rear, and a modest plume of smoke emerging via a spark-arrestor.

55 A business card for Robert Stephenson & Co., showing two trains crossing the 'high level' bridge over the Tyne. This opened in 1849, and Stephenson himself was the engineer. Like Hackworth's, the business was ready to build steam engines for any purpose.

EIGHTEEN

Imperial and Royal

Among the grandest of railway titles was that of the Imperial and Royal State Railway of Austria and Hungary, with its headquarters in Vienna and a network of lines running all through Austria, parts of northern Italy, and of what are now the independent countries of Poland, the Czech Republic, Slovakia, Hungary and the Balkan States. The kkStB (its German acronym) was established in 1884 and took into its embrace a number of struggling companies, and a heterogeneous collection of motive power. Moves towards standardisation began almost immediately. But it was with the appointment of Dr Karl Gölsdorf, an academically-trained engineer in the European tradition, in 1891, that Austrian locomotives began to assume a unique appearance, and to set new levels of performance. Gölsdorf, then thirty-two, had been supplementing his theoretical knowledge with seven years' practical experience at the State Railway Locomotive works. He was the son of the Chief Engineer of the Südbahn or Southern Railway, the other major system, who retained his post until 1907. Although Gölsdorf junior did not become titular head of the kkStB locomotive department until 1906, he had been given a free hand in locomotive design almost from the start, and in effect father and son reigned together over the imperial locomotive dominion for sixteen years.

His work thus began in the pre-superheater era, when compounding attracted many designers as a means of extracting more power from a given amount of steam, and so reducing fuel costs. Gölsdorf was among those who applied themselves to making this system work in practice as well as on paper.

In 1897 he introduced the Class 170 2-8-0, a design prompted by the building of the Arlberg mountain line from Switzerland via Bregenz into western Austria. Reliable traction was needed on the grades and in the long summit tunnel, and this two-cylinder compound proved to be extremely successful. With its flat 'baker's oven' smoke-box doors, wide-topped spark-arrester chimney, and a steam-pipe between its two lofty domes, it was an engine of striking rather than handsome appearance. In mechanical terms it was both up to date and powerful, with the largest heating surface of any locomotive in Europe, at 2,591sq ft (240.7m²). It coped easily with curves thanks to the Krauss-Helmholtz bogie, introduced in 1884, linking the leading single truck to the first coupled axle. Not far from Vienna was Munich and the Krauss works, where Dr Richard von Helmholtz was chief designer between 1884 and 1917. Remembered mainly for his very widely-used bogie, von Helmholtz was a designer of vast knowledge and he provided much of the theoretical basis for Gölsdorf's designs.

Up to 1918, 908 of the Class 170 were built, with some from all the main Austrian and Czech locomotive works, and they were used all over the Austrian empire. Even when superseded as an express type, they found varied employment on local passenger and freight services. Many were later fitted with superheaters. The last examples known to be in service were on the Graz-Köflacher Bahn in Austria, from where they were withdrawn in the 1970s. One from the GKB has been preserved, and the Czech Republic and Slovenia have one each.

Austria had already seen one or two 0-8-0 freight classes, but there was a need for more powerful goods engines, and Gölsdorf's first essay at an 0-10-0 came in 1900, with the Class 180, also a two-cylinder compound, designed to haul coal trains from the Bohemian mines. It too had an outside steam pipe between the two domes. It fulfilled the requirement of a light axle-loading (maximum 13.7t) and negotiation of 200m curves, helped by slight lateral play allowed in axles 1, 3 and 5. The drive was on the fourth axle. Although Gölsdorf has been credited with this development, it was actually pioneered in Vienna by John Haswell. Another outstanding success, 239 of this class were built and it led to a number of other ten-coupled types. No.180.01 is preserved in Vienna.

Among Karl Gölsdorf's earliest engines were 4-4-0s for passenger work, beginning in 1894 with the Class 6, and continuing in 1898 with the class 106. In 1903 the Class 206 appeared, representing the culmination of these express designs. They were all two-cylinder compounds, the cylinders outside, high-pressure on the right and bulkier low-pressure on the left, operated by an adapted form of Heusinger gear. Unlike its predecessor classes, the 206 had only a single dome and its exterior appearance was noticeably devoid of pipes and protuberances. In 1899 Gölsdorf had made a visit to Great Britain and had been impressed by the care taken by British designers with the external look of their engines. He did not imitate the British approach, but created his own unadorned style, giving his locomotives a sculptured look of a highly distinctive kind. Britain, too, was at this time the home of the most advanced crank axle technology; and Gölsdorf, realising that he had achieved about as much as was possible with two cylinders, was now contemplating four-cylinder locomotives, not on the Vauclain pattern but with high-pressure cylinders inside the frame, which meant inside cranks. In his system, live steam could be admitted to the low-pressure cylinders when full forward gear was engaged, for starting, through ports that would not be uncovered when valve travel was shortened as the driver reduced cut-off. The same applied in full reverse gear.

Four-cylinder compounds soon replaced the 4-4-0s on the international expresses; the first being a 4-4-2. Perhaps his finest express engine was the Class 110 2-6-2 of 1905; writing of Austrian locomotives, R.A. Whitehead refers to 'its authentic greyhound air', and it proved to be very free-running, helped by the fact that each cylinder had its own set of valve gear. Nevertheless, Gölsdorf pressed on for more power, with his celebrated Class 210 of 1908, which introduced the 2-6-4 wheel arrangement to the world – the four-wheel truck anticipating American 'super-power' practice by some seventeen years. This configuration was sometimes referred to as the 'Adriatic': its truck allowed for a big, wide firebox, 49.7sq ft (4.6m²), to burn the low-grade coal that the kkStB used. Unlike the 2-6-2, however, the bigger engine used a single piston valve to operate two cylinders at once on each side and as a result it was not so free-steaming.

Before 1911, Gölsdorf had used a steam drier, often in a pipe above the boiler, placed between two domes, but he abandoned this in favour of a superheater once the performance of the latter had been established, and from 1911 both 2-6-2s and 2-6-4s were built with superheat. The large-diameter driving wheels of the 2-6-4, 82.7in (210cm), suggested high speeds, but their purpose was in fact to reduce piston speed and consequent wear in the single large piston valve on each side. The maximum speed permitted in Austria was 62mph (100km/h), dictated by the lightweight track and steep curving gradients that prevailed throughout much of the system. Even the superheated version of the 2-6-4, Class 310, had a maximum axle load of only 14.4 tons (14.6t). 'It is hard to save a ton in one place but one can save two pounds in each of a thousand places,' said Gölsdorf, and those many weight-savings account for much of the stark but energetic look of these locomotives. The high-set tapering boiler somehow contrived to suggest that the engine had just taken a deep breath, inflating its lungs for action. Large acetylene headlamps completed the imposing effect. No. 310.123 has been preserved.

The need to use low-grade coal and often impure water had an impact on design. Among Gölsdorf's assistants was Johann Brotan, an Austrian engineer, who from 1906 developed a specialised boiler which was widely used on the Austro-Hungarian railways. The sulphurous Bohemian coal had a highly corrosive effect on copper fireboxes, and the Brotan system replaced the usual double firebox wall, copper inside and steel outside, with water 'legs' between them, by a set of close-packed vertical steel water pipes. As long as it remained sealed, this firebox worked well and generated steam quickly, but leakage of water, and of air through its outer casing, often reduced its efficiency. Around a thousand locomotives were fitted with it in Austria and Hungary, and it was used on some Swiss locomotives, but it aroused little interest elsewhere.

Gölsdorf was an anglophile, and took a strong interest in British locomotive practice. He sent accounts of his larger new designs to the *Locomotive* magazine, in London; an unusual procedure for a European engineer, and these were published with an amicable acknowledgement to 'our friend, Dr Gölsdorf'. Like his British counterparts, though, Gölsdorf was more forthcoming about the design features and planned services of his engines than he was about actual performance. But official policy about releasing information may also have played its part; the Austrian railways did not encourage too much public interest in their activities, and were far less indulgent of platform haunters and amateur photographers than the British. With many other friendly links, such communications came to an end with the outbreak of war in August 1914. In 1916 Gölsdorf died, aged fifty-five, but it was not until 1920 that the British railway press caught up with his death. He had designed more than forty classes of locomotive – the highest estimate said sixty – and set his mark on the steam power of all East Central Europe in a manner that few, if any, designers elsewhere could parallel.

NINETEEN

'Great Things Were Expected'

In the first decade of the twentieth century, most British railway companies were beginning to build larger locomotives, mostly 4-4-2s and 4-6-0s, for passenger service. In most cases, these were enlarged versions of what the designers, or their predecessors, had produced in the latter years of the nineteenth century, and the British 'line' prevailed. Typical of this was the Caledonian Railway's 903 class 4-6-0 of 1906, the same year as the Prussian P8. The CR had started a 'big boiler' trend in the 1895, and this small class of five inside-cylinder engines marks its fullest extent, with a heating surface of 2,400sq ft (223m²). Built at the line's St Rollox works in Glasgow, it was a distinctly old-fashioned machine in mechanism and also – though imposing and splendidly painted in royal blue – in appearance. But No.903 *Cardean* in particular had enormous prestige with the travelling public, as the regular engine on the Glasgow-Carlisle section of the 'Corridor', the 2p.m. Glasgow-London express, though its performance was unexceptional.

While old traditions persisted elsewhere, the foundations of British locomotive development in the new century were already in place at the Swindon Works of the Great Western Railway. The man in charge – Locomotive, Carriage and Wagon Superintendent – was George Jackson Churchward, who had joined the South Devon Railway as a premium apprentice in 1873, transferred to Swindon three years later, and worked his way up. Such a background – typical of British engineers until well into the twentieth century – might have produced a blinkered and traditionalist view, but Churchward was unusually open-minded for a British CME. He took a close and detailed interest in the designs and manufacturing processes being introduced by forward-looking companies in the United States and in Europe. Without introducing any radical departures from the fundamental Stephenson pattern, he subjected all aspects of the locomotive, and the locomotive building process, to thorough examination with a view to all-round improvement. Nor did he neglect the lessons of history, if the British locomotive historian J.N. Westwood is right in suggesting that: 'His espousal of generous steam ports and passages probably came from studying the legendary free-running of Crampton's locomotives.' His firm belief that great improvement was possible meant that in effect a revolution was in progress, and in this Churchward had his men behind him. In the words of the Swindon Works Manager, '... everyone was aware that boilers were being built from which great things were expected.' In 1906, addressing the Institution of Mechanical Engineers, Churchward said: 'The modern locomotive problem is principally a question of boiler.' If the boiler was unsatisfactory, it mattered little how good an engine might be in other ways. After intensive work, the GWR developed a tapered boiler, No.1 of what was to be a long continuous series. It owed more than a little to the American wagon-top pattern, and detailed drawings of an Illinois Central boiler had been carefully studied at Swindon in 1902. A steam dome was dispensed with, but it was matched with a Belpaire firebox, the combination providing good room for steam to collect above the water-level. Together with an operating pressure of 200psi ($14kg/cm^2$) or more, this assured plenty of steam. Another feature of this boiler was the top-feed system, through one-way clack valves. Though British designers generally avoided using feed-water heaters, this system, sending the feed water forward through a series of trays, did allow for a degree of heating before it mixed with the steam and boiling water around the firebox; and it was used fifty years later on British Railways standard locomotives. In 1903 Churchward fitted the No.1 boiler to Britain's first 2-8-0, the 28xx class, capable of hauling 1,000-ton coal trains between South Wales and London, and regarded as a giant among locomotives, as in British terms it indeed was.

Churchward had his full share of the competitive instinct. The GWR vied with the London & South Western Railway in running special mail trains between Plymouth and London in connection with transatlantic liner sailings, and he was determined to set the record. Aware that it would take some time for enginemen to get a feel for really high speed on the route, he told his Locomotive Inspector, George Flewellyn: 'Withhold any attempt at a maximum speed record until I give the word. Then you can go and break your bloody neck!' On 9 May, 1904, a Churchward 4-4-0, No.3440 *City of Truro*, heading the Plymouth–London 'Ocean Mail' of 148 tons (145.6t) on the hilly Plymouth to Bristol section, ran 127.8 miles (205.6km) in 123.25 minutes. During this run a speed of 102.3mph (164km/h) was recorded by Charles Rous-Marten during the 'hurricane descent' of Wellington Bank. For long it was considered the first authenticated occasion of 100mph plus, but later research has thrown serious doubt on the achievement. The true speed is likely to have been slightly under 100mph. *City of Truro* was in service until 1931 and saved from scrapping by a press campaign; it was restored to steaming order in 1957. In that year it reached 84mph (135km/h) on an eight-coach special train, on Wellington Bank, the high point of its epic run fifty-three years before. It is now kept at the GWR Museum, Swindon.

The 'City' class, introduced in 1903, shared some features of the old tradition – double frames and inside cylinders, with springs mounted above the running plate – with the new-style tapered and domeless boiler and Belpaire firebox. Churchward's new 4-6-0 design of 1902 had already revealed more drastic change. No. 100, *Dean*, set the pattern for the GWR's subsequent mixed-traffic 4-6-0s, with outside cylinders, having a long 30in (76.1cm) stroke, and Stephenson's link motion inside the frame. This was a composite frame, of British-style plate construction to hold the driving axles, and borrowing the American method of casting each cylinder in a single unit with half of the smoke-box saddle, resting on a bar bolted to the main plates. Somewhat horrifyingly to English eyes in Queen Victoria's last year, the running plate was raised, not quite to American heights, but almost fully exposing the driving wheels. The British locomotive was at last hoisting her petticoats. Still regarding the design as experimental, Churchward rebuilt one of the 4-6-0s, *Albion*, as a 4-4-2 'Atlantic' for purposes of intensive comparison both with the 'Dean' model and the three bought-in de Glehn compound 'Atlantics'. The first of these to appear, *La France*, drew 'astonishing crowds that had assembled alike at Paddington and along the line ... even the piles of milk-cans at the outer end of the down platform being converted into private boxes and dress circle for the occasion,' as Charles Rous-Marten wrote in the *Railway Magazine* of April 1904. With fortuitously good timing, the French engines caught the national mood: the French-British entente cordiale of 1903 was still very new.

By 1906 Churchward had resolved on simple-expansion 4-6-0s as the way forward. The decision was aided by the arrival of the superheater, which was fitted to new Swindon engines from that year. At first Schmidt's was used, but Churchward preferred a moderate degree of superheating, less fierce and abrasive than Schmidt's high superheat, and a 'Swindon' superheater, using fewer elements, was developed. Churchward was also among the first designers outside Germany to appreciate that to use the full potential of superheating, a reappraisal of the working of the valve gear was needed. The old form of Stephenson link motion, still in general use, relied on short-travel valves, which restricted the ease with which steam could be got in and out of the cylinders. Since 1903 the GWR had been fitting engines with larger valves with a longer range of travel, opening wider steam ports and allowing for admission of more steam. At the same time, they made possible a shorter 'cut-off' of the steam, to 20 per cent of the piston's stroke, or even less: very necessary with the expansive quality of superheated steam. Churchward was an early motor car owner and his close examination of the internal combustion engine is said to have led him to realise that the means of exhaust from the cylinders is at least as vital as that of admission. On the GWR 'Saint' class two-cylinder engines, Stephenson's link motion was adapted to allow for a short cut-off. On his four-cylinder 4-6-0s of the 'Star' and subsequent classes, Churchward used Walschaerts valve gear, again fitted internally. With the superheater, longer pistons, longer valve travel, and shorter cut-off, the driver had both more steam, more expansion of the steam, and greater control over its use. Extra valve length, and valve travel, was a matter of only an inch or fractions of an inch in machines of 70 tons weight, but those very small differences in apertures through which superheated steam was directed from a boiler at 225psi ($15.8kg/cm^2$), were of the greatest importance. An era was being inaugurated in which the performance and potential of a locomotive could be assessed more precisely, as well as dramatically increased. Science as well as engineering was now being exploited at the cutting edge of steam technology.

Churchward's 4-6-0s, nowadays seen as encapsulating the essential qualities of the English steam locomotive, were considered hideous when they were new; one designer of the old school, Patrick Stirling's brother James, wrote to Churchward to complain about his affront to British tradition. But their performance quickly silenced the critics. One of the directors of the GWR, inquiring of Churchward as to why new locomotives of the LNWR cost a third less to construct than the Swindon engines, is said to have been tersely informed: 'Because one of mine can pull two of their bloody things backwards.' Slow as they were to follow Churchward's example, other chief engineers found it impossible to ignore the GWR developments, both in terms of locomotive design and of the precision-based building methods maintained at Swindon. Right up to the 1930s, the Churchward design, refined and enlarged but not significantly altered by his successors, would set the standard by which other British companies' new locomotives were judged. Seventy-seven 'Saints' were built, up to 1911, and with their successors, the smaller-wheeled GWR 'Grange' and 'Hall' classes, two-cylinder types, totalling almost 490 locomotives, were by far the most numerous of the Great Western 4-6-0s. Although designated as mixed-traffic engines, their performance on express services could match that of the four-cylinder 'Star' and 'Castle' classes. The 'Saints' lasted until the 1950s, the last of them being scrapped in 1953. But even as they succumbed to the flame-torch, their mechanical genes were very apparent in the new 'standard' steam locomotives then being built for British Railways.

TWENTY

Big Boilers

For the locomotive designer, relieved of many problems by new developments, the main concern was how to provide the bigger boiler needed by modern operation. Locomotives could hardly grow higher or wider within their various loading gauges, but they could, and did, grow longer. Anatole Mallet had already shown one way in which boilers could be extended and greater power developed, and large Mallet articulated locomotives were used on many systems. In France, the *Est* railway imported two from the USA to bank heavy freight trains in the hilly districts around Verdun and Belfort. But the Mallet shared the same problem as rigid-frame locomotives: with the boiler sitting on top of the coupled wheels, its possible increase in diameter was strictly limited, especially when combined with the large-diameter driving wheels considered essential for speed. The English engineer Herbert Garratt developed a design which resolved this problem. The boiler was mounted on a low-slung frame suspended on pivots between two tractive units, and supplying steam via flexibly-jointed pipes to both. In this way greater diameter could be fitted into a constricted loading gauge. Born in 1864, Garratt had been apprenticed to the North London Railway works at Bow, and by his mid-twenties he was locomotive superintendent of the Central Argentine Railway. He gained more experience on a number of other overseas and colonial railways before returning to England in 1906. Retaining his colonial links, in 1907 he was inspecting construction at Beyer Peacock's works on behalf of the New South Wales Government Railway. In the following year he obtained a patent for his locomotive design. Just as Mallets had started small, so this other great articulated type had a modest narrow-gauge beginning, on a Tasmanian nickel-hauling line, in 1909. The first two Garratts (one is still preserved on the Festiniog line in Wales) were compound engines, with steam passing from high-pressure to low-pressure cylinders, and with the cylinders fitted at the inner ends of the bogie units. All subsequent specimens were to be superheated simples, with the cylinders at the outer ends (the drivers of the Tasmanians got very hot feet from cylinders placed under the cabs). A further advantage of Garratts was that they were normally designed to be run with the chimney at the rear – a benefit to crews on lines with long tunnels.

Garratt died in 1913, before his locomotives became widely-used. In the end over 2,000 were built, most of them by Beyer Peacock, to whom Garratt sold his patent. They promoted it as the Beyer-Garratt, which, with its double-hinged construction, could negotiate sinuous track and accommodate itself to sharp gradient changes, as well as develop very substantial power. It was also well-adapted to lightweight track, with its weight distributed over as many as sixteen axles. Although its pulling power on gradients was most appreciated, and consequently most were built to haul heavy trains at slow speeds, the design could be adapted to fast running. A real express version was built in 1930 for the Central Aragón Railway in eastern Spain, a 4-6-2+2-6-4 with 69in (175.1cm) coupled wheels; and a more striking and highly sophisticated design, also a 'double Pacific', was built in France for the Paris-Lyons-Mediterranean Railway's Algerian main line in 1938 (the PLM operated in Algeria until amalgamation with the state system created Algerian Railways in 1938). A blend of the Garratt format with French design, this engine was both elegant and muscular-looking, its cylindrical tank and tender of the same diameter as the boiler, giving it a more unified and streamlined appearance than other pre-war Garratts, with their square tanks mounted on the front bogie. It incorporated a variety of refinements, including electrically-operated, cam-worked Cossart valve gear, dual controls to help with driving in either direction, and fan ventilation for the enclosed cab. With 71in (180cm) coupled wheels, it was the fastest Garratt on record, achieving a maximum speed of 82mph (132km/h) on test between Calais and Paris. In scheduled service it ran the 262 miles (422km) between Algiers and Oran in seven hours. Like all engines with complex details, however, these required skilled maintenance, and in wartime conditions, this was not possible. By the mid-1940s, the Algerian Garratts were in quite decrepit condition, and all were scrapped by 1952.

North America, with its high clearances, never saw a Garratt locomotive, though many huge variants of the semi-articulated Mallet appeared there. Alco bought the rights to build Garratts in the USA, perhaps only to block other builders, and did not exploit them. Like great beasts enjoying mastery of their own territory, these types seemed to exclude one another. Garratts were supreme in South Africa. Portugal had Mallets; Spain had Garratts. The Ethiopian Railways acquired six large Italian-built Garratts after the Italian conquest in 1938. Numerous Garratts also ran in Australia and India. Surprisingly perhaps, their use in Britain was very limited. Only two types were built: a one-off engine for the LNER in 1925 and a class of 33 for the LMS introduced in 1927, intended for coal trains. Only one Garratt ever ran in Russia, where the railways had used articulated Fairlie and Mallet engines quite extensively in pre-Revolution times. In 1932 the Soviet Railways ordered a 4-8-2+2-8-4, designated Class Ya-01, from Beyer, Peacock, for testing on 2,500-ton coal trains. This was the largest steam locomotive to be built in Europe, with a total weight of 264.8 tons, though it was kept to a maximum axle load of 20 tons. Shipped to Leningrad, it was tested on the Sverdlovsk-Chelyabinsk line in the South Urals. There was some resistance to the design – Soviet engineers had a well-founded terror of seeming unpatriotic, as well as a belief in their own ability to provide solutions – and allegedly because its maintenance requirements did not suit the Russian operating conditions, the Ya was not approved. It remained a single-engine class, and the prototype was broken up in 1937.

The importance of good boiler design, and the demands of economics are illustrated by two Belgian locomotive classes, designed in that country's robust and highly individual tradition by J.B. Flamme, who took over Belpaire's chair in the State Railways locomotive department. The system now required new designs for both heavy freight and express passenger work, though not in large numbers; and Flamme designed a large new boiler, with a heating surface of 2,500sq ft (232m²) and 816sq ft (76m²) of superheating surface, and maximum pressure of 199psi (14kg/cm²) – an American-looking wagon-top design with a pronounced taper, to be shared by both types. However, the large-wheeled 4-6-2 of Type 10 had a longer frame than the small-wheeled 2-10-0 of Type 36, and while the boiler fitted the Type 36 exactly, the 'Pacific' was rather in the position of a big girl who has borrowed her younger sister's frock. There was an extent of uncovered frame. 'Space to mount a cannon' was one comment on the empty platform in front of the smoke-box of the 'Pacific', with the outside cylinders placed on either side and two further cylinders concealed beneath. But the Belgians had never balked at engines that looked strange to the foreigner. Flamme had looked long and hard at the French compounds, and, like his English contemporary Churchward, ended up by saying yes to four cylinders and no to compounding, for his express engines. The inside cylinders drove the front coupled wheels; hence their far-forward placement. Twenty-eight were built between 1910-1912 and proved their worth on heavy boat trains from Ostend into central Europe. By 1914 there were fifty-eight of them. After 1918 a number of alterations were made, including double chimneys, larger superheaters, the fitting of feed-water heaters, and smoke deflectors. German bogie tenders acquired as war reparations replaced the original small six-wheel tenders. Changes continued through the late 1930s, and the modernised Type 10s hauled expresses on the Luxembourg line until electrification in 1956; they were finally withdrawn in 1959.

On its appearance in 1910, Flamme's 2-10-0 was hailed as 'the biggest, strongest locomotive in Europe'. It too was a four-cylinder simple, the inside cylinders driving the second coupled axle; the outside cylinders driving the third. The initial order was for 136, of which all but two were delivered when the First World War engulfed Belgium in 1914. All were commandeered by the Germans, and their power became an asset to the German-Austrian alliance. Eighty were transferred to the Eastern Front in Galicia in north-east Austria. Some were captured as spoils of war by the Russians, who promptly designated them as Class F (for Flamme), converted them to the 5ft (152.4cm) gauge, and used them on the Ekaterina Railway. With some trouble, the Belgians eventually were paid for their engines by the post-war Soviet government. But fifty-eight of the class had in one way or another disappeared, and in 1922-1923 seventeen new members were delivered. From 1925 all were fitted with double chimneys designed by Flamme's successor Legein, and their superheating surface was increased to 816sq ft (75.8m²). Despite this, the Type 36s lacked the staying power of the Type 10s, and all were withdrawn by 1940.

Though large for its time, the Flamme boiler was of conventional design. A novel approach to maximising steam-raising capacity was devised by the Italian engineer Attilio Franco, and though first tried out in Belgium in 1932, its main development was undertaken by Franco in association with Dr Piero Crosti on the Italian state railways in the later 1930s. It was based upon deflecting the hot exhaust steam back through a large drum or pair of drums set parallel with the boiler, before ejecting it from a rearward chimney or vent at the right-hand side of the firebox. These drums were virtually secondary boilers, through which feed water from the tender was passed, and converted into steam at sufficient pressure to make its way into the main boiler. The effect was to maintain the boiler steam at a more consistent and also higher temperature than when cold or partly-warmed feed water was sporadically admitted. Secondary benefits, though important in hot, dry terrain, were reduction in the ejection of sparks and burning cinders, and conservation of water. The design resulted in one of the most unusual locomotive profiles ever seen. Unwary foreign visitors were often startled by seeing an engine which appeared to have no chimney: an omission otherwise seen only on very small industrial 'fireless' steam reservoir engines.

Strong claims were made for the system's ability to save fuel, up to 25 per cent compared to conventionally-boilered engines. After 1921, with its sights fixed on electrification, the FS produced no new steam designs, and instead various forms of modernisation were applied to existing locomotives. Over several decades, a large number of locomotives were equipped with Franco-Crosti boilers, the majority being Class 740 2-8-0s of 1922 vintage, which became Class 741. Mechanically the engines were unchanged, and there was no difference in the power output. The re-boilered engines were used interchangeably on the same schedules as the 740s. One expert commentator suggested that the claimed improvements owed almost as much to better boiler proportions and internal draughting as they did to the pre-heating system. Rather as the Brotan boiler hardly reached beyond Austria and Hungary, so the Franco-Crosti boiler had its greatest use in Italy, where the last of the class 741s survived until 1980. Several state railways, including the *Deutsche Reichsbahn*, built one or two prototypes without going for wholesale adoption. British Railways engineers built ten of the BR standard 9F 2-10-0s with Franco-Crosti boilers at Crewe works in 1955, and then reverted to conventional boiler design.

Up to the last, boiler design remained the crucial test of a designer's ability and a locomotive's quality. Computer-assisted design was not an option in the 1950s. Despite the valuable research work done under Wagner's direction on the *Deutsche Reichsbahn* on balancing the different elements forming the boiler, in the end there was no substitute for the expensive business of building a prototype and trying it out. For all W.A. Stanier's experience with Great Western boilers, the first boiler design of his LMS 'Pacifics' was a failure and had to be replaced, as were the first boilers of the New York Central's 'Niagara' 4-8-4s. The last British express design, the prototype No.71000 of 1953, suffered from flaws in the boiler design which were only cured when the locomotive was rebuilt by enthusiasts long after steam power had been officially abandoned.

TWENTY-ONE

Across Tundra, Veldt and Pampas

East and north of the Austrian Empire stretched the vast expanse of imperial Russia; its enormous distances considerably mitigated by the railways. Central control of such a strategic asset was as axiomatic for the Tsarist government as it would be for the Bolsheviks in 1918, although there were privately-owned railways as well as the state system. Locomotive design was a subject taught and researched at technical universities. It was not pursued in academic abstraction: the professors who sat on design committees had access to the building works and running sheds. Rather than rush into theory-based designs, they tended rather to dither and hesitate over the best way forward. Committees were not necessarily bad means of getting a design; they could prevent the kind of isolation from criticism which ultimately wrecked the reputation of Francis Webb, and if someone took a lead, a good design could be achieved. Perhaps the best sort of set-up consisted of a strong but open-minded chief, with a clear vision of what needed to be done, and how; with a team of able subordinates to back him. Such groups did occasionally occur. In the first decade of the twentieth century, the Russians were primarily concerned with the design of locomotives that could cope with heavy long-distance passenger trains and a steadily-increasing freight traffic.

Although British and American designs had been at the start of Russian railways, by the later nineteenth century French influence was strong, as it was in other aspects of Russian cultural and intellectual life. Compounding in the French style had been quickly taken up by designers like Aleksandr Borodin on the South West Railway. The expatriate Scot Thomas Urquhart, pioneer of oil-firing, was also an early compounder, beginning by converting an 0-6-0 simple to a two-cylinder compound in 1887. By the end of the century, the majority of his locomotives were either 2-6-0 or 0-8-0 compounds. The Class U 4-6-0, introduced in 1903, was a four-cylinder de Glehn-type compound, with the outside (high-pressure) cylinders driving the middle coupled wheels. Engineer A.O. Delacroa was responsible for the design of this passenger class, which was constructed up to 1910. Its maximum service speed was 65mph (105km/h). When new, the Class Us were sent east to the Ryasan-Ural and Tashkent railways. Two engines of this class played a part in Russian history – one headed the train which took Lenin on his fateful journey from Finland to St Petersburg in 1917; and another pulled his funeral train from Gorki to Moscow in 1924. Both are preserved, in Finland and Russia respectively. Locomotives had been saved from the scrap-yard before, because of their venerable age, or because they were the first of their kind, but this was preservation of a different sort: the locomotive U127 is seen as a national icon, symbolic of a convulsive and formative epoch, and a surviving participant of a definitive and profoundly historic moment in the nation's life; kept in much the same spirit as the embalmed corpse of Lenin himself. The lofty and commanding appearance of a Russian locomotive helped to create the right sense of awe.

Standardisation in Russia was such that only some two dozen locomotive types served all the needs of the vast system. As a result, some classes were built in very large numbers. The Class S 2-6-2 of 1912 eventually numbered more than 3,700 engines, and it was the staple motive power for passenger trains on most Russian trunk lines up to the 1960s. Its inception can be traced back to an Imperial Ministry specification of 1908, setting out the details of a 2-6-2 with a Helmholtz leading truck, a wide grate, and a Notkin-type superheater (an adaptation of Schmidt's). Compounding was now dropped, and the locomotive was to have two simple-expansion cylinders. The new design was first produced by the Sormovo Works in St Petersburg in 1910, and used for services around that city. It was recognised as an excellent one, and formed the basis of the S-class design. It was a big engine, with a haulage power equivalent to contemporary 'Pacifics', and its wide fire-grate, at 50.9sq ft (4.7m²) was at the upper limit for a single fireman. By 1918 around 900 had been built, and after a pause, construction continued under the Soviet government, at various builders, including the Kolomna works, south of Moscow. In 1925, Kolomna produced the Su, a longer-wheelbased version, and a number of other sub-classes appeared as the basic S was adapted to fit different requirements. Among these were the Class Sv (CB), built in 1915 to standard gauge and lower clearances for the Warsaw-Vienna line. Later, its axles were later widened to the normal Russian 5ft (152.4cm) gauge and it was transferred to the Moscow-Kursk line. Production of the S class continued, after an interruption during the Second World War, until 1951.

Inevitably it was Russia which produced the most numerous locomotive class of all, the famous Class E 0-10-0. From early in the twentieth century, the Russian railway bureaucracy had been pondering on how to fulfil the growing need for more powerful freight engines. The design that finally appeared in 1912 has been chiefly credited to the Polish designer V.I. Lopushinskii, a graduate of the St Petersburg Institute of Transport Engineers, and the first examples were built under his direction at the Lugansk works. They had two simple-expansion cylinders, fitted outside, operated by piston valves which were actuated by Walschaerts gear. The first of the class were oil burners, intended for the Far-Caucasus line. Coal burners, with larger cylinders, followed for the Northern Donetz line. With a maximum axle load of 15.9 tons (16.2t) they had very wide route availability. The area of the grate, 45.2sq ft (4.2m²), was large but still within the limits of hand-firing. At 171psi (12kg/cm²) the boiler pressure was moderate for the times; but this was a locomotive that would have to be maintained at a host of country depots far away from the major works, and higher pressure meant more rigorous servicing. With a heating surface of 2,231sq ft (207.3m²), and 547sq ft (51m²) of superheating, the Class Es usually had plenty of steam for the work they did.

From 1915, following successful performance of the first engines, production of the E class really got under way, at several different workshops. By 1923, about 2,800 had been built. The 1917 Revolution temporarily halted locomotive production in Russia, and the Soviet government placed huge orders with builders in Sweden and Germany for E class engines, 500 from Nydqvist & Holm of Sweden; 700 from 19 assorted German builders. These were built to the specification of the Lugansk engines of 1917, and the suspicious capitalist builders were said to have been paid with gold bullion. By 1926, the state-run locomotive industry had been established in Russia, and an improved version had been brought out by the Bryansk works, designated Eu, (*usilenny* = 'more powerful'). Between then and 1933 some 3,350 were built there and at the re-named Lugansk, now Voroshilovgrad; also at Kolomna, Sormovo and Kharkov. Its boiler pressure remained at 171psi (12kg/cm²) and its maximum axle load was 16.4 tons (16.7t). Meanwhile a further version appeared in 1931: Em 710xx, with a higher power-to-weight ratio, boiler pressure at 199psi (14kg/cm²) and maximum axle load 16.7 tons (17t) and about 2,700 of these were built, up to 1936. Many of these acquired a supplementary cylindrical water tank on the tender to increase their range; some E types were also fitted with condensing tenders for the same reason. In the early 1930s, the Murom repair works developed a heavier version, known as the Er, and around 850 of these were built at Bryansk and Voroshilovgrad. During 1944 some of the Er locomotives were rebuilt with 185psi (13kg/cm²) boilers, as originally designed for the Su 2-6-2, and these were designated Esu. In these the twin domes and sandbox were combined in a single boiler-top housing, and a clerestory-roofed cab was fitted, giving better ventilation. This style was perpetuated in E-class locomotives built after the Second World War. From 1945, with many locomotives destroyed or in dire need of reboilering or other major repairs, Er types were built in great numbers until 1952. Most of these were built not in Russia but in the satellite states, Poland, Czechoslovakia, Hungary and Romania. By 1960, the total number of the E class exceeded 13,000 locomotives.

Freight movement was the priority of the Soviet Russian railway system, and the E class was to be seen virtually everywhere on it. As late as 1959, engines first built in 1912 continued in use, and the class remained in service until the final abolition of steam power on the Soviet Railways. Though visitors marvelled at their size, these early twentieth-century Russian designs had no influence outside of Russia. Even the marine-style railings around the running plates – said to have been introduced as a safety measure by order of the Tsar Alexander II – harked back to the old British broad gauge, though its occasional use on some engines in France, like the US-built 4-4-2s of 1903 on the *Etat* railway, was probably a borrowing from Russia.

Elsewhere in the world there were wide-open spaces that approached the Russian scale, and where new or recent railway lines required modern motive power. Although Cecil Rhodes' notion of a Cape-to-Cairo railway through Africa was never to be realised, there were two substantial networks in southern Africa; one, centred on the British colony of Kenya, built to 3ft (91.4cm) gauge; the other, in British-controlled South Africa, to 3ft 6in (106.5cm). Both had lines that crossed wide areas of desert, and also long strenuous hauls up the coastal escarpments to the plateaux of the interior. There were no locomotive building works, and all engines were imported. British manufacturers were of course the prime suppliers. Pressure of business, and the 'bespoke' system, often made their delivery schedules very slow. Though Americans were adept at stepping into the gap, building engines at short notice for Egypt, Australia and South Africa at different times – and even a batch of 'Moguls' for the Midland Railway in England in the 1890s – their zealousness did not result in a permanent switch of customer loyalty. Like A.L. Beattie in New Zealand, his near-namesake H.M. Beatty, Chief Locomotive Superintendent of the Cape Government Railways, was well up to the mark on technical progress. His 4-6-0 design of 1903, constructed by the North British Locomotive Co., was the first British-built locomotive to have a Schmidt superheater, and the first superheated engine in South Africa. It also featured piston valves (using the version patented by Dr Schmidt) set above the two outside cylinders. The valves were actuated by Stephenson's link motion.

South Africa was to be one of the regions where the steam locomotive flourished best in the course of the twentieth century, not merely in numbers but also in terms of development and purposeful variation. On the other side of the South Atlantic Ocean, the story is less happy. Provincial governments owned and controlled the South African railways, but in South America, most lines were built and run by British, French or German companies as normal business propositions, expected to pay a dividend on the shareholders' capital. The British predominated, and a distinctly British style was maintained although generally the locomotives were larger than those built for home service, built to a broader gauge of 5ft 6in (167.5cm). Despite its portlier girth, and wooden cowcatcher, a visitor from the UK would have felt quite at home with an engine like the Class 12B 4-6-0 of the Buenos Aires & Great Southern Railway. Vulcan Foundry of Warrington built this class of eight two-cylinder compounds, without superheating, as an express type with 6ft (182.7cm) driving wheels. Its low running plate and wheel splashers are typically British. All were later converted to oil burning and superheaters were fitted from 1924. The maintenance difficulties of compound engines caused their withdrawal in 1937.

The typical freight engine of Argentina, and indeed of all Latin America from Mexico south, was the 2-8-0. The first were compounds, but after 1910, with the advent of superheating, compounding was generally abandoned on new engines, like the Class 11B 2-8-0, also a BAGS import, a large class numbering a hundred, built up to 1932. With fine impartiality for the time, the first order, in 1914, was divided between British and German builders. Though designated goods engines, they often worked branch passenger trains, as well as running freight over most of the BAGS lines. Most freight engines were two-cylinder simples, though the

Central of Uruguay had a three-cylinder simple 2-8-0, one of which remains in preservation.

Though primarily a country of grasslands and vast farms, Argentina also experienced rapid urban growth around Buenos Aires, and during the short heyday of the suburban steam train Vulcan Foundry supplied sixty-one of the Class 8E 2-6-4 tank engines in 1923. These three-cylinder simple-expansion engines worked heavy trains into and out of the capital's huge rebuilt terminus at Plaza Constitucion. Their side-mounted bunkers could hold 4 tons of coal, though all came also ready-fitted for oil burning.

Although there were brisk suburban services, and fast trains between Buenos Aires and Mar del Plata, the timetables of Argentinian and other South American railways were rarely taxing. The main problems of steam locomotive working were to do with water. Even when it was abundant, it was often rich in salts and minerals which caused priming and corrosion in the boiler, or lime which deposited scale and clogged the pipes. Boilers often had a short life. This was a difficulty with which British engineers were relatively unfamiliar, and although some depots had water purification plants, most were not considered large enough to justify this, and not a great deal was done to resolve it. After the early 1920s, the boom years of the South American economy had gone, and the railway companies were hard hit by reduced freight traffic. The purchase and maintenance of notoriously tricky devices like feed-water purifiers and heaters were beyond their resources. Instead they increasingly had to resort to a form of locomotive cannibalism, removing usable parts from the more decrepit members of a class in order to keep the others working. Lines of partially-dismembered locomotive corpses, lacking a pair of wheels, or rods, or regulator, rusted dismally on sidings near the running sheds. From the 1920s — and in sharp contrast to South Africa — the southern part of the South American continent made very little contribution to locomotive history. Apart, that is, from a brief, brilliant and very late flowering which is recorded in the Epilogue.

TWENTY-TWO

'Foreign Devils' Fire Carts'

Ever since the Mutiny of 1857, the railway locomotive had done more than any other single agent to hold British India together, making it possible for a few thousand administrators and officials to control a vast territory with its disparate peoples, languages and traditions. But as well as being the instrument of Empire, the locomotive was a friendly presence, which, like the holy cow, brought involuntary gifts to the poorest people. A visitor recorded this impression of a wayside station in *Rail Across India*:

> In front, lined up by the steam engine, women with pots and pans are receiving hot water from the boiler to do their washing etc. In some areas with a lack of clean water, this water will be used as drinking water. The water from the boiler is relatively safe and by comparison not worse than water coming out of the tap. After the train has left, women and children will search for coals between the rails.

Very early in the twentieth century, with the combination of impersonal benevolence and commercial calculation that characterised British rule in India, a committee of colonial administrators and locomotive engineers, based both in India and in Britain, got together to work out the specifications for sets of standard locomotives which would work on the two Indian gauges, of 5ft 3in (129.5cm) and one metre. These were the BESA (British Engineering Standards Association) engines.

The metre gauge (39.4in) was very important in India. The first metre-gauge line was opened in 1873, and the system quickly grew under a mixture of state and corporate enterprise. In 1969, the total route mileage stood at 16,060 miles (25,845km). Somewhat bizarrely, only the gauge was metric; every other measurement was expressed in imperial units of feet and inches. At first locomotive purchase was controlled by the various state governments, which had built the lines and leased them to operating companies; but from 1886, individual lines were allowed to order their own engines. This led to a wide variety of types and standards, though the old 0-6-0 F type still predominated. Around the turn of the nineteeenth century, increasing traffic and train weights, here as elsewhere, brought a need for more substantial motive power. In 1902, the Bengal & North-Western Railway ordered two 4-6-0s from Neilson & Co. of Glasgow. Class A, with 60in (152.3cm) coupled wheels and inside valve gear, was by some way the most massive engine to appear on the Indian metre gauge so far; Class B had 48in (121.8cm) driving wheels and Walschaerts valve gear, and was a closer indication of what was to come. In 1903, the British Engineering Standards Association set out a range of standard designs for Indian locomotives to run on the metre gauge; those for broad gauge engines followed in 1905. It included two 4-6-0 designs, one for a mixed-traffic type, and one for a passenger train engine, sometimes known as the 'Heavy Mail' engine. Accessibility of machinery, simplicity of operation, and a relatively light axle load (10 tons) were the keynotes. The tenders, Indian-style, had front canopies. The standard designs were widely adopted and served the Indian railways well for many years, though frequently very much adapted and modified as time went on. Large numbers of engines from the Indian metre gauge lines were shipped out for war work in Mesopotamia and East Africa during 1914-1918. Despite the formulation of new standard types (Indian Railway Standard) after the First World War, new engines continued to be built to the old BESA specification, with the addition of superheaters and piston valves, as late as 1939. BESA designs were constructed by various overseas builders – mostly British – as well as by Indian workshops like the Ajmer plant, the first Indian locomotive works, founded in 1902. The 4-6-0s numbered many hundreds, and many of these were still in active service well into the 1970s. Some Indian lines, like the Rohilkund & Kumaon, kept to 4-6-0s for all main-line traffic until the end of steam.

The old 0-6-0s badly needed to be supplemented by more powerful and faster haulage, and as part of the BESA programme, a two-cylinder, heavy goods type (HG) had been introduced to the Indian railways in 1906. The Class HS 2-8-0 of the Bengal-Nagpur Railway was a superheated version of it, originally with the Schmidt superheater, later with the adapted version patented by J.G. Robinson of the Great Central Railway in England.

The Bengal-Nagpur had 174 of these, making it the most numerous class on the line. The North Western had 132 of the HS class, and it was also built for several other Indian railways between 1913 and 1920. The builders were all British, Kitson of Leeds, North British, Vulcan Foundry, and Robert Stephenson & Co. Indian freight was hauled mainly by 2-8-0s, and by 2-8-2s on the metre gauge, until the introduction of diesel locomotives, which took place progressively in India, Pakistan and Sri Lanka from the mid-1950s.

Most people, when first introduced to the steam locomotive, reacted with interest or excitement; some with phlegmatic calm. Among all the peoples of the world, it was the Chinese who reacted in the most alarmed and negative way. Their ancient affinity with dragons might have suggested otherwise, but both public and official prejudice against 'the foreign devils' fire-cart' were strong. Railways were believed to create adverse *feng-shui*. Among the other reasons for hostility appear to have been the laying of rails across ancestral grave-sites; and their noise was held to disturb ancestral spirits. The first railway in China, which opened between Shanghai and Wusung in 1876, caused riots. Its first engine was a tiny 0-4-0, *Pioneer*, built in Ipswich, England in 1874, to help in track-building. An 0-6-0, *Celestial Empire*, followed to run the line from 30 June 1876. The name did not placate the opposers, and a fatal accident soon afterwards caused angry disturbances. The line was bought up by the Chinese authorities and closed in the following year. *Celestial Empire* and its carriages were shipped to Formosa (Taiwan) where the engine gradually rusted away. The next line was the Tangshan-Hsukochwang Railway, a narrow-gauge coal line. Traction was licensed only to mule-power, but the British resident engineer built a small engine, the 2-4-0T *Rocket of China*, without permission. When a Chinese inspection team was due to come, the engineer had to bury his locomotive in a hastily-dug pit, or so it was said. In fact this railway, set up by Chinese entrepreneurs, did lead to the building of others, though protest riots were frequent at the building of China's early railways. These were constructed piecemeal, by British, European and later Japanese interests, and locomotives were imported to work them. An eclectic collection of steam engines ran on the railways of pre-Communist China, and nothing that could have been called a typically Chinese locomotive appeared. It was only in the second half of the twentieth century that centralised control brought a range of standard types in vast numbers.

To designate the steam railway engine, most languages adopted some variation on the original 'locomotive', but in Bahasa Indonesia and its neighbouring language Bahasa Malaysia, as in Chinese, the term was more expressive of what it was than what it did: *kereta api*, 'fire chariot'. The great Indonesian archipelago was a Dutch colony until 1949, and Java in particular had a well-developed railway system on the 3ft 6in (106.5cm) gauge: the State Railways (*Staats Spoorwegen*), with a range of locomotives from small tank engines to articulated heavyweights. Dutch-owned and managed, it tended to buy from Werkspoor or German and Swiss builders. Like most colonial railways, it was usually short of capital, and its engines tended to have long life-spans. The forty Class B51 4-4-0s, two-cylinder compounds built between 1900 and 1909 for express passenger service, came variously from Hanomag in Hannover, Hartmann in Chemnitz, both German; and Werkspoor in the Netherlands. In the early 1970s around twenty were still active on local services. Their relative simplicity of construction helped, as did the fact that they could be employed, in their declining years, on light tasks. This was less possible for larger and more complex engines, like the Class DD50 2-8-8-0 Mallets of 1916. These were among the few American engines to run in Dutch Indonesia. Eight were built by Alco, with another twelve of the very similar class DD51 following three years later. Superheated compounds, they were built to haul heavy freight trains. The high-pressure cylinders were operated by piston valves, with slide valves on the low-pressure ones. All the DD50s were withdrawn and scrapped by the late 1960s. In the mid-1970s, 2-8-8-0 Mallets were still in use on the Indonesian PNKA system, but all were more recent German and Dutch-built DD52s.

Java was and is densely populated and in the 1920s the SS provided for fast short-haul passenger service, using tank locomotives of very similar sort to those which operated the same kind of traffic in Europe. On the SS, the Class C27 and C28 4-6-4 tanks were typical. The Swiss SLM works at Winterthur built the first fourteen C27s; twenty came from Werkspoor in the Netherlands, and five from Armstrong Whitworth in Newcastle, England. These last were delivered in 1922, by which time the enlarged C28 version, a fifty-eight-strong German-built class, had also come into service. Both types were widely employed on the Javanese network. The C27 had minimal side tanks, with most of its water capacity under the coal bunker, while the C28 had more conventional side tanks with downward-angled tops, though the tanks were not extended back alongside the wide firebox.

Large smoke deflectors also distinguished the C28, which was regarded as one of the fastest locomotives on the SS: its 59in (150.3cm) wheels took it up to at least 70mph (112.6km/h). This was said to be the Indonesian locomotive men's favourite engine type. Both classes were superheated two-cylinder simples, with piston valves operated by Walschaerts gear. Numerous examples of both survived until the last days of steam on the Indonesian PNKA system, working on slow-speed mixed-train services.

A very different tank type was the Class E10 0-10-0T of the Sumatra State Railways, also in the Dutch East Indies. They worked the steeply-graded, part-rack railway which had opened in 1891 from the port of Padang on the west coast up into the Equatorial mountain rainforest of the interior. Coal deposits made the railway an economic proposition, but such traffic required powerful locomotives. The first nineteen of the E10 class, later E101, were built by Esslingen in Germany in 1922. As elsewhere in Indonesia, the gauge was 3ft 6in (106.5cm). They were four-cylinder compounds, superheated, with outside valve gear and the inside cylinders driving the wheels that engaged on the central rack rail. They were very successful in their strenuous task, for as they wore out between 1964 and 1967, a further sixteen were built, as Class E102: ten from Esslingen and six from Nippon Sharyo in Japan. Mechanically the new engines were very similar to those of 1920s vintage, though more modern in appearance and with some significant modifications, including the fitting of Giesl ejectors and chimneys. These were the last rack and adhesion locomotives to be built for regular service.

The sound of the Mallet compound frequently joined the other noises of the rainforest, in Africa as well as South East Asia. In slightly less-demanding terrain than Sumatra, though still mountainous jungle, the Madagascar Railways (CFM), French-managed, were typical in their operation of 0-4-4-0 Mallet compounds. These dominated services on the metre-gauge lines until the arrival of diesel autorails. Most were built by the Société Alsacienne of Mulhouse, but Baldwin also supplied six in 1916. Fifty-six locomotives of this type were in use, of which about eighteen were super-heated. They were tank-tender engines, with side tanks alongside the boiler but also a four-wheel tender fitted with wood rails, as all were wood-burners with high spark-arrester chimneys. A few remained active on shunting duties in the late 1950s.

TWENTY-THREE

Engines of the Imagination

When he came to write *La Bête Humaine*, 'The Human Beast' in 1889, Émile Zola, already a celebrated novelist (and the son of a railway engineer) made at least one footplate journey between Paris and Mantes, recorded in *Mon Voyage*; spent a lot of time in the Gare St Lazare, that favourite terminus of painters, and accumulated a vast stock of background notes. There were good reasons, relating to the whole imaginative structure of his vast scheme of interlinked novels, why Zola could turn a locomotive virtually into a character; his concept of human nature was essentially mechanical. His vision of life was of the mechanical in the human, rather than of human qualities in the machine; his characters respond to regulation of which they are unaware, and move towards destinies not under their control. Unsurprisingly, he makes a point of recording the driver's empathy with his engine:

> On the dark horizon, there was no light but the bright gleam of signal lamps. He put on more steam for the stiff climb between Harfleur and St-Romain. Although he had been watching her ways for several weeks, he still felt uncertain about engine 608, she was too new, and her youthful skittishness still took him by surprise. That night especially, he felt as if she had strong ideas of her own, ready to set off on a wild highballing spurt if fed a few lumps of coal too many. Also, hand still on the regulator, and watching the fire, he was becoming more and more worried about his fireman. The tiny lamp on the water-level gauge made a dim light on the footplate, which was given a purplish tinge from the reddened glare of the fire-door.

However, this is no ordinary run, but the melodramatic climax of the story: the two men, once partners in making their engine give of her best, are bitter rivals in love. The fireman is murderously drunk, and they grapple on the swaying footplate as the engine races through the night with a packed troop train. In the end they pitch off together and are decapitated by the wheels. With no one at the controls, No.608 goes pounding onwards:

> At last the engine, self-willed, self-urged, could give way completely to the impetuous rush of youth, like an unbroken colt that has escaped its master and goes racing away over the level countryside. The boiler was stocked with water, the firebox had been fed and the coals were glowing fiercely; for the first half-hour, the pressure rose madly, the speed rose terrifyingly … The train passed Maromme like a thunderbolt. There was no whistle as it approached signal boxes or streaked through stations. It was racing at full tilt, the beast charging on, head low, uttering no cry, ignoring potential obstacles. On and on it ran, endlessly, as if maddened more and more by the hoarse urgency of its own breathing.

And so, with its passengers, 'a load of cannon-fodder', drunkenly singing patriotic songs, it disappears into the blackness of night, to a fate that may be imagined but is not recorded.

In its exploration of the relationship between man and machine, *La Bête Humaine* is a unique novel. To most authors as to most people, the locomotive was just a smoky contraption whose business it was to pull trains, and which was of no other interest. It had no claim on their imagination. This was as true of writers of non-fiction as it was of novelists – and why not? They were writing for the general public, the great majority of whom have a thoroughly utilitarian attitude to railway engines. The travel writer or even the novelist might cherish a private yen for locomotives but would let little of such schoolboyish interest show. In *The Great Railway Bazaar*, Paul Theroux's account of railway journeys across Europe and Asia, his only direct encounter with a locomotive – 'I had always wanted to ride in the engine [sic] of a steam locomotive' – is recounted as a disappointing episode, in the same tones of ironic self-deprecation as might be used to describe an unsuccessful attempt at seduction. Yet very occasionally in a novel one comes across a moment of movement and brightness, as the narrative meets the iron horse, not in anticlimax or a dully recorded event, but in an instant of vibrant vision. Here is a man trying to get across the track, just as a train is coming down:

… the gathering light bloomed quickly like a white fuse. Even as he saw the huge headlight emerge he twisted with the Doppler shriek of the whistle in his ears and leaped leftwards as the cleft and clamor of the freight locomotive hit him like a tarpaulin. As he stumbled back sidelong the loose-crying iron strode pistoning past, so deafening, so near, that it seemed Mattie had been shouldered aside by its shafts; he winced as the bright blinding firebox fled scorching past his hair.

This is from *Fools' Parade* by Davis Grubb, a thriller in which the railroad trains of Ohio and West Virginia form a constant moving background, rather as – in art – the tank engines of the Lancashire & Yorkshire Railway in the paintings of L.S. Lowry keep appearing between buildings and on long arched viaducts. And in rare moments locomotives can turn up in unexpected places. Occasionally, one such was the celebrated 'Cruiskeen Lawn' column in the *Irish Times*, written for many years by Brian O'Nolan under his pen-name of Myles naGopaleen. O'Nolan clearly felt the appeal of the steam locomotive, and indulged himself in writing about it by cleverly re-pointing the jargon to poke fun at himself as the steam-bore, writing 'For Steam Men':

> When it suits their book, some people do not scruple to drop hints in public places that I am opposed to poppet valves. It is, of course, a calumny. The fact is that I supported poppet valves at a time when it was neither profitable nor popular. As far back as the old Dundalk days, when the simple v. compound controversy raised questions almost of honour with the steam men of the last generation, I was an all-out doctrinaire compounder and equally an implacable opponent of the piston valve. I saw even then that the secret of a well-set poppet valve – short travel – was bound to win out against prejudice. I remember riding an old 2-8-2 job on a Cavan side-road, and my readers can believe me or not as they please, but we worked up 5392 IHP, with almost equal steaming in the HP and LP cylinders, a performance probably never equalled on the grandiose 'Pacific' jobs so much talked about across the water.

Such easy and gently mocking chat about the *arcana* of the steam locomotive was accepted by a readership which had been taught to expect all sorts of abstruse but comically-intended references. But the locomotive, in its rare figurings in modern literary usage, mostly retained the more sinister image which goes back to Charles Dickens. In André Malraux's novel *La Condition Humaine*, published in 1933 and describing the revolutionary events of 1927 in Shanghai, it is an overt symbol of death. The Kuomintang troops are rumoured to immolate their erstwhile Communist allies like the children of Moloch:

> 'They don't shoot them, they fling them alive into the furnace of the locomotive,' he was saying. 'Then that's that – they blow the whistle …'

– for the captive Reds, the distant wail of a locomotive whistle is a terrifying intimation of agonising death. Yet, anyone who has stood on a locomotive footplate would know that to thrust even one person through the fire-door would be extremely difficult. As a form of execution it is most improbable – there are many easier ways – but its symbolic value is very great. The steam locomotive, a potent element in modern industrial life, is used to consume, literally, those who stand against the system which exploits the workers. Malraux's vision, though it merely reflects propaganda statements of the time, seems now to anticipate the greater fires to follow; and the role of the locomotive in moving millions of captive people, in Germany, Poland and Russia, to a dreadful final destination. This is the other end of the line from its origin in the Romantic era, the heroic creation of mankind that would annihilate space and time and herald a better world. Yet even in that pristine era, as we have seen, it could stand for death and destruction, literally and figuratively. Equally, now, it was not always seen as an agent of doom. Like all powerful objects, it could lend form to a variety of ideas, emotions, even moods.

In his study of literary travellers, *Abroad*, Paul Fussell notes that: 'Ever since Whitman's "To a Locomotive in Winter" trains had been possible themes for art, but it's only in the '20s and '30s, with things like Spender's "The Express" and Arthur Honegger's musical composition Pacific 231, that the train theme became a fad. Graham Greene is said to have written *Stamboul Train* while listening to Pacific 231 on the gramophone.' Stephen Spender's poem 'The Express' was famous in its day, as much for its theme as for its treatment. It sets out to express the start and gradual increase of speed:

> *After the first powerful plain manifesto*
> *The black statement of pistons, without more fuss*
> *But gliding like a queen, she leaves the station.*

– and so out into the open country, 'Where, gathering speed, she acquires mystery' – this express's destination is no humdrum city, but night itself:

> *Ah, like a comet through flame, she moves entranced*
> *Wrapt in her music no bird-song, no, nor bough,*
> *Breaking with honey buds, shall ever equal.*

Even this rare attempt by a poet of distinction is more about the train than its locomotive. Before Spender, no serious English poet considered the locomotive, except for a few lines pronouncing a premature dismissal by John Davidson (d. 1908), the first poet to refer to 'the railway age', in The Testament of Sir Simon Simplex Concerning Automobilism: 'That railways are inadequate appears Indubitable now.'

Only in children's literature does the locomotive wear a friendly human face. In 1946 Graham Greene, a writer not renowned for cheerful optimism but who situated more than one novel on a train, published, anonymously, *The Little Train*: the story of an engine. In the previous year the Rev. F. W. Awdry had published *Three Railway Engines*, with *Thomas the Tank Engine* following in 1946, and many more to come. These brightly illustrated anthropomorphic stories captured children's fascination with trains and brought them down to their own scale, much as model railways did. Written originally by a vicar for his son, they show a railway-world with its own inhabitants and rules, yet superimposed upon our own; opening the pages we enter a world within the world, just as we do when passing through the booking-office. The engines have the ardours and emotions of children, while the Fat Controller can be relied on to keep their behaviour within bounds and maintain the whole system intact. Typecasting is heavy – Thomas is small and cheeky; Gordon the big express engine is loftily proud. Both must learn not to push those qualities to excess. The simple moralities of the Rev. Awdry capture an important aspect of the appeal of locomotives and railways, what L.T.C. Rolt described in *Lines of Character* as the blend of romantic freedom with classic order, within a self-contained and colourful world.

In grown-up literature as in life, the locomotive's prime purpose was to move characters from place to place, and occasionally knock them down. But it was so much a feature of daily life, in country as well as town, that insensibly, it entered that other realm of night, the human subconscious mind, and appeared in dreams. How many people dreamed of railway engines, and with what involuntary purposes these engines moved through the dreamscape, will never be known. But one of the prime subjects of dream research was the so-called 'Engine Man', an American entomologist who took the trouble to note down his dreams between 14 July and 14 October 1939, when he was in his mid-forties. Often his dreams were about locomotives, and sometimes he drew pictures of them in the margins of his dream journal. In 'Freudian' terms, of course, the steam locomotive is a fascinating construct, and it is easy to associate it in shape and movement with a phallic symbol. The motion of the piston rod is also, in a rather facile way, suggestive of sexual intercourse. No such associations were ever made by Sigmund Freud himself. But Ian Carter points out one rather extraordinary Freudian theory from the master's *Works*, Vol. 7: 'The shaking produced by driving in carriages and later by railway-travel exercises such a fascinating effect upon older children that every boy, at any rate, has at one time or another wanted to be an engine-driver or a coachman. It is a puzzling fact that boys take such an extraordinarily intense interest in things associated with railways, and, at the age at which the production of phantasies is most active (shortly before puberty) use those things as the nucleus of a symbolism that is peculiarly sexual. A compulsive link of this kind between railway-travel and sexuality is clearly derived from the pleasurable character of the sensation of movement.' Why boys alone should be supposed to derive such pleasure is only one of the oddities of this passage. But Freud lived too soon to read of the epiphanic moments described in such books as Hamilton Ellis's *The Beauty of Old Trains*, in which the authors record their first formative visual encounters with steam locomotives whilst still the merest infants, and before they had ever sat in a train. 'It was love – real passion – at first sight,' wrote David St John Thomas in *The Country Railway*.

The steam locomotive's presence in the mind is a subtle and complex one, a product of the senses, memory and imagination. It does not have a wholly masculine significance: its rotundities have a feminine quality, and no language refers to it as 'he'. The nature and function of the fire-door is entirely feminine: the fireman opens it and thrusts in fuel which is immediately consumed in a fiery womb; the product of this is sound, smoke, and movement as it bears him away on a ride which may be thrilling, or may be terrifying.

No wonder surrealist painters found it a source of inspiration. For them, it had an appeal of a different order to that which other modern artists had already felt. Among the first were the British Pre-Raphaelites, who, in the early stages of their movement, felt a moral duty to engage with modern themes. This yielded William Bell Scott's mid-century painting 'Iron and Coal', set on Tyneside, showing two children posed amidst a range of industrial activities, with locomotives in the background and a blueprint for a 4-4-0 in front. But the Pre-Raphaelites were unable to bear too much reality, even expressed in a romanticised way. In 1868, William Morris was insisting in *The Earthly Paradise*: 'Forget the snorting steam and piston stroke'. French painters took a more robust view. In 1873 Edouard Manet had painted 'The Railway', a scene in which a young girl gazes down through railings to a railway line from which clouds of steam rise, while her nurse or mother turns her back to it and reads a book. In the 1880s Claude Monet had painted his famous series of the Gare St Lazare, in Paris, recording its variations of light and colour as trains came and went; though his finest locomotive picture is 'Train Halted in Snow', intensely atmospheric with the headlights glowing palely through the grey murk. The Impressionists wanted to incorporate the railway as part of modern life, as well as to depict its novel atmospheric qualities. Vincent van Gogh's landscapes with railways, despite all the differences in style and setting, seem to reflect Turner's view of how the train marks a straight line across pastoral and traditional scenes, most notably in 'Les Moyettes', where the engine seems to cut its way through great vertical ranks of bare trees. Modernity was even more the theme of the *Futurist Manifesto* proclaimed by Tommaso Marinetti in 1909, though he chose strangely zoological metaphors: 'We will sing of ... greedy railway stations that devour smoke-plumed serpents ... deep-chested locomotives whose wheels paw the tracks like the hooves of enormous horses bridled by tubing...' Here the message was deliberately anti-classic. The locomotive was of today and should feature in today's art.

The Surrealists took a different stance. For them, everyday scenes and objects had an inner significance which could not be readily understood or described. Of his celebrated 1932 painting 'La Durée Poignardée', usually rendered as 'Time Transfixed', René Magritte later wrote: 'The image of a locomotive is immediately familiar: its mystery is not perceived. I decided to paint the image of a locomotive ... In order for its mystery to be evoked, another immediately familiar image without mystery – the image of a dining room fireplace – was joined.' The painting shows a locomotive rushing out from a fireplace beneath a mantelpiece which holds a mirror, a clock and two candlesticks, into a room which seems otherwise completely bare.

It is a Paris-Orleans Railway 4-6-0, vigorously puffing out steam. The time is 12.43. Magritte's professed aim in such juxtapositional paintings was to deepen knowledge, in a manner similar to the process of scientific research. This painting has certainly provided much food for thought. One wonders whether Magritte considered that the locomotive itself is a token of duration: its movements controlled by timetables, and its functions subject to measurement in every way. But his engine has no confining tracks. Around twenty years later, his fellow-Belgian, Paul Delvaux, spared time from some of his other obsessions to depict in dreamlike clarity of detail the Brussels suburban station of Watermal-Boistfort. In one of these paintings, 'Faubourg', an unmistakably Belpairean large-chimneyed 2-4-2 engine passes with its train before the inscrutable straw-hatted figure of a young girl. Unlike the intrusively thrusting Magritte engine, his appears as an absolutely integral part of the scene.

Other schools, Cubists, Expressionists, Fauvists, and unclassifiable artists like Edvard Munch, allowed the locomotive to penetrate their imaginations. But the total number of canvases is very small; other themes and forms were more compelling. Fine art relating to locomotives and railways is a slender peak rising above the vast output of the illustrators and depictors, often of great graphic talent, whose aim was to achieve a lifelike portrayal of a locomotive in action; or to convey a commercial message through advertising. The integration of the locomotive in public life was seen in the many more or less realistic depictions of brightly-painted engines hung on inn-signs outside many English pubs with names like 'The Railway' or 'The Locomotive'; and more impressionistic art-deco outlines of funnels, domes and wheels formed mural decorations in many a French Café-Terminus.

As in the previous century, musicians were among the twentieth-century creative artists who responded to the locomotive, though their enthusiasm is not always recorded in their music. Antonin Dvorak took time off from his post as Director of the New York Conservatory to go and watch trains at Grand Central Station, but opinion is divided between those who catch a whiff of steam and its rhythms in his symphonic works, especially the 'New World' symphony, and those who do not. Paul Hindemith studied timetables and played with model trains. Another musician who had a close affinity with trains was the English composer Peter Warlock (Philip Heseltine) who in 1912 wrote an article on the Van railway for *The Locomotive*, but did not publish music on any railway theme. The prime musical spokesman must be

Arthur Honegger, whose 'Pacific 231' mentioned earlier was composed in 1923. After its première, he said:

> I have always been passionately fond of locomotives. For me they are living beings and I love them as others love women or horses. What I sought to do … was not to imitate locomotive noises, but the translation of a visual impression and physical delight through musical construction.

A rural train ride in Brazil in 1930 was the inspiration of Hector Villa Lobos' 'The Little Train of Caipira', with rhythms recognisable as those of the little struggling puffer. In 1936 Benjamin Britten supplied a fine score to the British Post Office documentary film *Night Mail*. Otherwise, railway themes flourished best in 'light music' like Vivian Ellis's catchy 'Coronation Scot' of 1936. A railway enthusiast, he wrote the tune for his own diversion, and was pleasantly surprised by its popularity. Then in 1948, Pierre Schaeffer introduced musique concrète with *'Etudes aux Chemin de Fer'* – 'Railway Studies' from trackside recordings of steam locomotives at work (such recordings soon became popular in their own right among locomotive enthusiasts). Schaeffer's tradition was maintained in 1998 by László Sáry's *Locomotive Symphony*, an electro-acoustic composition assembled from actual locomotive sounds (Sáry's father had been a station-master in Hungary), but these were by no means mainstream musical works.

In an impressive piece of research, Philip Scowcroft has noted over 600 musical compositions on railway themes. Only a modest proportion of these address the locomotive directly; most of them have to do with trains, or railway incidents and accidents. In the last reckoning, the presence of the steam locomotive in the fine arts is a very small one: none of them would be any different today if the locomotive had played no part – with the possible exception of blues, in which the American steam railway maintains a presence, though mostly a background one. But it is perhaps more remarkable that it features at all. In the history of one modern art form, however, it is assured of an honoured place.

In 1895, the first moving films were made by the brothers Auguste and Louis Lumière. The very first was simply a scene of workers leaving their factory, but it was followed by a sequence filmed at the wayside station of La Ciotat, near Marseilles. When first shown it was known as 'Arrival of a Train at La Ciotat Station', but it was later more grandly, if less accurately, called 'Arrival of the Paris Express'. The star was a 2-4-2 locomotive of the PLM railway. When the movie, silent of course, was shown in London in 1896, the live musical accompaniment incorporated a hissing release of compressed air, bringing such a sense of realism that many of those watching thought the locomotive was going to roll right over them. The steam locomotive was a gift to early film-makers. It expressed movement as it travelled along: its spoked wheels revolved, its rods moved, it puffed out smoke. It gave wonderful action shots, and stopped promptly when required to. And while the locomotive itself was hard-edged and solid, its steam provided a soft, contrasting, enveloping diffuseness. The first feature film using locomotives was *The Great Train Robbery* of 1903, made on the Delaware & Lackawanna Railroad, using Baldwin 4-4-0s. The D&L was quick to appreciate the power of the new medium. Edwin S. Porter, director of *The Great Train Robbery*, had made a publicity film for them in the previous year, entitled *The Road of Anthracite*. This showed a journey taken by an attractive young lady, 'Phoebe Snow', on the line. Her white dress was still pristine when she arrived at her destination. The underlying message, which might as well have been the title, was No Smuts! Another film venture of Porter's, in 1902, was to make a series of journey films for Hale Tours in the USA. For these he used a camera mounted on the locomotive's pilot to give an engine's-eye view of the oncoming and passing scene. For the spectator, it was excitingly like being perched on the front of a racing train.

In a supplement to *Steam Magazine*, in 1995, the film historian John Huntley recorded over 230 movies with a railway theme. Some were documentaries, like the famous British *Night Mail* of 1936, some were dramatic re-creations of historical events, the majority were pure fiction. Often these were of the most melodramatic kind. Raids and robberies were usually involved. Anguished heroines were bound to the rails as the iron point of the cow-catcher came around the distant curve; stunt-men made flying leaps from car to car, or on and off the train from horseback; or ducked just in time for the tunnel. All these became standard items of popular imagery, as much associated with the train as any of its real everyday business. Stories involving drunk drivers, as in *The Flying Scotsman* of 1930; or mad ones, as in *The Last Journey* (1936) traded on the half-hidden fears of the travelling public. In the early days of movie-making, and for a couple of decades after, there was no lack of elderly locomotives, particularly in the USA, to re-enact historic scenes. Buster Keaton found his locomotives for *The General* on a lumber line in Oregon; they were 4-4-0s of 1870, little different to the true protagonists. By 1956, however, when *The Great Locomotive Chase* was re-made, facsimile engines had to be built.

Before long, film directors were demanding real smash-ups, and railway companies with superannuated engines were ready to oblige. Keaton crashed two, one of them by an unintended accident. The most dramatic was probably the triple crash in *The Train* (1964), laid on by the SNCF. There was a real accident when a locomotive, coming up too fast, smashed several cameras set up to film its approach. Directed by John Frankenheimer, this film became celebrated among locomotive admirers for its attention to correct detail. Often, directors had been untroubled by technicalities of interest only to railwaymen and enthusiasts. Alfred Hitchcock, though a master of train-situated drama, cared little for continuity of detail and was unrepentant to pedants who inquired how a Great Western engine could be hauling the Scotland-bound express in *The Thirty-Nine Steps*. The LNER provided facilities for the shooting of *The Flying Scotsman*, but H.N. Gresley was annoyed when the film showed a locomotive and its train parting company, and the train continuing to move: 'Apparently the LNER has not yet discovered the vacuum brake.'

One of the very few films in which the locomotive effectively had the starring role was the British comedy *The Titfield Thunderbolt* of 1952, in which a village community fights a rascally bus company to save its rustic branch line from closure. The title role is played by the preserved 0-4-2 *Lion*, built in 1838 for the Liverpool and Manchester Railway and the oldest working locomotive in the world. It is an exercise in pure nostalgia, of course – the gallant veteran, despite all opposition and adversity, puffs triumphantly into the junction to connect with the express; but at the time the film was made, the steam locomotive was already in full retreat. Its enduring appeal was still present at the start of the twenty-first century, when the immensely popular 'Harry Potter' stories and films used the steam-hauled 'Hogwarts Express' to transport the hero and his school-mates into the magical domain. In a wizarding context, anything is possible, including a GWR 'Castle' departing from King's Cross Station.

TWENTY-FOUR

Bigger Engines

The perceived advantages of more wheels and greater steam-raising capacity go back to the introduction of the 'Consolidation' in 1886, but the introduction in North America of heavier freight cars and of a more frequent pattern of long-distance bulk freight trains carrying oil as well as agricultural products and minerals, created a demand for power beyond what a 2-8-0 could provide. A precursor of the 'big engine' men was A.J. Stevens, master of machinery on the Central Pacific Railroad from 1870, who believed in building for himself. In 1882 the line's Sacramento shops turned out No.299, a 4-8-0, which proved effective on the mountain sections. He followed it with the legendary *El Gobernador*, a 4-10-0 built in 1883, the biggest locomotive in the world, weighing 146,000lb, but unfortunately its boiler failed to provide enough steam to satisfy its great 21 by 36in cylinders. The introduction and success of the 2-8-2 'Mikado', from 1897, have already been described.

Even as the 'Mikado' was being established on the standard gauge, however, bigger things were already on the way. The arrival in 1902 of the 2-10-0 compounds on the Atchison Topeka & Santa Fe Railroad has been noted; only a year later the 2-10-2 'Santa Fe' type was introduced on the same road. Seventy-six of this class were built, all for freight service; the first forty as coal burners; the rest oil-fuelled. The maximum boiler pressure was 225psi (15.75kg/cm²), and the driving wheels were of 57in (144.8cm) diameter. All were later converted to two-cylinder, simple expansion types, and with large cylinders, 28 by 32in (71.8 by 82cm), their nominal tractive effort was raised to 74,800lbs (33,922kg). The 'Santa Fe' type was undoubtedly a big engine, and it was the main freight hauler on many lines up to around 1930. Over 200 were eventually in use on the AT&SF itself. But it represented only a stage in the continuous push towards greater power. A bold effort was made in 1913 with a 'triplex' locomotive whose massive boiler was intended to power three sets of cylinders and driving wheels, which extended beneath the tender. This was the Erie Railway's Class P-1 2-8-8-8-2. Three engines of this configuration were built by Baldwin for the Erie and another, a single 2-8-8-8-4, for the Virginian Railroad, based on patent designs granted to George R. Henderson, then Consulting Engineer to Baldwin. His aim was to maximise the adhesive weight, and therefore the pulling power, of a big road engine. The six cylinders were of identical size and cast from the same pattern. Steam went direct from the boiler to the middle pair, which acted as high-pressure cylinders; they exhausted into the low-pressure cylinders to front and rear. Exhaust steam from the front cylinders then passed into the stack in order to create a draught for the fire; exhaust from the rear passed through a feed-water heater and out through a pipe behind the tank. The total length was 105ft 1in (32.03m). By now, locomotive naming was a rarity in the USA, but the first Erie engine was named *Matt H. Shay*, in honour of its oldest living engineman. It demonstrated its power on test by hauling a train of 250 loaded cars, weighing 17,912 tons (18,203t), and 1.6 miles (2.5km) long. The Erie Triplexes, with a tractive effort of 160,000lb (72,562kg), and weighing with their tenders 864,400lb (392t), were intended as pushers, or banking engines, on the line's Gulf Summit grades. Unfortunately, in normal action the steam distribution system was inadequate and performance was far below expectations. They were dismantled between 1929-1933, and the Virginian engine was converted to a 2-8-8-0.

These engines were built for slow, heavy slogging, but there was also a need for big engines that could move main-line freight along at a good rate. Heavy refrigerator cars in particular needed to be moved at passenger train speeds from the fruit farms of the west to the markets of the east. Passenger cars were also becoming more massive, with steel bodies replacing wooden-sided vehicles. In 1911, a new configuration for a fast locomotive was built by Alco in Schenectady – the 4-8-2 or 'Mountain' type. The first was for the Chesapeake & Ohio Railway, to haul passenger trains over its Clifton Forge Division in the Allegheny Mountains. At the time it was claimed as the most powerful non-articulated engine in the world, and the type became recognised as valuable where adhesion and tractive power were needed as well as speed. The driving wheel diameter of a 'Mountain' was generally around the 6ft (182.9cm) mark, a mid-way point between a typical freight engine and a passenger express locomotive. In 1918 it was one of eight standard types designated by the wartime US Railroad Administration, and many were built for lines with mountain sections. The Class M1 4-8-2 freight locomotive of the Pennsylvania Railroad began as a single test engine, at the PRR Juniata workshops in Altoona, but 200 others followed. In what was now standard US practice, it was a two-cylinder simple, with Walschaerts valve gear operating piston valves. The boiler tapered up from 84.5in (214.4cm) behind the chimney to 96in (243.6cm) and there was a long Belpaire firebox, supplied by duplex stokers. The running plate was stepped up to accommodate the air compressor equipment for the brakes. Braking power was as vital a feature of these locomotives as traction, for negotiating the long descents with trains of 140 coal hopper cars loading up to 4,700 tons. The 4-8-2 remained a popular type in the USA and Canada until the end of the 1920s, when most lines took up the 4-8-4, with its capacity for an even bigger firebox.

Essential to this process of growth of the locomotive was the corresponding growth of its tender. The later years of the 1900s saw a great leap in the size and capacity of the American tender in order to keep pace not only with the mechanical stoker and a much larger firebox, but also with a longer running schedule. The American tender in 1900 was not much bigger than the larger European version. Both ran on two four-wheel bogies, and might hold around 6,000 gallons of water and 10 tons of coal. By 1920 the European tender had scarcely increased in capacity but the American one had doubled its load of water and coal, and was normally mounted on two three-axle bogies. Tenders presented some difficulties of design: in a large square or oblong tank, water could move from side to side with enough force to cause derailment unless baffles were built in. Their great weight added to the engine's load. In the early 1900s, Cornelius Vanderbilt, grandson of the railroad magnate, patented a type of tender which carries his name: essentially a huge cylindrical tank with a coal (or oil) bunker mounted on its forward end. The weight-saving Vanderbilt tender was widely used both in the USA and in other countries, notably South Africa, where long distances were run by powerful locomotives through arid country. Greater capacity was always wanted – by the later 1920s an American 2-8-4 like the Erie Railroad's new 'Berkshire' had a tender holding 20,800 gallons and 28 tons. The peak was reached in the late 1930s with the Union Pacific's 'Challengers' and 'Big Boys', whose tenders had a capacity of 25,000 gallons of water and 28 tons of coal, and which were supported on seven axles.

In Europe, railways were opting for ten-coupled engines for heavy freight, especially when mountain terrain had to be traversed. Switzerland, though a small country, had numerous mountain lines, and also was responsible for the passage of heavy trains between Italy, France and Germany. The Class C5/6 2-10-0 of Swiss Federal Railways was the heaviest and most powerful steam locomotive to operate in Switzerland. Bigness of course is relative; it was almost exactly half the weight of the Pennsylvania M1 at 282,240lb (128 tonnes), and was hand-fired. As was usual in Switzerland and other central European countries, the design began with a work specification. Its predecessor, the Class C4/5 2-8-0, like it a four-cylinder compound, was specified as requiring 10,000kg of nominal tractive effort; or the ability to haul 200 tonnes up a 1 in 38 gradient at 12-15mph (20-25km/h). The bigger engine was required to work trains of 300 tonnes up a similar gradient at 15mph (25km/h). A tractive effort of 45,000lb (20,408kg) was needed, but by now a superheater was part of the specification. Thirty were built between 1913 and 1917, for passenger and goods trains over the Gotthard line. The first two were four-cylinder simples, later rebuilt as compounds; the rest were compounds from the start, with the high-pressure cylinders inside the frames. These drove the second coupled axle; the outside, low-pressure, cylinders drove the third. As very often with European locomotives, the front carrying wheels formed a Helmholtz bogie with the front pair of coupled wheels, giving some flexibility to the long wheelbase. It proved a highly reliable engine with ample power for its task: but this was essential. The thought of a locomotive stalling on an uphill grade in an Alpine tunnel several kilometres long was not a comfortable one.

Tunnels and steam locomotives were not a good match. The smoke problem was less acute where it was possible for a driver to shut off steam and let his engine coast through the bore, but when effort was necessary, it was extremely difficult to avoid producing smoke unless the engine was burning very high quality coal. Sometimes ventilation shafts could be provided, but often smoke and fumes remained trapped in the tunnel, making an infernal and scarcely breathable atmosphere for the next train. Drivers and firemen covered their faces with damp cloths and even lay down on the cab floor. Cases of near-asphyxia were frequent. The problem was not confined to mountain lines. When trains ran with great frequency, hardly any smoke dispersal took place even if, as in the tunnels under London, some ventilation was provided. 'As we grope our way into a mirk wherein the gas jets serve only to emphasize an ever-deepening gloom, the brimstone breath of the tunnels engulfs us...' wrote the historian Hamilton Ellis about the world's first underground railway, the Metropolitan, beneath central London. Its first custom-built engines, supplied by Beyer, Peacock of Manchester in 1864, were a 4-4-0 tank design, whose most distinctive feature was a condenser apparatus, intended for use in the tunnels. Exhaust steam was blown from the blast-pipe, through long lateral tubes, into the tank. This helped dissipate steam, and warmed the feed water, but did nothing for smoke emission. The original engines did not even have cabs.

Around 1900, the main British railways had a huge fleet of 0-6-0 freight engines which undertook almost all tasks from shunting and lightweight local pick-up goods trains to long-distance freight, often working double-headed in the latter role. Referring to a later period, the writer J.B. Snell commented that: 'Britain's railways were unique in that, like no others in the world, the largest and most powerful locomotives in the mid-twentieth century were used for passenger traffic. It is an exaggeration to say there had been no progress in freight locomotives since 1860; but there had been remarkably little.' His generalisation sweeps over engines such as Jones's 'Big Goods', but the Highland initiative was not copied, and further progress was marked only by the Great Western Class 28xx 2-8-0, introduced in 1903, until the Great Central Railway produced its 2-8-0 in 1911. The GCR needed a heavy engine for freight traffic in its Yorkshire-Nottinghamshire industrial heartland. The engine, designed by J.G. Robinson, had two simple-expansion outside cylinders driving the third pair of coupled wheels. Inside admission piston valves were placed between the frames, worked by a version of the Stephenson's link motion. The boiler pressure was modest for the time, at 160psi (11.2kg/cm²), as was its grate area of 26.25sq ft (2.4m²). During the First World War, when the need for locomotives to support overseas campaigns arose, this straightforward design was chosen by the government's Railway Operating Department, which had 521 built by several builders as well as the GCR's own Gorton works at Manchester. They were fitted with Westinghouse brake pumps to work French and Belgian stock, and also with steam heating apparatus for use in troop trains. After 1918, a number of British railways acquired the ex-ROD engines, and others remained in foreign service, both in Europe and in Mesopotamia and Persia.

At the same time, at the opposite side of Europe, the Bulgarian State Railways, first set up in 1888, were in need of a heavy freight locomotive, and, with a generous loading gauge, went for something a good deal more massive. Bulgarian locomotive practice, though strongly influenced by Austria and Germany, was distinctive in many ways even though the country had no locomotive works of its own. With no front plating, and the tail-rods of its four in-line cylinders protruding forwards like gun barrels, the Class 900 compound 2-10-0 of 1913 confronted the viewer like a weapon of war. Seventy were built, by Hanomag in Hannover. The high-pressure cylinders were inside, and a common piston valve drove the high- and low-pressure cylinder on each side. All cylinders drove the third coupled wheels, which had no flanges. Many of the class were fitted with chimney lids and a backwards-angled, smoke deflecting semi-collar behind the chimney. Some survived on remoter lines of the Central and Eastern operating districts into the 1960s. These were the most powerful Bulgarian engines before the modernisation policy begun in 1930, which produced a formidable 2-12-4 tank type in 1931, of German design and built by the Polish Cegielski works. With a nominal tractive effort of 70,200lb (31,826kg) they were employed on heavy coal trains. Bulgaria's northern neighbour, Romania, possessed two locomotive works, Malaxa and Resita, but tended to make use of German or Austrian designs, as in the Romanian State Railways Class 142 2-8-4 of 1936, which originated with the Austrian Federal Railways. This and other large Romanian locomotives incorporated an original feature, which was also used to some extent in Germany and Bulgaria. Developed by a Romanian engineer, H. Cosmovici, it was a dual coal-oil firebox, into which heavy oil could be jetted above the burning coal, to increase combustion when the locomotive was being worked particularly hard.

The British engineers Francis Trevithick and Walter Smith had been at the start of Japanese locomotive building, and before 1912 the Japanese National Railways had imported a variety of types, both British and American. But it was American design that was to prevail in Japanese locomotive building. The first big home-produced engine was the Type 9600 2-8-0 freight locomotive of 1913, built by Kawasaki Zosen Shipyard, Kisha Seizo Kaisha, and JNR's own shops at Kokura. The JNR's gauge of 3ft 6in (106.5cm), and tight clearance restrictions prevented an American height and bulk, but American influence was plain, from the bar-frames up to the boiler-mounted sandbox. The design was a success and 770 were built up to 1926, making it also Japan's first 'mass-produced' engine, and the first to be exported.

In most countries, the 2-8-0 and 2-8-2 remained the most common heavy freight locomotives. The PLM railway in France had 607 'Mikados'.

Argentina also had 4-8-0s, and the South African Railways favoured the 4-8-2, of which over 1,300 were acquired from 1904 onwards. Some railways also built or imported ten-coupled engines where greater power or lighter axle-weight were needed: Russia with its E class was by far the most notable. On one or two European railways, something with even more coupled wheels was tried; a single superheated four-cylinder compound 2-12-0 was produced by Karl Gölsdorf in Austria in 1911, and the German Württemberg Railway had a class of the same configuration.

TWENTY-FIVE

Express Elegance

The 'Pacific' had its beginnings in a need to provide good traction and a wide firebox for an engine that was certainly not expected to attain great speeds. But within a very few years, it was established as the big express engine. In some countries, including Germany, Great Britain, and Finland, it would retain that role to the very end; and for a period it was supreme, world-wide, as the peak of combined speed and power. Now, while freight locomotives might be supposed to labour obscurely, often at night, and out of the public eye, this could not be said of passenger engines, especially those that pulled express trains. Such trains, especially when providing international services, had long been considered special. Companies like Pullman and Wagons-Lits had been set up specifically to prove luxury transport on such routes. And even without the benefit of special rolling stock, prestige clung to the express trains that linked great cities, New York and Chicago, Oslo and Stockholm, Sydney and Melbourne, Warsaw and Berlin, London and Edinburgh, Cape Town and Johannesburg. For such trains, the locomotive of choice was for many years the 4-6-2.

The first European 'Pacific' was the Class 4500 of the Paris-Orleans Railway, introduced in 1907. With long inter-city runs through sparsely-inhabited countryside, the French railways had a need for large passenger engines, and this long, rangy-looking design was developed by the P-O and *Société Alsacienne* at Belfort, though the first thirty were built in the United States, by Alco's works in Schenectady. A four-cylinder compound of de Glehn-du Bousquet type, the class numbered seventy by 1908, and a further thirty, with superheaters, were delivered in 1910. All the later engines were built at Belfort. Piston valves, still relatively new, worked the high-pressure cylinders, while slide valves worked the low-pressure ones.

Soon after the French one came the first German 4-6-2, built for the Baden State Railways by Maffei in Munich, in 1907. In the early 1900s the firm was flourishing, with engineer-designers of great ability in Anton Hammel and Heinrich Leppla. They had purchased and explored Vauclain and de Glehn compounds from the USA and France before developing their own family of compound locomotives. These had bar frames, with the low-pressure cylinders outside. Their most celebrated locomotive of this type was the Class S3/6 4-6-2 for the Bavarian Railways, in 1908, of which 159 were built up to 1931, all at Maffei's Hirschau works except for the final eighteen, built by Henschel at Kassel. All four cylinders drove the second coupled axle, with the inside cylinders operated by the outside valve gear by means of rocker shafts. The big low-pressure cylinders, forged in a single block with the steam-pipes, combined with the conical smoke-box door and, untypically for Germany, a shapely, lipped chimney, gave the front end a powerful but elegant air. Small but significant details in the right place could have a large effect on a locomotive's appearance, and the chimney of the Bavarian engine gave it a touch of sophistication and refinement compared to Prussian locomotives with their no-nonsense stove-pipes. They were also quite light-footed, with a maximum axle load of 18t. This quality, combined with an impressive reputation for power, speed, economy and reliability, induced the *Deutsche Reichsbahn Gesellschaft* to order forty new S3/6s, for service on other lines.

The design of the S3/6 confirmed the establishment of an 'American' approach to design in Germany. Bar frames became standard, along with high running-plates and outside valve gear, and the somewhat English look of many German locomotives gradually vanished. The S3/6 has been described as one of the truly great designs of the early twentieth century. It displayed the ability most often sought but not always achieved, of hauling heavy trains at a consistent and high speed. Five engines were destroyed in the course of the Second World War, but the rest remained in post-war service. Thirty were rebuilt by the *Deutsche Bundesbahn* with larger, all-welded boilers between 1952 and 1956. Their final duties were still in hauling express trains, on the Ulm-Friedrichshafen and Munich-Lindau lines. The last were withdrawn in 1966 but numerous examples have been preserved.

Britain's first 'Pacific' type was built by G.J. Churchward at the Great Western Railway's Swindon works in 1908, but remained a lonely one-off. A stretched version of his 4-6-0 'Star' class, with four simple-expansion cylinders, a long domeless boiler and a straight-sided Belpaire firebox, it was an engine of imposing but plain appearance, named *The Great Bear*. The locomotive superintendent's intentions for it were never made wholly clear, though it was referred to as 'experimental'. It was too long (34ft 6in, 10.5m) and heavy to operate on any route other than London-Bristol, and its performance was not such an improvement over the GWR 4-6-0s as to justify the building of further examples. In 1924, as the British LNER company was developing its new 'Pacifics', the GWR quietly rebuilt their monster as a 'Castle' Class 4-6-0.

In 1914, the first 'Pacifics' in Scandinavia appeared in the form of the Swedish State Railways' Class F, eleven locomotives built by Nydquist & Holm between 1914 and 1916, to work on main-line expresses from the Norwegian border and on the Gothenburg-Stockholm line. Big headlights and snow deflectors elaborated the front end of what was anyway an engine of considerable presence. They combined compounding and superheating, using Vauclain's four-cylinder in-line pattern, all driving the second pair of coupled wheels. The high-pressure cylinders were inside the frame and the low-pressure ones outside; each set worked by a single piston valve operated by Walschaerts outside valve gear. The leading bogie and the trailing wheels ran on outside bearings. On the boiler top a large cover went over both regulator dome and sandbox. The cabs had wooden sides, a typically Swedish feature intended to provide better winter insulation than metal plate. The class did excellent work until electrification made them redundant in 1937. They were then sold to the Danish State Railways, reconditioned, refitted for right-hand drive, and put into service as the DSB's Class E for main-line express work. Between 1942 and 1950, the Frichs works at Aarhus in Denmark built a further 25, with steel cabs and some other modifications. The first of the original set, No.1200, was returned to Sweden where it is preserved.

In the same year as the F Class in Sweden, a prototype 'Pacific' emerged from the Pennsylvania Railroad's works at Altoona. The first US 4-6-2s go back to 1903, but hitherto fast express work on this line had been entrusted to locomotives of 4-4-2 'Atlantic' configuration. Something of greater stamina was now required for main-line work, and the result was the K4, one of the most successful and numerous 'Pacific' designs among the railways of the world. 'An engine among engines' wrote A.F. Staufer, author of *Pennsy Power*. The brief given to motive power chief J.T. Wallis was to produce a main passenger engine for the line, and the prototype of the design was built in 1914. By the American standards of the time it was a compact locomotive, but with a tractive effort rated at 44,460lb (20,163kg) it had ample power packed into it, and driving wheels of 80in (205.1cm) diameter were intended to give it high speed. It was superheated but, surprisingly perhaps, it was hand-fired, and a hand-worked screw reverser was fitted. The prototype was exhaustively tested, and line production did not begin until 1917. Only minor changes were made in the first fourteen years, testifying to the thoroughness with which the design had been prepared and tested at the Altoona test plant and on the road. Eventually 425 K4s were built, all but seventy-four of them at the PRR's own Juniata shops; the others came from Baldwin. They gave excellent main-line service through the 1920s and 1930s, and lasted on secondary duties into the 1950s. The decision to order a further 100 in 1927-1928 aroused controversy, as by then a 4-6-2 was a distinctly modest specimen among US breeds, and critics claimed that a more powerful 'Hudson' type should have been brought in. By the mid-1930s all K4s were fitted with power reversers and automatic stokers: its 70sq ft (6.5m²) grate had always been a very big one for a fireman to keep supplied on a long run.

The K4 could maintain 60-75mph (96-120km/h) with a 1,000-ton train over level or gently rolling terrain; its top recorded speed of 92mph (148km/h) was during test operations with No.5354. As cars became heavier, they were often used in double-headed formation. The last of the class in passenger service, No.5351, was retired in November 1957. The first of the K4s, No.1737, was due to be preserved, but its condition was too bad, and by a piece of sleight of hand not unknown on other lines too, its plates were transferred to No.3750, which remains preserved. Many other American lines used 'Pacifics' and the last of the type in the USA was the Reading Railroad's Class G-3, built in 1948.

Far from American high varnish, more modest 'Pacifics' hauled passenger trains on a great variety of railways, including the Djibouti-Addis Ababa line in Ethiopia. In 1915 a metre-gauge 4-6-2 was built at Haine St-Pierre in Belgium as part of an order of six for a Spanish railway. War conditions made it impossible to arrange delivery, and it was held in store for over twenty years. Finally, in 1936 it was sold for passenger service as Locomotive No.231 on the Franco-Ethiopian Djibouti-Addis Ababa Railway. Three identical examples were ordered from new and supplied in 1938. These were not among the high-speed 'Pacifics'; the trains were very slow, and though the engines boasted smoke deflectors in the best express-engine style, the operating speed scarcely required them.

Not all railways used the 'Pacific' type. The Russians and Italians preferred the 2-6-2 configuration, and the Austrians, as we have seen, turned it round to produce a 2-6-4. In some countries, bigger engines, the 4-6-4 and 4-8-4, came to replace it on the heaviest express trains. But most railways used it on their best expresses, and in due course the 'Pacific' would claim the world speed record for steam.

TWENTY-SIX

The Search for Super-Power

After the First World War, with its unprecedented mobilisation of men and machinery, and its equally unprecedented devastation of lives and landscapes, there was a sense in many fields of human activity that a new beginning had to be made. The physical, economic and political effects of war had a serious impact on railways. The great Austro-Hungarian system was dismembered. The German states' railways were about to be amalgamated into a single *Reichsbahn*. In Britain, government pressure was driving the hundred-plus companies to concentrate themselves into a 'Big Four', and American railways were struggling to shrug off the controls of centralised administration and standardisation imposed by wartime government in 1918. The old pre-war ways seemed far more remote than the mere gap of five years. The pressures of warfare had speeded up change and development in many technical fields, including that of the internal combustion motor. Armies that in 1914 had relied on trains and horses were still using trains in 1919, but the horses had been largely displaced by trucks and cars, and a flood of army surplus vehicles was taking to the roads. Commercial aviation was being actively planned. Electric traction had for ten years been a possible alternative to steam, but its high capital costs seemed likely to confine it to sections with particular operating problems, such as very steep gradients or lengthy tunnels. Now for the first time railway engineers had to consider the possible large-scale application of diesel or petrol-driven engines to the haulage of trains. Among them was the Russian Professor Lomonosov, soon to migrate to the USA, a distinguished theoretician of steam who became an influential advocate of diesel power.

Not that widespread dieselisation seemed very probable in the early 1920s. Steam was still supreme. In 1924 the railways of the USA had 70,000 steam locomotives in service. There was huge capital investment, of public and

private money, and there were substantial vested interests, from coal-owners to ironworks, linked with the manufacture and operation of the steam
fleets in every country. Steam locomotives were routinely hauling trains of
over 1,000 tons on many lines; were maintaining express speeds of 60mph
(96km/h) and more on many sections; and larger, more powerful designs
were always on the drawing boards. But the majority of designers were
conservators. They believed they had all the necessary elements for locomotive-building, and that what was now required was detail improvement,
in such matters as the testing and use of new metals and alloys in sliding
surfaces; and improved lubrication. In America, there was increasing use of
patent equipment. While most companies bought their new locomotives
from Alco, Baldwin or Lima, the locomotive superintendent could exercise
a degree of choice and personal preference in specifying particular makes
of add-on gadgetry. Abner Baker's version of the Walschaerts-Heusinger
valve gear, patented in 1905 and improved in 1911, was frequently specified
by companies buying from the big manufacturers, despite the fact that the
standard Walschaerts pattern was freely available (but the Baker gear did
allow more readily for very long valve travel). Generally speaking, there was
a 'US is best' attitude — not a new thing among American railroad engineers
— with a dismissal of, and reluctance to examine, European imports, whether
of mechanisms or ideas. American locomotives were so much bigger than
anyone else's that it seemed impossible for useful lessons to be learned from
the light-weight, narrow-boilered engines of Europe. But then, they had
almost half the world's locomotives. Export rather than import was the aim,
and the auxiliary companies produced some useful items, like the Franklin
wedge, to reduce axle-play in the horn-blocks, which the great Chapelon
was happy to buy in.

In Europe, where railways continued to build a high proportion of their
own locomotives, and where chief mechanical engineers exercised more
— sometimes total — control over design, the conservators were also the great
majority. As road competition bit more deeply into the business of the railways, managements became increasingly concerned about operating costs.
Locomotive costs had to be weighed along with all the other demands on
company funds, from new track to new coaching stock; and the pay demands
of a large and unionised staff. Allowing for a new boiler at some point, the
life expectancy of a steam locomotive was at least thirty years, and many
of those at work in the 1920s were much older than that. Engineers had to
compare the costs of replacing these old and uneconomical engines with

new standardised versions, against the cheaper short-term option of make-do and mend. In the 1920s, for all his power in some ways, the Chief Mechanical Engineer of the London & North Eastern Railway could not commit his company to an expenditure greater than £200 without Board approval. Some form of compromise inevitably ensued, and there was also a good deal of creative accountancy, a favourite tactic being to charge 'rebuilds', which might be in fact 90 per cent new engines, to the running account rather than to the capital account.

The basic technology of the steam locomotive was not highly complicated; despite its numerous add-on devices it remained a simple and robust machine. The places from which it emerged were laid out and equipped in equally simple fashion. Most locomotive workshops and assembly plants dated back into the previous century. Modern in their day, the largest ones had lofty erecting shops whose roof-mounted cranes could hoist a new locomotive up over its still uncompleted brothers. But other areas were dark and smoky, and, apart from the peace of the painting-shop, all were noisy, often deafeningly so. For employees they were often dangerous places, and sometimes deadlier than anyone knew. For many decades, asbestos was used as insulation to pack the space between the boiler shell and the outer plating, and asbestos dust joined in the cocktail of soot-laden and oily fumes that formed the normal atmosphere of a locomotive works. In these old plants, using basic machine tools, parts were cast or forged, and then clamped, riveted or pinned together in an assemblage that could not be called a product of precision engineering. But the system worked, largely because most of the locomotives built were still called on to perform very slow services which rarely called for full power output. In 1913, 7,200 of Great Britain's more than 22,000 steam locomotives were freight-hauling 0-6-0s; another 3,400 were 0-6-0 tank engines.

Traditional British design, with its plate frames and inside motion, did not lend itself to easy maintenance. The designer's attitude is shown, in not altogether unfair caricature, in a legendary exchange between Dugald Drummond, Chief Mechanical Engineer of the London & South Western Railway – a man who proved incapable of designing an effective engine bigger than a traditional, if handsome, 4-4-0 – and a driver who had a suggestion for some improvement. Drummond got up from his chair of office and motioned the driver to sit in it. When the man bashfully refused, Drummond said (he was a Scot): 'And why dinna ye like? Because ye know it's my bloody job to build the engines and yours to drive them.' With that, the driver was told to get out. Drummond ruled until 1912, refusing to the last to have anything to do with Schmidt's superheater.

One of the more trenchant commentators on the British locomotive scene, Professor W. A. Tuplin, wrote in *British Steam Since 1900*:

> ... there is ample evidence that even with the twentieth century a quarter spent, there were eminent locomotive engineers who did not in fact appreciate certain elementary points in basic design, and an expert in all the branches of basic design, detail design, construction, operation and maintenance was a rarity... many features in the development of British steam locomotives from 1910 onwards were inferior to what the Great Western was already demonstrating, and such failures to make use of existing knowledge may be regarded as causes for... little effort was made in Britain to design steam locomotives with the object of minimising the time and cost of daily labour in preventing the locomotive from being choked by dirt. The firebox and the ashpan had to be emptied, half-burnt coal had to be taken from the smoke-box, the firetubes had to be cleaned of soot, and their firebox ends had to be cleared of rings of built-up slag. Oil boxes had to be refilled daily or more frequently. Every week or so, the boiler had to be emptied and the sludge and scale removed as thoroughly as possible by water jets and rods with scraper ends inserted through holes from which the 'washout plugs' had been removed ... Every steam locomotive was the field of an endless battle against internal dirt.

The dirt was, of course, not only internal. Smoke and smuts were inseparable from the steam locomotive. This mattered much less up to the 1920s, for several reasons. First of all, the public accepted them as a necessary accompaniment to the blessing of mobility brought by the steam locomotive. Also, when engines were kept brightly painted and polished, the smoke seemed an almost embarrassing adjunct that should not be dwelt upon by polite folk. And in any case, there was no alternative. These reasons gradually fell away. In the uncertain economic dips and swings of the 1920s, and far more in the decade to follow, the care formerly lavished on the external appearance of steam locomotives dwindled to almost vanishing point except for the few which operated on the most prestigious services. Smoke and soot, when belched forth from a grimy, corrosion-streaked, sludge-crusted engine, were far more offensive than when emitted by a bright and shining one. From that period began a steady fall from public esteem. It was not an inevitable fall: well-kept in modern stabling, the steam locomotive was not unduly offensive as a neighbour. But lack of investment in maintenance resulted in the reeking ashpits, the pall of smoke, the oily puddles, the soot-blackened, decrepit buildings, and the begrimed engines that latterly characterised the shrines of the goddess of steam in such localities as Germiston, outside Johannesburg, La Chapelle in Paris, and Longsight in Manchester. For some enthusiasts, a kind of *nostalgie de la boue* remains inherent in the memory of such places, but to the wider public, they suggested that the steam locomotive messed up its environment and was not worthy of a place in modern life. Cars, trucks, and buses in increasing numbers showed that there now was an alternative.

Not all engineers and designers were content to be conservators. In several different places there were men, some of them quite grand and senior figures, others not, or not yet, so, whose technical ability and human zest were fired by the notion of making far better steam locomotives than had yet existed. Their zeal was encouraged by the fact that, around 1920, the progress of the steam locomotive seemed to have reached an impasse. This was particularly so in the United States. To the American traffic managers' desire for heavier trains and greater average speeds was joined an ever-more insistent demand from the financial side for lower operating costs. For the designers, the problem was that locomotives had reached their natural physical limits: there was simply not room for wider boilers or bigger cylinders. The locomotive building companies, well aware of their clients' needs, tried different ways of resolving the difficulty. Both Alco and Baldwin experimented with three-cylinder engines, despite the long-established American distrust of crank axles. Baldwin built a demonstration engine, a three-cylinder compound 4-10-2 with a water-tube firebox and conjugated valve gear (the company's 60,000th locomotive, it remained unique, and is preserved at the Franklin Institute, Philadelphia). As consultant to the Delaware & Hudson, James E. Mulhlfeld was about to begin his series of high-pressure experimental engines.

The company that showed the way forward was Lima. In 1921 it was bereft of orders and virtually shut down. It had grown on the building of the specialised patent 'Shay' geared locomotives for logging lines, but in 1916 had hired a new design chief, William E. Woodard, from Alco, and went for a share of the 'Class One' market – the big main-line railroads. Woodard, an engineering graduate of Cornell University, and with twenty years of practical experience, saw an opportunity for his hungry company. In May 1921 his assistant, Herb Snyder, presented a paper to the American Society of Mechanical Engineers, boldly entitled: 'The Need for Improvement in the Design of Present-Day Locomotives.' With his colours thus nailed to the mast, Woodard set out to develop what Lima's publicists would soon call 'Super-Power'. The process was described picturesquely by David P. Morgan in the November 1951 issue of *Trains & Travel*:

> Upstairs in Lima Locomotive Company's brick office building ... a thin little man bent over a drafting table and peered through silver-rimmed spectacles at an extraordinary blueprint ... The plan on the desk before him detailed a 2-8-2 with a fat boiler. It was unlike any engine taking shape in the shops behind Woodard's office. In point of fact it was unlike any other engine anywhere.

In fact, Woodard apparently did his design work in the New York office, was of stocky build, and wore horn-rimmed glasses. His point of departure was 'the combustion situation', and his first step was the Class H10 2-8-2 for the New York Central, based on a design of 1912. His rebuild had an almost identical boiler, and it was the firebox that was radically changed, increased in size by about 8sq ft and fitted with a double brick arch supported by eight 3.5in water tubes. An Elesco feed-water heater cylinder was mounted transversely across the smoke-box front. A large superheater of 'Type E' was fitted, giving 1780sq ft (165.4 m²) of superheating surface, 50 per cent more than the H10. In fitting such equipment, Woodard was aided by the fact that Lima's owners also owned a number of equipment suppliers, the Franklin Accessory Supply Company, the American Arch Company, and the Locomotive Superheater Company – all would contribute to, and benefit from, the new approach. In 1925, Woodard followed up with a much more radical design, the first 2-8-4 locomotive. Although several lines were showing interest, it was built by Lima as a speculative exercise, and known as the A-1. Everyone in the works was highly enthusiastic; the Plant Manager, John H. Wynne, wrote to his father on 8 February 1925:

> She is a beauty. She has an automatic stoker, feedwater heater, power reverse gear, cast steel cylinders (iron bushed) with outside exhaust pipes, a four-wheel trailer with booster engine attached ... and a firebox almost as large as your front room!

Their beauty was a 'tramp', out to charm the susceptibilities of motive power superintendents. It was a two-cylinder, simple-expansion locomotive, with a long firebox nearly a quarter the length of the boiler, supported by the four-wheel truck. Although this truck was seen as an American 'first', Woodard would certainly have known of the Gölsdorf 2-6-4. His truck was of quite different design, however, serving as a rear main frame, with the tender drawgear attached. The main frame itself did not extend back beyond the driving wheels. The truck also held the ashpan. The steam booster gave an additional 13,200lb (5,986kg) of tractive effort at low speed, to the engine's 69,400lb (31,473kg). Tested in April 1925 on the Boston & Albany's line through the Berkshire Mountains, the 2-8-4 took a 2,296-ton train east from Selkirk Yard to North Adams Junction in ten minutes less than its H10 predecessor with a train of 1,691 tons. It was also, in American terms, economical with fuel. The maximum cut-off was limited to 60 per cent of the piston stroke, making the steam work harder. Although this would reduce the initial tractive effort, Woodard compensated both by installing the booster engine and by raising the boiler pressure to 240psi (16.8kg/cm²). The case for super-power was proved. Indeed, even while the A-1 was still being tested, the same concepts, plus a combustion chamber, were built into ten 2-10-4s ordered in 1925 by the Texas & Pacific Railroad. The B&A was first to buy the 2-8-4, and the type was duly known as the 'Berkshire', except on the Chesapeake & Ohio, which preferred to call them 'Kanawhas'.

Lima 'super-power' was based on a new proportion of firebox (with a combustion chamber reaching forward into the boiler space), boiler, and superheater. It prompted a reassessment of steam performance: not simply brute dragging force, but force per unit of time, measured in horsepower in the cylinders and at the drawbar. The approach was rapidly adopted by the other builders, though some features, like the 'Woodard drive', an articulated connecting rod which attached to the big end of the main rod and imparted drive also to the next pair of coupled wheels, were not generally followed. Lima's pioneering work set the pattern for the final decades of American steam and also resulted in a satisfactory growth of market share for the smallest of the big three constructors.

Before the Woodard changes, at least the Americans knew they had a problem. It was not quite so apparent in Europe, where train-loads were lighter, but here too the search for greater power was on. The French magazine *Excelsior*, on 30 January 1925, hailed the arrival of the 'Superlocomotive' on the *Est* railway. Europe's first 'Mountain' type, it was a powerful four-cylinder compound, designed by Henri Mestre, the line's *Ingénieur Principal des Etudes*, with a tractive effort of 23,926kg. But it was not to retain its super-status. In 1925, the term 'Super-Pacific' began to be applied to the series of 4-6-2s begun under Georges Asselin in 1913 and capable of taking 550-tonne trains over the Calais-Paris route at an average of 60mph (96km/h). Also in 1925, a twenty-nine-year-old French engineer transferred from the PLM to the Paris-Orleans Railway. His name was André Chapelon, and he had a keen and incisive technical brain. As it happens, at this time his attention was chiefly focused on the opposite end of the boiler from Woodard's: what concerned him was the events that happened in a locomotive smoke-box when the engine was working hard, particularly how the blast-pipe functioned; and in 1926 he produced a new double blast-pipe, a modified form of one that had been worked out by the Finnish engineer Kilpi Kylälä, and soon to be known as the Kylchap blast-pipe. The design was highly successful, greatly improving the draught of the engines to which it was fitted. But it was just the start of Chapelon's investigations of the steam locomotive's innermost workings. In 1926 the decision was taken to rebuild a Class 3500 'Pacific' of 1907 to a design worked out by him. It was a radical operation, and the work, in the P-O workshops at Tours, took three years. The addition of a feed-water heater, the installation of a thermic syphon in the firebox, enlarging and redesign of the superheater, a rearrangement of the steam flow from boiler to steam chest, improved valve control using poppet valves, greater draught from the Kylchap pipes and a double chimney, and smoke deflectors, combined to transform the engine inside and out. Instead of a long, rather-rangy looking machine, it had acquired a purposeful, muscular look — less elegant of outline but more suggestive of power. And the power was certainly there. The improvement made in the old 4-6-2's performance startled not only Chapelon's colleagues but the whole engineering world. Rebuilding of the other 3,500s on identical lines began immediately and eventually 102 were either rebuilt or built new.

Fundamental to Chapelon's method, and its success, was a thorough appraisal of the way steam passed from the boiler, via high- and low-pressure cylinders, to the exhaust. 'Give her plenty of steam' had long been a saw of designers, but for the first time it was now scientifically established how to make the steam work to fullest effect, with the diameter of the pipes worked out and their direction made as straight as possible. The highest attainable degree of superheat was provided, at 750°F, sufficient to ensure that the steam entering the low-pressure cylinders was still in a superheated state.

To speed up express schedules on the Paris–Toulouse service, the P-O was considering new motive power options from 1930. At the suggestion of Chapelon, the former P-O four-cylinder compound 'Pacific' No.4521 was rebuilt as a 4-8-0, No.240.P1, to his design. This time, though the changes were even more drastic, the operation was faster. Between October 1931 and August 1932, radical alterations were made, again at the Tours workshops. The new boiler came from the *Nord* 'Super-Pacific', with a long, deep, narrow Belpaire firebox, into which a Nicholson thermic syphon was incorporated. The handsome, racy lines of the original were once again transformed by an accumulation of pipes, domes, pumps and cylinders, plus a steam turbine for generating electricity, into a husky-looking double-chimneyed engine of very different appearance. The arrangements of steam pipes and valves followed the plan already worked out.

Once again too, performance was increased by an astonishing degree. The free steaming circuits, the draught and blast arrangements, the excellent boiler and firebox allowed the engine to develop 4,000hp in the cylinders at a speed of 70mph (112.6km/h) with a train of 584t, and a further eleven were rebuilt in 1934, followed by twenty-five in 1940. These had mechanical stokers. The 240P.1 could run on grades or on the flat to the kind of schedule that post-war planners devised for electric traction, and with heavier trains.

Chapelon's approach was coolly logical as well as scientific: he saw the ways in which a steam locomotive could be made to perform to the utmost, and proceeded to make them a reality. His system needed a boiler pressure of 292psi (20.5kg/cm²), four compound cylinders and high-degree superheat; it needed the thermic syphon, the feed-water heater, and the precise action of the cam-operated poppet valves, in order to achieve what he knew the steam locomotive was capable of. Chapelon's genius brought these various items together within a high-powered functioning unity, but the French tradition of the skilled *mécanicien* driver was also a vital factor on his side. His work, publicised in technical journals as well as in railway enthusiasts' publications, had a rapid impact on practice in other countries. But, rather as if patronising a French restaurant where one can choose *à la carte* rather than accepting the *table d'hôte*, designers in those countries took what they wanted from his range of improvements and ignored others. What they all digested, as rapidly as they could, was his work on steam passages. This had as dramatic an effect on simple-expansion locomotives as it had had on the French compounds. Compounding remained a French thing; poppet valves were often tried on an experimental basis, without general adoption (Will Woodard and Nigel Gresley both put much work into poppet valve development); feed-water heaters and thermic syphons remained options for designers depending on the national tradition in the first case, and the designer's own urge to spread his wings a little in the second. Nowhere else was the full Chapelon treatment attempted – and nowhere else was the full Chapelon effect achieved.

But it was now clear that the use of certain fittings, if well-integrated into the design, could make a big difference to performance. The thermic syphon, a water tube leading up through the firebox from the lower front to the crown sheet, provided extra heating surface and up to three could be accommodated in a big firebox. The combustion chamber, a forwards extension of the firebox into the boiler space, ensured that more of the fuel was converted into heat. These were far from being new ideas; what was new was the thoroughness with which their function was examined and exploited. Nigel Gresley, who had sent his first Class P2 express 'Mikado' to Vitry in France for testing, explained to a meeting of the Institution of Locomotive Engineers:

> I did not hesitate to incorporate some of the outstanding features of the Paris-Orleans Railway's engines, such as the provision of extra-large steam passages and a double blast-pipe. There was no real novelty in these features but the French engineers had worked out the designs scientifically and had proved them by results obtained in actual service.

This was rather disingenuous, but designers often took a cool tone when, or if, acknowledging their borrowings. The whole point was that the French had taken the trouble to work out the designs scientifically, and nobody else had.

TWENTY-SEVEN

Getting Away from Stephenson

Brilliant innovators are few in any generation, and the mantle of tradition inherited by every chief engineer, while it perhaps helped to stifle innovation, may also have saved many a railway system from having thrust upon it untried and perhaps unsound designs whose novelty was more apparent than their value in regular service. Nor did all engineers, brilliant or not, have the thoroughness of approach and the scientific knowledge and methodology of a Chapelon. But there were other difficulties which hindered experimentation. Few countries had effective locomotive testing plants. Trials were generally made out on the road, with recording instruments measuring the cylinder performance and steam production; and the coal and water usage also being checked. A dynamometer car between the locomotive and the train would measure drawbar pull, and speed. Specially fitted brake-engines were sometimes used in order to provide a measurable drag force. But variables were always present: few lengths of track were straight and level; wind and weather affected running; constant speed was difficult to maintain; and communication between the recording engineers and the footplate staff was difficult or impossible. The first static testing plant was set up at Odessa, on the Russian South Western Railway, by its chief engineer, Aleksandr Borodin, in 1881. In his plant the locomotive wheels were jacked up and the drive was transmitted from the driving axle to the measuring instruments by belts. Static testing using roller wheels was begun by an American scientist, Professor William F. Goss of Purdue University at Lafayette, Indiana. He set up a test laboratory in 1891 and purchased a 4-4-0 from the Schenectady works to test various aspects of steam locomotive performance. Such intrusion of an academic into the commercial world of railroad engineering was remarkable; despite their far greater influence in their own countries, none of the technical professors in Austria, Germany or Russia equalled Goss' achievement. Columbia University followed with its plant in 1899, and Illinois also installed one later.

These university plants were intended to establish basic facts relating to the performance of the steam locomotive in general, and Purdue did valuable work, especially on smoke-box design. They were not intended for comparative testing of different types, nor were they concerned with potential innovation. In 1907, Goss wrote:

> The arrangement of steam piping on an American locomotive constitutes one of the many ingenious features which have so long served to perpetuate the general characteristics of the early machine ... The arrangement as a system of piping is perfect.

Dr Wilhelm Schmidt had by this time already managed to improve upon perfection, but it does not seem that news of the fire-tube superheater had reached Purdue by 1907.

The Chicago & North Western Railroad set up a test plant in 1895, but the best-known was the Pennsylvania Railroad's, installed at Altoona in 1906, having previously been made a popular attraction at the 1904 St Louis Exhibition. This was naturally used only for PRR engines, plus the occasional foreign locomotive bought for testing purposes, though a valuable series of bulletins was published, giving the results of the tests. In 1913, as part of the 'home building' programme, the Japanese built a test plant at Oi, on the outskirts of Tokyo. The German railways' test plant at Grünewald was established in 1930, and the French set one up at Vitry sur Seine in 1934. In Britain the Great Western had its own plant at Swindon from the later 1890s, though it was not until 1948 that a jointly-owned British testing plant was set up, at Rugby. The sight of a locomotive under static test was always awesome to visitors: the driving wheels revolving at speed, the reciprocal and rotating motion sliding and whirling in full play, the exhaust roaring out, and the carrying wheels quite static; the whole thing not moving forward an inch, being very firmly anchored to a steelyard at the rear, and with the driving wheels transmitting their motion to huge rollers set below rail level.

One of the main British agitators for a 'national' testing plant was H.N. Gresley, Chief Mechanical Engineer of the London & North Eastern Railway. Gresley, by temperament something of a radical, was compelled by the commercial realities of the 1920s and 1930s to be primarily a conservator. In fact this suited one aspect of his personality: he was also a stout believer in the 'horses for courses' approach to locomotive design, and he was happier to keep, and even continue to build, various older types than some other engineers would have been. Despite this, Gresley also sought to explore the further potential of steam power; supported, if not nudged on, by an enthusiastic assistant, Oliver Bulleid. In 1929 the LNER built the only 4-6-4 ever to run in Britain, No.10000, an experimental four-cylinder compound engine with a high-pressure (450psi, 31.6kg/cm²) water-tube boiler as used in ships. A bulbous streamlined casing was designed to cover it. It was intended to generate power comparable to the LNER's Class A3 'Pacifics' but with greatly reduced fuel consumption. Though its existence could hardly be a secret, it was known as the 'Hush-hush' engine, perhaps because it seems never to have appeared on a cost budget. It worked a number of scheduled services but was expensive and troublesome to maintain, and was rebuilt with the same boiler as the A4 'Pacifics' in 1938, though retaining its extra set of trailing wheels.

While Chapelon was at work pushing the potential of the conventional Seguin-Stephenson boiler to the full, experiments centred on new boiler designs – new to railway use, at least – were also being pursued by another British railway, as well as in Canada and France.

No.10000's boiler pressure, though almost twice any that had been tried in Great Britain before, was only half that applied in an experimental three-cylinder compound locomotive on the London Midland & Scottish Railway. Following the design developed up to his death in 1924 by Wilhelm Schmidt, of superheating fame, and known as the Schmidt or Schmidt-Henschel boiler, it was built by Henschel at Kassel. It had three separate pressure-systems: a steam generating circuit at a pressure around 1500psi (105.2 kg/cm²) which supplied heat to the primary steam drum at a pressure of 900psi (63.2 kg/cm²), which fed the high-pressure cylinder; and a 'low-pressure' fire-tube boiler at 250psi (17.5 kg/cm²), supplying the low-pressure cylinders. This boiler and associated works were applied in 1929 to the frame of a new 4-6-0 locomotive of 'Royal Scot' type and named *Fury*, a traditional name from the old days, but tragically apt. On the first test, a burst pipe allowed steam to escape into the cab, killing the Superheater Company's representative. Though it was repaired, and further tests made, the project was later abandoned and the engine rebuilt as a 'Royal Scot' 4-6-0, *British Legion*. The Schmidt-Henschel boiler was tried also on a Canadian Pacific 2-10-4 locomotive and on a French four-cylinder compound 4-8-2 of the PLM, both in 1930. Neither was successful.

The New York Central also tried out a Schmidt-Henschel boiler on a 4-8-4, No.800, in 1931–1932, but it was rapidly abandoned. Only one railway in the USA seriously pursued super-high pressure. Under its President, Leonor H. Loree, a great steam enthusiast, the Delaware & Hudson Railroad maintained a highly progressive design and maintenance policy during the late 1920s and early 1930s, employing as consultant James E. Muhlfeld, former motive power superintendent of the B&O and always keen to improve the basic steam locomotive. Three successive experimental high-pressure locomotives were built between 1924 and 1933. The final one, named *L.H. Loree*, was a four-cylinder triple-expansion compound 4-8-0, with front and rear cylinders driving the same set of coupled wheels. Boiler pressure was 500psi (35kg/cm²). The high-pressure cylinder on the right of the cab discharged to the intermediate-pressure cylinder on the left, and the steam finally was piped to the two front low-pressure cylinders. Rotary cam poppet valves were also fitted, and the firebox had over-fire air jets to improve combustion. A six-wheel rear bogie on the tender was fitted with a booster engine. With so many innovative features, the locomotive unsurprisingly remained a one-off, like its predecessors. The D&H continued to rely on its superbly-maintained conventional big engines to move its freight traffic.

In the end, it had to be accepted that the super-high pressure boiler was impossible to adapt to the constraints and working conditions of the steam locomotive. Notional economies of fuel consumption could not stand up against the very high cost and unreliability of the prototypes. In addition, the extreme working pressure inspired a fear among footplate staff similar to that of some drivers in the earliest days, who had felt good reason to mistrust the boilers of their steeds. Most railway companies and engineers accepted the results of the high-pressure experiments in a negative sense, as showing that there was no good reason to abandon the conventional tubular boiler.

Apart from experimental boilers supplying steam to conventional cylinders and motion, a number of locomotives were built in which boilers of standard Stephenson-Seguin type supplied power through a completely different kind of drive. Of the numerous efforts made, the most successful and promising were based on the steam turbine. Turbines were tried in two forms, in generating power to work electric motors, and in direct mechanical drive to the wheels. Some pioneering but unsuccessful work on turbine-electrics was undertaken by the North British Locomotive Company in Glasgow, in 1910 and 1920, but the greatest success was achieved in 1938 by the General Electric Company in the USA which built a 4-6-0+0-6-4 double unit locomotive of this type. Whatever its merits, the onset of war and of dieselisation ensured that it remained a one-off. These engines were all equipped with condensing apparatus. In marine engineering, steam condensers, apart from conserving water, improved the efficiency of turbines; and several turbine-condenser locomotives with mechanical drive were also built. Sweden was among the pioneers and a Ljungström condenser locomotive was sent to Argentina, a country with a natural interest in any system which promised to reduce water consumption by over 90 per cent. But its complexity in operation and heavy maintenance cost doomed it, and this was really the story with other condensing turbine locomotives. Yet some successful non-condensing designs appeared. The archetype was a tiny 0-2-2-0 tank engine built by an Italian engineer, Giuseppe Belluzzo, in 1907, with a turbine for each wheel. The Swedish Ljungström brothers worked on turbine application to larger engines, and claimed success with a 2-8-0 for the Grangesberg-Oxeløsund Railway in 1932. This helped to prompt the building of the 4-6-2 'Turbomotive' of the London Midland & Scottish Railway in 1935. Unique locomotive types all too often ended up under tarpaulins at the back of a shed, but this one spent fifteen years in revenue service, on express trains. Built by the LMS at Crewe, in collaboration with Metropolitan Vickers, it incorporated the Swedish-designed non-condensing turbine with the frames and boiler of a Stanier 'Princess Royal' 4-6-2. The turbines were at the front, with forward or main drive on the left, and backward on the right. Main drive delivered its maximum horsepower output at around 62mph (99km/h), appropriate for the aim of hauling heavy trains at moderately fast speeds. A double blast-pipe chimney was fitted, and three different boilers were tried, up to 1939. Test results both in tractive power on gradients and in coal and water consumption were favourable, but not significantly better than the piston-powered 'Pacifics'. The British experiment in turn encouraged the design of the solitary Pennsylvania Railroad Class S-2, a 6-8-6 built in 1946, though planned six years before. With this engine, the peak of steam turbine traction was reached: during testing, it drew a train of 980 tons at an average of 105mph (169km/h) for 30 miles on level track.

Perhaps more should have been achieved with turbine drive; as it was, it was never more than a footnote to the real business of steam power. But it was of concern to some serious engineers: Sir William Stanier was not a man to waste the LMS's money on chasing fancies. Yet in all these searches for a para-Stephensonian solution, one feels that the designers were pursuing a sort of mechanical Holy Grail – the vision of an efficiency beyond that which the conventional steam locomotive, however well designed and built, could ever achieve. The concept of thermal efficiency was always around to condemn traditional steam power. Arrived at by a fairly straightforward formula, it brought boiler efficiency, cylinder efficiency, and machine efficiency (this last a percentage factor obtained by dividing the locomotive's drawbar horsepower by its indicated or theoretical horsepower, and multiplying by 100: the difference between the two horsepowers is made by internal frictions and air resistance) together and expressed them as an overall percentage. The percentage was depressingly low: the best locomotive might not achieve more than 12 or 13 per cent on this scale. C.R.H. Simpson, the editor of *Locomotive Magazine*, wrote in 1959: 'It is a mistake to judge the steam locomotive as a thermodynamical machine, particularly so in the days when fuel was considerably cheaper than it is now.' But this 'inefficiency', the inadequacy of the work done in relation to the heat supplied, provided a convenient stick for the protagonists of other forms of power, as well as being seen as a limitation and challenge by steam engineers. It could not be ignored. But expensive experimentation had to be balanced against the fact that although thirteen decades of work and progress underwrote the Stephenson model, the full potential of conventional steam had not yet been completely worked out either in theory or in practice. Meanwhile, all that any steam-driven alternative had to show was a few one-off machines of varying degrees of unreliability and complexity. The only certainty they could offer was that further development would be extremely expensive.

TWENTY-EIGHT

The Standardisers

Experimental designs merely served to underline the point that, as soon as a railway owned more than a handful of locomotives, the virtues of having standard parts and fittings became apparent. Efficiency, speed and economy in maintenance and repair were improved; fewer one-off items had to be forged or cast, and the already vast index of the stores-clerk would not get even longer. This was noted by Marc Seguin in his book *Des Chemins de fer* in 1839, already looking forward to a time when constructional and mechanical details were so thoroughly established that further change would be of a minimal sort. But this ideal situation never arose. While the virtues of standard parts always shone brightly for the accountants, there were other priorities, which might compete. Additional locomotives of a certain class might be ordered from a constructor who had not built the originals, but who now offered a better price or faster delivery. Despite using the same drawings, there would be minor differences. The designer himself would be likely to take the opportunity to make modifications. The salesmen of auxiliary equipment were on a constant round, always proclaiming improvements. In the 1920s, *Locomotive* magazine would carry advertisements for six or seven different brands of feed pump and pyrometer. The arrival of a new chief engineer almost invariably signalled a significant change in design, as the new man set out to establish his own mark. The general progress of design was never at a standstill. When New Zealand Railways, pioneer of 'Pacifics', came to order a new 4-6-2 in 1906, the Class Q was still recent, but Beattie's new Class A had a quite different specification; and its updated version ordered by his successor H.H. Jackson, the Ab of 1916, was different again. Compared to the Class Q it was 20 tons lighter, and had a lower boiler pressure, but a higher tractive effort. Compared to the Class A, which had compound expansion, it had simple expansion, but 183sq ft (17m²) of superheating surface. Between-times, incidentally, ten standard US-style 'Pacifics' had been supplied by Baldwin in 1914 because of the long delivery schedule offered by Britain. Thus even a small system had four types of 'express' engine running at the same time: standardisation remained an ideal to which companies aspired with only limited success. Sometimes even the aspiration was absent; on the South African Railways, during the 1920s, the chief mechanical engineer, Colonel Collins, ordered such a variety of loco-motive types from different manufacturers and countries that his successor, A.G. Watson, had to institute a severe policy of standardisation.

Through the twentieth century, the imperatives of standardisation rang steadily louder. From early decades in Russia, a handful of locomotive types, built in very large numbers, began to dominate the world's most extensive single railway system. But Russia did not exert much influence beyond its own borders. The experience of world war, and the consequent strengthen-ing of economic control by governments, brought about a new phase of locomotive design in several countries. It was already apparent in Japan, and became even more so on the much larger German system, when in 1920 a national *Reichsbahn* (DRG) replaced the eight former state rail-ways. Operating conditions were desperately difficult because some 5,000 locomotives had been lost in war reparations and those which remained were often in dire need of overhaul and repair. A central engineering design department was established in Berlin under Dr Richard Wagner, formerly of the Prussian railways. He headed a Locomotive Committee on which the principal German manufacturers were represented, and a systematic plan of standard locomotive types to cover all traffic needs was launched.

Born in 1882, and a graduate of the Charlottenburg Technical High School, Wagner was a strong personality, described by E.S. Cox as: 'a big bear of a man ... earthy and practical and full of that realistic common sense which particularly appeals to railway engineers everywhere.' He was a frequent visitor to England, and became an honorary member of the Institution of Locomotive Engineers; like Gölsdorf, he supplied technical details of new classes to the British railway journals. Inheriting 284 locomotive types, he organised a unified classification and number-ing system to identify them, whilst superintending the design of the new standard types which were intended to replace them all. Eleven of these were complete by 1930 and a further eighteen were produced in the next decade. The first designs ranged from 0-6-0 tank engines to 4-6-2 express locomotives and 2-10-0s for main-line freight. Not all flourished. While 1755 of the Class 44 2-10-0 were built between 1926 and 1944, only ten of the Class 81 0-8-0T were built, in 1928. Such wide variations, and the relatively small numbers of many of the *Einheitslok* (standard locomotive) types, are due to a number of factors, including the effectiveness of proto-types, the priority of manufacturing needs, and the durability of the engines they were intended to replace. Not least, economic conditions played a part as the post-war German economy became mired in hyper-inflation and slump. But among the most important contributions of DRG standardisa-tion was the continuous programme of background work on boiler design and performance which went on under Wagner's direction. The number and dimensions of the tubes, large and small, and the arrangement of the boiler's interior space to minimise resistance to air-flow, and to ensure the most effective water circulation and efficient production of steam, were rigorously established. The published results had a strong influence on design on other railways, notably in Britain and the USA, during the 1930s and later.

For express passenger work, the 'Pacific' type was chosen, with a brief to haul a train of 800t at 62mph (100km/h) on level track, or 500t at 31mph (50km/h) on a rising grade of 1 in 100. Twenty went into service in 1925-1926. Ten were two-cylinder simple expansion engines and ten were four-cylinder compounds. Following comparative tests, it was decided to proceed with the simple expansion type, Series 01. Between 1925 and 1938, 231 were built (the ten compounds were also converted to simples in 1942).

Though designed and built in Germany, the 01s and other standard classes showed how the influence of American design practice had spread. They were bar-framed, with a flush-topped boiler and two domes, the leading one being the boiler inlet for the Knorr feedwater supply system, the rear one holding a Wagner-designed regulator. Between them was a sandbox holding sand for application to all coupled wheels in the event of slip-ping. Another American feature was the cylindrical heat-exchanger of the feed-water heater partly built across the upper section of the smoke-box. Walschaerts valve gear actuated piston valves, with all the motion out-side and easily accessible. The firebox however was of copper rather than steel as was normal in the USA. The trailing wheels, with inside bearings, were set behind the firebox, under the cab, a practice well-established on the old state railways. On the first engines, the running plate sloped down to the buffer beam, and large smoke deflectors were mounted on this. Later, smaller wing-type smoke deflectors were attached to the smoke-box sides, and the front sloping plates removed, further exposing the 'works'. The high running plate helped to make everything accessible, and all the DRG standard locomotives had built-in electric lights to illuminate vital lubrication areas. The boiler was of parallel shape, with a round-topped firebox — the Belpaire firebox never found much favour in Germany. A typical Central European feature, which would be retained by German locomotives, was long tail-rods protruding forwards from the cylinders.

The first 01s were built by Borsig and AEG, but Henschel and Krupp also contributed to the total of 241. From 1930 they were supplemented by a light 'Pacific' type, of very similar appearance, Series 03, of which 298 were built by 1937. With a maximum axle load of 17.5t, it had a much wider route availability, and once it went into production, no more of the Maffei S3/6 'Pacifics' were built. The original maximum operating speed was set at 81.25mph (130km/h), though many lines had a speed limit of only 62mph (100km/h) until the general train-speed increases from the mid-1930s. The 01 was a highly successful design and post-war rebuilds with welded boilers continued to operate on long-distance expresses.

For heavy freight haulage, the Class 44 2-10-0 was another very successful design, with 1753 built between 1926 and 1944. It was a three-cylinder simple expansion engine, bar-framed, with a copper firebox. Four-point suspension had been worked out, in order to make the ride easier, but its 20t axle load restricted it to main line services. The maximum operating speed was 43.5mph (70km/h).

An inevitable consequence of the standard approach was the abandoning of some effective and interesting types, often quite recent. The Württemberg Railways had one of the world's few locomotives with six driver axles, a 2-12-0 designed by Dr W. Daumer in 1917, a very effective design of which thirty-three were built up to 1924, but it was dropped with many others. It survived until 1957, when the last of the class was withdrawn from the Austrian Federal Railways. The unified German approach also largely ended the individuality of designs from the main builders; although they also built to order for export customers, these customers very often preferred a German design. The Portuguese Railways (CFP) were typical in this respect. Henschel, responsible for much of the CFP locomotive stock, built two 2-8-4T classes, 018 and 020, for Portugal's broad gauge lines (5ft

6in, 166.5cm); Class 018 was lighter and used for services in the south of the country; the twenty-four 020s were used mainly around Lisbon and Oporto. They were of typical German bar-frame construction, with two outside simple-expansion cylinders. A reliable heavy suburban class, most were still in service in the late 1960s. German practice was however most influential in countries to the east, notably Poland, Bulgaria and Turkey. Polish builders made regular use of German designs with only cosmetic modifications, while in Bulgaria and Turkey large numbers of German-built engines operated the main-line passenger and freight services.

In India, the BESA designs had already provided a degree of standardisation among the state railways, and this policy was carried forward with the work of the Indian Railways Standards Committee, set up by the Railways Board in 1924, which provided for three levels of 'Pacific' power, XA, XB, and XC, and a 2-8-2 XE, all two-cylinder simples with wide fireboxes designed to burn low-quality coal. The XC was intended for the heaviest expresses. The Bengal-Nagpur Railway, which had always tended to pursue its own locomotive policy, developed its own huge four-cylinder compound version of the XC, but most others followed the standard designs. Unfortunately, though built in large numbers by British manufacturers, the IRS classes demonstrated the adverse side of a standardisation policy. At best, they were of only moderate quality. Fractures of the plate-frames were frequent, and poor internal design limited their steaming capacity despite large boilers and modern valve gear. More serious was a tendency to distort the tracks and go off the rails. Minor adjustments to the bogies failed to solve this. Finally the catastrophic derailment of XB No.1916 at Bhita in July 1937, resulting in over 100 deaths, prompted a thorough enquiry, which, however, failed to identify the problem. A high-level British-French-Indian inquiry team was then asked to investigate, and identified the problem as quite inadequate side-control of the bogies. A heavy 'Pacific' needed to have a 7-ton initial resistance to lateral movement built into its bogies; the consulting engineers responsible for the X series had allowed for only three-quarters of a ton. French-originated methods of improving the suspension of big engines running on light or unstable track were put in hand. As the British engineer E.S. Cox frankly admitted, the British members learned things from the inquiry which they put to good use at home (*Locomotive Panorama*, I, p. 53).

In Britain itself, mixed attitudes to standardisation could be detected. From 1923 there were only four large companies, but each of those maintained its own separate locomotive design team. Within each company, there were differences of ideas and practice between the various workshops now brought under one ownership. The London Midland & Scottish Railway inherited six locomotive works of which three, at Horwich, Crewe and Derby, were very large and mutually hostile. The LMS's attempt to embark on a standardisation policy was vitiated and hampered by these internal tensions. On the London & North Eastern Railway, where H.N. Gresley was the locomotive chief, there were also old rivalries, but standardisation was not a major issue. Gresley was quite prepared to design small classes for specific routes and duties, like his solitary Garratt or his five Class P2 2-8-2s — Britain's only express 'Mikados', with 74in, 188cm driving wheels — for the Edinburgh-Aberdeen line. The Southern Railway, focused on electrification, had only a small though distinctive steam-building programme. The Great Western, least altered by the amalgamations, continued under Churchward's successor to build Churchwardian locomotives that still, through the 1920s, set the standards that others tried to match.

The weight of established tradition was so great that no-one seriously considered the possibility of bringing all British locomotive design under one roof. During 1926-1927, spurred by the combination of inter-company rivalry and a heightened sense of the value of good publicity, together with the need for more powerful express locomotives, all four companies brought out their own new designs. The GWR's contribution was the four-cylinder simple 'King', dubbed 'Britain's most powerful express passenger locomotive' on its appearance in 1926. This thirty-strong class represented the culmination of the design policy that had begun in 1907. The domeless tapered boiler reached a maximum diameter of 6ft (1.83m). The heaviest 4-6-0 on British railways, it was intended to haul the main West of England and Birmingham expresses to and from Paddington. A maximum axle load of 22.5 tons confined it to certain lines and though it cut the London-Plymouth timing of the 'Cornish Riviera Limited' to four hours for the 225.5 miles (363km), it was not allowed over the Royal Albert Bridge west of Plymouth. The maximum recorded speed of a 'King' was 108.5mph (174.6km/h), though its real value was in maintaining consistent speeds of the order of 60-65mph (96-105km/h) with trains loading up to 500 tons. They worked on express services until their final withdrawal in 1963.

In 1927, the difficulties of the LMS resulted in severe embarrassment for its locomotive department when it became plain that the company had no engine capable of pulling the new 'Royal Scot' London-Glasgow express on the 299.1 mile (481.3km) non-stop London-Carlisle stage. A compound 'Pacific' type, in the planning stage, was abandoned after tests made with a borrowed GWR 'Castle' showed that a simple-expansion 4-6-0 could outperform the proposed design. A very hurried order was placed with the North British Locomotive Company of Glasgow for fifty such locomotives. To assist with design, it was arranged with the Southern Railway that a set of drawings of its new three-cylinder 'Lord Nelson' 4-6-0 would be supplied, though relatively little direct use was made of the Southern design. The prototype, also a three-cylinder simple, turned out to be successful, able to take a 450-ton train unaided over the Shap summit; and a further twenty were built, known as the 'Royal Scot' class. It was a massive-looking engine, 13ft 2.5in (402.2cm) high, with a tiny chimney and low dome, and a straight-sided Belpaire firebox. After thirteen years' intensive service, the older engines began to be rebuilt with taper boilers and double chimneys; this sometimes amounted to virtually a new engine, with little beside the cab and tender preserved. But the operation was a great success and gave the 'Royal Scots' another two decades of express work. There was relatively little to choose between the 'Kings', 'Scots' and Southern Railway 'Nelsons', though their respective merits and failings were endlessly debated by enthusiasts. The slightly smaller driving wheels of the 'King' gave it a higher nominal tractive effort, but a single design could have accomplished all the tasks undertaken by the three.

Only with the arrival of W.A. Stanier from the Great Western, in 1931, was a sustained programme of standard design established on the LMS. It was not a root-and-branch exercise: economic depression limited it, and it was curtailed by war in 1939. But a range of tank and tender locomotives for suburban passenger and main-line mixed traffic work was brought out, including Britain's most numerous single class of tender locomotive, the two-cylinder 'Black Five' 4-6-0, of which 842 were built between 1934 and 1948, and its near relative, the Class 8F freight 2-8-0. With a weight of 159,040lb (72.1t), and a tractive effort of 26,000lb (11,790kg), there were few lines over which the Class Five could not run; and the great majority of services, both passenger and freight, were well within its capacity. While it is difficult to assess a locomotive's appearance with entire objectivity, most observers seem to have considered this design to sum up what the modern British steam locomotive was about. Combining something of the traditional reticence – no visible pumps or auxiliaries – with the new accessibility, which meant external valve gear and a running plate above the wheels, it was a harmonious composition. The matching curves of buffer beam and cab-side gave it balance; the gradual expansion from front to rear of its tapered boiler and high Belpaire firebox, acting against the diminishing effect of perspective, gave it a sense of bulk; the integration of the high-sided tender with the contours of the cab supplied a hint of streamlining; the chimney though large was set far enough back on the smoke-box top to avoid over-dominance. With no frills, no extras, it was an immensely competent piece of industrial design, resulting in an engine which expressed its own air of competence and solid efficiency, and lived up to it in service.

In the United States, freedom from the government control imposed by the short-lived Standardisation Committee of 1919-1920 in theory allowed each railroad to buy and operate its motive power as it liked. In fact, the concentration of main-line locomotive building among three companies continued to assure a high degree of standard practice. Most US and Canadian railway companies saw no need to design their own locomotives, when Baldwin, Lima and Alco, and the Canadian builders all provided a range that covered every likely need; and were happy to fit any patent auxiliary equipment that the operator might specify. A step forward by one of the big three was invariably quickly followed by the other two, as when Lima introduced its 'Super-Power' in 1925. Between 1928 and 1930, Baldwin built 2-8-2 locomotives for the Southern Railroad and the St Louis-San Francisco of identical driving wheel and cylinder dimensions, and very similar length and outline. The Frisco engine had a boiler pressure of 230psi (16 kg/cm^2) compared to the Southern's 20psi (14 kg/cm^2); that plus a booster in the truck gave it a higher tractive effort. It had a patent feed-water heater and pump, with external piping, which the other lacked. It was basically the presence and positioning, or the absence, of auxiliary equipment – such items themselves standardised by the makers – that gave engines a distinctive appearance, rather than separate designs. The most notable exception was the Pennsylvania Railroad, which liked to refer to itself as the 'standard railroad of the world' and was the only American line to make regular use of the Belpaire firebox. Within its own design conventions, though, the Pennsy also applied standardisation as much as possible. The K4 'Pacific' whose line production began in 1917 and the Class L1 2-8-2 of 1918, both built in their hundreds, shared the same boiler design and had many other interchangeable parts.

In most countries, multiple ownership of lines, and a lack of home-based building works, worked against any degree of standardisation. Japan was an exception to this, as the National Railways were the largest though not the only operator, and construction was almost entirely home-based, either at the JNR works or at one of the numerous large private builders, who by now also had a considerable export trade, mostly to Korea and China. In the case of the Class JF 'standard' 2-8-2 of 1935 for the South Manchuria Railway, in China, there was a form of standardisation by imitation, inasmuch as the type, later also named as the 'Liberation' class, was closely based on a US wartime standard Alco-built 'Mikado' supplied to the South Manchuria Railway in 1918. Over 2,500 were built between 1935 and 1957, at first in Japan at several shops including Kawasaki, Kisha Seizo Kaisha, Hitachi and Nippon Sharya Seisakusho, later in China at Dalian and Qingdao. During the 1930s a variety of other 2-8-2s were imported by independent Chinese railway companies, all denoted as sub-classes of JF. From 1957 a modified standard version was built at the Chinese works, of identical main dimensions but with longer piston valve travel, 6.3in (16.1cm) as against 6in (15.2cm). The 'standard' JF locomotives however continued to work freight over most parts of the Chinese railway network. Many were adapted for shunting, with sloping-backed tenders as often fitted on US switching engines, to improve the driver's view.

The JNR also went in for standard classes which could operate all over its 3ft 6in gauge network. With 1,115 built between 1936 and 1945, the D52 2-8-2 'Mikado' became the classic Japanese goods locomotive. Twelve plants were involved in building it, as well as JNR workshops. Although necessarily on a smaller scale than an American locomotive, the American influence was unmistakable. Lighter and shorter but with greater tractive power than its immediate predecessor, the D51, it had a flowerpot-style chimney, and a long boiler-top housing typical of Japanese locomotives, incorporating both dome and sandbox. In North American style, a feed-water heater cylinder was fixed crosswise in front of the chimney, and various other pumps for brakes and lubrication were fixed on the sides. Piston valves actuated by Walschaerts gear operated the two outside simple-expansion cylinders. After the first ninety-six had been built, some modifications were made, making the later ones marginally heavier. Although belonging unashamedly to the 'let it all hang out' school of design, the D52 was a robust and workmanlike engine, with a ready-for-anything air. In the words of one Japanese writer, it was: 'the truly representative steam locomotive of Japan.'

For designers, standardisation was most easily implemented in those aspects where there was general acceptance that a certain level of efficient performance had been reached. By the mid-1930s, this was the case with wheels, trucks or bogies, superheaters, and feed systems, among others. While improvements or at least variants were possible, it was also easy to adopt a standard approach. This could also be done with valve gear, where the long-lap piston valve was firmly established, but here the designers with radical leanings were haunted by the work of two Europeans, the Italian Arturo Caprotti and the Austrian Dr Hugo Lenz. Lenz introduced vertically-set poppet valves to locomotive use in 1905 and in 1907 produced an oscillating cam to work horizontally-set poppet valves. In 1915, Caprotti, trained as an automobile engineer, developed a form of locomotive valve gear in which vertical poppet valves were operated by a rotating cam. In both cases the cams took their motion from a gear set in a return crank on one of the coupled axles. Both approaches went through a whole series of adaptations, and both were most widely used in their inventors' native countries. But the potential benefits of poppet valves, including lightness of weight, steam tightness, and separate valves to control inlet and exhaust ports, offered enough improvement in efficiency and economy for many railways to continue experiments with them, and their use contributed to the success of Chapelon's locomotives in France. The last express steam locomotive in Britain, the prototype 4-6-2 No.71000, was fitted with a British-adapted Caprotti valve gear and on test it achieved one of the lowest consumptions of steam per single horsepower hour ever recorded. Though tried out everywhere, and widely used in some countries, notably Austria (homeland of Dr Lenz), poppet valves did not become universally used. The reliability of Walschaerts-Heusinger valve gear, and improvements to the effectiveness of piston valves, helped to keep them at bay. Also, completely new cylinder-blocks were needed for the installing of poppet valves: a major conversion task. A further point that concerned many engineers was that neither of the cam systems took on a definitive pattern: further improvement always seemed possible, and the conservators' instinct was to watch and wait.

TWENTY-NINE

Record Breakers

There was a certain cheerfulness and exuberance about the railway races and high speed attempts of the 1890s and early 1900s; the companies knew they could do it and wanted to show the world. In the next high-speed decade, one senses a rather different mood. By the 1930s, the railway companies were larger, wiser, soberer: they had adjusted to a world in which their monopoly was gone. The train was not the latest thing in transport – not even the fastest thing on land any more. Governments were more intrusive and demanding. And most railway companies were now more than fifty years old – many of their buildings and installations, and much of their equipment, were of similar age and in need of updating or replacement. Politically it was an edgy and disturbing time. The United States had lapsed into isolationism. Everywhere suffered from economic slump: in 1932 no new main-line locomotives were ordered in the USA. Europe was also shaken by political convulsion, and growing tensions between nations. Like all times, it had its high points and moments of achievement. The trains that ran in the 1930s were more drab than those of earlier times: most locomotives were painted utilitarian black and often showed signs of poor maintenance. But, on some occasions at least, the railways added some zest to the otherwise prosaic business of everyday life and of getting from A to B.

In 1926, the French businessman and locomotive enthusiast Baron Gérard Vuillet rode the Canadian National Railways' 'Intercity Limited' from Toronto to Montreal. Over the 334-mile (534km) run four different locomotives were used. The alternative routes between these cities were the cause of a needle match between the Canadian National and Canadian Pacific. The CPR had the longer road at 340 miles (547km) but for an exhilarating period between 1930 and 1933, it provided the world's fastest train over a distance exceeding 100 miles, from Smith Falls to Montreal West, 124 miles (199km) at an average speed of 68.9mph (110.9km/h). On his CN run, the stop-watch-wielding baron recorded a maximum speed of 82mph (132km/h) behind a new Class U1 4-8-2, and the whole journey took seven hours, fifty-six minutes and ten seconds. Between 1930 and 1933, this was reduced to six hours, while the CPR took fifteen minutes more. The CN's 'Mountain' type 4-8-2, built at the Montreal Locomotive Works, was praised by Vuillet as an excellent design, with a valve setting that was 'quite classical.' Then from April 1933 the two lines pooled the service and the schedule was promptly extended to six hours and thirty minutes.

While they lasted, these Canadian fireworks were not unnoticed elsewhere. In Britain, the Great Western Railway's lightweight afternoon express from Cheltenham to London had been the world's fastest in 1923, but had since been eclipsed by the Canadians and others. Its non-stop run from Swindon to Paddington, 77.3 miles (124.4km), was re-scheduled to seventy minutes in September 1929, which entailed long stretches at 80mph (128km/h) plus. The engines used were of the 'Castle' class, introduced in 1923, four-cylinder developments of the 'Stars'. In September 1931, three minutes were trimmed to make an average speed of 69.2mph (111.3km/h), but with a clear road, the train often arrived several minutes early, with a stop-to-start average of well over 70mph. On 16 September 1931, No.5000 *Launceston Castle* beat the old Atlantic City record of May 1905, when the American train had averaged 78.3mph, with a new world record of 79.7mph (128.2km/h). This was held until 5 June 1932, when *Tregenna Castle* averaged 81.7mph (131.4km/h) in a special run intended to score a point off the LNER and LMS who were both improving on the previously modest speeds of their north- and southbound expresses.

The maximum speeds hidden within the averages achieved in very fast runs were often very high, into the nineties or even more. Such performances could not fail to make some people consider the question of the absolute world record for steam power. Apart from *City of Truro's* downhill dash of 1902, there had been a few more or less well-authenticated occasions when a train had exceeded 100mph, as well as many more anecdotal accounts of super-speed. For engineers conscious of good publicity for the railway, and for steam locomotion – perhaps also conscious of the element of national prestige – it was not at all difficult to extend the road-testing of a new express engine to gauge its maximum speed potential. This is exactly what happened on a test run in 1936 with the new Class 05 4-6-4 of the German State Railways (DRG).

A small class of three, designed under Wagner's aegis by A. Wolff, built by Borsig in Berlin, and intended for the haulage of light-weight trains at very high speeds, the 05s showed Germany's steam engineers responding to the DRG's new fast diesel railcars. The DRG had stipulated the need for a locomotive to pull a 250t train at 93mph (150km/h) in normal service on level track, and with a maximum operating speed of 108mph (175km/h). Such a train would match the performance of the diesel railcars operating between Berlin, Hamburg, Cologne and Frankfurt, but with much greater passenger capacity and comfort. Three simple-expansion cylinders drove the first coupled wheels from the inside cylinder, and the second from the pair of outside cylinders, and three sets of Walschaerts valve gear were provided. The boilers were of the same diameter as the 01 Pacifics, but made of molybdenum steel plates, and the first two engines were bar-framed. The third was a much more experimental affair, built originally as a cab-front engine, to run on pulverised coal fuel. The huge driving wheels, 90.5in (2.30m) of all three were almost completely enclosed in a streamlined casing, painted in a red livery with a black, gold-lined band at footplate level. Double brake shoes were fitted to all wheels except the front wheels of the bogie, which had single shoes only, at the trailing end. In every detail Nos 05.001 and 002 were planned and built to sustain high speeds over long distances. Surprisingly perhaps, the copper-lined firebox was hand-fired: but with a grate area of 51sq ft (4.71m²) this was not impossible, especially as the engines were expected to be economical on coal. The tender was a large, seven-axle one, mounted on a four-wheel bogie with outside bearings, and three fixed axles with outside bearings set in the frame. Its capacity was 10t of coal and 8,200gals (9840US) of water. Germany did not use water troughs.

On 11 May 1936, in the course of a test run on the Berlin-Hamburg main line with a 197t train, No.05.002 driven by *Oberlokomotivführer* (senior driver) Langhans, took the world record for steam with a maximum speed of 124.5mph (200.4km/h) recorded in the dynamometer car. With the Reich's transport minister on board the train, it was clearly a premeditated exercise. This was achieved on virtually level track. Many other very fast runs were credited to Nos 05.001 and 002. From October 1936 until the outbreak of war in 1939 they operated Europe's fastest scheduled steam service, two hours and twenty-four minutes for the 178.1-mile (285km) Hamburg-Berlin route, requiring an average speed of 74.2mph (118.7km/h), which implies long stretches run at substantially higher speeds. They survived the war and in 1950 both Nos. 05.001 and 002 were rebuilt by Krauss-Maffei, and the streamlined casings were removed. No.003, which had not been a success and had been rebuilt conventionally in 1944-1945, was again rebuilt at this time. All three then participated in passenger express duties on the *Deutsche Bundesbahn* until 1957. No.05.001 is preserved, with its streamlined casing partly restored, but leaving the wheels and motion visible.

No.05.002 held its record for just over two years. Under its Chief Mechanical Engineer, H.N. Gresley, the British LNER had been building 'Pacifics' since 1923 and had had ample time to study the type and make the most of it. Since 1928 it had been building the class A3 'Super-Pacific' in large numbers, and these engines, typified by No.4472 *Flying Scotsman* (rebuilt from A1) were giving excellent service. They were three-cylinder simple-expansion engines, and their most notable feature was conjugated valve gear, a system of lever-linkage which enabled the middle cylinder to be worked by the two outside sets of Walschaerts valve gear. Early problems with it had been adequately resolved. A3s, fitted with corridor tenders to enable crew change (a feature unique to the LNER), ran non-stop between London and Edinburgh, and one, No.2750 *Papyrus*, had reached 108mph (173.7km/h). But now it was felt that something more was needed. The spark was lit by the high-speed *Fliegende Hamburger* two-car diesel express unit developed in Germany in 1933. At first the LNER management contemplated something like this for a four-hour London-Newcastle service, 268 miles (429km). But the best that the diesel could offer was four hours and twenty-five minutes, and test runs with the A3s showed that a steam locomotive could take a heavier train in less time. The new train was to be called the 'Silver Jubilee' in honour of George V's twenty-five years on the throne.

A new 'Pacific' design was drawn up, class A4, modifying that of the A3 in order to improve tractive effort and power output. Only six months elapsed between approval of the project and the delivery of the first engine of the class, No.2509 *Silver Link*, from the company's own Doncaster works, on 5 September 1935. At this time, as the railways faced up to motor and air competition, streamlining was widely practised, often of a crudely cosmetic sort, though Raymond Loewy was sculpting great engines in the USA. Gresley adopted the wedge-front used in French railcars designed by the Italian racing-car engineer Ettore Bugatti, and the streamlining of the A4s was done on a scientific basis, in a wind-tunnel, with a significant claimed reduction in air resistance. The angle-fronted cab, also borrowed from French practice, gave better vision to the driver. But undoubtedly the most significant streamlining was inside, where the casing concealed a 250psi (17.5kg/cm²) taper boiler with very carefully designed steam passages feeding three simple-expansion cylinders slightly smaller than those of the A3s. Here the LNER designers put into effect what they had learned from their earlier work with André Chapelon in connection with the P2 'Mikados'.

The launch of the new train, with streamlined articulated coaches and its gleaming wedge-fronted silver engine, was a sensation in itself, duly crowned by *Silver Link* breaking the British speed record with two maxima of 112.5mph (181km/h) on the demonstration run, and exceeding 100mph for 25 miles at a stretch. The four-hour London-Newcastle service was inaugurated on 30 September 1935. Between 1936 and 1938 a further thirty-one A4s were built at Doncaster, mainly for use on other extra-special services like the six-hour London-Edinburgh 'Coronation' train of 1937. This train had Britain's fastest-ever steam timing, requiring an average 71.9mph (116km/h) for the non-stop London-York section. The nine-coach train weighed 307 tons tare. But some of the glory of the A4s was taken by the rival 'Coronation Scot' of the LMS, whose demonstration run with its new streamlined 4-6-2 *Coronation* established a new British record of 114.5mph (184.2km/h).

In early 1938, a number of new A4s were fitted with Kylchap double chimneys, following successful experiment on an A3 'Pacific'. One of these was No.4468 *Mallard*. On 4 July that year, in the course of braking tests, this engine was authorised by Gresley to try for a maximum speed. In Gresley's mind was almost certainly not only the British record, but the world record for steam. With six 'Coronation' articulated coaches, and a dynamometer car, the train weight totalled 240 tons. On the East Coast main line south of Grantham, the train came over the low summit at Stoke at 74mph (119km/h) and with the engine kept by its driver J. Duddington at full regulator and first 40 per cent, then 45 per cent cut-off, accelerated down the 1 in 200 gradient until a maximum sustained speed of 125mph (201.1km/h) was reached, with an absolute maximum marginally higher. The record was snatched by a hair's breadth. Since that day, debate has gone on. The Germans pointed out that their record was reached on almost level track, with minimal assistance from gravity. It also became known that in being forced to its maximum effort, the British engine had broken the big end of its inside connecting rod, and instead of returning in triumph to London, had to be taken off its train for emergency treatment, like an athlete who has pushed past the physical limit. No.05.002 suffered no such over-strain. The suggestion that *Mallard* actually touched 126mph (202.7km/h) has recently been discounted, but computer-aided reviews of the dynamometer car records leave no doubt that the A4 attained the fastest verified speed of any steam locomotive. The work of this class and of its LMS 'Duchess-Coronation' rivals represents the high point of British express steam operation.

It took almost twenty years, until 1957, to provide all the single-chimney A4s with double Kylchap chimneys, and even in those twilight years of steam power, the class was still attaining speeds in excess of 100mph (161km/h). The exploits of the A4s are legion, both in high speeds and in powerful traction. A notable feat, again by *Mallard*, was the ascent of Stoke Bank, in the opposite direction to its record-breaking run, with a 415-ton train, at speeds up to 82mph (132km/h) and breasting the summit at 78mph (125.5kmh). Six of the class are preserved.

If anyone tried to beat the record set by *Mallard*, it did not work. A country that might have succeeded was the USA, where on certain routes speeds in excess of 100mph were a daily occurrence. One of these was the Chicago Milwaukee St Paul & Pacific Railroad. Travellers between Chicago and St Paul had a choice of three routes, all competing fiercely and offering the highest standards of speed and service. With no climbing to do, high speed was possible, and Alco built four highly specialised oil burning locomotives, the Class A 4-4-2, designed by the Milwaukee Road's mechanical engineer C.H. Bilty, to pull the 'Hiawatha' flyer, on a timing of six hours and thirty minutes for its 412-mile (663km) route, giving an average running speed of 66mph (106km/h). In Bilty's words (*Trains* magazine, December 1950), describing a preliminary test run with an F-6 4-6-4, 'We told our vice-president we thought the run [to Milwaukee] could be made in one hour. But he pointed out we would be hauling a regular service train, and if anything happened we would all land in jail.' One of the new engines, on a test outing, made one of the fastest-ever steam runs, 141 miles (227km) from Milwaukee to New Lisbon in 113 minutes. The 'Hiawatha' timing was later cut to six hours and fifteen minutes, despite five intermediate stops. Sustained speeds in excess of 100mph (161km/h) were necessary to maintain time. The engines were fitted with streamlined casings, and they and their trains were painted in a striking livery of yellow, orange, maroon and brown. It was not a lightweight train: with nine cars it amounted to 412.5 tons. These were the biggest and heaviest 'Atlantics' ever built, weighing (with tender) 528,000lb (234.6t) and with 300psi boiler pressure (21kg/cm²). In 1938, six similarly streamlined and equally speedy but coal-fired F7 4-6-4s replaced them, able to maintain the schedule with a twelve-car train, and from 1940 the Atlantics were diverted to the new 'Mid-West Hiawatha' operating between Chicago, Omaha and Sioux Falls. All ten of these engines achieved between a million and a million and a quarter miles in their running lives.

Other lines were using 4-8-4s for similar purposes, like the Union Pacific's semi-streamlined GS type operating the San Francisco-Los Angeles 'Daylight' streamlined train. But it is unlikely that any 4-8-4 has exceeded the speeds attained by the F7. With their streamlined front and boiler casing that also covered the cylinders, the F7s exemplified the tendency of American designers in the mid-1930s to play down the 'steamy' aspect of their passenger engines, but the wheels and running gear were left uncovered for easy access. They ran their twelve-car trains, 550 tons, at an average of 66mph (106km/h) including five stops. There is one verified account of 120mph (193km/h) averaged over a five-mile stretch, but no authenticated maximum speed above this. In 1940, they did however operate the fastest scheduled steam service anywhere, on the 'Hiawatha's' Sparta-Portage sector, 78.5 miles (126.3km) run at an average of 81.25mph (130.75km/h). The route length is almost the same as that between Swindon and London, but by 1940, with wartime loads and restrictions, the racing days in Great Britain were over, and the Great Western was in no position to claim back its lost laurels.

A potential rival in speed to the F7 was the Class J 4-8-4 of the Norfolk & Western Railway. This line's real business was moving coal in vast tonnages. It did not run many passenger services and its stud of express engines was not large. Their quality was however first-class. Eleven of Class J were built between 1941-43, to handle the line's principal passenger trains, and one was recorded as having reached 110mph (177km/h) on a test run with 1,025 tons on the Pennsylvania Railroad, near Crestline: at which speed its 70in (177.6cm) driving wheels were being turned at a rate which would have brought much greater speed with larger diameter. Speeds of up to 90mph (145km/h) in regular service with fourteen- or fifteen-car trains were also recorded.

But one is left with the feeling that the Americans had gone beyond playing the game of world maximum speed records for steam. After all, as far back as 1903, an experimental electric railcar had reached 130mph (209km/h) in Germany, and it did not seem likely that any steam locomotive would beat that. In 1937, of the ten fastest start-to-stop express train runs in the world, nine were being made by diesel multiple-unit sets; seven of them German, and two American. Only one was steam-worked, and that was the 'Hiawatha', at number 7. Many American railroads were about to embark on the commitment to change from steam to diesel power, and engineers would not be encouraged to invest time and money in proving points with steam. But there were other records which could be established. The real achievement of the N&W Class Js was not in absolute speed but in the intensive service which they gave. By 1950, the first had run well over 1,000,000 miles (1,609,000km) in service. The monthly distance run varied from 15,000 to 18,000 miles, (24,000-29,000km) and though the longest single run was from Roanoake, Virginia, to Cincinnati, Ohio, 424 miles (682km), their mileage was also assisted by smart turnaround times at the terminal stations. These engines were designed to travel about 240,000 miles (386,000km) before major overhaul. To many operators of steam locomotives such figures would have seemed like science fiction. But water-softening treatment and high standards of shed maintenance and preparation paid off for the N&W. Of all the American railroads, this was the one that worked hardest to modernise and retain its steam fleet, striving to match the levels of availability and use promised by the diesel-electric builders. In the end it could not buck the trend, but its steam services were all the more distinguished because of the hilly terrain in which it operated. By the time the Js were taken out of service in 1959, two had exceeded 2,000,000 miles (3,218,000km).

In France, where almost all lines were subject to a maximum speed of 75mph (120km/h), there was less interest in absolute speeds than in sustained running at averages close to the maximum. But in a valuable 'Profile' of the Nord 'Pacifics' (1971), Brian Reed noted that the Chapelon-designed 'Pacifics' of 1934-1939 exceeded 100mph (161km/h) on special tests and on one occasion No.3.1174 reached 108mph (174km/h) on the 1 in 200 falling gradient near Chantilly, with a hefty 400t train.

An intriguing postscript to the saga of high speeds with steam comes from Germany, where some remarkable tank engines were built in the 1930s. The role of the tank engine in the annals of steam is an honourable one that goes right back to *Novelty*, but in general it was also a secondary and workaday one, carried out in shunting yards and on suburban and minor lines, with little opportunity to shine. Some countries, like the USA and Russia, hardly used tank engines. But the Series 60 2-4-2T of the Lübeck-Büchen Railway in northern Germany was certainly special. In 1935 two Henschel-built streamlined engines of this class began running the 84km (52-mile) Hamburg-Travemünde service in one hour, start-to-stop, including an intermediate halt at Lübeck. Fast acceleration was essential, and they accelerated from 0 to 120km/h (75mph) in five and a half minutes. The train was a specially fitted push-pull unit; on the return trip the driver sat in a cab in the front coach, operating electrically-powered links to the controls. He communicated with the fireman by telephone. A third engine, with some modifications, was also built. They were a smaller precursor of the Series 61 4-6-6T of the German State Railways. The peak of Germany's streamlined high-speed tank operations was attained by this locomotive. Its prototype, a 4-6-4T, No.61 001, had been built in 1935 in a partnership between the Kassel firms of Henschel and Wagenfabrik Wegmann. The aim was to design a steam train that would emulate the performance of the new diesel-powered lightweight expresses, and be as convenient in operation. The locomotive and its four-car train were wholly streamlined. As on the Travemünde service, a driving cab was installed at the end of the last coach, so that on a return journey it became the front of the train. The engine was a big one, a three-cylinder simple, though its shrouding was so complete that it was only with difficulty recognised as a steam locomotive at all.

The *Henschel-Wegmann Zug*, as it was known, went into service in 1936 between Berlin and Dresden. In that year the solitary 60 001 ran a twice-daily express, doing the 109-mile (176km) journey in 100 minutes. It was clear, however, that its water and fuel capacity were too limited. On numerous occasions it arrived at the terminus with a dry tank, and for this reason the 4-6-6T was conceived, with an outside-frame six-wheel truck at the rear to carry increased supplies, 5t of coal and 1,010gals (1,210US) of water. The advent of war put an end to the service, and to further development of the super-tank express push-pull concept. No.61 001 was withdrawn in 1952; while the 4-6-6T was rebuilt by the *Deutsche Reichsbahn* in 1961 as a 4-6-2 tender locomotive for testing new rolling stock.

THIRTY

The Iconic Locomotive

Static machines have almost never been given individual names, however large or important they might be. The fancy of a separate identity has only been conferred on machines that move, under their own power. A practical reason lies behind it – the mobile machine needed to be recognised in different places. Trevithick felt no need to give his first locomotive a name: it was merely an engine on wheels, which could be taken off the wheels and applied to other uses, and was also of course unique. The Middleton Railway's *Salamanca* and *Prince Regent* were true locomotives, and their names heralded a practice that became official and was at first almost universal, the naming of locomotives. Very soon it was found necessary also to number them, as the species multiplied. With numbering, the naming of locomotives became sporadic – a traditional practice with some railways, an occasional whimsy with others; something never seen on most.

Although Charles R. King, writing in the *Railway Magazine* of February 1904, referred to it as 'an antiquated custom … abandoned by progressive railways', in the twentieth century, the country most addicted to naming its engines was his own Great Britain, where the express locomotives, at least, were normally provided with names. On the LNER, many of the 'Pacifics' were named after famous racehorses. *Hornet's Beauty, Bachelor's Button*, or *Pretty Polly* were quirky but somehow not silly names to affix to large locomotives. They were linked to the concepts of speed and the thoroughbred, had an individual sparkle and implied that the locomotive had a personality of its own. From the London & North Western, the LMS inherited a great and varied stock of names from folklore, like *Puck*, classical mythology from *Ajax* to *Venus*, and literature, though it mingled them with names of regiments and cities. Often names were quite dull: the custom of giving a locomotive class a standard form of name, as with the Great Western 'Castles', 'Manors' and 'Halls', lacked the variety and zest of the LNER's racehorse names. All companies often used names in an introverted way, to confer a compliment on some worthy person, one of its directors, or a politician. Instead of giving a personality to the locomotive, this gave the locomotive to a personality. Sometimes the complimentary gesture backfired: in the 1930s the Great Western began to name a series of rather antique-looking 4-4-0 rebuilds after various members of the aristocracy until one of them objected to being associated with such an uncharismatic type of locomotive. Another long-established standard practice was to underline the railway's links with the territory it traversed, seen equally in the Highland engines with Gaelic mountain names like *Ben-a-Bhuird* and the London Brighton & South Coast, or London Tilbury & Southend suburban tank engines named after their local stations. Some of the happiest names were those borrowed from literature, with Sir Walter Scott's works being an especially rich quarry. *Lord of the Isles* had a touch of grandeur, but the names of such North British Railway 'Scott' class and LNER D11/2 4-4-0s as *Jingling Geordie* and *Luckie Mucklebackit* also had a certain clankingly appropriate ring. Boring names or not, the GWR fixed very handsome nameplates to its engines, with raised brass lettering, as did some other companies. Surviving examples of these now fetch larger prices than the locomotives' own original cost. Prior to 1923, many other companies, notably the Scottish ones, were content to paint the names on the wheel-splashers.

In most other countries, the practice of naming individual locomotives was either dropped after the earliest years, or used very occasionally. In the later nineteenth century, Italy's Mediterranean Railway had a class of 4-4-0 engines named after celebrated heroines of history, including such un-Italian ladies as *Giovanna d'Arco* and *Carlotta Corday*; and Europe's first 4-6-0 class, introduced in 1884, were named after eminent men, beginning with the reigning Vittorio Emanuele II, but this was untypical. France, apart from some engines on the Alsace-Lorraine railways, early abandoned naming altogether, as did Germany and Austria, though Swiss engines often had names. Russian engines were not named, and in Central and Eastern Europe, China, Japan, and South America, the practice never really caught on. Some Spanish railways used names on occasion, as with the *Norte* railway's class of 0-8-0s named after rivers. In 1937, the Richmond, Fredericksburg & Potomac Railroad named all its twenty-seven new 'Northern' type 4-8-4s after Confederate generals and Virginian historic personages and state governors, but this was untypical of the USA, where named engines were rarities, as also in Canada. In places where British influence lingered, names were sometimes found on the more prestigious locomotives. Some Indian railways had a few named engines, and in Australia the Victorian Railways' S-class 4-6-2s of 1928, specially built to haul the new Melbourne-Sydney 'Spirit of Progress' train, were named after prominent Victorians.

Occasionally, a new locomotive or locomotive type might acquire such totemic significance within its native country that it would, exceptionally, be given a name. This happened with the Class 49 of the Norwegian State Railways (NSB). The 2-8-4, or 'Berkshire' type, introduced in 1925, remained an American exclusive until 1935. In that year the NSB, looking for a powerful locomotive to work through the Dovrefjell mountains between Oslo and Trondheim, particularly the steep Dombas-Trondheim section, opted for it and designed and built the first examples in Europe. The first three were built by Thunes Mekaniske Vaerksted of Oslo; 463 and 464 were classed 49a, and 465, with detail differences, including a feed-water heater, was 49b. They were four-cylinder compounds, with the high-pressure cylinders inside. Walschaerts valve gear, positioned outside, served both cylinders on each side. The tenders were of Vanderbilt type, mounted on outside-framed double bogies, with a covered coal bunker set on top of the water tank. Though smaller in dimensions than the US 'Berkshires' they were still among the largest and most powerful locomotives in Europe. From the first, the class was put into intensive use and despite the teething troubles inevitable with a new and complicated locomotive type, it soon operated very satisfactorily. High speed was not a requirement and the maximum running speed was 62mph (100km/h), but they proved to have excellent adhesion and acceleration, and climbed the Dovre grades with heavy trains at a steady 37mph (60km/h). There was a good deal of international interest in the new locomotives, and they occasioned much national pride, with the justifiable feeling that here was a considerable achievement for a small country. The first one, No.463, was duly named *Dovregubben*, 'Dovre Giant', after the mythical spirit that lurked in the mountains through which the big engines now rolled unchallenged.

After the German occupation of Norway in 1940, four more were delivered, two from Krupp in Essen and two from Thunes, classed 49c. These had single chimneys and smaller-diameter cylinders, and German-type smoke deflectors attached to the smoke-box sides. All seven worked on until the mid-1950s, and six were scrapped in 1958. *Dovregubben* can still be seen, though sadly for the Norwegian national spirit, the preserved engine is one of the Krupp-built pair, having been given the number and name-plates of the very first, and home-built, No.463.

A comparable national resonance clung to the Class 800 4-6-0 engines of the Great Southern Railway in Ireland. Locomotive design on the 5ft (152.4cm) gauge Irish railways was closely identified with the British tradition. The 'economic war' of the 1930s between the Irish Free State and Great Britain meant that there was little money available for new investment of any kind, and by 1939 the main Dublin-Cork line desperately lacked adequate motive power for heavy trains. The three '800s' were designed and built at the GSR's own Inchicore shops in Dublin to provide express services on this route. Three-cylinder simples, with three sets of Walschaerts valve gear, and double chimneys, they were the largest and most powerful locomotives built in Ireland, their dimensions comparable with the British 'Royal Scots'. Painted a glossy emerald green, they seemed to symbolise the ability of Ireland to construct its own future. They were named *Maedbh, Macha* and *Tailte* after legendary Irish queens endowed with magical powers. Soon, legends began to grow around them too, with rumours of speeds up to 100mph (161km/h). Nothing of this sort has been verified but they were undoubtedly fast as well as impressive engines. *Tailte* was withdrawn in 1957, *Macha* in 1964, but *Maedbh* is preserved. There is a little twist of historic irony in her story too: she resides at the Ulster Transport Museum rather than in the Irish Republic whose independent spirit she helped to characterise.

Apart from such rare exceptions, and the resolutely tradition-minded British, naming was confined to locomotive types or specific wheel configurations, when it occurred at all. It was a completely haphazard and somewhat disorderly business. Some names stuck, and some failed to survive; some were applied to more than one type; other types had more than one name. The great majority of these names arose in the USA and while a few, like 'Atlantic', 'Pacific' and 'Mikado' became universal, others were used patchily in other countries, like 'Mogul' for a 2-6-0, 'Prairie' for a 2-6-2, 'Hudson' for a 4-6-4 (though 'Baltic' was used in Europe for this configuration), 'Mountain' for a 4-8-2 (though the New York Central used 'Mohawk'). 'Decapod', usually applied to a 2-10-0, was used by the Southern Pacific for its 2-10-2s. 'Ten-wheeler', applied to the 4-6-0, was largely dropped because of its ambiguity after various other ten-wheeled configurations appeared.

Several names were applied to wheel arrangements rarely or never seen outside the USA, and these often had a public-relations whiff, bestowed by the builder on behalf of the first railroad to use the type. Thus the 2-10-2 became the 'Santa Fe', the 2-10-4 the 'Texas', the 2-10-10-2 the 'Virginian', and the 4-8-4 the 'Northern'. Disdaining the 'Texas' label, Henry Blaine Bowen, Chief Engineer of the Canadian Pacific Railroad, held a staff competition to find a class name for his great new 2-10-4 locomotives of 1929: the winner came up with 'Selkirk' after the mountains through which it would pass, and was duly awarded a prize of $50. Aspirational names later crept in, like 'Challenger' for the Union Pacific's 4-6-6-4, and this became a particular feature of Soviet and Chinese locomotives. In these cases, though, class names like 'Victory' or 'Aim High' were not intended also to classify specific wheel configurations.

In the years between 1927 and 1941, the locomotive as icon took on a new significance with the assumption of an ambassadorial role. Three different British locomotives were sent across the Atlantic, to make state visits to their American cousins. Unfortunately, the British loading gauge made return visits by 'Hudsons' or 'Northerns' out of the question. The first to make the trip was a Great Western 'King'. The original plan had been to name this class after famous cathedrals, but with the American invitation, it was felt that something even grander, and more royal, was desirable, and No.6000, *King George V*, was completed in the nick of time to go forth to the Baltimore & Ohio's centennial 'Fair of the Iron Horse'. The 'King' led the parades and made many demonstration runs. It returned wearing a large American bell, and this was to be the visible token of the others' visits also. Next was one of the new 'Royal Scots' of the LMS, sent to the Chicago World Fair of 1933, complete with its train. A polite fiction was perpetrated here. Naturally the eponymous class leader, No. 6100, was wanted. And No. 6100, *Royal Scot*, duly arrived. But it was actually a newly-built and somewhat improved engine, No. 6152, *King's Dragoon Guardsman*, which, having switched name and number for the occasion, went on to do a highly acclaimed 11,000 mile tour of North American railroads. In 1939 another World Fair, at Flushing Meadow, New York, which featured a Railroad Pageant including some of the latest American steam giants, was attended by another LMS locomotive, this time the streamlined 'Pacific' No. 6220 *Coronation*. Once again, however, everything was not quite what it seemed. The engine which appeared in the USA was actually No.6229, *Duchess of Hamilton*, which exchanged her identity with the class leader, and resumed it again on returning home in 1942. One or two sharp-eyed American observers noted with interest that its rods bore the number 6229. These visits, prompted by no commercial motive, created great public interest and goodwill. There was even some impact on American design: Colonel George H. Emerson, chief of motive power on the B&O, was sufficiently impressed by King George V's brasswork and neat lines to adopt a 'British' styling for his P-7 'President' class 'Pacifics' of 1928, including a brass chimney cap and low running plates, and with the pipe-work tidily hidden away. Many other American types of the 1930s show a similar tidying-up, without being streamlined, and for this the ambassadors can take some credit.

THIRTY-ONE

On the Footplate

Like the top-paying and top-drawer customers, who were able to place their chairs even on the stage of Shakespeare's theatre, so it had always been possible for a select few to demand, or accept, a ride on the footplate of a locomotive. It was only when cabs became more secure and capacious that this turned into the ordered system of the footplate pass. For the well-connected locomotive enthusiast, there was no greater privilege than to gain one of these, allowing travel on a particular engine at a specified time. Invariably, an inspector from the depot would also be present: for whose protection is not entirely clear. In Britain, railway companies were suspicious of speed freaks who might urge or even bribe a driver to make a record run from one point to another, or hit a maximum speed. But the inspector's job was chiefly to see that the guest survived the experience and did not get in the way of the engine crew. Most of the supercargoes were journalists, but wealthy enthusiasts like Baron Gérard Vuillet, with many friends on railway boards, were not uncommon. He rode on engines on many lines in Europe, Britain and North America, making careful logs of his journeys:

I spent the night of 9 March 1928 on the footplate of 2-8-0 No.4221 hauling coal train No.4104 from Lens to Creil. For the 100.3 miles five hours and thirty-one minutes were allowed, including a single stop of twenty-two minutes at Longueau. The time of departure was 9.32p.m. and the schedule was strictly kept, although fifteen minutes had been lost through signals towards Arras. The weather was cold, with snow falling during the second part of the journey. From Lens to Longueau we had fifty-six wagons (1,447 tons). Ten wagons were left at Longueau, leaving a train of 1,200 tons to Creil. From Lens there is a continuous ascent for 7.3 miles to km 199.7, nominally at 1/200, but in fact comprising stretches at 1/167 owing to track subsidences in the mining district. The summit is marked by a brick bridge over the tracks called *Pont à Lunettes* by the crews, on account of its shape when seen in the distance.

The Baron did his homework more thoroughly than most footplate guests, but then he had freely given his soul to the steel Mephistopheles. His iron disregard for such non-technical inconveniences as snowstorms was unshakeable; his Gallic nonchalance can only be admired. This note is from his footplate ride on one of the great 'Hiawatha' 4-4-2s, in June 1937, on train 101 between Chicago and St Paul:

> The locomotive rode remarkably well. At 96mph I wrote my notes conveniently standing up and not leaning against anything. At 106 mph I took them quite comfortably, sitting down.

Even grander personages than the Baron took not only the footplate, but the controls, sometimes. The best-known are probably King Ferdinand I and his son Boris III of Bulgaria. Both were thorns in the flesh of the *Compagnie Internationale des Wagons Lits*, which preferred the engine drivers of its expresses to be properly qualified. Drivers on the 'Orient Express' were strictly forbidden to admit them to the footplate. But in their own kingdom, they could not be gainsaid. Boris especially, the Mr Toad of railways, was an inveterate invader of the driver's side. On one occasion, as the king was driving fast towards Sofia, there was a flash-back when the fire-doors were opened, and the fireman, fatally burned, jumped from the engine. Boris drove on regardless, and the incident had to be expensively hushed up. More respectable royal steam men were king Frederik of Denmark, and the Duke of Segovia, a cousin of the ill-fated king Alfonso of Spain. The duke had gained an engine-driver's certificate, and sometimes took the regulator of the royal train during the 1920s. Frederik, who died in 1972, had planned his own steam-hauled funeral train, which duly ran from Copenhagen to Roskilde, hauled by two E-Class 'Pacifics' with the Danish colours banding their chimneys.

Almost always, however, the footplate was the preserve only of the professional driver and fireman. In egalitarian Soviet Russia, the latter was not always of the male sex. Hugh Hughes notes in *Middle East Railways*, how, towards the end of the Second World War, Allied servicemen in the Middle East were intrigued to find women sometimes doing the firing on the

Russian locomotives that took supply trains northwards from the Iranian-Russian border. This seems to have been a uniquely Russian practice. Driver and fireman normally worked as a two-man team, and the demands of running the engine and watching for signals made this co-operation essential, quite apart from the fact that operating rules spelled it out. But frictions might occur. Brian Fawcett, recalling the hard locomotive men of the Andean railways, told of one big fireman who had the habit of chalking a line down the centre of the cab floor, and instructing the driver to keep to his own side of it. This worked until he was partnered with a driver even tougher than himself, who stood him up against the tender front and beat him senseless, before asking the shed foreman for a replacement.

Far more often than not, there was harmony on the footplate. The triumph of *Mallard* in 1938 was that of Fireman Bray as well as Driver Duddington and Sir Nigel Gresley. Of similar calibre were Fireman Miot and Driver Gourault of the SNCF, the regular team in testing of Chapelon's new engines. Such men were the real kings of their trade, but their collaboration was reflected in the vast number of ordinary and unpublicised services of every day. Their work could easily be romanticised by the amateur enthusiasts. Catering for impressionable or youthful readers, some railway writers of an earlier generation liked to hint at their own footplate experiences, gained in an unspecified manner, mentioning lightly that nothing could taste better than ham and eggs fried on a burnished steel shovel thrust in through the fire-doors. Such culinary visions, located on express locomotives bucketing along at 70mph, were highly unlikely. Even on a stationary goods engine, and assuming that either driver or fireman, normally men of traditional mould, considered cooking to be an admissible skill, it would be a tricky feat. A bottle of lukewarm tea and a sandwich box provided the refreshment of most enginemen in tea-drinking lands; Argentinian crews had their *maté* and Brazilians their coffee; for many, water was enough, though in Italy or Spain, a straw-cased wine-flask might be stashed away in the cab. The most frequent hazard for men who worked on steam locomotives was damage to their eyes, caused by peering out into the cinder-laden slipstream to look for landmarks and signals. This could result in much more serious injury: in 1931, thirty-one French locomotive men were killed by lineside equipment while leaning out to look for signals. In France, drivers were compelled to wear goggles; in Great Britain, they were rigorously forbidden to do so. Partly because most engines were never required to move very fast, designers did little to improve forward sighting, despite the fact that the flat-fronted glass reflected any light in the cab. Only some express classes were later given wedge-front cabs, and only France and Germany experimented with aerodynamic or spinning-disc windows to prove all-weather visibility, though in Australia and some other countries, cab roofs were carried forwards to provide a degree of shade from direct sunlight, and from the 1930s it was normal on large German and Eastern European locomotives to have short hoods over the front glasses. The proximity of the fire, and the open sides and backs of cabs, often exposed men to simultaneous extremes of heat and cold. Best-protected were engine-men in the Communist countries, where they were high-status workers. Good, spacious cabs, sometimes completely enclosed, were common in Poland, Russia, Hungary and Czechoslovakia. The American 'hogger' too was usually well-enclosed, at least in cabs designed from the 1930s on. The lot of the fireman, or 'tallow-pot', so-called from the old greasing method, varied from the relative comfort of the cab of an oil-fired locomotive, to the perilously swaying tender deck of a 'Mother Hubbard' with virtually no protection at all. The use of 'hog' to refer to a locomotive went a long way back in US railroad slang, and did not seem to have any pejorative sense. Similarly the reliable Australian Class C36 4-6-0s of 1925, built by the New South Wales Government Railways, appear to have been quite affectionately known as 'pigs'. Drivers often addressed recalcitrant engines in much sterner language. But it was recorded at the official enquiry held in 1946 following an accident in England, that the driver said to his 'Pacific' engine, just before it jumped the rails and overturned: 'Steady on, old girl.'

THIRTY-TWO

The Biggest Engines

Why did North America come to construct such very large locomotives in the 1930s and 1940s? For the observer, there is a temptation to work by analogy and to compare this increase in size, so soon before the extinction of the species, to the fate of the dinosaurs in the natural world, hundreds of millions of years before. The unfortunate choice of 'Mastodon' as a name for the 4-10-0 locomotive, though neither the configuration nor its appellation gained very wide currency, rather underlined this. Now, however, we understand that the dinosaurs did not get too big for their own good, perishing beneath their own lumbering weight, but succumbed along with many other species to a global catastrophe. The fate of the giant steam locomotives was different. In their prime, they were confronted by a new and rival species possessing certain advantages, and which forced them out of their territory and into extinction. But while that rival species was still small and imperfect in operation, several factors encouraged the growth of the American steam locomotive.

One of these was simply the existence of space to expand into. 16.5ft of height and 10.5ft of width gave designers room to fit various auxiliaries, without compromising the size of boiler and firebox. Another was the Mallet articulated design, which was improved in various detailed ways. The desire of companies to have engines capable of running long distances encouraged growth. Among the great railroad companies, there was a sharp sense of prestige and consequent rivalry. They were joint stock corporations, with shareholders to please as well as reward; they also competed for traffic on numerous routes. On a scale larger in every way, their posture reflected that of the British companies in the 1920s, with their succession of express locomotives each boasting an attribute touted as superior to the others. But what it boiled down to in the end was that bigger engines hauled a greater tonnage.

One of the main impediments to building very long, heavy locomotives had been resolved in 1923. Great difficulty had been experienced in providing a frame that would support the weight of a massive boiler without itself being excessively heavy; and that would also provide the necessary flexibility on curving, undulating track. Neither the traditional bar nor plate frames were suitable, but the problem disappeared with the introduction of the single-piece cast steel frame. Running the whole length of the locomotive, and pierced as necessary for axle boxes and mounting fixtures, it was relatively light, very strong, and resistant to shocks, lateral forces, and pressures. Evolved from the wartime gun-carriage, eventually it would be the basis of most modern steam locomotives, but for twenty years it was used only in America. Another essential aid in operating the big engine was the mechanical stoker. By 1925 these had been around for twenty years and a number of reliable patent versions were available, powered by an auxiliary steam engine in the tender which operated a screw within a conveyor pipe, crushing the coal and funnelling it forwards to the firebox. A coal pusher at the back of the tender was normally part of the assembly. An array of steam jets then directed the coal to different parts of the grate area. Although the mechanical method used more coal than hand-firing did, it was cheaper than having two firemen. With grate areas now well in excess of 50sq ft (4.6m²), it was impossible for a single man to feed the fire. An alternative to coal firing that was looking increasingly viable, with the exploitation of vast American oil reserves, was the use of oil as fuel. As with the mechanical stoker, this reduced the fireman's task to operating a set of feeder valves, and made it possible for him to pay more attention to lubricators and other ancillary equipment.

Another precondition for very large engines was to have a road and roadbed that would support their great weight and in particular their maximum axle-weight. Whereas once 20 tons was seen as a heavy axle loading, the trend was moving towards a maximum half as heavy again, or even more. Such weight restricted the route availability of the very large engines, but as in most cases they were intended to operate on specific routes only, this was not considered to be a disadvantage, and the track and bridges were upgraded to accommodate the huge foot-fall of the behemoths.

Finally, the way forward, of integrating a very large boiler and firebox, feed-water heating, and ample combustion space in a balanced design, was shown by the Lima 'super-power' locomotive. From the later 1920s, then, the way was clear for very large locomotives to be built. In the United States, the need was also clear. Concentrating bulk freight into longer yet faster trains required fewer locomotives and train crews; it helped the railroad keep its costs down and its prices competitive; and it allowed more trains to be run over busy sections of line. In other countries, the need was not so evident. In Europe, apart from the loading gauge restrictions, freight trains were not often as long and heavy as those of the USA; and distances run were usually much shorter. Southern Africa opted for the Garratt articulated locomotive. South America was getting by with eight-coupled engines, and with Mallets or Garratts on some mountain lines. Australia was still very much a British protectorate in locomotive terms. Russia, however, whose state-owned railways enjoyed a monopoly of long-haul transport, and which was anxious to show that anything the capitalist Americans could do, the Soviet system could do too, was interested in big engines, although many Russian engineers felt that the real need was for a modernised, faster and more powerful version of the trusty but slow old carthorse, the E-class 0-10-0. By 1931 this need was urgent as the Soviet Railways' lack of motive power was threatening the success of industrial development plans. A number of strategic main lines were quickly upgraded to take locomotives of 20-ton axle load and the Class FD 2-10-2, named for Felix Dzerzhinsky, the tough commissar who reorganised the Russian railways in 1921, was designed. The work took place under uniquely Stalinist circumstances – the engineers were under arrest by the OGPU secret police, and their drawings were made in the ill-reputed offices of that organisation. A two-cylinder simple, the FD shows numerous American features, including bar frames, a mechanical stoker, and a thermic syphon in the firebox. In 1933 series production began at the Voroshilovgrad works and over 3,000 were built. In the late 1950s and early 1960s, around 1,250 of these locomotives were transferred to China and regauged to standard gauge, as Chinese Class FD.

As big engines go, the FD, though over 16ft high, was still relatively modest. It weighed 302,085lb (137t) and had a tractive effort of 64,500lb (29,251kg). A typical American 2-10-2, like the Chicago & Illinois Midland's Class H-1, of 1930, weighed 405,600lb and had a tractive effort of 77,000lb plus another 10,500lb from its booster. And in American terms this was a middleweight. There was strong pressure on the Soviet Railways to come up with something bigger. As a rule, Russian locomotive engineering was eminently practical, and even its more arcane experimental designs were entered into in a spirit of serious scientific enquiry. Consequently the one and only member of class AA20, which appeared in late 1934, a 4-14-4 with seven driving axles, the largest non-articulated locomotive in Europe, and with the longest rigid wheelbase ever built, was something of an embarrassment. Named after its sponsor, Andrei Andreyev, it was intended to demonstrate maximum freight locomotive dimensions and performance within the Russian gauge and with the recently increased maximum axle loading of 20 tons. Numerous engineers opposed the proposal, saying that more 2-10-2s would be far more useful. The original intention was for a 2-14-4, to be built by Krupps in Germany, but at a late stage in the design a front bogie was substituted and it was built in Russia at the Voroshilovgrad works. It never entered revenue-earning service. A publicity visit to Moscow was made in January 1935, and the huge engine was duly hailed as a triumph of Soviet technology. No comment was ever made on its further activities, and three decades went by before the Russian technical press was able to admit that the AA20 had been a total failure. Its 207-ton (465,920lb) weight spread the tracks and broke points, and it regularly derailed on curves. It was hidden away and at some point was unceremoniously scrapped.

The only essay at seven driving axles proved unworkable, and most companies would fight shy of six in a row, though some heavy-duty tank engines of this configuration were used in Austria, Bulgaria and Indonesia. But in 1926 the Union Pacific Railroad acquired the first of eighty-eight 4-12-2s of the 9000 class from Alco's Brooks Works. These were until 1934 the longest and largest non-articulated locomotives in the world. The length of the coupled wheelbase was 30ft 8in (9.34m). A company statement announced the aim as 'to haul mile-long freights at passenger train speeds.' Unusually for the USA, they were three-cylinder engines, though employing simple expansion, with the inside cylinder driving the second set of wheels and the outside cylinders the third. In an unusual employment of overseas technology, the British Gresley conjugated valve gear was used, to avoid having three sets of valve gear. To help the engine traverse curves, the first and last sets of coupled wheels were allowed a degree of lateral play; and the fourth was originally flangeless, though this was later found to be unnecessary. The 4-12-2s were successfully employed on the UP until 1956, and the first engine, No.9000, is preserved. With a tractive effort of 96,650lb (43,832kg), they represented the maximum power to be got from a rigid-framed locomotive.

For still-greater power, the American railroads stayed with the Mallet format but using simple expansion only. Just as the 4-12-2 was unique to the Union Pacific, so the 4-8-8-2 'Cab-first' Class ACs were to be seen only on the Southern Pacific Railroad. The 'cab-first' concept goes back to Europe in 1900, but the SP took it up in the biggest way. Between Truckee and Blue Canyon, on its Sierra Nevada line, there were 38 miles of snow-sheds, built to prevent huge snowdrifts from blocking the line. In these long snow-sheds and the many tunnels, smoke blowing back into the cab had been a source of distress and indeed danger to the engine crews, and the design was intended to deal with this problem. As the engines burned oil, the question of access to the fuel supply was easily dealt with: oil and water were towed in a box-like twelve-wheel double bogie tender, with oil supplied at 5lb (2.2kg) pressure to the burners. The first AC locomotives had been Mallet compounds turned back-to-front in 1910; these were rebuilt from 1927 as simple-expansion engines, and the AC5 locomotives of 1928 were four-cylinder simples from the start, of greater mechanical dimensions than the AC-1s, and with an estimated tractive effort of (124,300lb). In all, the SP had over 200 AC locomotives, constructed up to 1937, of which only Class AC-9 was not cab-forward. Like the Adriatic Class 500 of Italy, these locomotives ran permanently 'backwards'. Despite the relative freedom from smoke, though some from preceding trains always hung about in tunnels, the enginemen were not entirely happy at first. Many expressed concern at what might happen in a collision at one of the many unguarded road crossings. But the cab-firsts had a long career; the last in action was No.4274 in December 1956; the last of the line, No.4294, is preserved.

In 1929, another railroad with long-haul routes across wilderness and mountain introduced what was, until the advent of the Union Pacific 'Big Boys' in 1941, the biggest locomotive in the world. In some respects, such as grate area, evaporative heating surface and superheating surface, it was never exceeded. This was the Class Z-5 2-8-8-4 of the Northern Pacific Railroad. A prototype was built by the American Locomotive Co. in that year, and in 1930 a production run of eleven was ordered, rather oddly from Baldwin rather than Alco. Known as the 'Yellowstones', they were designed to haul 4,000-ton freight trains on the 216-mile (347.6km) sector of the transcontinental route through the 'Badlands' between Mandan, North Dakota, and Glendive, Montana, up grades of 1.1 per cent, and they worked on such tasks into the late 1940s. These engines stood 17ft 2in (5.23m) from the rails to the chimney lip, and weighed 1,010,475lb (499t) with their twelve-wheeled tenders. They were built Mallet-fashion, with the pilot and front coupled wheels forming an articulated truck; the rear coupled axles fixed to the frame, and a pivoted four-wheel trailing truck, but the four cylinders were simple-expansion only. The immense firebox of over 200sq ft (18.6m^2) was intended to burn lignite, or 'Rosebud coal', from a NP-owned mine in Montana. A booster engine was fitted to the trailing truck to assist with starting off, and delivering an additional 13,400lb (6077kg) of tractive effort to its own 140,000lb (63,492kg). All the 'Yellowstones' were later fitted with roller bearings, in the use of which the NP was a pioneer among American railroads.

The advantages of tapered roller bearings, already used in the automobile industry, were dramatically introduced to the American railroads in 1930, when the Timken Roller Bearing Co. took a leaf out of Lima's book and sponsored a demonstration locomotive. Apart from having roller bearings fitted on all axles, it was a standard Alco Schenectady-built 4-8-4 'Northern', given the road number 1111 and consequently known as the 'Four Aces'. Fifty-two manufacturers of special parts and fittings supplied their products at no charge until the locomotive should have run 100,000 miles. Thirteen railroads tested it over the next two years. A great publicity stunt, when the 355-ton giant was shown to be so free-rolling that three men could pull it from a standing start with a rope, was exceeded only when the same thing was done in Chicago by three nubile young ladies. The case for roller bearings was well and truly made. In February 1933, after the 100,000 miles were accomplished, the Northern Pacific bought No.1111 and ran it for a further twenty-three years and a further 2,025,000 miles (3,258,225km).

Engines of the 'Yellowstone' configuration were the biggest steam power on several major railroads, including the Baltimore & Ohio and the ore-hauling Duluth Missabe & Iron Range, and were built into the 1940s. They established the double set of simple-expansion cylinders as the standard for the biggest and most powerful locomotives. Everything on the largest possible scale, well-built from first-class materials, utilising all that was known of efficient steam circulation, ensured that they did a very effective job. In terms of their own tonnage, and the tonnage they could move, they overshadowed all other locomotives. Their absolute power was unchallengeable. And yet, measured by tonne of weight against tonne of tractive effort, they were not supreme.

From 1936, André Chapelon had been engaged in rebuilding a 6000-Class 2-10-0, one of a class of four-cylinder compounds which, with various alterations, had been running freight trains on the Paris-Orleans system since 1909. The aim was to produce a big freight engine (in European terms) which would perform economically at low speeds – something steam locomotives were historically incapable of doing. The rebuild was even more comprehensive and drastic than the designer's previous efforts, and the result, not completed until 1940, was a six-cylinder, six-driving axle locomotive: No.160.A.1 of the French National Railways (SNCF), which had been formed from the old provincial companies in 1938.

A six-cylinder steam locomotive might seem destined to be one of these design freaks destined for hiding at the back of a locomotive shed. Two, three, or four were established as the standard forms. But Chapelon's was a thoroughly considered approach. He had to construct a locomotive that worked within the loading gauge and the axle-weight constraints imposed by the civil engineer. The six coupled axles were needed because the long boiler and firebox required adequate support and a sufficiently low maximum axle-loading. Naturally, a compound-expansion system was planned: maximum utilisation of steam was a basic principle for Chapelon, and compounding was the norm on big French locomotives. Six cylinders were considered necessary, as a single pair of low-pressure cylinders able to provide the requisite power would have had to be so large as to break the loading gauge. Four in-line low-pressure cylinders were set ahead of the first coupled axle, with the inside pair driving the second axle and the outside pair the third. The high-pressure cylinders, set inside, towards the middle of the locomotive, and receiving steam via a Houlet superheater, drove the fourth coupled axle. Thus three of the six coupled axles were directly driven. The cylinders were equipped with double walls with steam admitted between them - steam 'jackets' to keep the insides as hot as possible. The boiler was divided into two parts, in an adaptation of the Italian Franco system, the front end being a pre-heating drum, from which almost-boiling water was fed by an overflow system into the main boiler. A thermic syphon was fitted in the firebox. Every effort was made to generate, to conserve, and to make the most effective use of steam. Exhaust steam drove the feed pump that supplied the pre-heater. Steam was re-superheated in a Schmidt superheater between the high-pressure and low-pressure cylinders. Lenz poppet valves were used to work the pistons, actuated by oscillating cams driven by Walschaerts gear, all of it outside the frames. Kylchap double exhaust pipes were fitted. The original frame was substantially reinforced as well as lengthened. The three driving axles were fixed, while the first, fifth and sixth were given a degree of lateral movement to enable the long wheelbase to negotiate curves.

The rebuilding was completed in June 1940, just before the fall of France. There was no opportunity to undertake testing, and the new engine was sent out on a regular freight working and stored away at Brive, in the south-west, until after the war. Tests were finally begun in 1948, when they were made both on the Vitry static testing plant, and on the road. The aim of the design was fully met. At low speeds, the locomotive showed no decline in thermal efficiency. Its fuel consumption went down, not up as had been the norm hitherto. A valuable result, not anticipated, was that the steam jackets on the high-pressure cylinders, combined with moderate superheat in the low-pressure cylinders, removed the need for ultra-hot superheating, whose extremely high temperatures were a constant source of expensive damage to castings, joints and lubricated surfaces.

Although high speed was not a pre-requisite, the engine recorded 59mph (95km/h) on test. It took a train of 65 vehicles, 1,686t, on level track between Laroche and Dijon at a steady 30mph (48km/h). The maximum actual tractive effort recorded on the move in these tests was of the order of 49,000lb (22,200kg). On one occasion, starting a 1,686t train on a curving 1 in 125 gradient, the dynamometer car registered a tractive effort of 87,840lb (39,836kg). The Union Pacific 4-12-2, weighing 515,000lb (257.7t), had a tractive effort of 96,650lb; the French locomotive, at 137.5 tonnes, had a power-to-weight ratio close to twice that of the American giant. The 2-12-0 was inevitably a test engine; its designer considered it as a mobile labora-tory. But there was no question that it worked. However, from the SNCF's beginning, the management had been determined to pursue a policy of electrification. Despite the success of the prototype, no further conversions were authorised. No.160 A.1 remained a single-engine class until it was scrapped in November 1955, two years after Chapelon had retired from the SNCF.

With his six-coupled engine, Chapelon had gone a long way towards resolving what had always been a problem of the steam locomotive: how-ever great its full tractive potential, it was unable to exert it to the maximum at starting and at low speed. In the years before 1938, steam designers might have shrugged this off as a regrettable but inevitable feature. It was the main reason for applying booster engines to rear bogies or sometimes to tender wheels. This practice went back a long way, to the St Etienne-Lyons line in France in 1843, when the engineer Claude Verpilleux, Seguin's successor, fitted one to a locomotive called *La Jumelle*. Archibald Sturrock patented a 'steam tender' to supplement the power of his 0-6-0 locomotives on the coal trains of the Great Northern Railway in Britain in the 1860s. By 1938, however, this deficiency was a serious disadvantage in comparisons made with the competing diesel-electrics (General Motors had set up its Electro-Motive Division shops at La Grange, Illinois, in 1935). Though individually much less powerful than a big steam locomotive, these could be worked multiple-unit, and through their gearing could deploy full power over a much wider spectrum of speeds. The American steam designers were unaware of Chapelon's continuing work on this very aspect, and even if they had been, it is unlikely that they would have been influenced. By now, the two traditions were too far apart. The American answer was to provide locomotives of such power that their relative inefficiency at low speed did not hinder them from getting massive train-weights on the move. They had ceased to be simply concerned by how many tons a locomotive could pull, probably at a low speed. Driven by the demands of commercial and traffic managers who wanted to combine haulage power with speed and efficiency, they were thinking in terms of what horsepower could be developed by a really big locomotive, working hard. Performance of this kind was exemplified by the Santa Fe Class 3765 4-8-4s built between 1937 and 1944, which ran the 1,788 miles (2,877km) from Kansas City to Los Angeles in twenty-six hours and at an average speed of 68.8mph (110.7km/h), with nine crew changes on the way. They had driving wheels of 80in (203.2cm) diameter and a boiler pressure of 300psi (21kg/cm²). But the culmination of this approach was seen in the Union Pacific Railroad's Class 4000.

These articulated 4-8-8-4s were the 'Big Boys' – the name was chalked on a smoke-box during construction by an unknown employee of Alco, and it stuck. No public-relations consultant could have improved on it. The twenty-five engines of this class were the largest and most powerful steam locomotives ever built, surpassing the Northern Pacific 'Yellowstones' of 1928 in weight and with a length of 132ft 10in (40.57m) compared to 122ft (37.157m); though their nominal tractive effort, at 135,375lb, was slightly less. Although the Union Pacific was an early user of diesel locomotives for its passenger express trains, it did not begin to use diesels for freight until 1947. In this department, steam was still unchallenged. But the requirements were severe. The design was worked out by the Research & Standards department of the UP, in close association with the American Locomotive Company, which built the engines. The presiding spirit was Otto Jabelmann, whose career had begun as a call-up boy in Cheyenne, waking the engineers for the dawn shift, and who had been the UP's head of motive power and machinery since 1936, and vice-president in charge of research and mechanical standards since 1939. He had also overseen the design of the line's other giant steam locomotives including the 'Challenger' 4-6-6-4s of 1936.

The frame was a single massive cast steel piece. Welding was extensively used in building, notably in the construction of the boiler, pressed to 300psi (21kg/cm^2) – the highest pressure used with a conventional 'Stephenson' tubular boiler. Multiple-jet exhausts fed out through a double chimney. All axles were fitted with roller bearings. A significant new feature was the redesign of the joint between the front truck and the frame, to allow lateral movement only. Any changes in gradient or unevennessses in the track were absorbed by a highly effective suspension system. This solved what had been a problem with big articulated engines: the occasional tendency of weight to shift from one set of wheels to the other with consequent loss of adhesion by the lightened wheels.

Although they could and did operate on other parts of the Union Pacific system, the 'Big Boys'' operating requirements were defined by the mountainous Sherman Hill main line through the Wasatch Mountains between Ogden, Utah, and Green River, Wyoming, a 176-mile (283km) stretch rising from 1,933ft (596m) to 8,013ft (2,444m) with a ruling grade of 1.14 per cent. The section length was just about right. At full power, a 'Big Boy' consumed 22,000lb (9.9t) of coal in an hour, and the tenders, running on five fixed axles plus a four-wheel bogie in front, held 28 tons of coal and 20,800gals (25,000US) of water. Two mechanical stokers kept the vast grate supplied with coal. The longest, strongest turntables in the world were installed at Green River and Ogden, 135ft (41m) to turn the 560t 'Big Boys'. The 4000s could haul trains of up to seventy refrigerated fruit cars, weighing 3,200 tons, over this road without assistance. Nor was it a matter of slow dragging as in former years. Full power output was obtained at 70mph (112km/h), though they could operate at up to 80mph (130km/h). This maximum equated to around 10,000ihp developed in the cylinders, an output beyond that of any other steam locomotive and far beyond that of contemporary diesel units. But in a 1974 article in the *American Trains* magazine, W. Withuhn pointed out: 'Big Boy's profitable capacity was not so much determined by its 6,200hp at 35mph (56km/h) as it was limited by its

5,200hp at 20mph (32km/h).' In other words, at the crucial phases of starting off and accelerating with a heavy train, the 4000s were unable to put
more than half their full power potential to use.

Even half that potential was very considerable, and despite this ostensible
limitation, the 'Big Boys' were immediately effective in service and the first
batch, built in 1941, all achieved more than a million miles (1,609,000km)
of running. Wartime traffic gave them much heavier loads, and they often
worked double-headed on immensely long trains. Their last revenue-earning duties were in July 1959, and withdrawal began from 1961. Four of the
4000s survived on the active list at Green River depot until July 1962, and
eight are preserved as static museum and display items. In one bizarre experiment at the Los Angeles City Fairplex (curiously evocative of the furnace
immolations hinted at by André Malraux) it was found that the firebox of
No.4014, with its grate area of 150.3sq ft (14m²), could accommodate thirty-
two schoolchildren. Although the technologies involved are very different,
it is not altogether fanciful to see in those mighty locomotives a presaging of
the Saturn rocket that would take men to the Moon. They gave American
engineering the opportunity to develop confidence in working on a grand
scale and in pushing machinery to its maximum power.

THIRTY-THREE

A Sort of Zenith

The decade between 1935 and 1945 saw the steam locomotive performing at its peak in both passenger and freight service. The speed
achievements of the 'Hiawathas', A4s and 05s stood out all the more brightly
against a general pattern of distinctly modest speeds in many countries, and
on most services even in the USA, Britain and Germany. The great majority
of passenger trains made frequent stops, and the quality of locomotive work
was assessed as much in brisk starting, acceleration and braking as in maintaining high speeds. But even reflected glory was not to be dismissed. The
glamour and fame of the racers, if they could not be emulated everywhere,
still had a widespread effect in the phenomenon of streamlining, which
seized the railway world in the 1930s.

Streamlining began in France, in 1894, when the PLM's C-Class 4-4-0s
were modified by Théophile Ricour, giving them a backwards-angled plate
above the buffers, a pointed smoke-box front whose line was carried up to
the top of the lofty chimney; and a sharply V-fronted cab. These engines had
to pull heavy expresses up the Rhône valley between Marseille and Lyon,
in the teeth of the southwards-blowing Mistral wind, and their casing, of
which an extended version was applied to a further 120 new engines after
1898, was intended to be functional, as their by-name *Coupe-Vent*, 'Wind-
Cutter', suggests. Even when the Mistral was not blowing, fuel savings were
hoped for as a result of lessened wind-resistance. Although pointed conical
smoke-box doors enjoyed quite a vogue in several countries, including Italy,
Hungary and Sweden, the entire wind-cutting package was not emulated
anywhere else, and in France was confined to this one class and the 4-6-
0 Class 3401 that succeeded it. A hint of the style returned with the big
wedge-front chimneys fitted to the last eight of the *Nord* 'Super-Pacifics'
in 1931. For twenty years, little was heard of streamlining, and all the fast

new express designs of the 1920s retained the traditional shape. There was an innovation, however, and this was the introduction of smoke deflectors, metal panels set up alongside the smoke-box in order to help force the exhaust stream upwards and thus improve the driver's view, which was already much reduced by the large diameter of modern boilers. Deflectors were first seen in Germany, and were first fitted as standard on the Class P10 2-8-2 of 1922, after testing in the aerodynamic laboratory at Göttingen. It was one of the curiosities of modern locomotive construction that these 'wings' or 'smoke lifters' appeared very frequently on the locomotives of some countries, and hardly ever in others. North American locomotives, apart from a small number of exceptions, did not possess them. Italy, Austria, South America, India, Australia and New Zealand were other territories where they rarely sprouted. In Germany, Russia and China, very large deflectors rising from buffer beam to chimney were common, though from the early 1940s most German ones shrank to smaller fittings on the smoke-box sides. They were common in France, where a main-line locomotive was likely to have tall deflectors with a hint of an aerodynamic roll at the top. Britain was ambivalent: express and even mixed-traffic locomotives on the Southern Railway had half-height deflectors; other lines had them at full height; others had none at all. Poland produced an individual variant of little deflectors mounted right up alongside the chimney, with some resemblance to pigs' ears, and one or two locomotive types in other countries also acquired these, like the Norwegian Class 31b 4-8-0 of 1921. As 'blinkers' were often fitted to locomotives after they had been running for some time, it must be presumed that the front end design of certain classes was more likely to encourage smoke to cling low rather than to rise. Most railway systems used wind-tunnel tests to establish the most effective form of deflector. Nevertheless, surveying all this range of shapes and sizes, it is hard to resist the piquant comparison which can be drawn with the various and widely-differing horn formations of the members of the antelope family, whose primary purpose is display.

In the early 1930s, more extensive change to the basic appearance began. The man chiefly responsible was not a locomotive engineer. He was a post-war German immigrant to the USA, Otto Kuhler. Greatly admiring the New York Central's new J-1 'Hudsons' of 1928, he fell to sketching ways in which their long, powerful lines could be smoothed off and yet emphasised. A railway magazine published his draft designs in 1931, and Alco was sufficiently impressed to hire him as a design consultant. Product styling was a driving force of new industry, from radio to automobiles; and as the top railroad men ordered their latest-model Buicks or Oldsmobiles, they acknowledged its power.

Kuhler was the pioneer of American railroad streamlining, and designed the 'Hiawatha' trains, among others. The involvement of industrial design with locomotive engineering was confirmed by the work of such men as Henry Dreyfuss with the New York Central and Raymond Loewy with the Pennsylvania Railroad. When Loewy, already with a reputation in his native France, first applied to the Pennsy, in 1932, he was assigned the task of designing a trash-can for Penn Central Station, which he duly did. Soon he was working with the motive power chief, Fred Hankins, on grander projects. Though he may not have been able to tell a Johnson bar from a journal box, Loewy's approach was thorough. He rode the engines and sought to combine practical needs with slick appearance. Caught short one day while riding at high speed in the cab of a K-4 'Pacific', he wanted to instal a crew toilet in his new design (on long runs, locomotive crews usually had a bucket tucked away somewhere, or climbed into the tender). His approach was to begin with a clay model, and later in the decade he would also use wind-tunnel tests in order to tackle problems like low-hanging smoke.

British engineers did not enlist the help of high-profile style gurus, but the London & North Eastern Railway did look abroad, to Ettore Bugatti, whose petrol-mechanical railcar, with rounded, wedge-shaped ends, built for the French railways, inspired the shape of the LNER A4 'Pacific' in 1935. W. A. Stanier's LMS team themselves created the design of the 'Coronation' 4-6-2 of 1937, which was less elegant than the A4. Indeed, few of the many streamlined casings placed on locomotives throughout Europe and beyond looked as if they were anything other than an afterthought. Among the most perfunctory-looking (though actually wind-tunnel tested) were two Great Western engines, provided in 1935 with bulbous fronts and with fairings behind the chimneys and safety-valve casing. They seemed expressive of a stand-off between a demanding public-relations team and a deeply sceptical mechanical engineering department. The LNER designers, with a greater sense of conviction, also created the impressive look of the partly-streamlined first P2 express 'Mikado' of 1934, whose hood was intended to help lift the smoke; and this was borrowed in 1935 for the Class 1 four-cylinder 4-6-2 of the Belgian National Railways, designed by Raoul Notesse, and built in Belgium by Cockerill. It was among the heaviest of all European 'Pacific' types, with a maximum axle load of 23.3 tons (23.7t), and coupled wheels, of 82.75in (210.2cm) diameter. Kylchap double blast-pipes, and feed-water pumps and heaters, were fitted. Thirty-five were built, for use on the heaviest main-line expresses. In 1939, Notesse undertook a more thorough exercise in streamlining with the Class 12, the last 4-4-2 type to be designed anywhere. Also built by Cockerill, this small class of six locomotives was intended to operate lightly-loaded high-speed inter-city services. Its outer shell was effective in providing streamlining while leaving working parts accessible, and the yellow speed-stripes on its green paint helped to give it the look of a flyer. They had bar frames and inside cylinders; four had Walschaerts valve gear with outside return cranks to the leading coupled wheels; the others had rotary cam valve gear. The six-wheel tenders were cannibalised from redundant engines, and given a streamlined casing to match the new engines. The 'Atlantics' worked 246 ton (250t) trains between Ostend and Brussels, 71.5 miles (115km) in one hour, with a maximum speed of 87mph (140km/h), though at high speed their ride was reputedly uncomfortable. The Second World War brought the service to an end. After 1945 they worked similar trains on the Brussels-Lille route, and were still doing so in 1960. One member of the class has been preserved.

In 1937, with the international enthusiasm for streamlining at its height, the Polish State Railways (PKP) decided to begin a two-cylinder 'Pacific' class for high-speed express work. Only two were built, at the Chrzanov works in Warsaw, and only the first, Pm-36.1, as a streamliner, the second as a conventional engine. Both were planned to run at speeds up to 87mph (140km/h) and had the largest-diameter driving wheels of any Polish engine. As in all modern Polish locomotives, the driving cab was fully enclosed; more unusually its entrance was built into the tender frame. The German invasion and occupation of Poland in 1939 put a stop to any further development of the class.

The Russian Railways produced their streamliner with the Class 232 4-6-4 in 1938. This was intended as a small class of ten streamlined engines, specially built to haul the *Krasnaya Strela* ('Red Arrow') express between Moscow and Leningrad (404 miles, 650km), on an eight-hour schedule with two engine changes en route. In the end only three were built, two at Kolomna, one at Voroshilovgrad. All had varying features. The first, known as 232.1, reached the maximum recorded speed of any Russian steam locomotive, with 106mph (170.5km/h) near Kalinin on 29 June 1938. War and the German invasion put a stop to development, and work on the class was not resumed afterwards, though Nos.2 and 3 remained in active service on the 'Red Arrow' into the late 1950s.

The ripples of streamlining went far beyond North America, western Europe and Russia. In the 1930s, Iraq was a British Protectorate, and shortly before the outbreak of war, new streamlined two-cylinder 'Pacifics' were ordered from Robert Stephenson & Hawthorns, of Darlington, England, for the Iraq State Railways. This was the Class PC, and three were delivered, despite wartime conditions, in 1940. A fourth member of the class was lost on the way. Handsome engines, reminiscent of the British 'Coronation' and A4 classes, painted green and with individual names, they were ordered originally for the completion of the line from Baghdad via Tel Kotchek into Syria and Turkey, the route of the 'Taurus Express' from Istanbul. Despite the streamlining, the schedule was a distinctly slow one, taking seventeen hours and thirty minutes from Baghdad to the border, where they relinquished the train to a far from smoothly-contoured ex-Prussian G8 or – after 1945 – perhaps an ex-British War Department 2-8-0. The PC class were still operating the service in the 1950s. A very similar design also clothed the Chinese SL7 4-6-2, operating a rather faster pre-war service, the 'Asia Express' between Dalien and Shenyang.

Loewy's design work for the Pennsylvania Railroad culminated in two locomotive types, the S1 6-4-4-6 duplex-driver and its successor, the T1 4-4-4-4. In the late 1930s, the PRR was looking for a replacement for the now ageing K4 'Pacific' class. For some time Baldwin had been promoting the concept of duplex drive – two sets of cylinders driving two sets of coupled wheels within a single rigid frame. The intention was to produce power beyond that of a 4-8-4, and speed beyond the maximum of a Mallet. The advantages of this form were that the operating machinery could be lighter; the cylinders could be smaller and the stroke shorter; the stress on moving parts significantly less, with a reduced thrust from the piston. In addition, the rigid frame promised stable running at high speeds. The boiler, with a maximum pressure of 300psi ($21kg/cm^2$) was designed to provide adequate power for all four cylinders. The S1 had a bullet front; for the T1 Loewy devised the famous 'shark-front' styling, with inter-cooler, air pump and bell all tucked under the pilot. In every respect they were thoroughly up to date. Poppet valves worked the cylinders, and all axles had Timken roller bearings. Although the S1 was reputed to have exceeded 120mph (193km/h) on numerous occasions, its utility was limited by an excessively heavy axle-load of 33.5t. It remained a one-off, and the lighter T1 was commissioned. Trials of its two prototypes brought in good reports. Both could achieve 100mph (161km/h) in service with 1,020 ton (1036t) trains. One of the prototypes had a booster on the rear truck, but this was not specified when another fifty T1s were ordered, twenty-seven from Baldwin, the others from the Pennsylvania Railroad's Juniata works. In addition, twenty-six 4-4-6-4s of Class Q2 were delivered in 1944-45: these had slightly smaller drivers and a rear-truck booster and were intended for heavy fast freight trains. Streamlining was dispensed with, though the enormous boiler, with the biggest Belpaire firebox to be built, was smoothly cased. The Q2 duplex-drivers were the most powerful rigid-framed locomotives ever, capable of hauling 12,000-ton trains. No.6175 was recorded as developing 7987 indicated horsepower at a speed of 57.4mph (92.3km/h). At such a power output, the locomotive was evaporating 16,600 gallons of water an hour, and burning 12.5 tons of coal. Even a vast tender holding 19,200 gallons, and 37.5 tons, was beginning to look inadequate in the face of such an appetite. Many superlatives were lavished on the new designs, but as the engines came into service, problems began to mount. A major one was the lack of adhesion. Wheel-slip was endemic, not only at low speed, and drivers struggled, often in vain, to cure it. Other mechanical and operating problems arose. For all its thrusting appearance, the T1 did not gain the reputation of a successful design. One railroad historian described it as 'impressive in every way except grate area and boiler capacity.' Nevertheless, it was capable of very high speed, and No.5500 was unofficially credited with achieving 135mph (217km/h) in 1950. It had been rebuilt with rotatory cam gear. By 1953 they, the Q2s and the S1 had all gone, most of them with less than ten years' service. Though his contribution shaped the externals rather than the mechanical essence of the passenger locomotives, Raymond Loewy may be left with the last word, recalling how he stood at Fort Wayne station, watching the S1 go racing by at: '120 miles an hour... It flashed by like a steel thunderbolt; the ground shaking under me ... I felt shaken and overcome by an overwhelming feeling of power, by a sense of pride at the sight of what I had helped to create ... '

The shark-fronted design of Pennsylvania locomotives found an echo in Australia, on the Class 520 4-8-4 of 1943, the last steam design for the South Australian Railways. But by the early 1940s, the novelty and impact of streamlining were wearing off, and the steam locomotive was returning to its 'natural' shape. The tenet 'form follows function' implied a

cylindrical boiler and smoke-box; and streamlined variants failed to dominate. Any gains in fuel consumption were hardly noticeable, and were only
attained at very high speed, which by no means all streamlined engines
were capable of. They also had to be set against the need to remove casings
to get at pumps or lubricating points. During the Second World War, many
engines, like the Polish Pm-36.1 and the British 'Coronation' class 'Pacifics',
were stripped of their casings and emerged in conventional form. The flimsy
and rather unconvincing angular lightweight casing applied in the late 1930s
to a large number of Italian locomotives also soon vanished. Most designers
showed little concern with external streamlining after 1945, though two
important exceptions were France and Germany, where partial streamlining
was employed with the final express steam designs. By the beginning of the
1960s, only the A4s, still in action on British main lines and all now fitted
with double blast-pipes, served to remind people for a little longer of the
streamlined era and the zenith of express steam.

THIRTY-FOUR

A Consideration of Chimneys

Of all the features that made up a conventional locomotive's appearance, the one most instantly noticeable was the chimney. With its prominent location at the front end, its width, height and shape had a strong influence on the 'look' of an engine, and made it an important element in class-identification. Some observers have read a great deal into chimney styles, seeing engines which 'smile' or 'frown' or even 'leer' according to the design and positioning of their chimneys. Designers, especially those brought up in the British school, often went to some trouble to provide their locomotives with visually pleasing chimney designs. It was a time-honoured process, going back to the fretted crown worn by *Rocket* and the finely-flared copper bell-mouth of *Adler's* chimney top. Hundreds of variations on the basic theme arose, with subtle variations in curve or taper, and rims, lips and caps of carefully-chosen width and height. Several British railways embellished chimneys with bright copper rings; in Denmark, the national colours were painted round the chimneys of some engines. Such details were purely decorative, but others were justified in the name of efficiency: Certain Belgian State engines, most express types on the Great Western, and some on the Midland Railway of England, among many others, had a raised cap round only the front half of the chimney top – this 'capuchon' was said to improve smoke-lifting, though it was never applied systematically. Among the most imposing chimneys were those fitted to Belgian engines by Alfred Belpaire, beginning in 1884 with massive funnels square in plan, with trapezoidal tapering sides, and a high capuchon. From 1893 to 1898 he used an equally large oval design, though there was a short return to the square base in 1894-1895. These huge chimneys were explained as necessary to provide draught for the large fireboxes, but in truth, all the different designs had a purely cosmetic effect. The excellent Prussian engines had no-nonsense stove-pipes. Designer chimneys were expensive to make, requiring careful machining and turning, and made up of several different parts.. Occasionally an engine working hard might blow its chimney cap right off. Many engines had several different forms of chimney fitted during their working lives.

What really mattered was the blast-pipe design, unseen within the smoke-box. A straight up-and-down unadorned stove-pipe served perfectly well as a conduit for whatever came up through the exhaust system. But that might include sparks and red-hot coals. Many chimneys were given the additional function of holding a spark arrestor. Wood-burning engines were particularly likely to spread sparks, and this accounts for the wonderful variety of smokestacks on American locomotives up to around 1870. More than a thousand patents were issued in the USA for different designs of smokestack and spark arrestor, during the nineteenth century. Most often seen on wood-burners was the wide-tapered bonnet stack, with a netting cap over the mouth, which might be as much as 5ft wide. Most of its space was for holding cinders, with a release catch at the base to let them out; an inner stove-pipe funnelled the exhaust up from the blast-pipe. Of very similar shape was the centrifugal stack, whose inner pipe was fitted with curving baffle plates which made the exhaust spin around, with the effect of throwing heavier sparks and cinders to the side, where they would fall harmlessly into the hopper space. The 'diamond stack' was devised for coal-burning engines by George S. Griggs, around 1856-1857; it dispensed with the hopper aspect, but had a widened upper section containing a spark deflector and, usually, also had a wire netting cap. Some American engines, and many on Swedish private railways, had spark-arresting baffles installed in the bases of the chimneys; this gave the Swedish locomotives an oddly clerical air, like pastors wearing their ruffs. The other frequently-seen kind of spark-arrestor chimney was the balloon stack, familiar in illustrations of Finnish and Austrian engines. It took the form of a widened top section fitted on the lower stove-pipe, incorporating one or more spark screens, and sometimes with a further narrow stove-pipe section above it. It too conferred a distinctive air, somehow oriental, with a hint of a turban, to the engines which carried it. Hamilton Ellis claimed that Austrians called them *Nachttopfschornsteine*, 'chamber-pot chimneys'. By the 1920s, spark arrestors were normally contained within the smoke-box. All such devices, to a greater or lesser degree, interfered with the force of the blast, and a rough-and-ready balance had to be maintained between keeping in the sparks and letting out the exhaust, which was vital to maintaining the draught. Depending on how near they were to the hottest part of the exhaust, the screens often had a short life, and unless regularly renewed, offered increasingly little hindrance to sparks and burning cinders.

Other things were done to chimneys. On European railways, many had lids which could be swivelled on or off, and which added to the racy look of the first French 'Pacifics'. In northern lands, such lids were a protection against severe frost, which had a damaging effect on the interior piping and plumbing, but they were also employed in Indonesia, Uruguay, and other places, to damp down smoke emission and to protect the inner works. In the interest of lifting the exhaust stream, many modern locomotives in eastern Europe were given an outwards-tapering, semi-circular fitting rising from the rear base of the chimney, with the look of a turned-up shirt collar. To cope with changes in the loading gauge, chimneys were sometimes adjustable. The join visible in the centre of the typical German stove-pipe chimney was to allow the upper section to be removed if the engine ran on a line with limited clearance. When Germany annexed Alsace after the Franco-Prussian war of 1870, taking over the railways in the process, many locomotives seconded to work there suffered from bashed funnels on the lower over-bridges. On the Highland Railway in Scotland, David Jones fitted unique chimneys with a set of louvres cut in the front of the outer stack; this was intended to produce an upwards draught which would help lift the exhaust, carried in an inner pipe. It was an innovation which the rest of the railway world felt able to ignore. On the basis that the taller the chimney, the more draught it would produce, some engines had chimneys that could be lengthened. Locomotives of the Santa Fe Railroad's oil-fired Class 3765 and 2900 4-8-4s were fitted with an extendable stack that could be automatically hoisted up when running through open country. At much the same time, the Southern Pacific fitted its 4-8-8-2 Classes AC 11 and 12 with 'smoke-splitters', a hinged frame over the chimney top, worked by compressed air, which divided the blast and helped to protect the wooden roofs of snowsheds. The US Southern fitted 'Wimble ducts', which could be engaged to deflect upwards thrust along the boiler top, to its 'Mountain' engines for the same reason. In China during the 1930s some engines, fitted with armour plate to push armoured trains, had their chimneys joined to a pipe of the same width that bent through two right angles to pipe the smoke down to rail level, in the hope of disguising its presence to aircraft.

Many railways were content to provide the basic stove-pipe, with a strengthening rim at the top, and no more. They included most North American, German and Central European lines. Indeed, one of the features that was most noticeable about Will Woodard's first modified 2-8-2 was that ' … there was a lip to her stack' (D. P. Morgan). Professor Goss's team at Purdue University tested seven stacks of different diameters and lengths, either straight or tapering slightly outwards, without reaching definite conclusions. Australia, which had followed British practice with shaped, lipped, and capped chimneys, began to adopt a new look from the late 1920s, with the 'basher front end' incorporating alterations to the blast-pipe and an unadorned stove-pipe chimney, first seen on the Victorian Railways' X-Class 2-8-2 of 1929.

The double chimney is of some antiquity. Even in 1889, three LNWR compounds were fitted with double chimneys, of almost Belgian proportions, for a time; and from the 1920s, wider or longer chimneys were used to accommodate double or multiple blast systems, and again designers by choice left them plain or provided them with rims and caps. The Kylchap double chimney was usually incorporated in a single fitting, but a few locomotives, like the first 2-6-6-4s, built for the Pittsburgh & West Virginia Railroad in 1934, or the one-off 'Heavy Harry' of 1941, Australia's first 4-8-4, built by the Victorian Railways, had two separate chimneys set close together. Some of the biggest US locomotives had spotlights fitted behind the stack, so that the fireman could monitor the exhaust in the dark; in a few cases, like the Rio Grande Class L131 2-8-8-2 of 1927, the stack, with its rim curved up at the front, seemed to owe more to the design of battleships than of locomotives. Another highly distinctive chimney was the Lemaître type, exceptionally wide, set above a ring of blast nozzles; overshadowing the brow of engines like the Southern Railway 'Schools' Class 4-4-0s in Britain like a conspirator's hat. At a very late stage in the steam locomotive's career, 1951, an entirely new kind of chimney appeared: the narrow, oblong Giesl ejector. This was developed in Austria by Dr A. Giesl-Gieslingen, who had trained as an electrical engineer. At its base was a line of seven fan-like jets whose effect was to give a continuous reduction of exhaust pressure. The advantages of this were to reduce back-pressure on the pistons, to improve air distribution through the firebed – an important consideration with low-grade coal – and reduce disturbance of the incandescent upper region of the fire. In 1954 Giesl-Gieslingen also introduced his micro-spark arrestor, which in combination with the ejector was claimed to all but eliminate the spark problem. Most railways still using steam tried the system on at least one or two locomotives, and around 2500 engines were fitted with the Giesl ejector, 452 of them being in Austria, where almost all the locomotives earmarked to work on after 1966 were thus equipped. It was also quite widely used in Czechoslovakia, but China, the last country to build main-line steam, did not make use of it at all. It improved the steaming capacity of older engines but its arrival on the scene came too late to establish whether it would have made a significant positive improvement to an already-efficient modern locomotive. Whatever its effectiveness, most steam enthusiasts thought it detracted from a locomotive's appearance; some considered it an aesthetic abomination. But what Giesl-Gieslingen showed, and what applied work on the draughting system in the late 1940s at some other places, like the British Railways works at Swindon, also showed, was that by dint of applied science and experiment, substantial improvements to steam locomotive performance still could be made without any fundamental alterations or additions.

THIRTY-FIVE

War Engines

The perception of the locomotive by governments and government departments was not restricted to its commercial uses. At first, official interest was most apparent in Europe. Belgium, France and the German states all exercised more control on railway development than the United Kingdom and the United States. But it was done to the greatest degree of all in Tsarist Russia. From the beginnings, the Tsar and his advisers had seen the value of the railway in administering a vast country, and the usefulness of having a locomotive-building industry. To them the locomotive was a tool of strategy, not only civil but military. Railway mythology had it that Tsar Nicholas I defined the line of the St Petersburg-Moscow railway by laying his sword on the map between the two cities' names. It was the same desire to maintain control that led to the building of the Trans-Siberian line.

The British government learned the lesson with the Indian Mutiny of 1857, when its native Indian regiments rose in revolt. At this time Indian railways consisted of only a few short lines, with the lightweight locomotives whose arrival has been noted. The supply lines of the British army were greatly overstretched and lack of transport slowed its response. Once the colonial order had been restored, the previous dilatory approach to railway construction was condemned, and contracts were rapidly placed for long-distance lines based on a combination of government funding and private capital.

The position was very different in the USA, when the outbreak of civil war in 1861 sharpened the interest of government in railways. Although the northern states had double the mileage of the south, both sides had well-developed networks. For four years, on both the Confederate and Federal sides, locomotives became instruments of war, hauling troop trains, ammunition and supply trains, and ambulance trains. They propelled armoured gun carriages, and were often attacked and derailed in the war zones. The most celebrated event in later times, though a sideshow in the war, was the 'Great Locomotive Chase' of 12 April 1862. By this time the 'American' type 4-4-0 had developed into the brightly-painted form, with shiny brass and copper-work, often with huge spark-arrester smokestack and a big oil headlamp, familiar from many illustrations and Western movies. One of these, *The General*, built at Rogers Locomotive Works, Paterson, NJ, for the Western & Atlantic Railroad, was hijacked at Big Shanty, Ga, on the Atlanta-Chattanooga line, by a party of northern saboteurs. They were chased along the single line by southern railwaymen and troops in a hair-raising pursuit until their engine finally ran out of wood and steam beyond Dalton. Apart from its shared adventure with the pursuing *Texas*, this engine was typical of very many others, which led less dramatic lives as the basic work-horses of the now much busier American railway network. *The General,* much restored and now discreetly oil-fired, is preserved at Chattanooga.

The Baltimore & Ohio ran an armoured train and found that the locomotive was the most vulnerable part of such a unit, when it was disabled by a shell which hit the boiler. Later, locomotives would be armour-plated. The Confederate General Stonewall Jackson was quick to appreciate that locomotive power was a key aspect of warfare. He waited until the B&O Martinsburg Yard was full of engines, then cut off access to it and later tried to destroy the engines, apart from some that he had removed to run in the South. The B&O lost sixty-seven locomotives. But soldiers also found that steam engines were quite hard to put out of action, and unless thoroughly destroyed, could be quickly repaired. A favourite tactic of saboteurs in a hurry was to smash the valve gear with sledge-hammers – this was an aspect of accessibility that designers had certainly not reckoned with.

When a country was waging total war, then all its locomotives were 'war engines' and the railways were pressed into the national war effort, coping with levels of demand and pressure unknown in peacetime, quite apart from the hazard of destruction. The steam locomotive fleet was a vital strategic asset, and indeed was one of the main items that made 'total war' possible. In the World War of 1914-1918, as we have seen, Belgian locomotives could end up on Russian tracks. By British government order, many 0-6-0 freight locomotives from the Indian metre-gauge railways were shipped across the Indian Ocean to help in the campaigns against German East Africa. Following visits from the shrewd Samuel Vauclain, by then vice-president of the Baldwin Locomotive Works, to Russia in 1914 and 1915, it was arranged that the Imperial railways would purchase locomotives from the United States. This resulted in the Class Ye 2-10-0, of which 1,300 were ordered between 1915 and 1917. A total of 881 were delivered before the Bolshevik revolution halted trade between the two countries. One consignment is believed to have been lost at sea. One hundred of the embargoed engines were bought by the US government, converted to standard gauge and sold on to the Erie, the Seaboard Air Line, and other lines. The rest were cancelled. When Russia was again on the Allied side in World War II, arrangements under the 'Lease-Lend' scheme were made to rebuild the same design, denoted as class Ye,a. Alco and Baldwins built a further 2,120 between 1944 and 1947. With the commencement of the 'Cold War' in the post-war years, the last twenty were diverted to Finland, which shared Russia's 5ft gauge. Some engines of the first vintage were still in operation in Siberia in the late 1950s. In World War I, US engines also went to France. Quite apart from main-line and standard gauge power, both sides set up networks of narrow-gauge track to serve the trenches. British engines under the control of the Railway Operating Division of the Royal Engineers ran behind the front lines in Flanders, with munition and other supplies and troop and ambulance trains. By the end of the war there were 675 of them, the later ones specially built for the war effort, but many others were commandeered from the railway companies. Even when returned, these kept their oval brass R.O.D. plates, like campaign medals, and the British locomotive enthusiast Norman Marlow, a teenage engine-watcher in 1923, was particularly excited by one such, a Midland Railway 0-6-0, 'famous as having been captured by the Germans.'

Locomotive sabotage was normally a grim business but occasionally it was conducted in a light-hearted vandalistic spirit. The British writer Peter Fleming described one wartime exploit, shared with his fellow officer Norman Johnstone, at Larissa in Greece in 1941:

One of our jobs earlier in the campaign had been to destroy some rolling stock which could not be moved away. Norman had a splendid time blowing up about twenty locomotives and a lot of trucks, but towards the end we ran out of explosives. At this stage a sergeant in the 4th Hussars turned up, who was an engine driver in civilian life. With Norman helping him, he got steam up in the four surviving engines, drove them a quarter of a mile down the line, then sent them full tilt back into the station, where they caused further havoc of a spectacular and enjoyable kind.

Of this piece of licensed delinquency, the writer adds nonchalantly that, ' ... the whole thing was carried out under shell fire.'

Under the umbrella of the military engineers, armies also owned a number of locomotives of their own, usually small ones, used for the training of drivers and for moving stores in large depots and bases, but the numbers of these were modest. It might also be truer to call these 'engines used in war activities' rather than war engines, as this term acquired a rather different meaning in the Second World War. 'War engine' came then to mean a locomotive designed and built under government control to a wartime standard, and deployed according to the instructions of those directing the military campaigns. The Americans, the British and the Germans all built locomotives that fitted those criteria. Although British railway writers in the post-war years were fond of referring to any of three locomotive types as 'the engine that won the war', none of them, the LMS Class 5 4-6-0 and the LNER Class V2 2-6-2 and B1 4-6-0, were war engines in the true sense, as they were built and operated as civilian locomotives.

The classic example is German, partly because the name '*Kriegslokomotive*' was borrowed into English as 'war engine', chiefly because it was built in greater numbers than any other. Its genesis goes back to 1938, when the *Deutsche Reichsbahn Gesellschaft* introduced its Class 50 as a standard two-cylinder 2-10-0 heavy freight locomotive. It was very much in Richard Wagner's DRG tradition, with bar frames, round-top boiler, and wide firebox. After the outbreak of war in 1939, production was stepped up, and the design was modified in order to speed up building. The modified engines were classed as 50ÜK (*Übergangskriegslokomotive*, 'transitional war locomotive'), and a total of 3164 were built. In 1941, when the German war effort on two fronts created a heavy demand for extra motive power, a massive increase in locomotive production was begun. Now emerged the 'war engine' proper, the Class 52 2-10-0, whose details were worked out by a technical group from the DRG and the principal manufacturers. The prototype 52.001 was built by Borsig, a two-cylinder engine, with simple expansion, and Walschaerts gear operating piston valves. Speed of construction, and the minimum of materials consistent with durability, were essential. Welding was used to a greater extent than in any previous locomotive type;

they had completely welded boilers and welding was used wherever possible to join parts that would once have been riveted or bolted together. Most of the Class 52s had plate frames, of steel 3cm (1.2in) thick, far thinner than the 8cm (3.1in) bar frames of the Class 50. Square steam-pipes and a box-like steam-chest above the cylinders emphasised the 'no frills' approach, though from 1943, lightweight smoke deflectors of the type developed by Friedrich Witte, Wagner's successor, were fitted to the smoke-box sides and slightly softened the gaunt outline.

In a huge and sustained effort, around 6,700 *Kriegsloks* were built between 1942 and 1945. All German locomotive manufacturers except the bomb-damaged Krupps built the Class 52, as did the Skoda works at Plzen in Czechoslovakia, Graffenstaden in occupied France, and the Polish Chrzanov and Cegielski works. It was never a totally homogeneous class; the different makers, the need to improvise with materials, and a constant flow of revised detail instructions from the technical committee, ensured considerable variety. Some major variations formed effective sub-classes.

The Germans had found in the Russian campaign of 1941 that their locomotives were liable to break down in the extreme cold of Russian winters, and a number of special features, including a chimney cowl, insulation of outside-mounted pumps, fully-enclosed cab, and in some cases insulated tender tanks, were fitted to some of the first *Kriegsloks*. Feed-water heaters, standard on the Class 50, were not however fitted to the Class 52s. The original version was coal-fired, but an oil-burner later appeared, with a tank fitted in and around the coal bunker space on the tender. Another variant was fitted with a condensing tender: a number of the class were equipped in this way to run supply trains to the German armies fighting on the Russian front, as the retreating Russians had razed all their engine sheds and refuelling facilities. Armour plating was fitted to some of these engines. Some Russian lines were re-gauged to standard by the Germans, but many of the Class 52s were provided with extended axles to fit the Russian 5ft (152.4cm) gauge.

The *Kriegslok* had a maximum speed of 50mph (80km/h) running either forwards or backwards. With a tractive effort of 51,000lb (23,140kg) they were powerful engines, and their weight of 185,220lb (84t) spread over six axles enabled them to run on all but the flimsiest trackwork. From 1943, their standard tender was the welded Type 914, known as the *Wanne*, or 'bath-tub' from its rounded sides. It was a remarkable piece of design in itself. Riding on two four-wheel bogies, it could be built in one third of the time of a conventional tender, held more coal and water, and used less metal in construction. Its capacity was 10t of coal and 7,000gal (8,400US) of water.

These engines were rostered in an intensive network of conventional freight trains running normal goods services, in addition to regular or specially timetabled supply trains carrying military equipment to the German army groups spread across Europe from Brittany to Norway and the Balkans. Over a thousand operated under military control in the eastern occupied territories; and hundreds of others were sold or sent on loan to Croatia, Hungary, Romania, Serbia, and Turkey. Most of their activity, however routine, was considered a military secret; in wartime Germany — as in Great Britain — to be found with a camera or notebook near a locomotive was to invite summary arrest. But some of their work was cloaked in deadlier secrecy and menace. It was chiefly *Kriegsloks* which had the sinister task of drawing the long, dreadful trains of closed wagons and cattle trucks which transported human beings by the hundred thousand across the railway network and out of it, on to newly-built tracks which led right into the concentration and death camps, into zones of horror beyond the last vestiges of civilised life.

Built to serve the immediate war effort, the *Kriegsloks* were not expected to have the life-span of a conventional locomotive, but their construction proved robust enough to ensure many years of service. After the end of the European war in 1945, they played a vital part in keeping things moving on the battered and patched-up railways of central and eastern Europe. Large numbers were taken over by the liberated nations, or commandeered by, or given in reparations to, the Russians. Construction of new Class 52s, on a limited scale, went on until 1951, in Poland, Belgium and West Germany. In Germany itself the stock was divided between the Federal and Democratic Republics, operating the *Bundesbahn* and *Reichsbahn* systems respectively. Their life on the *Reichsbahn* was longest, with the reconstruction of 200 during 1960-1967 as Class 5280. Some of these *Rekolok* rebuilds were also given Giesl blast-pipes and double chimneys. The 52s formed the DR's most numerous steam class, and the last ones remained in service until the 1980s.

Russia after the war held around 2,130 *Kriegsloks*, as 'trophy' locomotives. Regauged, repaired, rebuilt, cannibalised (sometimes one locomotive was resurrected from the wrecks of three) as Class TE, they were widely deployed in the western Soviet Union and its satellite states until the late 1950s. Many were converted to oil firing. In 1963, the Russians sold 100 oil-fired former Class 52s to Czechoslovakia. Large numbers also went to Poland, Bulgaria, and Hungary; in all some 700 were redistributed as the Russian diesel and electric construction programmes began to take effect. On the Yugoslavian system they were designated Class 33 and were the largest single class on the JDZ. After the collapse of Yugoslavia, some were brought from storage into active use in Bosnia during the warfare of the mid-1990s. The furthest-flung were twelve from Russia and Poland, supplied to North Vietnam for use in another war, around 1984. Some of the longest-lived survivors were in Turkey, where their 15-ton axle-load enabled them to run on branch lines in eastern Anatolia. Up to 1990 they could sometimes be seen part-nered with their wartime rivals, war surplus American S-160 2-8-0s. Large numbers of the *Kriegsloks* survive in preservation, in several countries. Once Germany had invaded Russia, and America had entered the war, the likeli-hood of German victory became increasingly slim. No-one was ever going to call the Class 52 'the engine that won the war', but of all war engines, this one made the greatest contribution.

In the Second World War, it was estimated that 42,000 locomotives in the USA did more than double the work done by 64,000 in the First World War. This was less because they were modern engines, than because great strides had been made in water treatment and consequently in prolonging boiler life and reducing the need for heavy boiler servicing. These war efforts were made by the civilian railway companies, under close government supervision. Strictly military locomotive power was the responsibility of the United States Army Transportation Corps, which provided direct support for army operations. As in Germany, there was close collaboration between it and the manufacturers, once it became plain that there was a need for military locomotives on an unprecedented scale.

The USATC's pre-war standard designs were small engines for work on military tracks inside camps and depots, typified by the 0-6-0T switcher side-tank type. This became a familiar sight especially in French, Greek and Yugoslavian station yards after the end of World War II. Three US builders, Davenport, Vulcan, and Porter, built 382 for service in Britain, Europe and the Middle East, in dimensions to fit the British loading gauge. Two sand-boxes and a dome on a short boiler, with the stove-pipe chimney, gave them a characteristic look. The two outside cylinders were operated by Walschaerts gear. The first ones arrived in England in July 1942. Thirteen were acquired after the war by the Southern Railway, for working in Southampton Docks, and some of these remained active until 1967. Seventy-seven were bought by the SNCF, where some lasted until 1971. Yugoslavia received 120, and built twenty-three more to the same plans in 1956-1957. Twenty went to Greece, where some were converted to tender 0-6-0s. During 1943, thirty engines, oil-fired, were sent for work in the Middle East, operating in Iraq, Palestine, and Egypt, and some of them remained in civilian service after 1945. Four were supplied to the Jamaican Government Railways in 1943-45.

Compared to its bigger brothers, the USATC tank engine's numbers were modest. The S160 class of 2-8-0 tender locomotives, commissioned as one of four standard steam types, reached a total of 2120, including its variants. They were built to standard gauge, by the 'big three' constructors, Alco, Baldwin and Lima, between 1942 and 1945. It too was a small engine by American standards, built to fit within the relatively tight British loading gauge, but it was a typically US design, with bar frames, two outside simple-expansion cylinders, operated by piston valves, actuated by Walschaerts gear; a high-set boiler, and a wide, round-topped steel firebox. Steam brakes were fitted, as well as a Westinghouse air brake pump, with air cylinders placed under the running plate on each side. The compressor pump was fitted to the left of the narrowed smoke-box door. For use with British rolling stock, dual air/vacuum brake equipment was fitted. On the boiler top, dome and sandbox were in a single housing. The standard American three-point suspension system gave them a stable ride even over ill-maintained and bomb-blasted tracks. A number of American 'convenience' fittings, including rocking grates and hopper ashpans in the firebox, were built in, which made the locomotives popular with British and European crews, but there was no power reverser, though this was by now standard on civilian US locomotives. The great majority were coal burners, though some oil-burners were built or converted, including 106 for the south-west region of France, which had oil-fuelling facilities. Two types of standard eight-wheel tender carried 8 or 10 tons of coal and 5,400gals (6,480US) of water. The design was a very sound one, with only one significant defect that emerged with time, a weakness in the screw fixing of the firebox roof stays, which caused a number of firebox collapses, with fatal results for the crews in some cases.

The first overseas destination for the S160s was Britain, partly to provide its railways with extra motive power under the Lease-Lend scheme, partly as a holding base for the invasion of Europe. In September 1943, the Great Western Railway's repair shops at Ebbw Junction, Newport, in South Wales, became the HQ of No.756 Railway Shop Battalion, US Army, and engines were stored and prepared for use here. To support the North African campaign, 139 were shipped to Oran by mid-July 1943. By late 1944 they were being shipped across the English Channel to Europe in large numbers, to operate behind the lines in liberated territory. Apart from military use on troop, munitions and general supply, and ambulance trains, they were loaned to the national railway authorities to supplement the lack of available power on civilian services. Usage was at a peak in 1945; but with the end of hostilities in Europe, the S160s, like the troops, were ready for demobilisation. Many were gathered together in a huge 'dump' at Louvain in Belgium, and also at other depots. A vast redistribution took place. Almost the only country not to take some into permanent service was France. Thirty went to the ÖBB in Austria, 244 to Italy (twenty-five of these were sold on to Greece in 1959), twenty-seven to Greece, sixty-five to Yugoslavia, forty to the DB in Germany, fifty to the TCDD in Turkey, around 500 to MÁV in Hungary, and a similar quantity to PKP in Poland, eighty to Czechoslovakia, 101 to South Korea, twenty-five to China. Around thirty engines remained in North Africa on the Tunisian and Algerian railways. The remainder probably ended up in Russia, joining the 200 that had been sent directly there in the course of 1943. Another sixty had been built to Indian broad gauge, shipped out in parts, and assembled at works near Bombay and Calcutta. They went into service with the Indian Government Railways from August 1944. Locomotives of the same type also went in small numbers to Jamaica and Peru (1943) and Mexico (1946).

In civilian use, the war engines gradually acquired fittings or adaptations normal to their new owners, most often taller chimneys, and in time some were more substantially rebuilt. In Poland and Hungary large numbers were still in regular service in the early 1970s. In these two countries particularly, the S160s were invaluable freight engines during the hard years of the later 1940s, running in service with the German Class 50 and 52 2-10-0s.

The S160 was a standard-gauge locomotive, and for narrower gauges the USATC produced another standard type in large numbers, the Class S118 2-8-2, generally known as the 'MacArthur' in honour of US General Douglas MacArthur, whose star was high at the time. Like the other war engines, this type not only performed valuable service during the Second World War, but was a staple engine on many systems for a long time after that. The design work was done by Alco, to fit both the metre and the 3ft 6in (106.5cm) gauges. Between 1942 and 1945, 859 were built, with Baldwin, Davenport, Porter and Vulcan also involved. Maximum route availability was demanded, so its heaviest axle load was set at 9 tons and it was built to clear even restricted loading gauges. Various different kinds of drawgear and braking equipment could be fitted, and it could easily be switched from coal to oil firing. It was intended to be as economical and simple as possible both in construction and in operation.

Most of the MacArthurs went to the Indian metre-gauge lines, delivered in crates for assembly on arrival. In the later stages of the war, and after it, some were dispersed to Burma, Malaya, and Thailand. Others were in service – in some cases into the 1970s – in Iraq, Algeria, Tunisia, Nigeria, the Gold Coast (Ghana), the East African Railways system, the French Cameroons, the Manila railroad in the Philippines, the Queensland Government Railways in Australia, the United Fruit Co. lines in Honduras, and the White Pass & Yukon Railroad in Alaska. After the war some were built for the Peleponnesus Railway in Greece and the Djibouti-Addis Ababa line in Ethiopia. It was the most widely-dispersed locomotive type ever built: the only continent in which a 'MacArthur' did not run was rail-free Antarctica.

As in the First World War, the British looked first to existing designs for locomotives to support the military campaigns, and the 2-8-0 freight engine of the LMS, introduced in 1935, was selected by the Ministry of Supply on behalf of the War Department as the standard engine for military use at home and abroad. This was already a 'standard' type, produced in large numbers and with a large supply of spare parts already in stock. The only adaptation was to fit Westinghouse brake pumps to the right of the smoke-box, for working air-braked stock. By 1945, over 700 had been built, and virtually every locomotive works in the country had contributed some. Many remained in the Middle East after the war, and some were still working in Turkey more than twenty years after steam had been abandoned in Britain. But the LMS engine had not been designed for wartime building, and some component materials, like the molybdenum-manganese steel of the connecting and coupling rods, were in very short supply. From 1943, an 'Austerity' 2-8-0 design appeared, in many ways a pared-down version of the LMS locomotive, using many identical parts, but with a round-topped rather than a Belpaire boiler. In 1944 a larger ten-coupled version was produced, at first intended particularly to work in overseas theatres. The only previous ten-coupled engines to run in Britain had been two exceptional one-off designs. But the private British builders had sent many hundreds abroad. The requirement was for an engine combining a light maximum axle-weight of 13.3 tons, low enough to run on lightweight or improvised track, and a good tractive effort. Another required factor was a tight turning circle, achieved here despite a wheelbase of 21ft (639.6cm) by making the third driving wheels flangeless, and allowing a degree of lateral play to the front and rear coupled axles, of 0.5in (12.7cm). Many features show its 'Austerity' background: as with the 2-8-0, the round-topped parallel boiler and firebox lent themselves to quantity production; fabricated parts were used instead of heavy forgings and castings; some wheels and wheel parts were cast iron, not steel. The wide firebox, designed to convert readily from coal to oil fuel, was made of steel, a departure from previous British practice which invariably employed copper; and for coal firing its base was in two parts, which could be rocked separately to remove ash and stimulate the fire. The boiler pressure, the two cylinders, the motion and 56.5in (143.5cm) wheel diameter were all identical to those of the 2-8-0, so that its theoretical tractive power was the same, but the capacity for making steam was much greater, and it had an extra 5 tons of adhesive weight, and its haulage power was significantly greater. Both vacuum and air brake equipment was fitted, and the engine also had its own steam brake. An eight-fixed-wheel tender carried 9 tons of coal and 5,000 gals (6000US) of water. Many ran on post-war freight duties into the 1960s, and the class provided a basis for the new British standard 2-10-0 of the 1950s.

A reversal of the usual economy war-engine pattern was seen in Japan, when a set of ten 4-6-2s was built in 1942 by Hitachi for use on the railways of occupied Thailand. Perhaps to impress the conquered Thais, these were built to opulent standards for wartime, with feed-water heaters, copper-capped chimneys, smoke deflectors and a handsome lined-out black livery. For its own railways, Japan did not produce an equivalent to the war engines, but continued to build standard pre-war classes, like the D52 'Mikados'. From 1943 to 1946, when demand for steel was far outrunning supply, many new engines were provided with smoke deflectors and running plates of wood boarding, and lighter frames than the original design. They had to be weighed down with concrete blocks to make up for their lack of adhesion. These locomotives were brought up to normal specification after 1946.

The designs of the war engines had a considerable effect on the post-war generation in Britain and Europe; particularly in the development and use of welded boilers and other uses of welding in the construction process.

As a final item, there is the solitary case of a 'war-begotten' locomotive. In war reparations, the handing over of existing engines and the building of further examples of existing classes was usual. But the big Class Ma 2-10-2 of the Hellenic State Railways was an entirely new design. Greece had traditionally bought German and Austrian locomotives, but the twenty Mas came from Ansaldo of Sampierdarena, Italy, in 1953-1954, as part of Italian war reparations. Italy, long converted to electrification, had no tradition of large modern steam designs, and this belated production was not a success. The plate frame was too lightweight to support the huge boiler, and the firebox was too small to generate the amount of steam required. A number of Austrian 2-10-0s had to be borrowed between 1957 and 1961 to supplement them. They were scrapped in the late 1960s.

The steam locomotive was essentially a civilian machine. As an offensive weapon, it was of little use. In war as in peace, it was a helper to human activity and intentions. It could not be converted into a kind of battle-tank, and it did not take kindly to being girded in heavy armour-plate. There was no space to mount guns. Rather than make it a gun-platform, it was easier to convert it into a fire-pump, to help deal with the effects of air-raids, as some American railroads had long done for dousing lineside and snowshed fires. In wartime use, it even-handedly hauled fresh troops and munitions to the battle-fronts, and took away ambulance trains laden with the wounded. The good machine fulfilled the tasks set it by its human masters.

THIRTY-SIX

Post-War Engines

Although the USA in particular possessed the technology to build powerful diesel locomotives, the war engines were nearly all steam-powered. Steam was still the basis of railway operations in 1939, and in the countries where the war engines were used, the servicing and maintenance facilities and workshops were all set up for steam. Above all, in the countries where they were built, there were huge workshops dedicated to, and skilled in, the construction of steam locomotives, and large numbers of experienced drivers, firemen, and fitters.

When American army engineers entered the great Henschel works at Kassel, in May 1945, they found a remarkable locomotive, the 2-8-2 No.19-1001. This experimental type, a DRG design begun in 1935, was virtually complete in 1941, but was set aside when the demand for war engines came. It was an eight-cylinder locomotive, each driving axle being turned by a two-cylinder   V-format driving unit suspended from the main frame and outside the wheels. Piston valves operated the cylinders by means of eccentrics, with the eccentric shafts chain-driven from a main crankshaft. Impressed by this piece of advanced steam technology, the Americans removed it to Fort Monroe, in the USA. It was kept there for some years, but little or no interest was shown by locomotive designers, and it was broken up in 1952.

During the war, while Baldwin, Lima, Alco and the smaller American builders laboured on a three-shift day basis to turn out steam locomotives, the development of diesel-powered traction did not come to a halt. General Motors' EMD plant and other diesel builders continued to build both switchers and freight road engines, though building of passenger diesel engines was officially brought to a stop in 1942. Acknowledging the emergence of diesel power, Alco and Lima had already set up joint ventures to build diesel-electric locomotives with General Electric and Hamilton respectively; and Baldwin later began collaboration with Westinghouse. By 1945 and the end of the war, many US railroads were using diesel freight engines; and the manufacturers had their plans already prepared for the resumption of building passenger units. The US steam fleet was showing the marks of several years of intensive use, combined with reduced and often less-skilled maintenance. Even before the war, in 1937, Baldwin had published an estimate that over 90 per cent of current American motive power could be regarded as obsolete. This took account of the fact that though the 1930s had seen the introduction of various new classes, the production numbers were usually small. Much of the locomotive stock predated the 'super-power' era. In 1938 Alco said of the steam locomotive: 'Although it is over 100 years old it is still in process of evolution.' Promoting the 2-6-6-6 type of which sixty were built between 1941 and 1949 for the Chesapeake & Ohio, Lima said: 'Where the amount of power that can be packed into a single unit is important – where you want 6000, 8000, even 10,000 horsepower in one engine – the steam locomotive is unchallenged… They are fine pieces of machinery. Modern in every respect, they are establishing remarkable records for economy, reliability, and low maintenance.' It ended on a rather desperate note: 'Don't sell these steam giants short. They have their place – and in their place are unsurpassed.' Despite their efforts to push the virtues and potential of steam, however, the steam builders were not about to reap the benefits of stock replacement, as the railroads proceeded to invest millions of dollars in new motive power.

North America was the battleground, and the battle for supremacy was immediate and swift. Any thought that steam and diesel might peacefully coexist was soon abandoned. This was the only hope for steam, but it was shot at from several different directions. One of these was the preference of the great majority of enginemen for diesel working. Another was the railroad companies' natural reluctance to maintain the expense of dual facilities, especially when – in most cases – the diesel service depots were new and the steam depots old and badly in need of refurbishing. Also of great importance were the frequent shortages in coal supply: disastrous relations between workers and management in the US mining industry resulted in a series of lengthy strikes and lock-outs through the later 1940s. But in the end, what turned the slow defeat of steam into a rout was the highly effective propaganda campaign of the diesel-electric builders, which had its effect not only on railroad operators but, most significantly, on American public opinion. Diesels were there, they were cleaner, more economical, more efficient; they looked smarter – they were the modern thing. The travelling public came to want and expect them. The railroad managers, looking with justified concern at the rapid increase in domestic air traffic, found that diesel-powered services gained customers from competing steam routes.

The economic argument for steam was based mainly on the fact that steam locomotives were cheaper to build. The counter-argument for diesel-electrics was that they were cheaper to run, and, needing less maintenance, were able to run greater mileages. One of the few lines to undertake extensive comparative cost and mileage tests of diesel-electric and steam power was the New York Central. In October 1946, the new S1- or 'Niagara'-class 4-8-4s were tested against a pair of twin E7 General Motors diesels, on the New York-Chicago run, starting from Harmon. This was no set-up for either side's benefit; the steam locomotives were the NYC's own, twenty-five of them, built by Alco, to the specifications of Paul Kiefer, the NYC's head of motive power. The 'Niagaras' were built for consistent high speed and heavy-duty performance, to a degree that has probably never been equalled with steam. The entire 928-mile (1493km) Harmon-Chicago run, once requiring up to four locomotive changes, was to be run by one engine, with a pause for a rapid top-up of coal in the huge fourteen-wheeled tender. Water could be picked up from troughs, 'pans' in the USA, laid between the tracks. An annual mileage in excess of 275,000 (442,000km) could be expected. And average speeds were high. The prime train was the 'Twentieth Century Limited' and its timing was sixteen hours, requiring an average of 58mph (93km/h) including stops. Mile after mile at 80mph (128km/h) and more was needed to maintain the schedule. Quick work in the depots at each end was needed to keep the engines serviced to a peak of efficiency. Only the Norfolk & Western's shed facilities matched or bettered those of the NYC. EMD's E7 was equally new; its twin units capable of developing 4000hp and a tractive effort of 53,080lb against the 61,050lb (27,936kg) of the 'Niagara'. The results of the tests were closer than perhaps anyone had expected. Over the month, the 'Niagaras' averaged 27,221 miles each, and the E7s 28,954. Average operating costs per mile were calculated as $1.22 for the steam locomotives and $1.11 for the diesels. The E7s were in front, but the publicity put out by GM's Electromotive Division had promised a far greater margin of economy compared with steam – and diesel locomotives were much more expensive to build. At that time it was also assumed that their operating lives would be shorter.

But few railroads had the level of steam servicing that the NYC provided for its fast flyers, and elsewhere, against the average performance of a run-down stud of ageing steam locomotives, serviced in depots thirty to fifty years old, the diesel units lived up to their manufacturers' claims. The press and the general public preferred them. With long-distance railways now facing serious competition from internal coach and air services, the managements desperately wanted to show a modern face. That was something steam could not do. The railroads which handled substantial coal traffic held out longest – the coal companies were their largest customers and it did not seem politic to offend them. Also, they usually got their locomotive coal at a substantial discount, if they did not actually own their own mines. As late as 1957, the Norfolk & Western still operated 408 steam locomotives when many other Class One railroads had none at all, but in the following year it capitulated, ordering 268 new diesel-electric units. By then, the New York Central was down to 122 steam locomotives, with ninety-three electric units and almost 2,000 diesels. In *Dropping the Fire*, Philip Atkins records that the company was so obsessed by the need to present a new image that it would not allow the Smithsonian Institute to preserve one of the 'Niagaras'. The Pennsylvania Railroad, the NYC's great rival, was quick to follow the NYC's example. Its late run of modern 'duplex' steam locomotives had not been the anticipated success and by the end of 1949 most were already out of use.

The mental process behind the steady withdrawal of steam power can be followed in the successive announcements made by the Chesapeake & Ohio, a line which earned most of its revenue from coal haulage. It annual report for 1944 stated: 'There is no economic justification for the use of diesel freight or passenger power on the Chesapeake & Ohio.' In 1947, the Chairman said: 'I do not think it is in the public interest to operate diesels at all.' He went on to warn about the depletion of oil reserves. By 1952, however, the company President was saying: 'The greatest single advance in railroad efficiency in recent years has been the introduction of the diesel-electric locomotive, and the Chesapeake & Ohio is making use of this new tool.'

Naturally, the rest of the railway world followed events in North America with great interest. At the end of the Second World War, the railways of Europe were in far worse condition than those of the USA and Canada.

Quite apart from damage to track, stations and installations, many locomotives had been destroyed by bombs, shells, mines and sabotage. In Austria, the proportion of heavily or totally damaged locomotives was put at 70 per cent of the stock. Four thousand French locomotives were destroyed or heavily damaged. The Dutch railways had suffered greatly, though well before the end of the war the government-in-exile, based in Great Britain, had with careful provision ordered two locomotive classes from Nohab in Sweden, and delivery began very soon after liberation. The Netherlands also acquired a number of redundant Swiss 4-6-0s. Spain had remained neutral but had suffered its own damaging civil war in 1936-1938. As they surveyed their battered systems and took stock of their over-used and ill-maintained locomotives, the European railway managements found themselves compelled to take both a long-term and a short-term view of what was necessary. Although they had seen America opt wholeheartedly for diesel-electric, the long-term view, for most, was of a largely electrified system, with diesel-worked minor lines. In the shorter term, however, there was no alternative to continuing with steam. New forms of traction, especially the construction of an electric catenary, would require huge capital investment and take a large number of years. The steam locomotive must therefore soldier on. But all countries needed new engines. As locomotive works that had also been busy building tanks and armoured cars returned to civilian business, they found their order books filling up rapidly. Their problem was at first to obtain the steel and special metals required, and fuel to drive their own machinery. The orders came not only from the war-torn countries but from others not directly involved, but which had been unable to import new locomotives during the war years. So began the last years of active steam locomotive building in Europe, with a general sense that although steam was on the way out, the process might well take several decades. Most designers were content to be conservators, putting together locomotive designs that embodied the best current practice, sometimes in compromise with their own traditions and personal ideas. Thus the post-war generation of steam locomotives was based on the tried-and-true pre-war designs, with necessary concessions to the comfort and convenience of engine and depot crews. But there were still a few radicals around – not all designers wrote off the steam locomotive's future – and, even if the fastest speed had been reached, and the heaviest load pulled, there was still vigour and capacity for development: some fine fireworks were still to come before the great display ended.

The lessons learned in wartime construction were immediately applied to peacetime conditions. This was particularly so in Germany and Czechoslovakia, where the welding of boilers, tenders and other items had been developed to a high level of effectiveness during the war, with the Skoda works at Plzen perhaps leading the field. In Great Britain there was more of a reversion to traditional methods of riveting and bolting. All countries continued to build pre-war locomotive types, mostly of a mixed-traffic kind, while new steam designs were being evolved. In Germany, divided into two nations for fifty years to come, the *Deutsche Bundesbahn* embarked on a similar exercise of standardisation to that which the *Reichsbahn* had initiated in the 1920s. Britain's 'Big Four' companies remained independent and pursued their own policies until they were all brought into a single national ownership in 1948. The SNCF, though it resumed its plans for electrification, also had to acknowledge a need for new steam power. Only Italy and Switzerland, both more advanced in electrification, did not build or buy new steam engines.

By the end of the war, an old bug-bear that had always afflicted the steam locomotive was finally disposed of. Two kinds of water treatment had been developed, both of which ensured the admission of purer water to the boiler than ever before. In the United States it was the 'hundred per cent lime soda' solution, which was mixed with the feed water in treatment plants. In France it was the patent TIA, *Traitement Intégrale Armand*, developed by Louis Armand of the PLM, an engineer who became director-general of the SNCF and transferred his interest to electric and even nuclear-powered locomotion. The TIA system was installed in the tender tanks. Use of either method minimised the accumulation of scale, eliminated corrosion, reduced the frequency, time and cost of boiler maintenance, greatly extended the boiler's life, and reduced fuel consumption by about a fifth. While this external aid improved the locomotive's diet, the quality of the coal on which it was fed declined sharply. During the war years, there was a steep rise in the price of coal – in Great Britain by 57 per cent – and in the immediate post-war years it was also in short supply. Once again, the steam locomotive's toleration of ill-treatment did harm to its public esteem. Burning lowest-grade coal, it made less steam and more smoke, and went less fast – but nevertheless it went. Diesels allowed no such compromises.

One of the first railway administrations to come to grips with post-war circumstances was the Indian Railways. In 1946 they introduced a new express locomotive, the Class WP 'Pacific', for the 5ft 6in (167.5cm) broad gauge. It represented a significant change of locomotive policy on the IR. India was still a British colony, though independence was clearly on the horizon, but the attitudes of colonial deference and 'Mother-country knows best' were gone. Though designed in India, these were wholly American-style engines, with the prototypes built by Baldwin and nearly half of the class, 320 engines, being built in the USA or Canada. The Chrzanov works in Poland and Vienna Lokomotivfabrik of Austria also built thirty each. After the unhappy experiences with pre-war 'Indian Standard' types, these reliable and free-steaming engines were received with great relief. It was the most numerous 'Pacific' Class in the world, with a total of 755 built between 1947 and 1967, the last 435 at the new Chittaranjan works, set up in India – with British investment support – in 1950. Given a massive appearance by their big boiler, small chimney, and bulbous smoke-box front, they were built in the classic American manner, with bar frames, two simple-expansion cylinders, and Walschaerts valve gear actuating piston valves. The parallel boiler was topped by a long parallel casing concealing all fittings except the just-protruding chimney. The quality of Indian track had not improved in the war years, but their suspension system was well-adapted to the problems created by soft or uneven ballast. The bullet-headed green front end of a WP, with its eight-pointed silver star around the centrally-placed headlamp, was one of the most familiar sights to the foreign traveller in India. Among the many express trains they hauled was the 'Grand Trunk Express', between Madras and Delhi, and some were fitted with tender water scoops when water troughs were laid on one section of the line. On long hauls there might be a crew of four, with two firemen and a coal breaker in addition to the driver. In the late 1980s they were still to be seen, though often in a wheezy, leaky, neglected state in their latter years. Even after class withdrawal and the official end of Indian steam in the 1990s, some still remain in special service.

In Britain, in a sense, the post-war locomotive era began quite early in the war, and in a surprising place. The Southern Railway had already embarked on a policy of large-scale electrification when it appointed Oliver Bulleid – for long Gresley's assistant on the LNER – as its Chief Mechanical Engineer in 1937. But it also had long non-electrified main lines running west and south-west. Bulleid was a firm believer in the ability of steam power to meet the needs of a modern railway, and set about designing large new engines. He began with the most traditional type, the

0-6-0, and produced a squat, boxy locomotive looking so much like some scaled-up toy that Sir William Stanier is said to have inquired: 'Where's the key?' But it was also the fastest and most powerful of any British 0-6-0. To avoid wartime restrictions on construction, his 1939 design for the 4-6-2 'Merchant Navy' express passenger engine was presented to the Ministry of Supply in 1941 as a 'mixed traffic' type. At 6ft 2in (188cm) its driving wheels were not quite too large for that description to be completely mendacious. In the eyes of its designer, it was a new-generation locomotive intended for an era when trains loading up to 600 tons would be hauled at average speeds of 70mph (113km/h) or more. It was a prescient vision. The squared-off 'air-smoothed' casing was intended to suit automatic washing plants as well as to reduce air resistance. It gave the engines a bold new look, and some of the novelties incorporated inside it were no less bold. Bulleid was an authority on welding, and much weight was saved by welded construction of an all-steel firebox and boiler. At 280psi (19.6kg/cm²), it carried the highest pressure of any conventionally-boilered British locomotive. The three simple-expansion cylinders were operated by piston valves, actuated in turn by his unique chain-driven valve gear, enclosed within an oil-tight casing. This 'oil-bath' also enclosed the middle connecting-rod, crosshead and crank. These novelties were to present incessant repair and maintenance problems. Between 1948 and 1950 one of the class, No.35005, was fitted with a mechanical stoker. The 'Merchant Navies' were followed by a lighter-weight 'West Country' class, 110 strong, of the same design.

From 1954, all the 'Merchant Navy' class and over half of the 'West Country' were rebuilt in conventional form without the outer casing and inner oil bath, and with three sets of Walschaerts valve-gear. Their story illustrates the degree of personal power, even into the 1940s and in wartime, which a British chief mechanical engineer possessed within his domain. No other country had a railway system in which some two hundred new engines could be built with an untried and inaccessible system for such a crucial part of the works. Nor would Britain after 1948. But for his part, Bulleid was a man with a vision of modern steam power, using coal, still the country's prime natural resource (North Sea oil was still thirty years away). He was prepared to throw the dice for a high stake. In 1948 he followed up his 'Pacifics' with an even more radical new design, the 0-6-6-0T 'Leader'. An attempt to build a steam engine with the operating characteristics of a diesel, it was dogged by design troubles and the single prototype never got beyond the test phase; work on three part-built engines was abandoned

at Brighton works after 1949. With a driving cab at each end, and a tor-
rid space for the fireman in the middle, it bore some resemblance to the
Prussian Class S9 of 1904, though the inner works were completely different. It was mounted on two articulated six-wheel bogies, each driven by a
three-cylinder engine on the centre axle, with steam distribution by sleeve
valves. All the motion and cranks were encased and automatically lubricated. Four thermic syphons were fitted in the firebox. By 1951, all were
dismantled.

One radical at a time was enough for the British railways. Other designers followed the path of the conservator. The next wholly new 'Pacific'
design was the last to come from the LNER, and it took over the class
designation A1 from the first LNER 'Pacifics'. British practice invariably
credited the whole design to the presiding chief mechanical engineer,
and these were thus designed by A.H. Peppercorn. Three-cylinder simple-expansion locomotives, forty-nine of them were built at Doncaster
under the nationally-owned British Railways regime which began in
1948. One writer noted with entire approval that it was: 'every inch a
Doncaster Pacific... The original theme first postulated by Gresley in 1922
was still substantially there in 1948.' Nevertheless, there were some significant changes. Gresley's conjugated valve gear was replaced by three sets of
Walschaerts gear. A stubby, stove-pipe-style double chimney and Kylchap
blast exhaust were fitted, and electric lighting was provided. The boiler
had a steam collector in its 'banjo dome'. Compared with the A4, still the
benchmark performer on the East Coast route, it had a reduced heating
surface despite a bigger firebox. Peppercorn's A1 was an effective engine
in service, free-steaming and relatively fault-free. There were those who
commented that, with so little in the way of new or original ideas, this
was no more than should have been expected. The last five of the class
had roller bearings on all axles, and four of these ran over a million miles
(1,609,000km) in relatively short careers. The last one withdrawn was in
June 1966.

When the Railway Executive was set up to run the nationalised railways
of Great Britain, the German example was followed in the setting-up of a
Locomotive Standards Committee, in 1948. Headed by R.A. Riddles, chief
designer of the 'Austerity' war engines, it was to lay out policy for future
motive power, based on a small number of standard types. Remembering
how the old LMS had been crippled in its early years by ancient rivalries among the companies forming it, Riddles acted with considerable

diplomacy. A number of road trials were carried out, with the aim of testing locomotives of the old companies on the main routes of their rivals. But despite, or more probably because of, the great variety of relatively recent locomotive types, the decision was made to ignore them all, and to design a new set of standard locomotives which could cope with all traffic requirements. The design leaders drew most on the work of the former LMS, not merely because most of them came from it, but because it had already advanced furthest along the road of 'standardisation'. Many component parts were taken from, or modelled on, existing equipment, but the range of 'modern' features was greater than on any predecessor. Most of these were intended to be labour-saving, like self-cleaning smoke-boxes (these were fitted with grids for shaking ash and cinders down to a hopper), rocker grates, self-emptying ashpans, mechanical lubricators and roller bearings — nothing new in themselves. Some features of proved effectiveness, like the thermic syphon, were not employed. For engines designed by a committee, and with working groups at several different locations, the British standard types were generally successful. The first to appear, in 1951, was the 4-6-2 'Britannia' Class 7MT — for 'mixed traffic', though it was just as much an express passenger engine as the 'Merchant Navy' Class. Unlike any previous British 'Pacific' for home use, it had only two cylinders. Fifty-five were built, and after some initial problems with driving wheels which fell off at speed, and a few hair-raising incidents when engine and tender (plus train) came apart from each other, they performed reliably in an era when maximum power output was rarely required. The 'thrashing' times were far in the past. A larger and more advanced standard express 'Pacific' was also planned, but only the prototype of this was built. In 1951, reviewing different forms of traction, Riddles put the economic case for steam power: 'There is also a case for steam, and it is that at present in a considerable range of circumstances, a pound will buy more tractive effort than in the case of any other form of transport.' A further report to the British Transport Commission in 1952 said: 'The steam locomotive is reaching the end of a long phase of evolution and it is unlikely that any revolutionary developments will be made in the future... within its inherent limitations, this form of motive power will continue to provide efficient service for some time to come.' Three years later, it seemed the time had come. The British Railways Modernisation Plan of 1955 announced the complete replacement of steam by diesel or electric traction. Phasing-out was planned to take fifteen years, but in fact it took slightly less.

Though by no means revolutionary, among the British 'standard' types, the most original was the Class 9F 2-10-0, the first ten-coupled class built specifically for home use in the UK. A 2-8-2 was first considered for the post-war standard heavy freight locomotive, but the success of the wartime 'Austerity' 2-10-0 was decisive in making this the adopted configuration. The boiler was similar to that of the 'Britannia' 4-6-2 class, but 21in (53.3cm) shorter, and set high, in order to provide the widest possible space for the ashpan. The resultant space between boiler and frame earned the class the nickname of 'spaceships'. Nevertheless, the compromise necessary between a wide, deep ashpan and the 60in (152.5cm) coupled wheels was perhaps the weakest point in a generally excellent design. As in the 'Austerity' engines, the driving wheels, on the central axle, had no flanges, in order to help in traversing curves. Many of the class were provided with a concrete arch in the firebox instead of the conventional brick arch. The provision of smoke deflectors, unusual in a freight engine, may have been in anticipation of a low-pressure exhaust which would not rise clear of the boiler. The British Railways designers were reluctant to use double blast-pipe chimneys, partly because they believed these were really only useful at full power output, which, as with the standard 'Pacifics', they did not expect to be a frequent occurrence. However, later engines of this class were so equipped, and one was experimentally fitted with a Giesl ejector. In 1955, Crewe works built ten engines with the Franco-Crosti boiler. Feed-water heaters were a normal sight on American, French and German locomotives, among others, but had never been widespread in Britain. British engineers' distaste for external fittings may have played a part. This was by far their most serious attempt to provide such an aid to efficient steam generation. Unlike Italian Crosti-boilered engines, the 2-10-0 retained its front chimney in addition to the exhaust vent fitted on the right-hand side of the boiler, though it was used only when the fire was being started up. Sulphur dioxide corrosion of the tubes was a problem, and the Crosti variation was not particularly successful. In another trial scheme, three 9Fs were fitted with mechanical stokers in 1958, apart from the solitary 'Merchant Navy', the only British locomotives not to have hand-firing.

The 9F Class numbered 251, not a large fleet by comparison with the big freight engines of other major industrial countries. They were employed chiefly on vacuum-brake fitted mineral trains. Although not fitted with train heating apparatus they did run passenger trains in summer, notably on the Somerset & Dorset line. Once one of them was put on the

'Flying Scotsman' express between Grantham and Kings Cross, and celebrated this promotion, from infantry to cavalry, as it were, by completing the run at an average 58mph (93km/h) start to stop, including a maximum of 90mph (145km/h). At least one other authenticated 90mph was recorded, before the operating authorities placed a maximum of 60mph (96.5km/h) on the class. The 9F was the last steam locomotive designed for British railways, and No.92220, built – with a conventional boiler – at Swindon in 1960, and named *Evening Star*, was the last steam locomotive built for regular service on British Railways. Its service career was no more than three years, and it has been preserved, with some others of the class.

The great home of radical steam design continued to be France. In the SNCF, André Chapelon was head of the Department of Steam Locomotive Studies until 1953. Although steam design was increasingly side-lined in an organisation focused on electrification, some remarkable new locomotives appeared. The most notable was a 'Northern' design, the 242 A.1 4-8-4. Chapelon's English biographer, H.C.B. Rogers, describes this as 'the greatest steam locomotive of all'. And yet only one was ever built. Its beginning was as a prototype 4-8-2 express passenger type for the *Etat* railway. Built at the Fives-Lille works in 1932, it proved on test to be a bad steamer and a rough rider; it was never put into regular service, and the design was abandoned. In the late 1930s, when SNCF authorities were planning the future development of large engines, permission was given for this engine to be rebuilt under Chapelon's direction as a three-cylinder compound. Wartime delays meant that the work did not begin until 1942, at the Forges et Aciéries de la Marine et d'Homecourt, at St Chamond. The reconstruction was radical, beginning with the frames. Though Chapelon had adopted the American-style single-piece steel chassis for new locomotives, he was obliged in this case to strengthen the frame by a combination of transverse steel stays and welded steel plates along the sides. This increased the weight to a point where the additional carrying axle was needed in order to keep the maximum axle load at 20.6 tons (21t), and the engine became a 4-8-4 (242 in French notation). Maximum boiler pressure was set at a high 292psi (20.4kg/cm^2). The single high-pressure cylinder, driving the first coupled axle, was fitted inside, in line with the external low-pressure cylinders. Each was operated independently by Walschaerts valve gear, with that for the inside cylinder worked by a crank on the third left-hand coupled wheel, as with some Czech locomotives. The low-pressure cylinders drove the second coupled axle. Poppet valves in the original machine were replaced by double piston valves. Naturally very close attention was paid to the size and positioning of steam passages and to the draughting and exhaust system, with a triple Kylchap ejector and chimney. A large Houlet superheater was installed, and two Nicholson thermic syphons were fitted in the firebox, which was made of steel and mechanically stoked. The front and rear bogies had roller bearings. Many minor details were attended to: in locomotives, the chafing effect between axle boxes and the horn guides had always been a source of vibration and weakening of the frame; for the first time in Europe, American Franklin automatic wedges were fitted, to minimise the effect, which they did with great success. The big engine rode with remarkable ease and silence. The effect of the rebuild was to increase the weight by 20.3t but to virtually double its potential power output. The work was completed in May 1946.

The exhaustive tests that followed quickly showed that there was nothing theoretical about this power. Measuring the output in horsepower, this was the first European locomotive to sustain a continuous 4,000hp or more at the tender drawbar, corresponding to more than 5,000hp developed in the cylinders, while running at speeds of up to 75mph (120.7km/h). It achieved these results without excessive use of fuel or water: its fuel economy was as great as that of the French four-cylinder compounds, and considerably greater than that of, for example, the most powerful British 'Pacifics' of the 'Coronation' class. A further important consideration was its ability to start off heavy trains on rising gradients without suffering the problem that had always dogged steam locomotives, slipping of the coupled wheels. In such situations, a calculated tractive effort of 56,000lb (25,400kg) was produced. None of these were freak results or the product of specially favourable situations. The tests ran between 1946 and 1948, on some of France's most challenging main lines, in all seasons, including winter, when steam had also to be provided for heating a long train of passenger cars.

Whilst the 4-8-4 was a large engine in European terms, it was only of moderate size compared to American express locomotives. But with it, as with Chapelon's 2-12-0, any former notion of correlation between dimensions and power output had to be set aside. The Southern Pacific's GS-4 Class 4-8-4 weighed 475,000lb (215.4t), more than half as much again. The New York Central's Class S-1a 4-8-4 had 44 per cent more evaporative heating surface, 40 per cent more superheating surface, and almost double the grate area. These were regarded as first-rate express passenger locomotives, but the A.1 could at least match them in performance, and leave them far behind in economy. If the design had been reproduced, it would have created a most formidable class of engines, but 242.A1 was destined to remain a solitary example of excellence.

The fact that a steam engine could out-perform the French electric designs was an embarrassment, not a triumph, for the SNCF. At this time the delayed tests of the Chapelon 2-12-0 were further reinforcing the steam case. The fuel economy displayed by his engines also challenged the argument that the capital costs of electrification would be balanced by lower running costs. The principal effect of the A.1 was to send the electrical engineers back to the drawing board so that their new 2-D-2 locomotives tcould be upgraded to match its performance. Placed at the Le Mans depot, the A.1 took its turns with 'Pacifics' at running Paris expresses which were easily within its power. Its capacity could only be revealed when having to make up time after delays. In 1960 it was withdrawn from service and broken up.

When in 1948 the SNCF identified a need for new steam express power in the south-east region, it seems strange that it should have ignored the 242.A.1, and chosen as the prototype an ex-PLM 4-8-2 'Mountain' type, 241.C. However, André Chapelon was given the task of effecting improvements to the design, which went back to 1931, before series construction began. New cylinders, with an improved steam circuit, were made, and the frames were strengthened to some extent by transverse steel members. The external design closely followed Chapelon's established pattern. But it was impossible to incorporate the range of radical changes that marked his 'Pacific' rebuilds, and they were moderate rather than exceptional performers in service. Between 1948 and 1952, thirty-five 'Mountains', known to the enginemen as '*Moumoutes*', were built by the Le Creusot Company, as Class 241.P, replacing forty 2-8-2s of the 141.P class. The 241.Ps were first based at Marseille, and hauled heavy expresses up and down the Rhône valley between there and Lyon; when this stretch was electrified, they were dispersed among a number of depots in the North, East and West regions. They were to be the last of France's big four-cylinder compounds in regular service, operating until 1970; their final service being between Nantes and Le Mans. Several ran more than two million miles. The last three were taken out of service at Le Mans depot in May 1970, but have been preserved. New locomotives otherwise reflected pre-war designs. Marc de

Caso, Chief Mechanical Engineer of the old *Nord*, had designed a four-cylinder, superheated compound 2-10-0 in the 1930s, capable of hauling 2,000t coal trains. As Class 150.P, 115 were built for the SNCF up to 1950. These were equipped with mechanical stokers and supplemented the thirty *Nord* engines. De Caso's express masterpiece was the striking but solitary Class 232.U1, laid down before the war as a four-cylinder simple 4-6-4 of Class 232.R, but completed in 1949 as a compound engine, with Houlet superheater, long-travel piston valves and roller bearings on all its axles. No further examples were built, but 232.U1 is preserved at Mulhouse.

While following the last phases of the steam locomotive's career, it is important to remember that new, post-war designs everywhere formed only a small minority of the engines in service. The natural longevity of the steam locomotive, combined with the economic depression of the 1930s, the hiatus of a six-year world war, and the slow initial pace of post-war reconstruction, meant that many elderly engines, large and small, in an immense variety of types, survived in use into the 1950s. The continued employment of so many virtual museum pieces, in the age of the jet plane and the mass-produced motor car, was in itself one of the factors that contributed to the steam locomotive's demise. In almost every country, locomotives with cabs open to the weather and unprovided with seats, with heavy manual reversing gear and cumbersome hand-operated fire-doors, with smoke-boxes and ashpans whose cleaning was a long and grimy task, formed the majority. Sometimes they were well-maintained, most often they were not. Providing spare parts was often difficult, and added to costs. These were also the locomotives most likely to be worked by newly-trained staff. Driving, or firing, such engines, or preparing them for service, became less and less appealing to workers, especially as adverse comparison could be made not only with other trades, but with the comfort and relative ease of driving diesel and electric locomotives. Particularly in the United States and Australia, the engine-men's unions had been successful in compelling reluctant companies to improve working conditions on the foot-plate, but all railways were finding it more and more difficult to recruit and retain steam locomotive crews.

For amateur locomotive enthusiasts, by contrast, the range of types and varieties to be found at that time was a source of delight. With a strong element of historical interest and nostalgia, tours and visits were made to inspect, and ride behind, the last representatives – often wheezing and decrepit – of classes that had once swept with dash and sparkle along main-line tracks, or done stalwart service in freight yards.

In 1950 the observer could still see 4-4-2 'Atlantic' locomotives at work in England, Denmark, Pakistan, and Mozambique (in the latter until 1978), of designs that in the first three cases went back to the first decade of the century. 'Mother Hubbard' 4-4-2s of 1918 or earlier, with boiler-mounted cabs, could be found on the Central of New Jersey. The visitor to Vienna or Prague could see Gölsdorf engines that still had balloon chimneys and two domes connected by a wide steam pipe. Among the numerous locomotives hauling the 'Taurus Express' on its various stages between Istanbul and Baghdad would be ex-Prussian G8 0-8-0s of 1902 vintage, belonging to the Syrian Railways. In Britain, the last few of Churchward's 'Saints', the first modern 4-6-0, also introduced in 1902, were still in main-line service. In Thailand, German Hanomag-built 2-6-0s, of a type first supplied to the Royal Siamese Railways in 1906, were still hauling freight trains. Russian Class E 0-10-0s still numbered several thousands, their design hardly changed since 1912. The Pennsylvania Railroad ran fast trains with its K4 'Pacifics', first seen in 1914, up to the end of 1957, the same year as the last of New Zealand's Q-class 'Pacifics' of 1901. In the Dalmatian mountains of Yugoslavia, the rugged 2-6-6-0 Mallets of Class 601, built in Budapest in 1914, still had ten years of hard slogging on the gradients between Split and Zagreb ahead of them. Local trains in Scotland were pulled by the last generation of the 'Dunalastair' 4-4-0s, built in 1916. But these were all twentieth-century locomotives. In 1950 it was not hard to find working engines whose career had begun well over fifty years before.

Japan still possessed examples of the Beyer, Peacock Type 5500 4-4-0, imported from England in 1894 and typical of many built for colonial and foreign use, with its low running plate angled up over the outside cylinders. The South African Railways, which always excelled at conserving the old while introducing the new, were still using the Class 7 4-8-0 built for the old Cape Government Railway in 1892. In New Zealand, the 1 in 15 Rimutaka incline had not yet been by-passed and was still worked by Fell rack engines supplied in 1876 and 1886, with up to four on each train. Three Canadian Pacific 4-4-0s of 1883, much-rebuilt but retaining an antique look, were working on local passenger trains in New Brunswick. Great veterans were often to be found in Spain. The *Norte* railway's 'River' class of 0-8-0 of 1879 was still busy in 1950 and most of its forty-seven engines, with a variety of chimney cowls, survived for another ten years. Even more ancient was an 0-6-0 freight locomotive built by E. B. Wilson in Leeds, England, for the Madrid Zaragoza and Alicante Railway in 1857. It was still at work in 1961, aged 104. The New South Wales Government Railways' 93-class 0-6-0, introduced in 1877, had its last two examples still in harness until 1972. The supreme survivor was probably in Indonesia, where a Glasgow-built 2-4-0 of Class B50 was still working in 1972, aged 122. Reasons for long survival included light axle-weights, making engines especially suitable for certain routes; light duties that did not overtax frames or motion; and the owning company's lack of cash to buy new engines. But the veterans also had to be good, free-steaming examples of their kind.

Thus, to the traveller, whether it was a source of pleasure or not, the steam railway presented a distinctly old-fashioned and dilapidated appearance in the middle of the twentieth century. It was the superannuated engines, rather than the new types, which afforded propaganda to the diesel sales-men: one diesel could easily replace two or more of them. Their only merit to the operators was that they had long ago paid for themselves, and they were cheap to operate, as long as they did not need heavy repairs. As they wore out, they went to the breakers' yards, and the range and number of older steam types diminished with increasing speed through the 1950s.

In the 1960s, with the number of new diesel and electric locomotives and multiple units becoming greater year by year, more and more of the older steam locomotives were taken off the road, even if still in good working order. In Great Britain and France, the scrapping of steam locomotives was proceeding wholesale, and by this time, the programme consisted mostly of engines which had a decade or more of useful life in front of them. Rail travellers became accustomed to seeing lines of condemned engines standing on sidings at locomotive depots. At first, as if officials feared that all diesel engines might suddenly acquire some fatal disease, or the fuel sup-ply run out, this was referred to as 'storage'. To write off and dump large numbers of usable modern engines was a heavy responsibility. The book value and potential earning power was far greater than their scrap value. But the managements kept their nerve and forced the process through. The transition period was not long. The railway writer Roger Lloyd predicted in 1956 that it might take fifty years for the phasing-out of steam in Britain to be complete. He overestimated by thirty-four years: Britain's last regular steam passenger train ran in December 1968. The steam locomotive was highly resistant to the insidious modern concept of built-in obsolescence:

its structure had to be made strong enough to withstand such high internal pressures, intense heat and powerful thrusts that it could hardly fail to last for many years. But against the judgement that it was, simply by virtue of what it was, obsolete, there was no defence. In 1928 the world population of steam locomotives was around 227,000; fifty years later it was 25,000 and shrinking fast.

Not all countries destroyed their steam locomotives with the haste that overcame the United States in the 1950s, and Great Britain in the 1960s. A more measured approach was taken by several European countries, including Czechoslovakia, where a number of interesting locomotive types were built in the 1940s and 50s, for use in both passenger and freight service during a transitional period before main-line electrification. The Czechoslovak National Railways (CSD) loading gauge allowed engines of a height of 15ft 2in (461.9cm) and a width of 10ft 2in (309.6cm) which gave designers useful scope, and they did not hesitate to build big. The Class 476 4-8-2 of three three-cylinder compound engines, introduced in 1950, was a development of the two-cylinder 475-class 4-8-2 of 1947. Before the imposing of the 'Iron Curtain' in 1948, Czechoslovak practice had been very much influenced by France, which explains the compounding, which by that time was rare outside France. The high-pressure cylinder was set inside the frame. However, the compounding system was not judged a success, and only three were built in this form; with the remaining twelve built as three-cylinder simples, in which form they gave good service on long-distance east-west expresses.

A much more numerous class was the CSD's Class 556 2-10-0. Between 1952 and 1958 the Skoda works built 510 of these powerful two-cylinder simple engines, in a worthy finale to almost sixty years of Czech-built steam power. The welded boiler and firebox with thermic syphon, arch tubes and combustion chamber were now established as standard, as were mechanical stokers, Kylchap double blast-pipe chimneys, and roller bearings. These engines could haul 1,200t trains at 50mph (80km/h) on the level and frequently took much heavier loads, up to 4,000t. Numerous examples remain in preservation.

Among the last steam locomotives designed and built at the Skoda works was the simple-expansion express 4-8-2 of Class 498.1, in 1954, in essence an improved version of the Class 498.0 of 1947. In a typical feature of modern three-cylinder Czech steam locomotives, the valve gear for the inside cylinder was operated by a long rod from a return crank fitted to the crank-pin of the third coupled axle on the left side. Although like most post-war Czech engines it was rather German in styling, many of the internal arrangements were derived from Chapelon's work in France. The firebox, of welded construction, had a combustion chamber, a thermic syphon and two tubular arches. Roller bearings were fitted to all axles. In anticipation of eventual displacement from main-line services, there was a provision for adjusting the axle load between coupled and supporting wheels, to enable it to run on secondary lines. As electrification of the network advanced, the express engines of the CSD were required to run certain routes, such as that from Prague to Kolín, to schedules devised for electric traction. The two 498 classes rose magnificently to this demand. No.498.106, on a test run on 27 August 1964, achieved the maximum speed on Czechoslovakian rails, of 100.6mph (162km/h). This engine, and one other of the class, are preserved. In 1972, the Czechoslovak railways resolved to eliminate the use of steam traction within five years. In fact it took nine, but on 1 April 1981, No.556.0506 worked the last scheduled steam service on the CSD.

In the various countries of South America, there was a variety of railway development on several different gauges from narrow gauge to the Argentinian 5ft 3in (160cm). Common to all was the need to import locomotives: although each company had its repair works, no main-line locomotives were built. The South American railways remained an important market for builders in the United States and Europe, though by the early 1950s, the USA had dropped out of steam locomotive supply. One consequence of this was that a line which had long used only American engines, the Cerro de Pasco Railway, in Peru, was compelled to order new steam traction in Britain. But the engine was a thoroughly American design, and one of the sturdiest locomotive types ever built, the 'Andes' 2-8-0 of the Central Railway of Peru (FCC) and its two neighbouring lines, first introduced in 1935, and built by the thoroughly English firm of Beyer, Peacock, in Manchester, in 1951. Perhaps only such ultra-specialised types as the Fell rack engines were more highly adapted to their terrain and tasks than these locomotives, whose work is graphically described in *Railways of the Andes*, Brian Fawcett's memoir of railways in that supremely unwelcoming environment. On the Central, they reached the highest point of any railway, at 16,693ft (4,783m). Cerro de Pasco was the remote Andean mining town reachable only by pack-mule in the mid-1820s, when Richard Trevithick's wanderings had taken him there as a mining engineer.

High altitude was not a problem for steam locomotives: with a significantly lower atmospheric pressure, their boiler pressure of 200psi (14.1kg/cm2) actually became more efficient. Steep and long gradients, tight curves, and ice-railed tunnels were the everyday reality. Air-powered sanding gear, rail-washing pipes, and a twin-pipe air braking system were fitted. Oil was the fuel.

The numerous railway systems of Brazil had engines from most of the exporting companies, though the United States predominated. In 1948 Brazil still had the world's biggest metre-gauge network, even more than India at over 22,000 miles (35,200km). Much of it by this time was in poor condition and with out of date equipment. In 1949 the National Railways Department (DNEF) set out to buy new traction, and an order for new locomotives, both 4-8-4 and 2-8-4, was won by a specially-formed French consortium, GELSA, which appointed André Chapelon as its designer. Although not as complex as French standard-gauge loco-motives, being two-cylinder simples, they had Kylchap double exhausts and mechanical stokers, and Belpaire fireboxes fitted with two thermic syphons. Some were still at work in the 1970s, not only in Brazil but also in Bolivia. However, they do not appear to have been particularly successful in service.

Most other South American railways were in financial difficulties and their motive power efforts centred on keeping enough pre-war types on the road to provide a service. But in 1948, just before the Argentinian railways were nationalised, the Central Argentine Railway placed an order with the Vulcan Foundry Co. in Warrington, England, for no fewer than ninety of a new 'Pacific', Class 12L. Only forty were delivered, before the balance of the order was cancelled in favour of twenty-one metre-gauge diesel-electrics. The 12L was Argentina's last steam type. Three-cylinder simples, they had Caprotti cam-operated valve gear and parallel boilers with wide round-topped fireboxes. Their big tenders, with two six-wheel bogies, built for running through territory with poor water supplies, weighed more than the locomotive, when fully loaded. They were withdrawn in the late 1960s.

Africa continued to be a strong market for steam locomotive builders after demand from the other continents had ebbed away. There was only one locomotive builder on the continent, the South African Railways' Salt River works, at Cape Town, which had only been building new engines since 1945 and supplied only a small part of the SAR demand for loco-motives. In Southern Africa, lack of oil was a prime reason for continuing to burn coal in locomotives. But an interesting variant was built in 1951 for the Benguela Railway (CFB) in the Portuguese colony of Angola. The Class 11 4-8-2 was a sophisticated wood-burner for the 3ft 6in (106.5cm) gauge, supplied by the North British Locomotive Company. Its fuel was quick-burning eucalyptus wood, from plantations specially sited alongside the tracks, and split into 24x10in (60.9x25.3cm) chunks for hand firing. Modifications to the firebox included ashpan ventilation and a dust protection plate, and a spark arrester was fitted inside the smoke-box. The 4-8-2s were largely used on passenger services, taking 500-ton trains over sections with a ruling gradient of 1 in 80.

South Africa had ample coal reserves and throughout the twentieth century had developed a successive line of ever-larger and more powerful locomotives on its 3ft 6in (106.6cm) gauge lines. These were mostly of eight and ten coupled wheels, and straightforward in design. In the 1920s and 1930s, German and American builders were used as well as British; and though the SAR's engineers contributed their own ideas, they increasingly leaned towards American techniques like solid-grease lubrication, 'self-cleaning' smoke-boxes, and shaking grates which British designers were slow to adopt. Design on the SAR and its close neighbour, Rhodesian Railways, was thus conventional though up-to-date. A more searching response to local conditions, notably the long desert haul from Cape Province on the Cape Town-Johannesburg trunk line, which crosses the arid Karoo Desert, into the Transvaal, was seen in the Class 25 4-8-4. The prototype was built by Henschel – pioneers of condensing since 1933 – in 1948, and eighty-nine of these very big condensing locomotives were built between 1953 and 1955, by the North British Locomotive Company. The tenders (built by Henschel) were longer than the engines, though most of their space was occupied by the condensing apparatus. South Africa and the Soviet Union were the two countries to make most use of condensing. The condenser had a dual effect. An effective system offered a 90 per cent saving on water use, and around 10 per cent on fuel. Primarily it conserved the locomotive's water supply, an extremely valuable function in arid country; recycling the exhaust steam which would otherwise be lost through the chimney and various other vents. Having passed through the cylinders, the steam was transferred via a flexible pipe to the tender, in which a grease separator and turbine fans were mounted. Assisted by air vents in the tender sides, the fans cooled the steam back to water, which could then be returned to the tank and re-used to make steam. The exhaust steam also drove a smaller turbine fan which provided draught in the smoke-box to draw heat through the boiler tubes and maintain the fire at a suitable temperature. As a result, with no blast up the chimney, these engines did not 'puff'; instead the whine of the fan was heard.

Despite the extensive testing with the 1948 engine, an expert observer noted that the condensing locomotives 'were not an unqualified success.' But they lasted until 1974, from which year they were rebuilt with conventional tenders, joining the fifty non-condensing engines which had been built at the same time, Class 25NC, of which ten were from NBL and forty from Henschel. The dimensions of these locomotives were considerably greater than those of many on the standard gauge. The grate area was 68.9sq ft (6.4m²); the heating surface within the boiler 3059sq ft (284.1m²) and the superheating surface 630sq ft (58.5m²). The comparable figures of the standard-gauge Czechoslovakian Class 556 2-10-0 freight engine of 1951 were grate area: 46.3sq ft (4.3m²), heating surface: 2015.5sq ft (187.2m²), and superheater: 777sq ft (72.2m²).

Along with the condenser engines, latter-day steam locomotion in southern Africa is perhaps most closely linked with the Garratt type. It was here that the Garratt reached its peak of effectiveness, and the SAR had more of them than any other railway. Its first Garratts, Class GA, were delivered in 1919. They were already giants for their time; and a variety of Garratts and other articulated types followed. In the late 1920s the original Garratt patents expired, and though Beyer, Peacock of Manchester worked to maintain their monopoly by patenting new features, the way was now open for other manufacturers to use the principle. The Germans were foremost in this, and from 1927 Hanomag, Maffei, Krupp and Henschel feature among the suppliers of locomotives of the Garratt type, as well as Beyer, Peacock. The North British Locomotive Company of Glasgow also contributed from 1924, though its 'Modified Fairlies' were not true Garratts. In South Africa, Garratts were a familiar part of the railway scene, and hauled all kinds of traffic. The most powerful South African Garratts were the Class GL, of 4-8-2+2-8-4 configuration, built by Beyer, Peacock in 1929. These had a nominal tractive effort of 78,650lb (35,669kg) at 75 per cent of maximum boiler pressure.

In 1954 no less than three new classes were introduced, GMA, GMAM, and GO. The first two were identical in their main dimensions and power rating, the difference being that GMAM carried 14 tons (14.2t) of coal and 2160gals of water (2592US) and GMA 11.6 tons (11.8t) and 1650gals

(1980US). The maximum axle load was the same, 15 tons (15.2t), enabling them to work on lightweight 60lb (29.6kg) rails, but GMAM weighed an extra 13.1 tons (13.3t). Both had a water-cart tender in addition to the front-end tank, which had had the curved-front, round-edged streamlined style of most post-war Garratts. Its water was treated as a reserve supply, the engine normally drawing from the detachable tender, and this helped to maintain the locomotive's total adhesive weight. US-made 'Commonwealth' cast steel bed-frames were used. Welding was extensively used in the boiler and firebox, and all axles had roller bearings, with – another US feature – Franklin spring-loaded wedge horns fitted in the horn-blocks. All were equipped with a mechanical stoker, and mechanically-rocked firebars in the grate. Some GMAs were altered to GMAM, and vice versa; the combined total number built between 1953 and 1958 was 120, making it by some way the most numerous Garratt class ever built. Henschel, Beyer, Peacock, and North British were the builders.

The SAR Garratts were moved around the country as the tide of electrification caught up with them. Their last great stronghold was in Natal, when for a time more than half of the GMA/Ms were stabled at Pietermaritzburg. Increasingly, their use was on freight only, often working double-headed on coal trains loading up to 900 tons on such lines as the long Franklin and Greytown branches, where the ruling gradient was 1 in 30. Although GMA/Ms were still very much in use in the late 1970s, chiefly on industrial branches, some had been put into storage, and the SAR was able to hire twenty-one to the National Railways of Zimbabwe in 1979; others were hired out to Mozambique. In these countries, combined steam and diesel operations went on until the mid-1990s, when the GMA/Ms were finally phased out.

Another notable Garratt class operated on the East African Railways (EAR) system in Kenya. Its 59 class 4-8-2+2-8-4s were the most powerful locomotives ever to run on metre-gauge tracks anywhere in the world. When the American 'Big Boys' were retired from the Union Pacific Railroad in the late 1950s, they became the largest steam locomotives in regular service anywhere, their 7ft 6in (228.4cm) diameter boilers being more than twice the width of the rail gauge. The line from Mombasa on the coast to the Kenyan capital, Nairobi, climbs from sea level to 5600 ft (1705m) over a distance of 330 miles (531km), at a ruling gradient of 1 in 66. The summit level of the East African Railway, 530 miles (853km) inland, was at 9,000ft (2,956m). The EAR had a stock of heavy rigid-frame engines, the most recent being 2-8-2s supplied in 1951, but since 1926, it had also made use of Garratt-type locomotives. These were ideal for the slow, heavy hauling the EAR required, and engine crews and depot fitters had built up a tradition of expertise in handling them. But the need for engines to haul greater loads at greater speeds was clear. The 59 class was ordered in 1950, with detailed design entrusted to the manufacturers, Beyer, Peacock of Manchester. The original order was for nine, increased to thirty-four before deliveries began in 1955; all were in service by the end of 1956.

The design was influenced by various technical uncertainties which hung over the railway at this time. Oil was the fuel of preference, but coal might become cheaper. Discussions were going on about widening the gauge to 3ft 6in (106.5cm), in order to make a unified system with South Africa and Rhodesia. New engines had to be built so that their axles could be readily widened; and also be convertible to coal firing. In the 59 class that meant providing for the installation of a mechanical stoker if necessary, though these were in fact never installed. Pumps for both vacuum and air braking were fitted on the left-hand side of the smoke-box. As normal with Garratts, they were simple-expansion engines; the four cylinders operated by piston valves which were actuated by outside Walschaerts valve gear. Long connecting rods, tapering towards the crosshead, drove the third sets of coupled wheels. Roller bearings were fitted to all axles and to the big ends of the connecting rods.

With the introduction of this class, the schedules between Mombasa and Nairobi were improved by up to a third. The 59s could take a 1,200 ton (1219t) train unaided up the gradients of 1.5 per cent at 14mph (22.5km/h) and round curves where sometimes the driver could see the tail end of his train running parallel to him in the opposite direction. Development work continued after delivery and the class was fitted with Giesl ejectors in the early 1960s. The Giesl exhaust was said to reduce back-pressure in the cylinders, and thus to allow freer steaming and better load-hauling up the grades. Pride in these great engines was reflected by the unusual policy of giving them names, after the highest East African mountains. Further enlargements of the Garratt design were also drawn up by the EAR during the later 1950s, including one with a condensing tender, but the decision to adopt diesel-electric traction meant that they remained paper projects. When diesel-electric locomotives took over the mail trains, the Garratts continued to haul freights and mixed trains on some of the long branches. Withdrawals began in 1973 and by 1980 all were out of service, ending a great tradition and also one of the world's most spectacular steam locomotive sights, to rival the 'Big Boys' on Sherman Hill, of the 59s forging slowly but steadily up into the mountains with immensely long trains curving away out of sight behind them.

Australia, whose various state railways had large numbers of quite elderly steam locomotives in the 1940s, proved to be a ready market for the American diesel-electric builders in the post-war years. At the same time, several new steam designs were introduced, and some controversy arose later about the rapidity with which relatively new locomotives were withdrawn from service and scrapped. Traditionally, Australian locomotive design policy had always been based on British models, whether imported or home-built. There had been only occasional exceptions, with American locomotive classes brought in when British delivery schedules were too long. This began to change in the 1930s with the arrival of American railway managers in one or two states and a conversion to the notion, much more American than British, that a locomotive should be made as easy as possible to service, and as easy and convenient as possible to operate. Several Australian designs were modelled on American 'streamliners'. Orders still tended to be placed with British builders, but the scale of the engines and their specifications were determined by Australian designers. The Class C38 'Pacific' of the New South Wales Government Railways, which appeared in 1943, was Australian-built, designed by Harold Young, the chief mechanical engineer, on thoroughly American lines, and the first five of the eventual thirty were streamlined in a manner similar to the Norfolk & Western J-Class. It represented a great step up in power from the C36 4-6-0 which it replaced on express services. All had cast-steel frames, and roller bearings on all axles, and Canadian-type 'Boxpok' unspoked wheels. Power reversers were standard. They were at first painted in a distinctive green livery, with buff and red lining, replaced by standard black in the 1950s. Their main employment was on the Sydney-Albury section of the 'Melbourne Limited' sleeping car train, and after 1955, when diesel-electrics took over the 'Limited', many C38s were transferred to fast goods work, though they worked on Sydney-Newcastle expresses until 1970. The last to be in regular service, No. 3820, was withdrawn in December 1970. Examples have been preserved both streamlined and unstreamlined. This engine also produced a rare instance of Australian steam technology being exported, when its cab design, fixed to the boiler rather than the frame, was used for the British 'standard' Pacifics nine years later.

In the late 1940s the Victorian Government Railways (VGR) embarked upon 'Operation Phoenix', intended to modernise its somewhat run-down system. The main passenger motive power was the A2-class 4-6-0, dating back to 1907. As part of this exercise, seventy Class R 4-6-4 locomotives were ordered from the North British Locomotive Co. These 'Hudsons' were two-cylinder simples, of very solid bar-frame construction. A 'Pacific' had been originally intended, but the inclusion of mechanical stokers in the design necessitated the four-wheel bogies. The grate area was only 42sq fit (3.9m²) but Australian firemen were increasingly disinclined to do heavy stoking. Belpaire fireboxes were fitted, and considerable care was put into cylinder, valve and steam circulation design, in order to make the engines free-steaming. Provision was made for later conversion from the VGR's 5ft 3in (160cm) to standard gauge. The running plate was deepened and curved at each end; and with the smoke deflectors and buffer beam they were painted scarlet, though otherwise the engines were finished in unlined plain black. Though full use of their potential was never made because of the simultaneous introduction of B-class diesel-electrics, the R class was not considered a success. Careless deck stowage on the sea voyage had let sea-water corrode their bearings, and the VGR complained about poor workmanship as well. The 'Hudsons' were quickly relegated to secondary and freight work. A proposal to fit them with 'Stug' apparatus for burning pulverised coal was also dropped. Withdrawals began in 1961 and all were out of service by the 1970s, though four have been preserved.

American influence was also apparent on the Western Australian Government Railways (WAGR) 3ft 6in (106.5cm) gauge, where the W-class 4-8-2 was introduced in 1951. Designed by the WAGR and built by Beyer, Peacock in Manchester, sixty of these engines were delivered in 1951-1952 and were altogether more successful. They were chiefly intended for branch freight work, but were versatile enough to operate main line passenger trains and all but the heaviest freight workings. Ease of operation and maintenance was by now increasingly important, and the class had self-cleaning smoke-boxes, self-emptying ashpans, power reversers, and roller bearings on all axles. The last eleven of the class were taken out of service in December 1973, and several are preserved.

The biggest and busiest of the Australian state railways was the New South Wales Government Railway (NSWGR). Rather surprisingly, it did not use articulated locomotives until 1952, when the Class AD60 4-8-4+4-8-4 Garratt type was introduced. Often referred to as 'the most powerful locomotive in the southern hemisphere', it was in fact less powerful than the East African Railways 59 class, but was the largest and heaviest steam locomotive to run in Australia. Its maximum axle loading did not exceed 16 tons, enabling it to work over most of the system, including branch lines if they generated enough bulk freight traffic to require the AD60s' 1500-ton capacity. The class, all built by Beyer, Peacock, was originally intended to number sixty, but the order was reduced to fifty, and in the end only forty-two were assembled, the last of them entering service in January 1957. They were handsome and imposing engines, with the curved-front water tank similar to those of post-war African Garratts. The boiler was supported on a one-piece American-made 'Commonwealth' cast steel frame with integral cylinders, and all axles and the main crank pins had roller bearings.

The AD60 was an effective engine, though its overall power in relation to its great weight has been criticised as less than it could have been. At 85 per cent of maximum boiler pressure, its tractive effort was calculated as 63,600lb (28,843kg), compared to the South African GL Garratt with 89,130lb (40,421kg) but which weighed only 471,870lb (214t). Nevertheless, the boiler and firebox were of exceptionally favourable dimensions: the boiler had an outer dimension of 87in (220.8cm) and the mechanically-stoked firebox had a grate area of 63.3sq ft (5.8m²). Twenty-five of the class had two thermic syphons fitted in the firebox, plus two arch tubes; the others had two arch tubes only. Thirty were fitted with dual controls, enabling them to be easily driven in either direction, a useful facility on branch lines where the terminal depot might not have a turntable of the necessary great length. The class worked until the 1970s, their last years spent working from Newcastle, north of Sydney, often in a poor state of maintenance, and mostly hauling coal trains to the docks at Port Waratah. No.6042, withdrawn on 18 March 1973, was the last steam locomotive in regular government service in Australia. It remains in working order, and another three of the class have also been preserved.

By 1950, 125 years on from the appearance of *Locomotion* on the Stockton & Darlington Railway, it might have been supposed that nothing much could go wrong with the design of a new steam locomotive. Or, if it did, that it would be due to some new aspect of technology, like the tiny cracks in the welded boilers of the New York Central's 'Niagaras' which necessitated twenty-four expensive carbon-steel replacements. That it wasn't necessarily so was shown by the Class 65 2-8-4T of the German Federal Railways (DB). One of the first products of the DB's post-war new building programme, built by Krauss-Maffei in Munich, it was intended to be a standard type. Full advantage was taken of modern engineering techniques in the all-welded boiler and firebox, the latter with combustion chamber; Heusinger valve gear operated the two outside cylinders, driving the third coupled axle. Other modern basic equipment included a feed-water heater, compressed air sanding gear operative either in forward or reverse gear (boxes not on the boiler-top but built into the side tanks), pressure lubrication, and electric turbo-generator. It was a mixed-traffic engine, designed for frequent stops, rapid acceleration, and a top speed of 53mph (85km/h) in either direction. Unfortunately, it was not as successful as was anticipated. Water spilled from the tanks when the brakes were applied. Its fuel bunker was too small for an effective day's work. At speeds in excess of 31mph (50km/h) it developed an increasingly strong hunting motion, caused by an imbalance in the reciprocating and revolving masses of the machinery. Whilst eighty-seven of the 'rival' Class 6510 of the DR were built, Class 65 numbered only eighteen. The first withdrawal was in 1966 and all were gone by 1972, while numerous older tank types still worked on.

Such a failure was quite untypical of the *Bundesbahn*, whose small range of post-war designs included some excellent locomotives. Perhaps the most distinguished was the Class 10 4-6-2. These two 'Pacifics', Nos10.001 and 002 of the DB, were the last high-speed express steam locomotives to be built. Krupps of Essen, long associated with iron and steam, were the constructors. The two were identical in shape but differed in certain details. Both were three-cylinder simple-expansion types, with the inside cylinder driving the leading coupled axle, and the outside cylinders driving the second. Three sets of Walschaerts valve gear operated long-travel piston valves. Double blast-pipes and double chimneys were fitted. All axles and main bearings were of the roller type. Their front look-out windows had revolving clear-vision screens as fitted to torpedo boats; they had air-assisted power reversers, dual-pressure air brakes and a range of instrumentation that would have amazed drivers of an earlier generation. Below boiler level they were partially streamlined, with a deep valance covering the cylinders, partly obscuring the wheels and motion, and terminating in a rounded casing covering the front end between smoke-box and buffer-beam, with inset electric headlights.

No.001 began as a coal burner, with an oil supply on the Cosmovici system providing supplementary fuel on long grades or with heavy loads; 002 burned oil only, and 001 was eventually converted to this form. As with the last US express locomotives, these were steam engines designed to compete with diesels on the diesels' own terms, with comparable economies of maintenance and similar levels of availability, capable of an average monthly running of 12,400 miles (20,000km) and a fuel consumption of around 11 tons per 620 miles (1,000km). 'The finest riding and most responsive steam locomotive on which I have ever travelled,' was the comment of the British author P. Ransome-Wallis after a 320-mile (515km) footplate journey. But in Germany as elsewhere, the fate of steam power had been sealed; and no more of Class 10 were built. Steam lasted longer on the East German *Reichsbahn*, which, like the *Bundesbahn*, relied very much on wartime and pre-war engines, and built only a handful of post-war designs, in small quantities. One aspect of development which was being explored there was the use of pulverised coal as a fuel, which had aroused interest in some other countries, including Australia.

In Russia, electrification began to expand from the early 1950s, but there seemed to be no hurry to oust steam power, which was also being modernised. Passenger traffic in Russia had long been a secondary consideration to the movement of freight, but in 1953 a modern express locomotive, the Class P36 4-8-4, went into production. Designed by I. S. Lebedyanskii at the Kolomna Works, its prototype, P36.001, appeared in March 1950. It was the first 4-8-4 to be built in Russia, and the first Russian locomotive to have roller bearings on all axles. Between 1954 and 1956, Kolomna built 250, and the last one, P36.0251, was also the last main-line steam locomotive constructed for the Soviet Railways. This was an effective design which, if government decree had not put a sudden stop to steam construction, would undoubtedly have been produced in far greater numbers.

It was, typically, a two-cylinder simple, built on conventional lines and with an obvious debt to American design, though its nominal tractive effort, at 40,040lb (18,160kg) was less than that of the typical American 4-8-4. In North American locomotive style, the heat exchanger of the feed-water heating system was fitted transversely on the smoke-box top, in front of the chimney. A more individual touch was seen in the backward-slanted upper part of the cab, and the main steam-pipe was carried from the dome to just behind the chimney inside an insulated 'skyline' casing which was continued back to the cab. A few P36s were painted blue, but most were in standard Russian light green passenger engine livery, with red wheel centres and white rims. Large smoke deflectors extended from the buffer beam back alongside the smoke-box.

In 1954, steam power still seemed to have a vigorous future in Russia; Lazar Kaganovich, the Commissar of Transport, announced: 'I am for the steam locomotive and against those who imagine we will not have any steam locomotives in the future.' In that year a large new steam locomotive type was designed, the Class P38, an articulated 2-8-8-4. Two prototypes were built. In order to haul freight trains of 3,500 tons it was calculated that the engine should have an adhesive weight of 160 tons; to stay within the maximum axle load, this required eight coupled axles, and so the Mallet type, with simple expansion, was chosen. Once again, a resemblance to American practice of two decades earlier is discernible: but there had been little real technical progress in the design of very big engines since that time. The two P38s were built at Kolomna Works in December 1954 and January 1955. Although lighter than the Ya-01 Beyer Garratt of 1932, these were the biggest engines actually built in Russia. On test, P38.001 was recorded as having pulled a 3500-ton train at 15mph (24km/h) up an incline of 1 in 110. The new engines were tried out in southern Siberia on lines between Krasnoyarsk and Ulan Ude. Further details of their performance were not published, but it was later stated that they had not functioned well in conditions of extreme cold. Line production was not established, and after a brief working life, both prototypes were withdrawn. Meanwhile, by 1957, Kaganovich was disgraced and dismissed from his post, part of the case against him being that: '… he stubbornly insisted on developing steam traction, though it is well known that steam traction is uneconomic and out of date.' A decision was made by the Supreme Soviet to make a rapid transition to diesel and electric power, with steam to be phased out as early as possible; and ongoing work on new steam designs was stopped forthwith.

Spain, for many locomotive enthusiasts a happy hunting ground in the 1950s and 1960s, was one of the last countries to build main-line steam. On its formation in 1943, Spanish National Railways (RENFE) inherited a huge range of locomotive types, many of which continued to work until steam was being phased out in the late 1960s and the 1970s. But a few new classes of larger engines were designed. Spain had a number of locomotive builders at Bilbao and Barcelona, but no distinctively Spanish school of design emerged. Spanish locomotives were usually of a somewhat heavy or massive aspect, because of relatively small driving wheels, but mostly showed a mixture of German and French ancestry. Many were built in Britain, however, including the first twenty-five of the Class 141F express mixed-traffic 'Mikado' 2-8-2, of which another 216 were built between 1953 and 1960, at the Spanish works of Euskalduña, Babcock & Wilcox, Maquinista Terrestre y Maritima, and Macosa. All were two-cylinder simples, with different types of feed-water heaters; the final 116 were oil burning, with double chimneys. Walschaerts valve gear was fitted in all cases. Until electrification of the trunk routes, the 2-8-2s took their turn on international express trains as well as on internal services between Madrid and major provincial cities. Prestige services were also hauled by the ten 4-8-4s of 1955, built by Maquinista Terrestre y Maritima of Barcelona. This was Spain's most advanced steam design. Spanish railways had a long history of using eight-coupled engines, which suited both the hilly terrain and the often lightly-laid tracks. RENFE had also built a 4-8-2 type, and the 4-8-4s were in most respects a stretched and enlarged form of these. They were chiefly used to haul international expresses to and from France on the not-yet electrified main line section between Avila and Miranda del Ebro. These sleeping car trains could weight in excess of 750 tons, but this was well within the compass of the 4-8-4s. The old Spanish railway companies, influenced by French practice, had built mostly compound locomotives, but RENFE design policy was focused on simple-expansion, two-cylinder types. The ubiquitous Walschaerts motion was used, but the 4-8-4s were equipped with Lenz-type poppet valves, actuated by oscillating camshafts. All had double blast-pipes and Kylchap double chimneys. Auxiliary equipment included a water treatment system to reduce boiler scale, feed-water heater and pump, and a turbo-generator which provided train lighting. Roller bearings were fitted on all axles. The engines were oil-fired. With driving wheels of 74.75in (190cm) diameter, they might have been capable of considerable speed, but the general speed restriction in Spain to 68mph (110km/h), meant that their quality was shown rather in maintaining a high average pace with heavy trains. They worked until steam power was finally withdrawn in mid-1975. One of the class has been preserved, and they might be said to form a fine climax to the Spanish steam tradition, except that they were not the last. In 1961, ten oil-burning Garratt 2-8-2+2-8-2 freight locomotives were constructed for RENFE by Babcock & Wilcox's Bilbao works – rather strangely, they were built, with no more than minimal differences, to a design first supplied by the same builders to the Central Aragón Railway in 1930.

Vying with the Spanish Garratts as the last European main-line steam locomotives to be built were two 2-10-0s constructed by the Turkish Railways (TCDD) at their own workshops in 1961. The majority of Turkey's engines had come from Germany, and these were based on German designs, with 'bathtub' tenders. Steam power in Turkey lasted into the 1990s. Hungary finally abandoned steam traction in 1986. Poland, which in 1972

had announced that steam power would end in 1980, was still making occasional use of a few steam locomotives in the 1990s. But the country where
the steam locomotive proved most durable is of course China, the original
objections to it long forgotten. Although the state railway system finally
phased out steam traction in the 1990s, some industrial lines were still using
large steam engines into the twenty-first century.

With the formation of the Railways of the People's Republic, in 1948,
China embarked on a grand-scale standardisation scheme. Within this programme, the largest freight type, and also the most numerous, was the Class
QJ 2-10-2, introduced in 1956. QJ, 'Qian Jing' means 'March Forward'. More
than 4500 were built from 1957 until the late 1980s, mostly at the giant
Datong works but also at five other locomotive works in China, and they
were to be seen in almost every part of the country. The basis of the type
was the Russian Lv class, whose specifications and detailed drawings had
been sold or given to the Chinese after 1951, but subsequent modifications
included the provision of a combustion chamber with a shorter boiler. In
response to an insatiable demand for more motive power, they were being
built at maximum speed, with intensive use of fabricated parts and wholly
welded boilers. The British engineer David Wardale, who assessed the QJ in
1983, recognised their merits as powerful freight engines with good tractive
power and adhesion characteristics. The latter were helped by an 'adhesion
booster' which used air pressure to alter the spring equalising system, shift-
ing weight from the carrying to the coupled wheels on starting. But he
was critical of many aspects of design and building which led to heavy
vibration, 'hunting' and a sense of instability. He also observed that many
features were unchanged from American designs of the 1930s, rather than
using more up-to-date practice, including the brake system, power reverser,
mechanical stoker, power fire-doors, feed-water heating system, mechanical
lubricator, and grate-shaking mechanism. The standard tender was an eight-
wheeler, with capacity for 14.5t of coal and 8,700gals (10,400US) of water,
but engines operating in the drier eastern provinces were provided with
twelve-wheel tenders of greater water capacity.

In 1969, the Chinese railways introduced a new, smaller freight type, the
Class SY 'Aim High' 2-8-2, the last of the standard Chinese steam classes
to enter production. Constructed at the Tangshan workshops, its design
appears to derive from the JF6 2-8-2 introduced in Japanese-occupied
Manchuria as long ago as 1934. This in turn had been based on a United
States Railway Administration design of the First World War. The SY was

fitted with a railed bogie tender with a sloping back, again on an American model. Extensively used on industrial lines, this class was an unusual sight on main line services. The total number produced is believed to have exceeded a thousand.

Two themes emerge from the development of the steam locomotive in the second half of the twentieth century. The first is the posthumous triumph of the American school of design. Lima gave up building steam locomotives in 1949. In 1956 Baldwin's last steam locomotives were built, a 2-8-2 freight class for New South Wales; production for home use had already ceased and in that year Baldwin stopped all locomotive building. Alco followed them in 1959. But even when these great names had gone, even when the last American engines had been taken off the road, for honourable preservation in the case of a few, for the breakers' torches and hammers in the case of the vast majority, new locomotives were still being built to American design, in American style, or with American features. Even in Britain, which maintained the integrity of its own style in general respects to the end, design had moved towards what E. S. Cox discreetly called 'the world trend' in many details, such as self-cleaning smoke-boxes, rocking grates, hopper ashpans, roller bearings, and high-mounted running plates fixed to the lower flanks of the boiler; Cox also noted that the post-war British designers wanted to use bar frames, rather than the traditional plate frames, but that the railways' workshops were not equipped to build and repair them. The last steam locomotives built for export by private British builders were all of basically American type.

The second theme is the 'Unfinished Symphony' one. Through continuous development for a hundred and fifty years, locomotive engineers had seen Trevithick's brain-child grow under their hands, in power, in size, and in ease of operation. Two men could manage a 'Big Boy', weighing 500 tons plus with its tender, as readily as the 5-ton locomotives of the Rainhill trials. In almost all the countries where steam locomotives were built, development work was still going on, until brought to an abrupt halt; and none of the people involved felt that they were near the end of the line. Even without 'New Generation' steam, the haulage capacity, reliability and availability of steam locomotives had been very much improved and further improvement seemed entirely possible. It is easy to exaggerate the possible results that continued research might have achieved, but the fall of the axe leaves the question open.

By the best estimates that have been made, the total number of steam locomotives thought to have existed is around 650,000. In *Dropping the Fire*, Philip Atkins notes that the greatest number were built in the USA, 177,000. Germany produced 155,000; Britain 110,000; Russia 50,000; France 39,000; Belgium 16,000; Austria 15,000; Japan 11,000; China 10,000; Hungary 7500; Canada and Czechoslovakia each 7000. Significant numbers also came from Australia, Denmark, Finland, India, Italy, Korea, The Netherlands, Norway, Poland, Romania, Spain, Sweden, and Switzerland. Portugal is recorded as having built one. Of that total, only a tiny fraction remains, the majority of which are static display items that will never steam again.

A Smoky Epilogue

Though it took fifty years, the demise of the steam locomotive was a steady and apparently inexorable process. Lingering longer in some countries than in others, even now still to be found in protected 'heritage' corners, as well as on a handful of Cuban and Javanese sugar railways and one or two Chinese industrial lines, by the end of the twentieth century to the great majority of people it was only a memory or a museum-piece. Yet, like some exiled dynasty that might one day come back over the water, it kept the loyalty of little bands of devotees here and there. Such groups are rarely united, and tensions soon became apparent between those who felt the remaining steam locomotives should be preserved as they had been built, and those who felt they should be improved, particularly if they were to keep working. Most were content to dwell on the glorious past, but in some places the words 'Second Generation' were murmured, and some dyed-in-the-wool believers were in a position to take action on its behalf.

Railway companies everywhere had abandoned research and development, at a time when much interesting and promising work was in hand and some remarkable new locomotive classes had been produced in prototype. One of the many people who had worked with steam, or designed steam locomotives, and felt strongly that there was unfinished business, was L. Dante Porta. An Argentinian engineer, born in 1922, he had acquired both a university degree and an engine-driver's certificate. In 1949, as a personal venture, he rebuilt an elderly Argentinian 4-6-2 as a streamlined 4-8-0 on Chapelon-inspired lines (inauspiciously, this was the year in which the Argentinian railways part-cancelled an order for British-built 'Pacifics' in favour of diesels). For some years, Porta managed a programme for the modernising of the State Railways' steam fleet. In 1957 he became engineer of the world's most southerly railway, the 29.5in (75cm) gauge Rio Turbio line in Patagonia. Coal-hauling was its business, using 2-10-2 steam locomotives supplied in 1956 by Mitsubishi. A further batch was supplied in 1963 but by that time Porta had revamped the earlier engines and substantially remodelled the design of the new ones. At the centre of his work was what he termed the Gas Producer Combustion System, a firebox which admitted scientifically worked-out amounts of air through primary and secondary intakes, and mixed exhaust steam with the primary air intake, in order to create a zone of combustion above a thick layer of low-quality coal, burning at a relatively cool temperature, with the greatest heat, around 1,400°C (2,520°F), generated in the space above it. The value of air inlets and steam jets into the firebox had long been recognised, and used as long ago as the 1850s, but in a somewhat haphazard way. Now, exhaust steam was piped to the ashpan and mixed with air, keeping the temperature down and preventing the formation of clinker. Live steam jets and air intakes from above helped in the gasification process by creating a controlled turbulence, holding coal particles in suspension rather than blasting them almost instantaneously through the tubes and out of the chimney. Although reduced coal and water consumption was the main aim, less soot and smoke were produced. Porta also made substantial improvements in locomotive draughting and lubrication systems. The efficiency and economy of the altered 2-10-2s improved dramatically, but were overshadowed by the outstanding performance of the new engines. In 1960 Porta returned to Buenos Aires but continued his work on thermodynamics and locomotive development; and kept in contact with the Rio Turbio locomotive department. He was looking ahead not only to Second Generation Steam but to the Third Generation.

The climate was hardly favourable, either in Argentina or elsewhere, though in the 1960s Porta provided his Kylpor exhaust – a development of the Kylchap type – with valve gear and firebox improvements, for seventy-four 0-6-0 industrial saddle-tank engines of the British National Coal Board. His work and ideas brought him into contact with others who foresaw a future for steam, one of them being David Wardale, who was then Assistant Mechanical Engineer (Steam) on the South African Railways. Using Porta's methods, in 1979 Wardale successfully modified a German-built Class 19D 4-8-2, built in 1938, which had been a notoriously poor steamer. In 1981 he was allowed to tackle a non-condensing Class 25 4-8-4, No.3450, built in 1953. The Class 25 was still considered an epitome of steam design, with virtually every modern feature from Timken roller bearings to a self-cleaning smoke-box. Thirty-four significant modifications were implemented at the

SAR Salt River workshops in Cape Town. Among the most important were the fitting of a GPCS firebox, a Lempor (Lemaître-Porta) double-exhaust system, a longer and internally aerodynamic smoke-box, and an enlarged superheater with a superheat booster, achieving temperatures of around 440°C (792°F). New steam pipes, an enlarged steam chest, and a feed-water heating system (this last not used before on SAR locomotives) were fitted, the cylinders were insulated, and improvements were made to the valves and pistons. Wardale seized his opportunity to show what a modern technological approach to steam power design could achieve. He named the engine *L.D. Porta*, after his mentor, but its bright red paint coat earned it the popular nickname of 'Red Devil'. Tests of the engine in service revealed a 28 per cent reduction in coal consumption and a 30 per cent drop in water consumption, compared to the Class 25. But in addition, the maximum recorded power output of No. 3450 was 3,784hp at 46mph (74km/h), showing a 43 per cent improvement on the Class 25. The transformation was such that the locomotive was given a new classification as Class 26. Like all prototypes, it had weaknesses and problems, including difficulty in managing the GPCS fire with a mechanical stoker, and a definite proneness to slipping; but such technically resolvable items were minor compared with the levels of economy and performance promised. But SAR policy was by now firmly committed to the phasing-out of steam. Wardale left South Africa in 1983, and the 'Red Devil', though remaining in service, suffered from the effects of neglect and unspecialised maintenance. In 1992, steam locomotives were finally taken off main line work in South Africa, but fortunately No. 3450 was saved from cutting-up and has been both preserved and restored to running order.

In 1980, Porta became involved with American Coal Enterprises, a private US group which believed that, with high oil prices, the time was ripe to sponsor a return to coal-fired steam power, in a modern form using 'clean coal technology'. He produced a detailed design for the ACE 3000, a four-cylinder 4-4-4-2 with a condensing tender or 'support unit' and a driving cab at each end. The ACE businessmen failed to raise the necessary funds to construct this locomotive, or any other new-generation machine. In the winter of 1984-1985, in the hope of generating sympathetic publicity, a preserved Lima-built Class J3a 4-8-4 of 1948, formerly of the Chesapeake & Ohio Railroad, was hastily overhauled and used on an ill-judged series of display runs, which inevitably only showed up the weaknesses of a 1930s design, poorly prepared, and all too obviously 'First Generation Steam'.

Far from promoting 'clean coal' use, it produced vast amounts of smoke, its booster engine failed, and on one occasion it ran out of fuel. The *Wall Street Journal* reported: 'If there are any doubts about why steam faded from the nation's rails 30 years ago, a ride on ACE's locomotive, No.614, puts them to rest.'

This was unfair, but the fault was not the reporter's, who merely described what he saw; but that of the ACE promoters, whose over-confidence, lack of preparation and overall self-delusion would have made the Jacobite court of St Germain seem a haven of cool reality and common sense by comparison. Wardale, also briefly recruited by ACE, wrote in *The Red Devil* that: 'What really killed it was the falling oil price', but one is left with the feeling that its promoters – unlike the engineers – could never have got the project successfully under way.

New Generation steam remains a theoretical possibility, though the passage of time is steadily removing both the people who might maintain some continuity with the first generation, and the workshops that could undertake construction. If steam power should return as a serious force in transport, it will only be as the result of greatly changed circumstances, and its form will bear little resemblance to its predecessors. The steam locomotive, offspring and handmaid of the Industrial Revolution, has now become an item in the 'museum culture' which we have devised to ease the communal and personal stress arising out of rapid and unsettling change from one form of technology to another. With the covered wagon and the clipper ship, it represents a time, recent and in its case still remembered, but not reclaimable – the heroic age of surface transport.

Bibliography

1. Books (excluding books on individual locomotive designers and classes)

Ahrons, E.L., *British Steam Locomotives, 1825-1925*. London, 1927
Armitage, W.H.G., *A Social History of Engineering*. London, 1961
Atkins, Philip, *Dropping the Fire*. Clophill, 1999
Bailey, Michael R. and Glithro, John, *The Engineering and History of the 'Rocket'*. York, 2000
Beebe, L., and Clegg, C., *Hear the Train Blow*. New York, 1952
Botkin, B.A., and Harlow, A.F., *A Treasury of Rail Road Folklore*. New York, 1953
Brown, Dee, *Hear That Lonesome Whistle Blow*. London, 1977
Brown, J.K., *The Baldwin Locomotive Works, 1831-1915*. Baltimore, 1995
Brown, William H., *The First Locomotives*. New York, 1871
Bruce, A.W., *The Steam Locomotive in America*. New York, 1952
Burton, A., *Richard Trevithick, Giant of Steam*. London, 2000
Carter, Ian, *Railways and Culture in Britain*. Manchester, 2001
Catchpole, Paul, *The Steam Locomotives of Czechoslovakia*. Birmingham, 1995
Clark, Peter, *Locomotives in China*. Waterloo, NSW, 1983
Clarke, T.C., and others, *The American Railway*. New York, 1889
Colburn, Zerah, *The Locomotive Engine*. London, 1851
Conte, Arthur, *L'Epopée des chemins de fer français*. Paris, 1996
Cookridge, E.H., *Orient Express*. London, 1978
Cox, E.S., *Locomotive Panorama, Vols 1 and 2*. London, 1965-1966
Cox, E.S., *World Steam in the Twentieth Century*. London, 1969
Cox, E.S., *Speaking of Steam*. London, 1971
Crush, Peter, *Woosung Road: China's First Railway*. Hong Kong, 1999
Dambly, Phil, *Vapeur en Belgique, Tome I*. Brussels, 1989
Daumas, M., and others, *Histoire Générale des Techniques de la Civilisation Industrielle, Vol. 1*. Paris, 1978
Dendy Marshall, C.F., *A History of Railway Locomotives Down to the End of the Year 1831*. London, 1953
Dickens, Charles, *Dombey and Son*.
Dickinson, H.W., and Titley, A., *Richard Trevithick, the Engineer and the Man*. Cambridge, 1934
Dodd, G., Railways, *Steamers and Telegraphs*. London & Edinburgh, 1867
Durrant, A.E., *PNKA Power Parade*. Kenton, 1974
Durrant, A.E., *Australian Steam*. Newton Abbot, 1976

Ellis, C.H., *British Railway History. 2 Vols*. London, 1954

Ellis, C.H., *Lore of the Train*. London, 1971

Ellis, C.H., *Railway Art*. London, 1977

Fawcett, Brian, *Railways of the Andes*. London, 1963

Freeman, Michael, *Railways and the Victorian Imagination*. New Haven and London, 1999

Fryer, Charles, *Experiments with Steam*. Wellingborough, 1990

Fussell, Paul, *Abroad*. Oxford, 1980

Galeries Charpentier, *Un Siècle du Chemin de Fer et de l'Art*. Paris, 1950

Glover, G., *French Steam Locomotives*. Chichester, 1974

Gölsdorf, Karl, *Lokomotivbau in Alt-Österreich*. Vienna, 1978

Goss, William F., *Locomotive Performance*. New York & London, 1907

Grinling, Charles, *History of the Great Northern Railway*. London, 1903

Grubb, Davis, *Fools' Parade*. New York, 1969

Highet, Campbell, *Scottish Locomotive History, 1831-1923*. London, 1970

Hirsimaki, Eric, *Lima: The History*. Washington, 1986

Hollingsworth, Brian, and Cook, Arthur, *Steam Locomotives*. London, 2000

Hughes, Hugh, *Middle East Railways*. Kenton, 1981

Hughes, Hugh, *Indian Locomotives, Parts 1-3*. Kenton, 1990-96

Kalla-Bishop, P.M., *Italian Railways*. Newton Abbot, 1971

Kalla-Bishop, P.M., *Italian State Railways Steam Locomotives*. Abingdon, 1986

Kinglake, A.W., *Eothen*. London, 1844

Kubinszky, M., *Ungarische Lokomotive und Triebwagen*. Basel, 1975

Lablache, J.-J., *Chemins de fer et création artistique au 19ième siècle*. Paris, 1978

Lake, C.S., *World Locomotives*. London, 1905

Lloyd, Roger, *The Fascination of Railways*. London, 1951

Lloyd, Roger, *Farewell to Steam*. London, 1956

Loewy, Raymond, *Industrial Design*. Boston & London, 1979

Mallet, Anatole, *Evolution Pratique de la Machine à Vapeur*. Paris, 1908

Malraux, André, *La Condition Humaine*. Paris, 1933

Marshall, L.G., *Steam on the RENFE*. London, 1965

Marx, Leo, *The Machine in the Garden*. New York, 1964

Morgan, Bryan, *The Railway-Lover's Companion*. London, 1963

naGopaleen, Myles, *The Best of Myles*. London, 1968

Nock, O.S., *Steam Locomotive,* 2nd ed. London, 1968

Nock, O.S., *Rail, Steam and Speed*. London, 1970

Oberg, Leon, *Locomotives of Australia*. Sydney, 1975

Palmer, A.N., and Stewart, W.W., *Cascade of New Zealand Locomotives*. Wellington, 1957

Peddie, R.A., *Railway Literature 1556-1830*. London, 1931

Pet, Paul C., *Rail Across India*. London, 1985

Poole, Peggy, *Marigolds Grow Wild on Platforms*. London, 1996

Purdom, D.S., *British Steam on the Pampas*. London, 1977

Ramaer, R., *The Locomotives of Thailand*. Malmö, 1984

Ransome-Wallis, P. (ed.), *Illustrated Encyclopedia of World Railway Locomotives*. New York, 1959

Rogers, H.C.B., *Turnpike to Iron Road*. London, 1961

Rolt, L.T.C., and Whitehouse, P.B., *Lines of Character*. London, 1952

Sauvage, A., *La Machine Locomotive*. Paris, 1945

Seguin, Marc, *Des Chemins de fer*. Paris, 1839

Sekon, G.A., *The Evolution of the Steam Locomotive*. London, 1899

Smiles, Samuel, *Lives of the Engineers, Vol. 3*. London, 1858.

Snell, J.B., *Mechanical Engineering: Railways*. London, 1971

Staufer, A.F., *Pennsy Power*. New York, 1957

Theroux, Paul, *The Great Railway Bazaar*. London, 1975

Trevithick, Francis, *The Life of Richard Trevithick*. London, 1872

Tuplin, W.A., *British Steam Since 1900*. Newton Abbot, 1969

Vance, J.E., *The North American Railroad*. Baltimore & London, 1995

Veitch, George S., *The Struggle for the Liverpool & Manchester Railway*. Liverpool, 1930

Vuillet, Gérard, *Railway Reminiscences of Three Continents*. London, 1968

Wardale, David, *The Red Devil*. Inverness, 1998

Warren, J.G.H., *A Century of Locomotive Building by Robert Stephenson & Co*. Newcastle upon Tyne, 1923

Westwood, J.N., *Locomotive Designers in the Age of Steam*. London, 1977

Westwood, John, *Railways at War*. London, 1980

White, John H., Jr., *American Locomotives: An Engineering History, 1830-1880*. Baltimore, 1997

Whitehead, R.A., *Austrian Steam Locomotives, 1837-1981*. Tonbridge, 1982

Wood, Nicholas, *A Treatise on Railways*, 3rd ed. London, 1838

Zola, Emile, *La Bête Humaine*, in *Les Rougon Macquart, Vol 5*. Paris, 1970

2. Periodicals

Jahrbuch für Eisenbahngeschichte

Locomotive Magazine

Locomotive Profile series, 1970-1973

Locomotive, Railway Carriage and Wagon Review

Railway Engineer

Railway Gazette

Railway Magazine

Railway & Canal Historical Society Journal

Railway & Locomotive Historical Society Bulletin

Steam Railway Magazine

Stephenson Locomotive Society Journal

Trains & Travel

Transactions of the Newcomen Society

3. Websites

www.mercurio.iet.unipi.it

www.musicweb.uk.net/railways_in_music.htm

Index

Abroad, 192
ACE see American Coal Enterprises
Ackerman, Rudolf, 88, 97
Addington works, 156
Adler, 57
'Adriatic' type, 163
AEG works, 234
Agenoria, 36
Ahrons, E. H., 141
'Aim High' class, 330
Ajmer works, 184
Alco see American Locomotive Company
Alexander II, Tsar, 180
Algeria, 172, 295, 296
Alkan, Charles-Valentin, 89
Allan, Alexander, 71
Allen, Horatio, 33-35, 45, 77
Alley, George, 98
American Arch Company, 220
American Coal Enterprises, 335-336
American Locomotive Company, 133, 134, 143, 153, 154, 202, 209, 216, 219, 238, 239, 247, 264, 265, 266, 269, 270, 274, 294, 296, 299, 300, 331
American Society of Mechanical Engineers, 220
'Andes' type, 317-318
Angola, 99, 319
Ansaldo works, 298
Arend, De, 62
Argentina, 83, 85, 121, 132, 157, 181, 182, 207, 229, 317, 333-334
Arlberg line, 161
Armstrong Whitworth works, 186
Arnoux, Claude, 60

Ashcroft, E.H. 74
Aspinall, Sir John, 146
Asselin, Georges, 222
Atchison Topeka & Santa Fe Railroad, 132, 201, 269, 283
Atkins, Philip, 302, 332
'Atlantic' type, 141-142, 159, 167, 211, 247-248, 254, 276, 314
Auden, W.H., 242
Australia, 83, 84, 106, 133, 173, 181, 253, 260, 263, 274, 279, 284, 296, 313, 323, 327, 332
Austrian Federal Railways (ÖBB), 206, 234, 295
Awdry, Rev. F.W., 193

Babcock & Wilcox, Bilbao, 329, 330
Baird, Matthew, 100, 108
Baker, Abner, 216
Baldwin, Matthias, 59, 61
Baldwin works, 59, 100, 108, 110, 111, 132, 134, 153, 157, 187, 198, 202, 212, 216, 219, 232, 238, 265, 277, 278, 289, 294, 296, 299, 300, 331
Baltimore & Ohio Railroad, 37, 40, 46-47, 52, 58, 79, 101, 102, 107, 133, 154, 228, 255, 256, 266, 288
Bavaria, 76
Bavarian State Railways, 210
Bayonne-Biarritz Railway, 128
Beattie, A.L., 156, 181, 231
Beatty, H.M., 181
Beauty of Old Trains, 194
Beaver Meadow Railroad, 60
Beebe, Lucius, 88

Belfast & Northern Counties Railway, 130
Belfort works, 209
Belgian State Railways, 121, 148, 173, 276, 281
Bellevue disaster, 90
Bells on locomotives, 42
Belluzzo, Giuseppe, 229
Belpaire, Alfred, 121, 131, 152, 173, 203, 234, 281
Belpaire boiler, 121-122, 166, 238, 278, 297, 318, 324
Bengal & North Western Railway, 184
Bengal-Nagpur Railway, 184-185, 235
Benguela Railway, 319
'Berkshire' type, 203, 221, 253-254
Berlioz, Hector, 89
B.E.S.A. designs, see British Engineering Standards Assoc.
Bessemer, Sir Henry, 105
Best Friend of Charleston, 45, 59
Beuth, 75
Beyer, Charles, 121, 124
Beyer Garratt, 172
Beyer, Peacock works, 84, 121, 154, 171, 172, 173, 205, 314, 320, 321, 322, 325
'Big Boy' class, 203-204, 265, 269-271, 322, 323, 332
Bilty, C.H., 247
Birkinshaw, John, 23, 27
Birmingham & Gloucester Railway, 58-59
Bissell, Levi, 107
Blackett, Christopher, 19, 20, 22
Blakslee, James I., 108
Blenkinsop, John, 21
'Bloomers', 79
Blücher, 23
Bolton & Kenyon Railway, 49
Bolton & Leigh Railway, 32
Bombay-Thana Railway, 83
Booth, Henry, 32, 33, 40
Borodin, Aleksandr, 177, 225
Boris III of Bulgaria, 258
Borsig works, 75, 154, 234, 243-244, 290
Boston & Albany Railroad, 221
Boston & Maine Railroad, 101
Boston & Providence Railroad, 100
'Bourbonnais' type, 110
Bourdon, Eugène, 73-74
Bourne, John Cooke, 88

Bowen, Henry Blaine, 255
Braithwaite, John, 40, 51
Brakes, counter-pressure, 114
Brazil, 83, 110, 318
Brazilian National Railways Department, 318
Brighton works, 307
British Engineering Standards Association (BESA), 183, 184, 235
British Railways, 11, 169, 175, 285, 309, 310
British Railways Standard classes, 175, 308-310
Britten, Benjamin, 197
Brook, James, 60
Brooks works, 134
Brotan boiler, 164, 175
Brotan, Johann, 164
Brother Jonathan, 54
Brown, William H., 35, 55
Browning, Elizabeth Barrett, 91
Brunel, I.K., 64
Brunton, William, 21
Bryansk works, 179, 180
Budapest Locomotive Works, 155
Buenos Aires & Great Southern Railway, 181
Bugatti, Ettore, 245, 275
Bulgarian State Railways, 206, 235, 293
Bulleid, O.V.S., 227, 305-307
Burstall, Timothy, 40
Bury, Edward, 49, 55-56, 57, 58, 63

Cab-front locomotives, 134-136, 265
Caledonian Railway, 118, 122-123, 138, 139-141, 153, 165
Cail, J.F. works, 131, 154
Cairo-Alexandria Railway, 83
Camden & Amboy Railroad, 53, 67, 106
'Camel' type, 101, 107
'Camelback' type, 102, 141, 260, 314
Campbell, Henry R., 60-61
Canada, 62, 85, 96, 106, 107, 154, 227, 228, 238, 242, 303, 332
Canadian Locomotive Co., 154
Canadian National Railway, 154, 242-243
Canadian Pacific Railway, 154, 228, 242, 255, 315
Cape Government Railway, 181
Caprotti, Arturo, 240

Caprotti valve gear, 240, 319
Carlyle, Thomas, 43
Carter, Ian, 10, 194
Catch-me-who-can, 19
Cegielski works, 206, 291
Central Aragón Railway, 172
Central Argentine Railway, 171, 318
Central Pacific Railroad, 106, 201
Central Railroad of New Jersey, 314
Central Railway of Peru, 317
Central Railway of Uruguay, 182
Cerro de Pasco, 20, 317
'Challenger' class, 203, 255, 270
Champlain & St Lawrence Railway, 62, 63
Chapelon, André, 131, 136, 152, 216, 222-224, 225, 227, 240, 246, 267-268, 269, 310-313, 317, 318, 333
Chapman, William, 20-21, 54-55
Charleston & Hamburg Railroad, 45, 59
Cherepanov, E.A., 63
Chesapeake & Ohio Railroad, 98, 202, 221, 300, 302, 336
Chesapeake, 107
Chicago & Illinois Midland Railroad, 263
Chicago & North Western Railroad, 226
Chicago & Rock Island Railroad, 138
Chicago Milwaukee St Paul & Pacific Railroad, 247
Chicago World Fair 1933, 255
China, 153, 185, 239, 252, 255, 263, 274, 285, 295, 330-331, 332
Chittaranjan works, 305
Chrzanov works, 276, 291, 305
Churchward, G.J., 152, 165-169, 174, 210-211, 314
City of Truro, 166-167, 243
Coalbrookdale 16
Cockerill, John, 77
Cockerill works, 77, 122, 276
Cockshott, F.P., 138
Colburn, Zerah, 55
Collins, Colonel, 232
Columbia University, 226
Conner, Benjamin, 118
Consolidation, 108-109
'Consolidation' type, 108-109, 111
Cooper, Peter, 46
Coppernob, 56
Cornwall, 15

Cork, 56
Cosmovící, H., 206, 326
Cossart valve gear, 172
Country Railway, The, 194
Coupe-vent, 273
Cox, E.S., 145, 232, 235, 332
Crampton, T.R., 66-67, 166
Crewe works, 76, 81, 128, 129, 229, 236, 309
'Crewe' type, 118, 175
Cruickshank, George, 89
Cuba, 102, 333
Cugnot, Nicolas, 14, 16
Currier & Ives, 88, 97
Czechoslovakia, 154, 180, 260, 285, 291, 293, 304, 316, 332
Czechoslovakian State Railways, 295, 316-317, 320

Danforth & Cooke, 107, 134
Danish State Railways, 211
Darlington Railway Museum, 28
Darrell, Nicholas, 45
Datong works, 330
Daumer, W., 234
Davenport works, 293, 296
Davidson, John. 193
Davis, Phineas, 52
DB see Deutsche Bundesbahn
Dean, William, 125
De Caso, Marc, 313
Decken, Heinrich von, 29
De Glehn, Alfred, 130-131, 167, 178, 209, 210
Delacroa, A.O., 178
Delaware & Hudson Canal Company, 34, 35
Delaware & Hudson Railroad, 219, 228
Delaware & Lackawanna Railroad, 198
De l'influence des chemins de fer, 33, 231
Delvaux, Paul, 196
Dendy Marshall, C.H., 18, 29, 32-3
Denmark, 154, 155, 211, 314, 332
Derby works, 236
Derwent, 66
Des Chemins de fer en Angleterre, 29
Deutsche Bundesbahn, 210, 254, 292, 295, 304, 326-327
Deutsche Reichsbahn, 292, 304, 326, 327

Deutsche Reichsbahn Gesellschaft, 175, 210, 215, 232, 233, 243, 250, 290, 299
De Witt Clinton, 53, 54
Dickens, Charles, 95, 96, 193
Dickinson, Emily, 93
Dixon, John, 40
Djibouti-Addis Ababa Railway, 212-213, 296
Dom Pedro Segundo Railway, 110
Dombey & Son, 95, 96
Domes, presence and absence of, 125
Doncaster works, 76, 125, 307
Dorchester, 62, 96
Dovregubben, 253-254
Dresden-Leipzig Railway, 57
Dreyfuss, Henry, 275
Dripps, Isaac, 53, 67, 106-107,
Dropping the Fire, 302, 332
Drummond, Dugald, 217
Dublin & Kingstown Railway, 50
Du Bousquet, Gaston, 130-131, 152, 209
Dübs works, 84, 154, 155
Duddington, driver, 246, 259
Duluth Missabe & Iron Range Railroad, 266
'Dunalastair' type, 123, 314
Dundee & Newtyle Railway, 55
Dvorak, Antonin, 196
Dzerzhinsky, Felix, 263

Earthly Paradise, The, 194
East African Railways, 180, 296, 321-2
Eastern Counties Railway, 51, 127
Eastwick, Andrew, 60
Eastwick & Harrison, 61, 63, 64
Egyptian Government Railways, 158, 181
Einheitslok, 233
Ekaterina Railway, 174
Elesco feed-water heater, 220
Ellis, C. Hamilton, 194, 205, 282
Ellis, Vivian, 197
Emerson, George H., 256
Emerson, Ralph Waldo, 92
'Empire State Express', 142
'Engine Man', the, 194
Eothen, 90
Ericsson, John, 40,
Erie Railway, 102, 107, 108, 127, 202, 203, 289

Essen, 105
Esslingen works, 75, 187
Est Railway, France, 67, 152, 171, 222
Etat railway, France, 153, 180
Ethiopian Railways, 173, 212, 296
Etudes sur la stabilité des machines locomotives, 51
Euskalduña works, 329
Evans, Oliver, 14
Excelsior, 222
Experiment, 36
'Experiment' class, 129
Experiment (US), 54, 59
Express, The, 192-193
Express Trains, English & Foreign, 137

Fairbairn & Sons, 56
Fairlie locomotive, 173
Fairy Queen, 83
Far Caucasus railway, 179
Farrer, Lord, 137
Fawcett, Brian, 259, 317
Fell engines, 315
Ferdinand I of Bulgaria, 258
Fernihough, William, 51
Findlay, George
Finland, 154, 282, 289, 332
Fitchburg Railroad, 92
Fives-Lille works, 310
Flamme, J.B., 122-123, 173-174
Fleming, Peter, 289
Flewellyn, George, 166
'Fliegende Hamburger', 245
Floridsdorf works, 154
Fools' Parade, 191
Forges et Aciéries de la Marine et d'Homecourt, 310
Forrester, George, 50, 70
Foster, Rastrick, 34, 35, 57
'Four Aces', 266
Foxwell, Professor, 137
Franco-Crosti boiler, 43, 174-175, 267, 309
Franklin Institute, 219
Franklin wedges, 311
Fraser, Charles, 94
Frederik, king of Denmark, 258
Freeman, Michael, 10, 87
Frescot, Cesare, 107
Freud, Sigmund, 194

Frichs works, 155, 211
Fulton, Robert, 32
Furness Railway, 56
Fury, 227
Fussell, Paul, 192
Futurist Manifesto, The, 195
Garbe, Robert, 145, 148
Garratt, Herbert, 152, 171-173
Garrat locomotive, 8, 171-173, 263, 320-323, 325-326, 330
Garrett & Eastwick, 60
General, The, 288
General Electric Co., 229, 300
General Motors, Electromotive Division, 269, 299, 301
Georgetown-Plaisance Railway, 66
Giesl-Gieslingen, A., 284-285
Giesl exhaust, 187, 284-285, 309, 323
Giffard, Henri, 80-81, 122
Glasgow, 57, 123, 154, 155, 157, 184, 229, 315
Glinka, Mikhail, 89
Goliath, 50
Gölsdorf, Karl, 136, 152, 161-164, 207, 221, 232, 314
Gooch, Daniel, 65, 66, 71, 125
Gorton works, 205
Goss, William, 225-226, 284
Gotthard railway, 133, 204
Gourault, driver, 259
Gowan & Marx, 63
Graffenstaden works, 291
Grangesberg-Oxeløsund Railway, 229
'Grasshopper', 52
Gray, John, 71
Graz-Köflacher Bahn, 162
Grazi-Tsaritsin Railway, 103
Great Bear, The, 211
Great Central Railway, 205
Great Eastern Railway, 130
Great Indian Peninsula Railway, 83, 109
Great Northern Railroad, 111
Great Northern Railway (GB), 76, 120, 125, 126, 138, 139, 269
Great Northern Railway (Ireland), 136
Great Railway Bazaar, The, 190
Great Southern Railway, 254
Great Western Railway, 64, 65, 75-76, 87, 88, 125, 131, 138, 152, 165-169, 199,
205, 210-211, 226, 236, 243, 248, 252, 255, 275, 281, 295
'Greater Britain' class, 129
Greece, 289, 294, 295, 296, 298
Greene, Graham, 192, 193
Gresley, Sir Nigel, 152, 199, 224, 226-227, 236, 245, 259, 307
Griggs, George S., 100, 282
Grubb, Davis, 191
Gurney, Goldsworthy, 49

Hackworth, Timothy, 22, 24, 28, 36, 40-44, 61, 63, 66
Haine St-Pierre works, 212-213
Hall, Joseph, 76
Hallette, Alfred, 30
Hamilton works, 300
Hammel, Anton, 210
Hankins, Fred, 275
Hanomag works, 148, 186, 206, 314, 321
Harrison, Joseph, 60, 61
Harte, Bret, 106
Hartmann works, 121, 186
Haswell, John, 77, 152, 162
Hawthorn, R.&W., 146
Hawthorne, Nathaniel, 92
Hazeldene & Rastrick, 19
Hear the Train Blow, 88
'Heavy Harry', 284
Hedley, William, 22
Hellenic State Railways, 298
Helmholtz, Richard von, 121, 162
Helmholtz truck, 178, 204
Henderson, George R., 202
Hendrie, David, 155-156
Henschel & Sohn works, 75, 135, 147, 154, 210, 227, 234, 235, 250, 299, 319, 320, 321
Hercules, 61
Hero of Alexandria, 23
Heusinger, Edmund, 73, 149, 162, 326
'Hiawatha' class, 247-248, 258, 273, 275
Highland Railway, 155-156, 205, 283
Hindemith, Paul, 196
Hirschau works, 210
Hitachi works, 239, 297
Hitchcock, Alfred, 199
Hogan, driver, 142
'Hogwarts Express' 199

Holland Iron Railway Company, 62
Homfray, Samuel, 17, 19, 37
Honegger, Arthur, 192, 197
Hornblower, Jonathan, 127
Horwich works, 236
Houlet superheater, 148, 267, 311, 313
Howe, William, 71-72
'Hudson' type, 212, 254, 274, 324
Hudson, William, 109
Hughes, Hugh, 258-259
Hull & Selby Railway, 71
Hungarian Railways, 123, 152, 295
Hungary, 154, 161, 164, 175, 180, 260, 273,
    293, 330, 332
Huntley, John , 198
'Hush-hush' engine, 227
Huskisson, William, 42

Illinois Central Railroad, 98, 166
Imperial Austrian Railways (kkStB), 123,
    161-164
Inchicore works, 254
India, 84-85, 109, 132, 155, 173, 183-185,
    253, 274, 332
Indian Railways, 295, 304
Indian Railways Standards Committee,
    184, 235
Indonesia, 186-187, 283, 315
Indonesian State Railways, 186, 187
Indus Valley Railway, 155
Injector, 81-82
Institution of Civil Engineers, 80, 120
Institution of Locomotive Engineers, 224,
    232
Institution of Mechanical Engineers, 80, 128
Iraq State Railways, 277, 296
Ireland, 50, 56, 136, 191, 254
Irish Times, 191
'Iron Duke' class, 65
Iron Horse, first use of term, 29
Italy, 64, 132, 134, 174-175, 213, 252, 273,
    274, 298, 332

Jabelmann, Otto, 270
Jackson, H.H., 231
James, William, 71
Japan, 110, 158, 187, 206-207, 232, 252, 297,
    314, 332
Japanese National Railways, 206, 239-240

Java, 102, 154, 333
'Jenny Lind' 78-79, 128
Jervis, John B., 34, 35, 53-55, 66
John Bull, 52-53
Jones, Casey, 98
Jones, David, 155-156, 205, 283
Joy, David, 78, 128
'Jumbos' see 'Precedent' class
Juniata works, 203, 212, 278
Jupiter, 106

Kaganovich, Lazar, 327, 328
Kaiserin Elisabeth Bahn, 124
'Kanawha' type, 221
Kassel, 154, 210, 227, 250, 299
Kawasaki works, 206, 239
Keaton, Buster, 199
Kemble, Fanny, 44, 125,
Kennedy, James, 49
Kentucky State Fair, 151
Kershaw, J., 109
Kiefer, Paul, 301
Killingworth, 23
Kilmarnock & Troon Railway, 27, 36
'King' class, 236, 255
King, Charles R., 251
Kinglake, A.W., 90
Kirtley, James, 100
Kisha Seizo Kaisha works, 158, 206, 239
Kitching, W. & A., 66
Kitson works, 83, 185,
Knorr feed-water system, 233
Koechlin, André, 62
Kokura works, 206
Kolomna works, 178, 327, 328
Krauss, Georg, 121
Krauss works, 121, 162
Krauss-Maffei works 121, 154, 244, 325
Kriegslokomotive, 290-293
Krigar, Friedrich, 29
Krupp works, 105, 108, 234, 253-254, 264,
    291, 321, 327
Kuhler, Otto, 274
Kyläläla, Kilpi, 222
Kylchap exhaust, 222, 246, 247, 268, 307,
    311, 317, 318, 320
Kylpor exhaust, 334

La Bête Humaine 189-190

La Condition Humaine, 191-192
La Portenta, 83
Lancashire & Yorkshire Railway, 146, 191
Lancashire Witch, 32, 34, 37, 77
Landwührden, 121
Langhans, driver, 244
'Leader' design, 307
Lebedyanskii, I.S., 327
Le Chatelier, Louis, 51, 114
Le Creusot, 128, 135, 312
Leeds, 21, 79, 83, 185, 315
Lehigh & Mahanoy Railroad, 108
Lehigh Valley Railroad. 108, 157
Leicester & Swannington Railway, 42
Lemaître exhaust, 131, 284
Lempor exhaust, 335
Lenin, V.I., 178
Lenz, Hugo, 240, 268, 330
Leppla, Heinrich, 210
'Liberation' class, 239
Liège & Namur Railway, 67
Lille, 89, 154, 157,
Lima Locomotive Works, 153, 216, 219-
    221, 238, 263, 294, 299, 300, 331, 336
Lines of Character, 193
Lion, 199
Little Train of the Caipira, 197
Liverpool, 49, 50, 88
Liverpool, 49, 56
Liverpool & Manchester Railway, 39, 43,
    44, 45, 49, 50, 52, 57, 62, 84, 88, 199
Lives of the Engineers, 33
Ljungström condenser, 229
Lloyd, Roger, 315
LMS see London Midland & Scottish
    Railway
LNER see London & North Eastern
    Railway
Locomotion, 28, 41, 326
Locomotive banknotes, 96
Locomotive colours, 78, 119, 120, 129
Locomotive dreams, 194
Locomotive hell-bound, 87
Locomotive in art, 88, 194-196
Locomotive in films, 197-199
Locomotive magazine, 164, 230, 231
Locomotive music, 89-90, 196-197
Locomotive naming, 78-79, 93, 119, 251-
    254

Locomotive Panorama, 236
Locomotive postage stamps, 96
Locomotive Superheater Co., 220
Locomotive testing plants, 225-226
Locomotive type-names, 254-255
Loewy, Raymond, 245, 275, 277-278
Lomonosov, Professor, 215
London & Birmingham Railway, 55-56, 88
London & North Eastern Railway, 173,
    199, 211, 217, 226-227, 236, 243, 245-
    246, 251-252, 275, 290, 307
London & North Western Railway, 71,
    75, 79, 81, 119, 128, 139-141, 158, 168,
    251, 284
London & South Western Railway, 166,
    217
London Chatham & Dover Railway, 154
London Midland & Scottish Railway, 173,
    175, 227, 229, 236-238, 243, 246, 251,
    255, 275, 290, 296-297, 308
Long, Col. S.H., 57
'Long-boiler' type, 56
Longridge & Co., 62, 64
Longridge, Michael, 28, 77
Lopushinskii, V.I., 152, 179
'Lord Nelson' class, 237
Loree, L.H., 228
Louisville & Nashville Railroad, 89
Lowry, L.S., 191
Lübeck-Büchen Railway, 250
Lugansk works, 179
Lumbye, Christian, 89
Lumière brothers, 197-198

'MacArthur' type, 296
'Mac's Mangle', 85
McConnell, J.C., 79, 85, 146
Machine in the Garden, The, 94
McIntosh, J.F., 122
Macosa works, 329
Madagascar Railways, 187
Madrid Caceres & Portugal Railway, 121
Madrid Zaragoza & Alicante Railway, 315
Maedbh, 254
Maffei, Josef, 76
Maffei works, 210, 234, 321
Magritte, René, 195-196
Malaxa works, 206
Malayan Railways, 157, 296

Malcolm, Bowman, 130

Mallard, 246-247, 259

Mallet, Anatole, 33, 128, 171

Mallet type, 102, 133, 134, 172-173, 186,
    187, 261, 263, 265, 266, 277, 314

Malraux, André, 191-192, 271

Manet, Edouard, 195

Maquinista Terrestre e Maritima, 329

Maribor workshops, 76

Marinetti, Tommaso, 195

Markham, Charles, 100

Marlow, Norman, 289

Martin, John, 87

Martineau & Taylor, 30

Marx, Leo, 10, 94

Mason, William, 118

Massachusetts, 42

'Mastodon' type, 261

MÁV see Hungarian State Railways

Mechanical stoker, 159, 262

Mechanic's Magazine, 23, 42

Mediterranean Railway, 252

'Merchant Navy' class, 306, 308, 309

Merchant's Magazine, 94

Merthyr Tydfil, 17, 18

Mestre, Henri, 222

Metropolitan Railway, 205

Metropolitan Vickers, 229

Middle East Railways, 258-259

Middleton Railway, 21, 29, 97, 251

Midland Railway, 100-101, 129, 153, 181,
    281, 289

'Mikado' type, 110-111, 207, 236, 239, 246,
    254, 275, 298

Mill, John Stuart, 94

Miller, E.L., 45, 59

Millholland, James, 107

Miot, fireman, 259

Missouri Pacific Railroad, 157

Mitchell, Alexander, 108

Mitsubishi, 334

'Mogul' type, 64, 107, 108, 181, 254

Mohawk & Hudson Railroad, 53, 142

Moncheuil, M., 146

Monet, Claude, 195

Monkhouse, Cosmo Gordon, 91

Monkland & Kirkintilloch Railway, 57

Monster, The, 106

Monterau & Troyes railway, 146

Montreal Locomotive Works, 154

'Moral Influence of Steam', 94

Morgan, David P., 220, 284

Morris, William, 194

'Mother Hubbard' type see 'Camelback'

Mount Clare workshops, 101, 102

'Mountain' type, 202-203, 222, 243, 254,
    283, 312

'Mucca' type, 134-135

Muhlfeld, James E., 133, 219, 228

Mulhouse, 62, 131, 187, 313

Munch, Edvard, 196

Munich, 76, 162, 210, 326

Murdoch & Hill, 57

Murdock, William, 14-15

Murom works, 180

Murray, Matthew, 21, 24, 69

naGopaleen, Myles, 9, 191

Naples-Portici Railway, 64

Neilson & Co., works, 118, 123, 154, 184

Netherlands, 62, 154, 186, 303

Neville, James, 32

Newcastle on Tyne, 23, 27, 31, 55, 146, 186

Newcomen, Thomas, 13

New South Wales Government Railways,
    171, 260, 315, 323, 324

New York, 34, 53, 137

New York Central Railroad, 8, 142, 176,
    220, 228, 274, 275, 301, 302, 311, 326

New York World Fair, 1939, 255

New Zealand, 85, 156-157, 274, 314, 315,
    318

New Zealand Railways, 156, 231

'Niagara' class, 176, 301, 325

Nicholas, Tsar, 29, 287

Nicholson, John, 127

Nicholson thermic siphon, 223, 311

Nigeria, 296

Night Express, 91

Nippon Sharya works, 187, 239

Nizam's State Railway, 155-156

Nohab see Nydqvist & Holm

Nord railway, France, 8, 63, 89, 110, 120,
    130-131, 153, 223, 249, 273, 313

Norfolk & Western Railroad, 154, 248,
    249, 301, 302, 324

Norris, William, 58, 59, 62, 67, 75

Norris works, Vienna, 75

Norte Railway, Spain, 314
North British Locomotive Co., 154, 181,
    185, 229, 237, 319, 320, 321, 324
North Eastern Railway, 130, 137, 138, 140
Northern Pacific Railroad, 265, 266, 269
'Northern' type, 255, 310, 312
Northern Donetz Railway, 179
Northern Railway, Canada, 107
Northumbrian, 43-4, 50
Norway, 132, 211, 253, 292
Norwegian State Railways, 274
Notesse, Raoul 276
Notkin superheater, 178
Novelty, 40, 42, 45
Nüremberg-Fürth Railway, 57
Nydqvist & Holm, 155, 179, 211, 303

Oeynhausen, Karl von, 29
Oi testing plant, 226
Old Ironsides, 59
'Old Maud', 133
Oldenburg State Railways, 121
Ouest Railway, France, 81
'Outrance' class, 120-121

'Pacific' type, 155, 156-157, 173, 175, 209-
213, 223, 227, 229, 231-232, 233, 235, 249,
    251, 254, 258, 260, 273, 275, 277, 283,
    305, 314, 318-319, 326-327
PCM works, 124
Papin, Denis, 13
Paris Exposition, 102, 121
Paris-Lyon-Mediterranée Railway, 66, 172,
    198, 206, 222, 228, 273, 304, 312
Paris-Orleans Railway, 62, 196, 209, 222,
    223, 267
Paris-Sceaux Railway, 60
Parker, Theodore, 94
'Patentee' class, 51, 57, 62, 64, 97, 113
Pennsy Power, 211
Pennsylvania Railroad, 53, 109, 114, 131,
    141-142, 154, 159, 203, 204, 211, 226,
    229-230, 238-239, 248, 275, 277-278,
    302, 314
Pennsylvania Society for Internal
    Improvement, 29
Penydarren Tramroad, 17, 28, 151
Peppercorn, A.H., 307
Perdonnet, J.-A., 31

Perkins, Thatcher, 89
Peru, 20, 95, 317
Pétiet, Jules, 8, 110, 146
Philadelphia, 15, 58, 59, 81, 134, 137, 141,
    219
Philadelphia & Columbia Railroad, 58, 59
Philadelphia & Reading Railroad, 63, 102,
    107, 119, 141-142
Philadelphia, Germantown & Norristown
    Railroad, 59, 60
Pittsburgh & West Virginia Railroad, 284
Plancher system, 135
'Planet' type, 50, 51, 59, 62, 63,
Plant System, 142-143
PLM see Paris-Lyons-Mediterranean
    Railway
PNKA see Indonesian State Railways
P-O see Paris-Orleans Railway
Poland, 154, 180, 235, 260, 292, 293, 330
Polish State Railways, 276, 279, 295
Porta, L.D., 152, 333-335
Porter, Edwin S., 198
Porter works, 293, 296
Portugal, 124, 154, 173
Portuguese Railways, 234-235
'Prairie' type, 254
'Precedent' class, 129, 140-141
'Precursor' class, 129
Pre-Raphaelites, 195
Pride of Newcastle, 34, 36
Prince Regent, 21, 251
'Problem' class, 81
Promontory Summit, 106
Puffing Billy, 22, 55, 77
Punch, 89
Purdue University, 225, 284

Qian Jing class, 330

Race to the North, 138-141
Rail Across India, 183
Railway Magazine, 115, 147, 151, 153, 167,
    251
Railway Operating Department (ROD),
    205, 289
Railways of the Andes, 317
Rain, Steam and Speed, 87
Rainhill Trials, 35, 39-42, 73, 77
Ramsbottom, John, 81, 84, 152

Ransome-Wallis, P., 327
Rastrick, J. U., 35
Reading Railroad, 212
'Red Devil', 335
Reed, Brian, 155, 249
RENFE see Spanish National Railways
Report on Canals and Railroads, 29
Resita works, 206
Rhode Island works, 134, 143
Rhodesian Railways, 319
Richmond Fredericksburg & Potomac
    Railroad, 252-253
Ricour, Théophile, 273
Riddles, R.A., 307-310
Rio Turbio railway, 334
Robert Stephenson & Co., 28, 30, 33, 34
    41, 49, 50, 53, 57, 62, 66, 71-72, 84, 185
Robert Stephenson & Hawthorns, 277
Robinson, J.G., 205
Rocket, 32, 37, 39-43, 77, 78
Rocket of China, 185
ROD see Railway Operating Department
Rogers Locomotive Works, 59, 108, 134,
    288
Rohilkund & Kumaon Railway, 184
Rolt, L.T.C., 193
Romanian State Railways, 206, 292
Rosario & Puerto Belgrano Railway, 121
Rossini, Giacomo, 89
Rous-Marten, Charles, 142, 153, 167
Royal George, 36, 46, 61
Royal Prussian Railways, 130, 131, 135, 143,
    148-149, 165, 210
'Royal Scot' class, 227, 237, 235
Rugby, 226
Ruskin, John, 95, 124
Russia, 85, 106, 128, 132, 152, 154, 173, 174,
    177-180, 207, 213, 232, 260, 263, 264,
    274, 287, 289, 293, 295, 314, 327-328,
    332

Sacramento Valley Railroad, 79
Sacramento works, 201
'Saint' class, 168, 169, 314
St Etienne-Lyons railway, 29, 269
St Lawrence & Champlain Railway, 62, 96
St Louis-San Francisco Railroad, 154, 238
St Petersburg, 63, 64, 178, 179
St Petersburg & Tsarskoe-Selo Railway, 63

St Rollox works, 165
Salamanca, 21, 251
Salt River works, 319
Samson, 50, 62
Sans Pareil, 39-44
'Santa Fe' type, 201, 255
Sáry, László, 197
Savery, Thomas, 13
Schaeffer, Pierre, 197
Schenectady, 202, 209, 225, 266
Schmidt superheater, 131, 145-147, 148,
    168, 178, 181, 218, 268
Schmidt, Wilhelm, 145-147, 149, 227
Schneider works, 135
Schubert, J.A., 57
Schwartzkopff works, 121, 154
Scientific American, 94
Scott, Sir Walter, 252
Scott, William Bell, 195
Scowcroft, Philip, 197
Seaboard Line, 143, 289
Segovia, duke of, 258
Seguin, Marc, 29-33, 44, 62, 231
Sekon, G.A., 128
'Selkirk' type, 255
Sellers, William, 81
Semmering trials, 76-77
Seraing, 77
Shanghai & Wusung Railway, 185
Sharp, Stewart works, 81, 109, 154, 155
Shay locomotive, 219
Silesia, Upper, 29
Simpson, C.R.H., 230
'Single-driver' type
Sirhowy Railway, 37
Skoda works, 154, 291, 304, 316
SLM (Schweizer Lokomotive und
    Maschinenfabrik), 186
Smiles, Samuel, 32-33
Smith, Walter, 206
Smithsonian Institution, 53, 302
Smoke deflectors, 274
SNCF, 199, 259, 267, 268, 294, 304, 310,
    312
Snell, J.B., 205
Snyder, Herb, 220
Société Alsacienne de Constructions
    Mécaniques, 62, 131, 154, 187, 209
Sormovo works, 178

Soutar, driver
South Africa, 84, 110, 173, 180, 181, 203, 207, 232, 263
South African Railways (SAR), 156, 232, 315, 318, 325, 334-335
South Australian Railways, 279
South Carolina Railroad, 77
South Korea, 295, 332
South Manchuria Railway, 239
South West Railway (Russia), 177, 225
Southern Pacific Railroad, 135-136, 265, 283, 311
Southern Railroad, 238
Southern Railway, 274, 284, 294, 305
Soviet Railways, 173, 180, 263-264, 276-277, 328
Spanish National Railways (RENFE), 329-330
Spender, Stephen, 192-193
Staats Eisenbahn Gesellschaft (StEG) works, 76, 123, 154, 161
Stamboul Train, 192
Stanier, Sir William A., 175, 229, 230, 237, 275, 306
'Star' class, 168, 169
Staufer, A.F., 211
Steam Magazine, 198
Stephens, Adrian, 42
Stephenson, George, 20, 23-28, 36, 39-44, 49, 69, 80, 145
Stephenson, Robert, 20, 23, 32, 37, 39-44, 55, 56, 77
Stevens, A.J., 201
Stevens, John, 33, 60
Stewart, William, 21-22
Stirling, Patrick, 102, 124-125, 126, 138, 168
Stockton & Darlington Railway, 27, 28, 42, 46, 66, 95, 326
Stockton & Stokes, 46
Stourbridge Lion, 34-35
Strauss, Johann, 89-90
Strong, G.S., 157
Sturrock, Archibald, 120, 138, 269
Südbahn (Austria-Hungary), 152, 161
Sumatra State Railways, 187
'Super-power' 220-221, 263
Surrey Iron Railway, 27
Susquehanna, 102
Swainson, Taylor, 29

Sweden, 78, 155, 179, 211, 229, 273, 282
Swindon works. 76, 165, 169, 226, 285
Swiss Central Railway, 133
Swiss Federal Railways, 204, 303
Syrian Railways, 314

Taiwan, 185
Tangshan-Hsukochwang Railway, 185
Tangshan workshops, 331
Taunus Railway, 73
Tay Bridge disaster, 98
TCDD see Turkish Railways
Tenders, 203-204, 292, 320, 331
'Teutonic' class, 129
'Texas' trype, 255
Thailand, 157, 296, 297, 314
Theroux, Paul, 190
Thomas, David St John, 194
Thomas the Tank Engine, 89, 193
Thoreau, Henry David, 92
Thuile, M., 135
Thunes Mekaniske Vaerksted, 253-254
TIA (Traitement intégrale Armand), 304
Times, The, 42
Timken roller bearings, 266, 278
To a Locomotive in Winter, 93, 192
Tokyo, 158, 226
Tom Thumb, 46
Tours works, 222, 223
Trains magazine, 220, 247, 271
Treatise on Rail-Roads, 25
Trevithick, Francis, 157-158, 206
Trevithick, Frederick, 158
Trevithick, Richard, 15-23, 36, 146, 151, 317, 332
Triplex locomotive, 202
Trollhättan works, 155
Tubize works, 133
Tuplin, W.A., 218
'Turbomotive', 229
Turkish Railways, 148, 154, 234, 292, 295, 296, 330
Turner, J.M.W., 87, 195

Über Schienenwege in England, 29
Union Pacific Railroad, 106, 203, 248, 255, 264, 268, 269-271
United States Army Transport Corps, 293-296

United States Railroad Administration, 203, 238, 331
Upper Italian Railways, 107
Urquhart, Thomas, 103, 177-178
Uruguay, 182, 283
USATC see United States Army Transport Corps
Utica & Schenectady Railroad, 99

Valve gear, 10, 69-73, 118, 149, 264
Van railway, 197
Vanderbilt tender, 203, 253
Van Gogh, Vincent, 195
Vauclain, Samuel M., 132, 141, 152, 210, 211, 289
Verbiest, Father, 22-23
Verlaine, Paul, 92
Verpilleux, Claude, 269
Victorian Government Railways, 253, 284, 323
Vienna, 75, 123, 161, 162, 179, 314
Vienna Lokomotivfabrik, 305
Vietnam, 293
Vigny, Alfred de, 90
Villa Lobos, Hector, 197
Virginian Railroad, 202
Vitry sur Seine, 224, 268
Von Borries, A., 130, 146, 152
Voroshilovgrad works, 179, 180, 264
Vuillet, Baron G., 242-243, 257-258
Vulcan works, UK, 83, 154, 158, 181, 182, 185, 318
Vulcan works, USA, 293, 296
Vulkan works, Germany, 147

Wagenfabrik Wegmann, 250
Wagner, Richard, 152, 175, 232-234, 243
Walden, 92
Wall Street Journal, 336
Wallis, J.T., 211
Walschaerts, Egide, 72, 121, 149
Walschaerts valve gear, 134, 149, 157, 159, 168, 187, 203, 211, 216, 233, 240, 244, 268, 276, 307, 322, 330
Wardale, David, 330, 334-335
Warlock, Peter, 197

Washington Country Farmer, 57
Watson, A.G., 232
Watt, James, 14-15
Webb, F.W., 119-110, 128-129
Weber, Max von, 90
Werkspoor works, 154, 186
West Point Foundry, 34, 45, 54, 57
Western & Atlantic Railroad, 288
Western Australian Government Railways, 325
Westinghouse, George, 114-115, 122
Westinghouse brake pump, 114, 157, 205, 294, 296
Westwood, J.N., 146, 166
Whistler, George Washington, 37
Whistles on locomotives, 42
White, John H., Jr., 79, 102, 105
Whitehead, R.A., 162
Whitman, Walt, 93, 192
Whyte, F.M., 8
Wilkes-Barre works, 157
Williams, William, 71
Wilson, E.B., 79, 315
Wimble duct, 283
Winans, Ross, 40, 46, 79, 101-102, 107
Withuhn, W., 271
Witte, Friedrich, 291
Wolff, A., 243-244
Wood, Nicholas, 25, 70
Woodard, W. 152, 219-221, 222, 224, 284
Wootten, John H., 102
Wordsworth, William, 95
Worsdell, T.W., 130
Württemberg Railway, 207, 234
Wylam Colliery, 22
Wylam Dilly, 22
Wynne, John H., 220-221

'Yellowstone' class, 265-266, 270
York, 52
Young, Harold, 323
Yugoslavia, 293, 294, 295

Zara, Giuseppe, 135
Zimbabwe, National Railways of, 321
Zola, Emile, 189-190